Requiem
of the
Rose King

4

AYA KANNO

Based on *Henry VI* and *Richard III*
by William Shakespeare

REQUIEM OF THE ROSE KING

VOLUME 4
VIZ Media Edition

STORY AND ART BY
AYA KANNO

TRANSLATION	JOCELYNE ALLEN
LETTERING	SABRINA HEEP
DESIGN	FAWN LAU
EDITOR	JOEL ENOS

BARAOU NO SOURETSU Volume 4
© 2015 AYA KANNO
First published in Japan in 2015 by AKITA PUBLISHING CO., LTD., Tokyo
English translation rights arranged with AKITA PUBLISHING CO., LTD.
through Tuttle-Mori Agency, Inc., Tokyo

The stories, characters and incidents mentioned in this
publication are entirely fictional.

Additionally, the author has no intention to discriminate
with any of the depictions within this work.

Printed in the U.S.A.

Published by VIZ Media, LLC
P.O. Box 77010
San Francisco, CA 94107

10 9 8 7 6 5 4 3 2 1
First printing, May 2016

www.viz.com

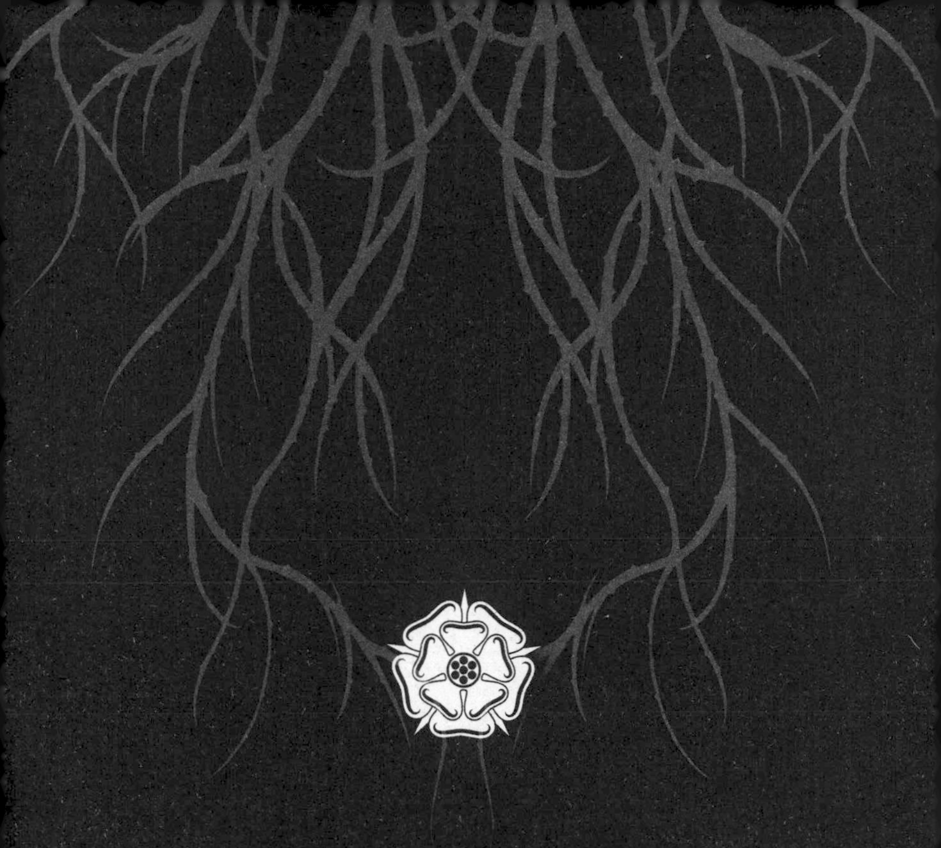

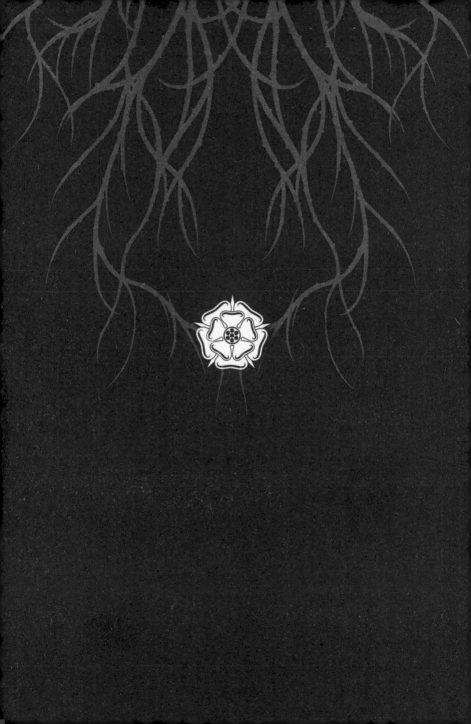

Story Thus Far

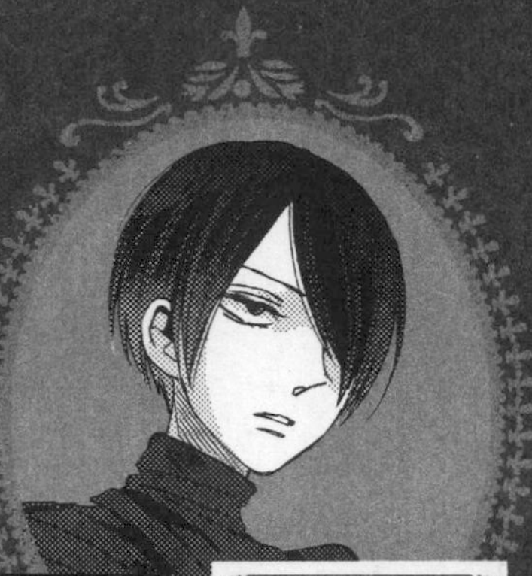

WHITE ROSE

House of York

RICHARD

The third son of York, he has been shunned by his mother since childhood.

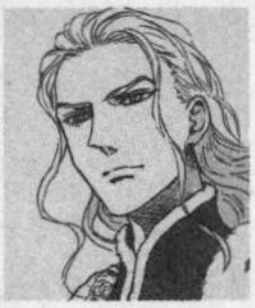

Richard, Duke of York

Father of Richard. He was the light of hope for Richard, but he was killed by Lancaster.

Cecily

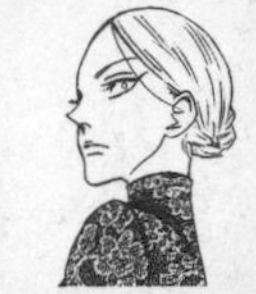

Mother of Richard. She despises him.

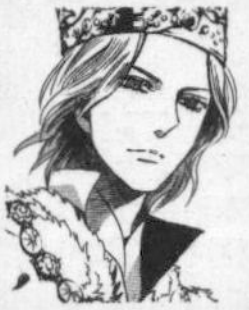

Edward

Current king. The oldest son of the House of York. He's very good with women.

George

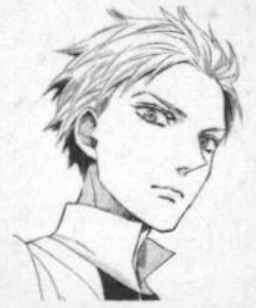

The second son of the House of York. He is the type who doesn't think too deeply about things.

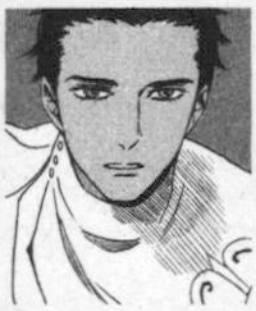

Catesby

Richard's attendant since childhood. He knows Richard's secret.

House of York Allies

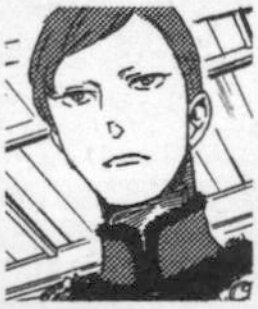

Earl of Warwick

He knew Richard's father for a long time and is a trusted ally but lost honor after being betrayed by the king.

Anne

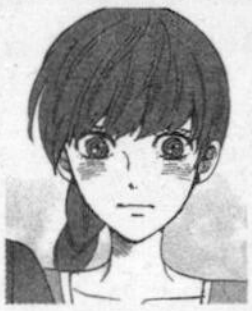

Daughter of the Earl of Warwick. She's curious about Richard.

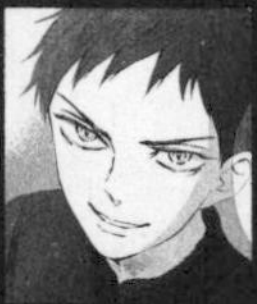

Buckingham

Very ambitious. He has come forward and named himself Richard's kingmaker.

Elizabeth

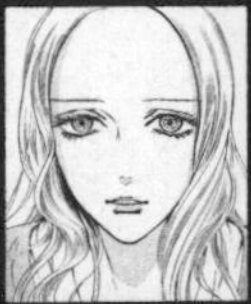

Married Edward and is now queen. She lost her husband in the war and harbors a grudge against the House of York.

Characters &

RED ROSE

House of Lancaster

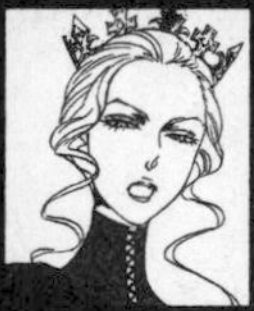

Margaret

She is Henry's wife, but she feels little love for him. She aims to restore her family to power.

Edward

Son of Henry. Strong willed. He has taken an interest in Richard.

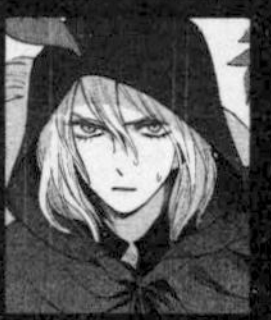

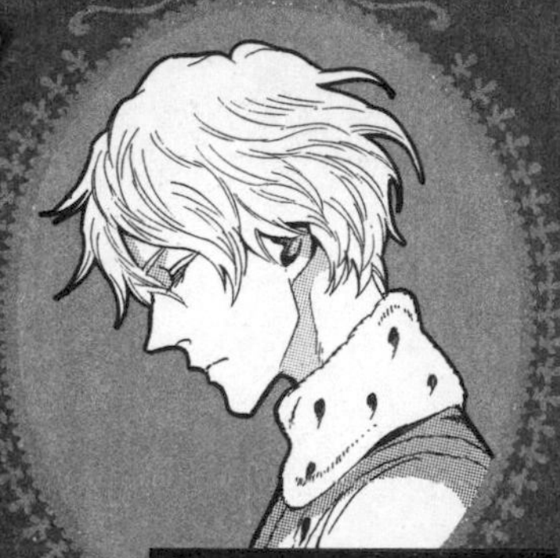

HENRY THE SIXTH

The former king. He's very pious and hates fighting. Occasionally, he disguises himself as a shepherd and slips out of the castle.

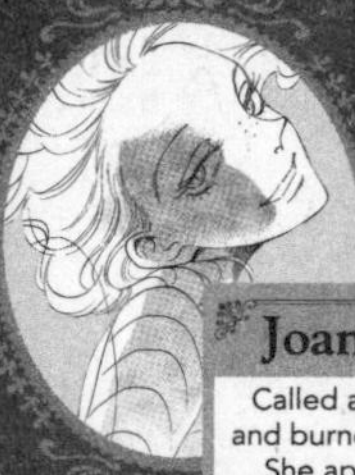

Joan of Arc

Called a French witch and burned at the stake. She appears before Richard as a ghost.

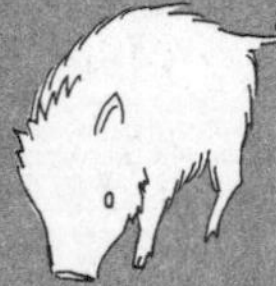

White boar

Saved by Richard when it was injured. The boar is very close to Richard.

Story thus far...

ENGLAND, THE MIDDLE AGES.

The two houses of York and Lancaster are caught in repeated royal contest, the age of the War of the Roses.

The House of York appears to have the upper hand in the battle, but then Richard's father is killed by Margaret in front of the throne. Learning of his father's cruel death, Richard cuts down soldier after Lancaster soldier on the battlefield and resolves to live a life in the darkness. The battle ends with a York victory.

Several years later, his older brother Edward becomes the new king, and peace comes to the land—until one day, Edward falls in love with the beautiful widow Elizabeth. But she seeks the fall of the House of York. Edward decides to marry her in a secret ceremony without consulting his retainers, and Richard is left in the woods as an alibi while his brother gets married. When Henry suddenly appears there, they spend some time alone together, and Richard's heart begins to soften toward him.

Warwick, having proceeded with talks to marry the new king Edward to the sister-in-law of the French king for the security of the nation, discovers that Elizabeth has been formally placed upon the queen's throne and trembles with anger.

Meanwhile, Richard encounters Buckingham and learns of the possibility of he himself becoming king. And then comes a notice that villagers have come bearing the head of the former king Henry...

Requiem
of the
Rose
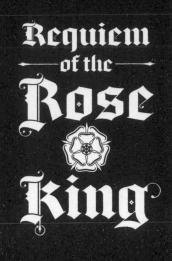
King

Contents

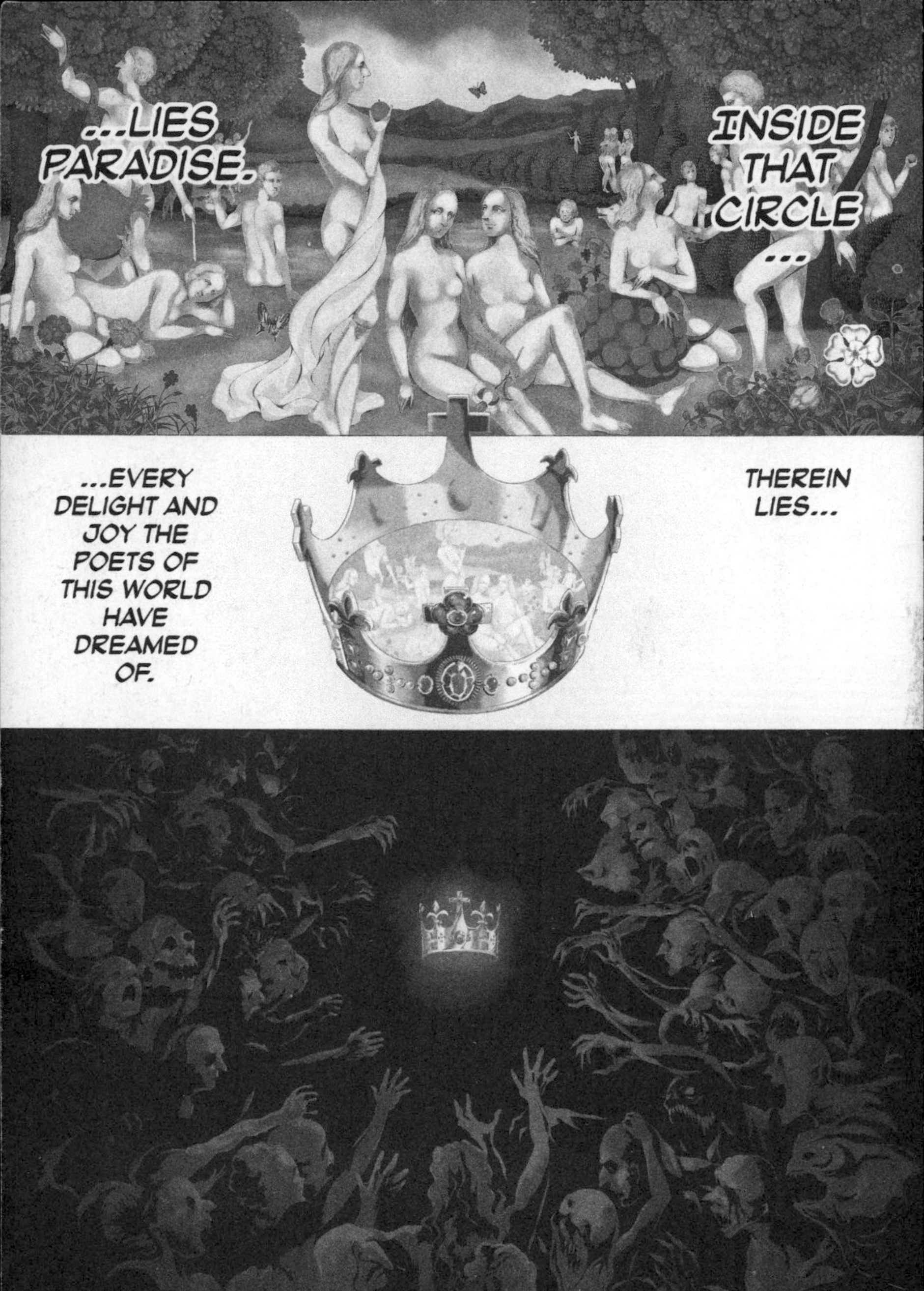
INSIDE THAT CIRCLE ...
...LIES PARADISE.
THEREIN LIES...
...EVERY DELIGHT AND JOY THE POETS OF THIS WORLD HAVE DREAMED OF.

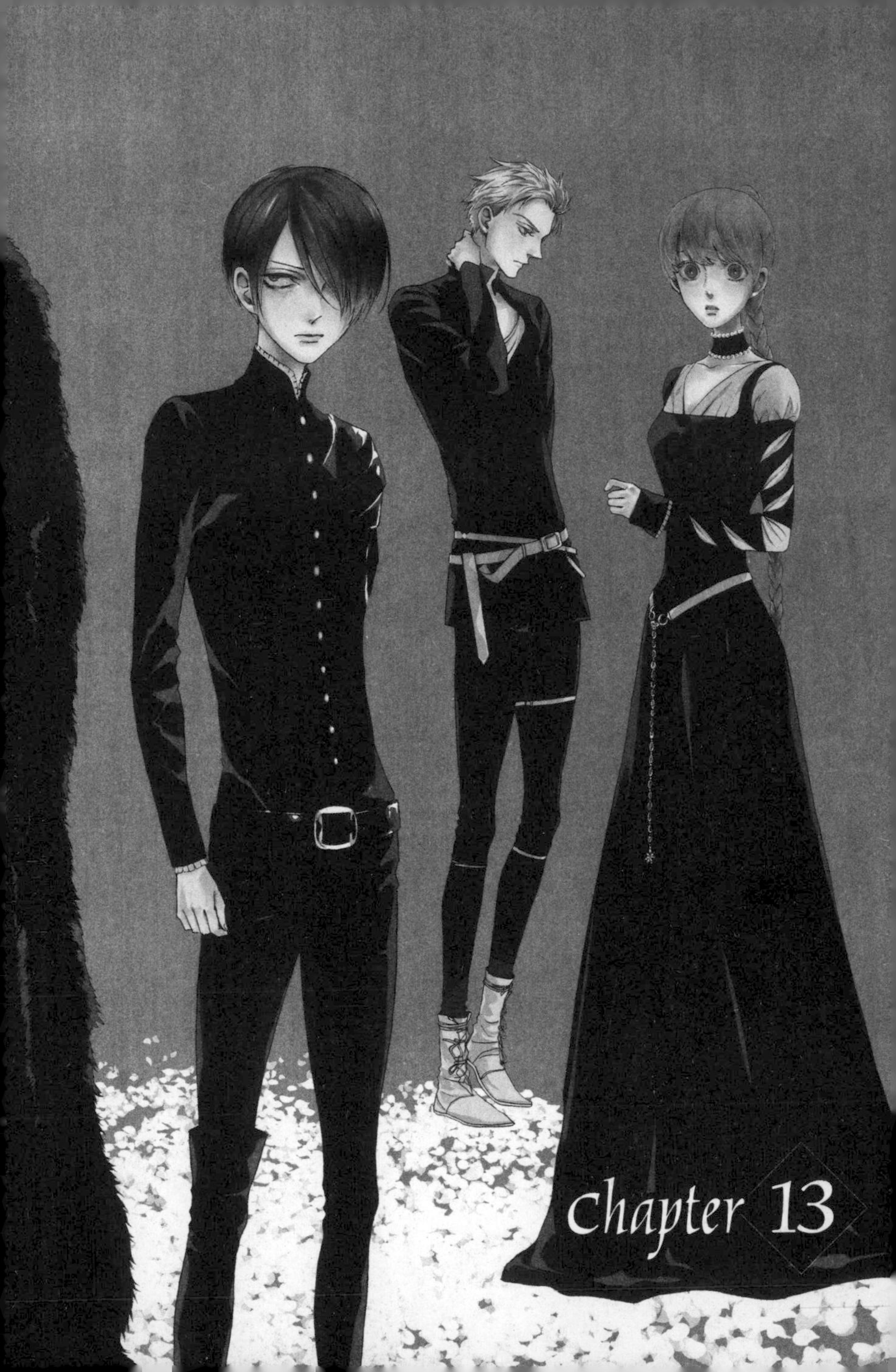
Chapter 13

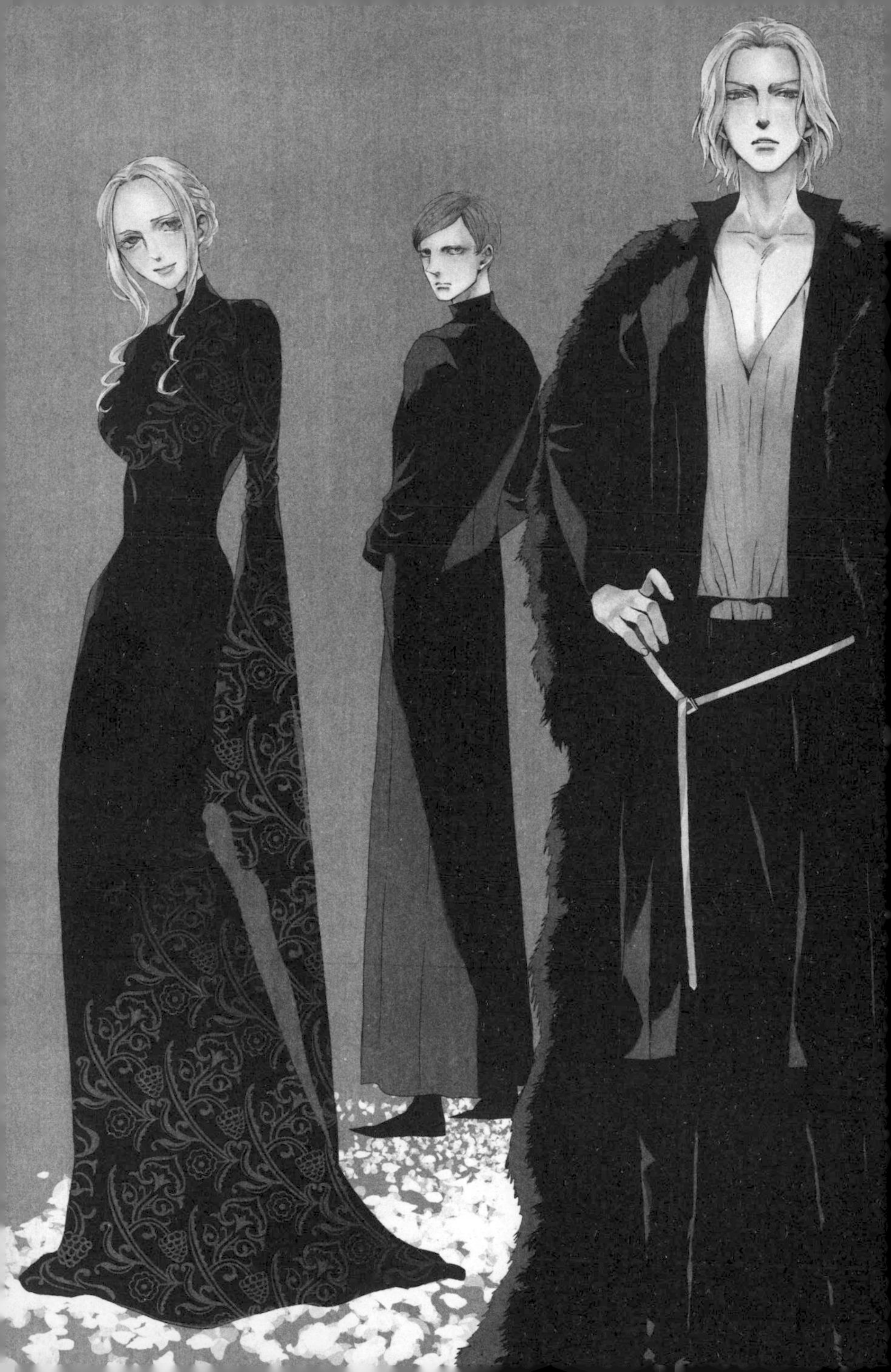

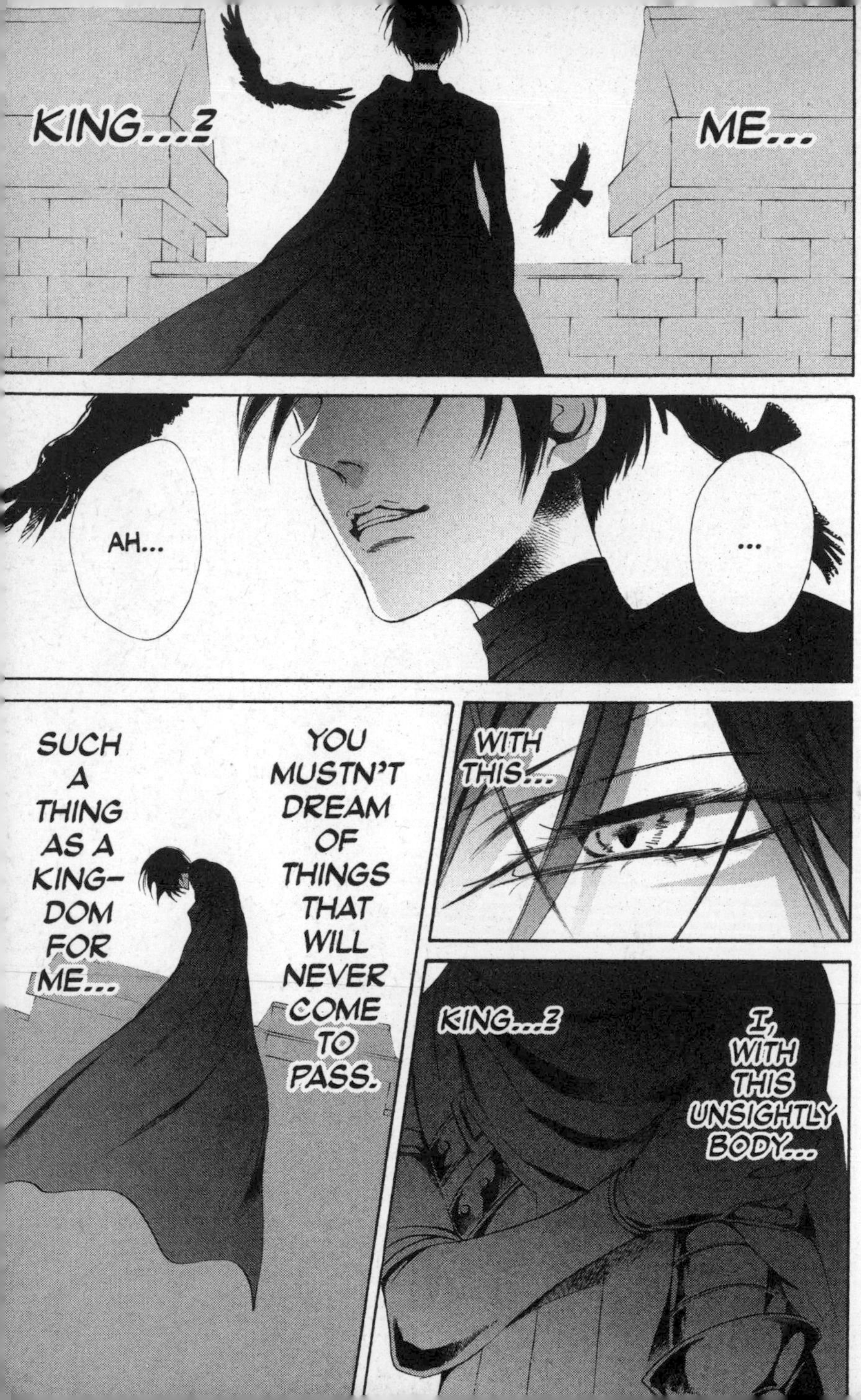
ME...
KING...?
...
AH...
WITH THIS...
I, WITH THIS UNSIGHTLY BODY...
KING...?
YOU MUSTN'T DREAM OF THINGS THAT WILL NEVER COME TO PASS.
SUCH A THING AS A KING-DOM FOR ME...

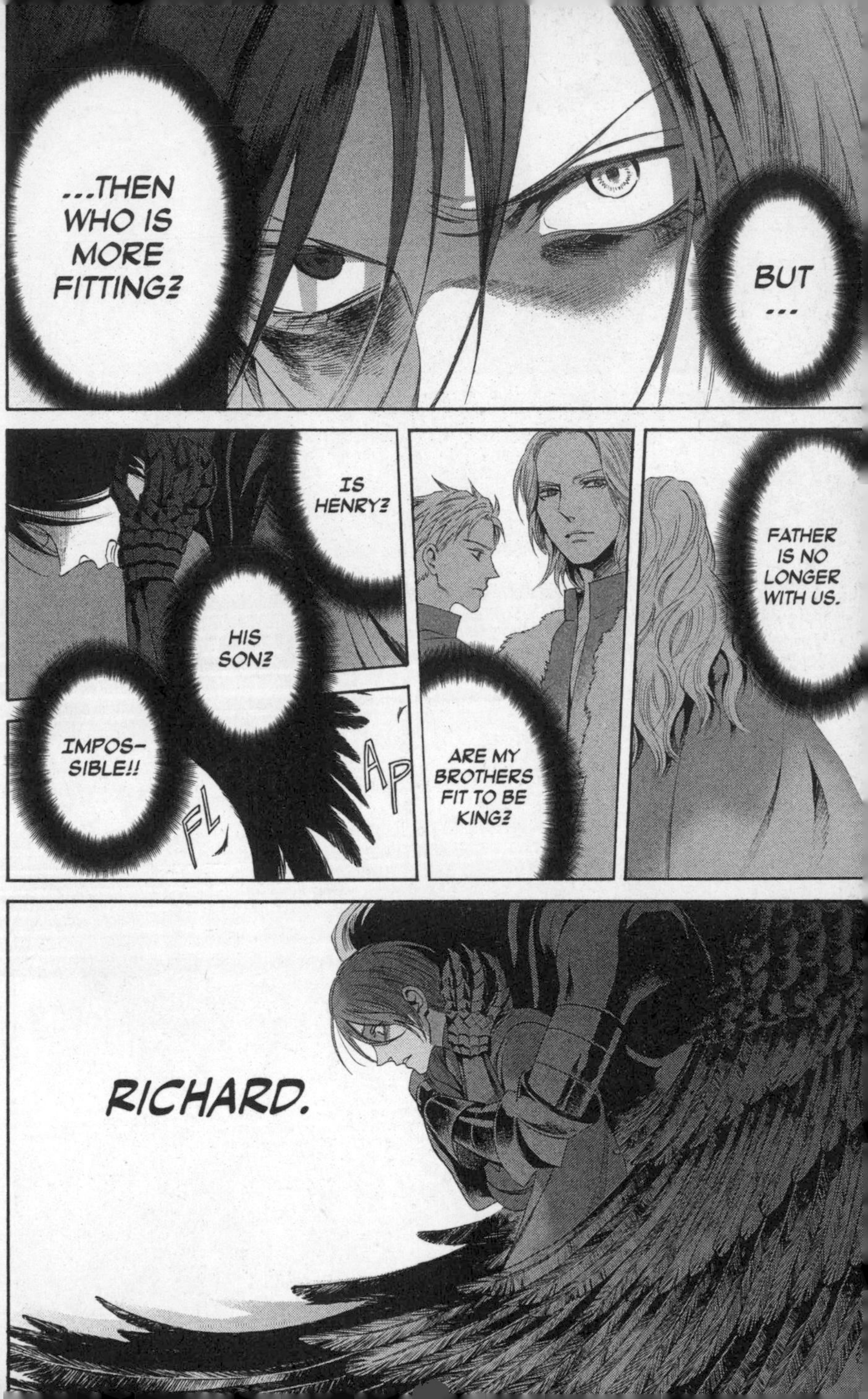
BUT ...
...THEN WHO IS MORE FITTING?
FATHER IS NO LONGER WITH US.
ARE MY BROTHERS FIT TO BE KING?
IS HENRY?
HIS SON?
IMPOSSIBLE!!
FLAP
RICHARD.

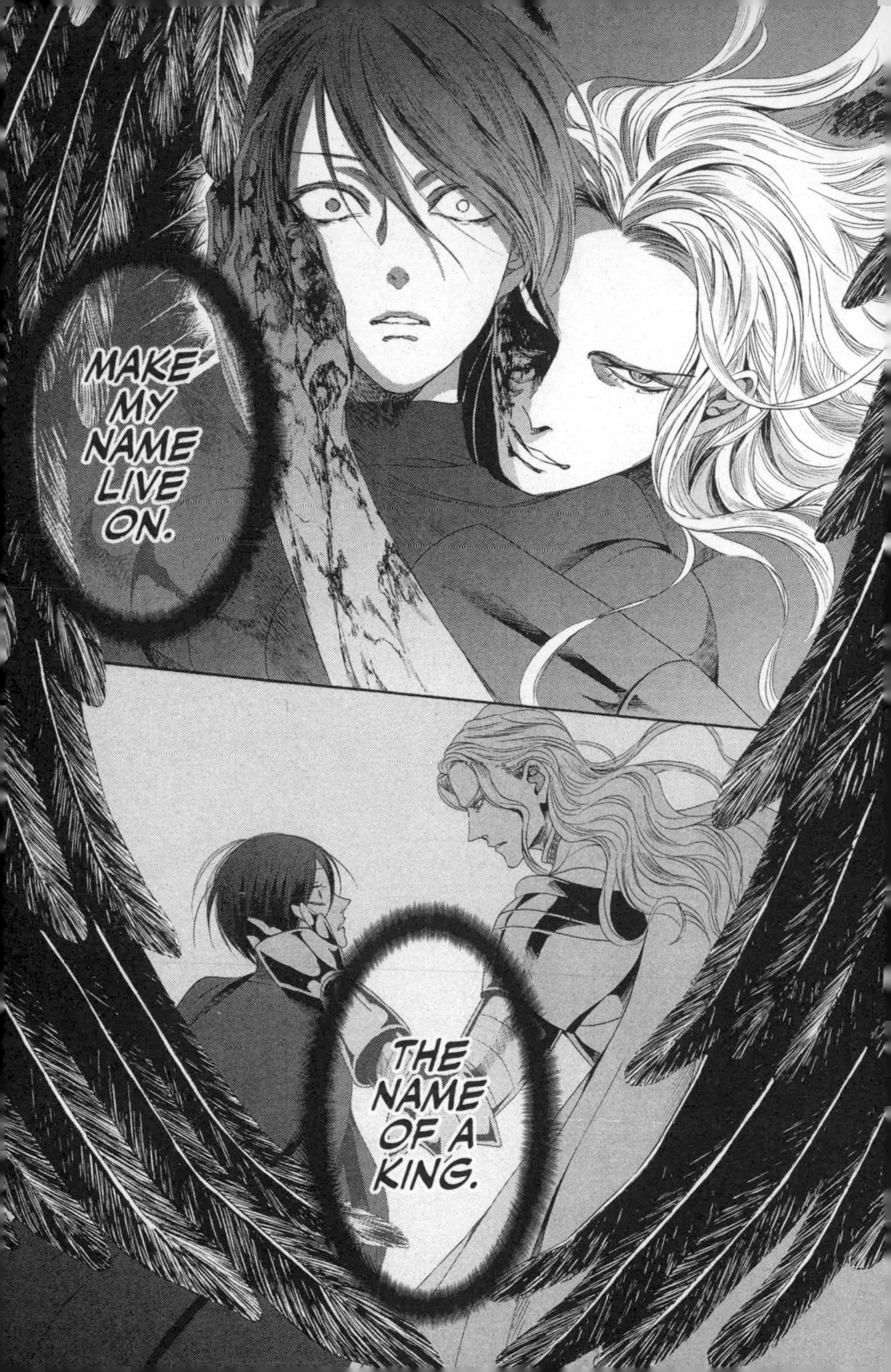
MAKE MY NAME LIVE ON.
THE NAME OF A KING.

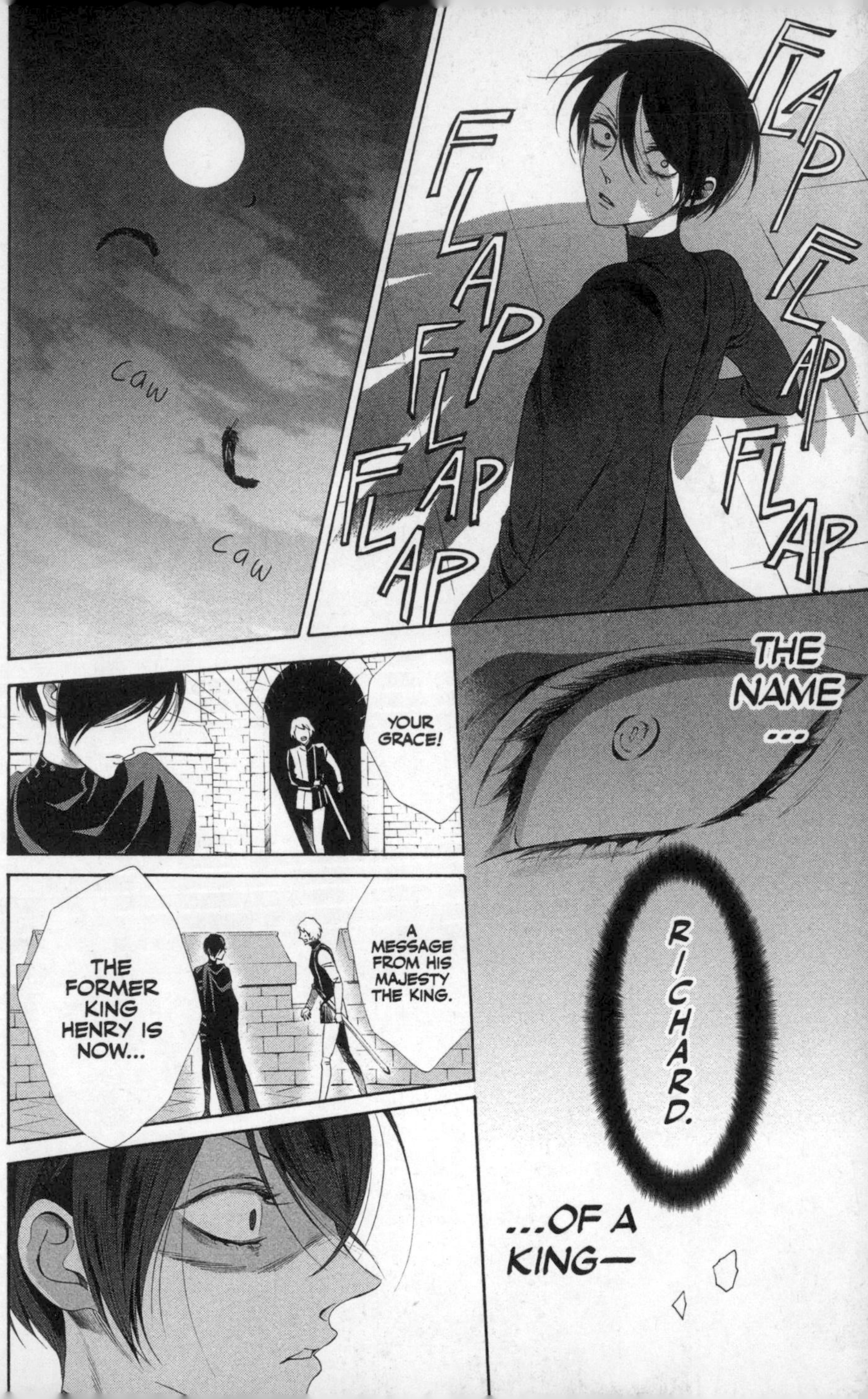
FLAP FLAP FLAP
FLAP FLAP FLAP
FLAP FLAP
caw
caw
THE NAME...
RICHARD.
...OF A KING—
YOUR GRACE!
A MESSAGE FROM HIS MAJESTY THE KING.
THE FORMER KING HENRY IS NOW...

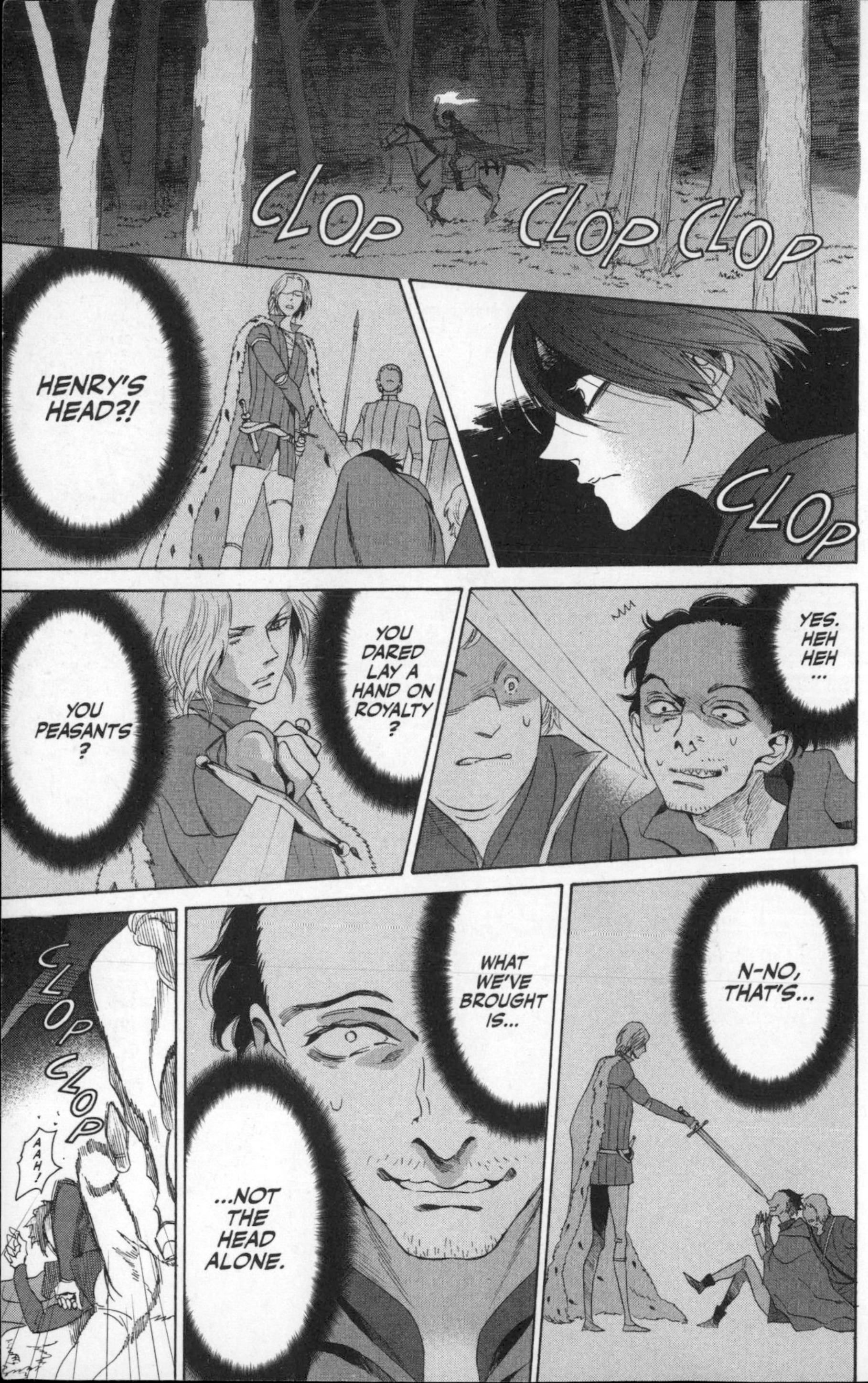

CLOP
CLOP CLOP
CLOP
CLOP
HENRY'S HEAD?!
YES. HEH HEH...
YOU DARED LAY A HAND ON ROYALTY?
YOU PEASANTS?
N-NO, THAT'S...
WHAT WE'VE BROUGHT IS...
...NOT THE HEAD ALONE.
CLOP CLOP CLOP
AAH!

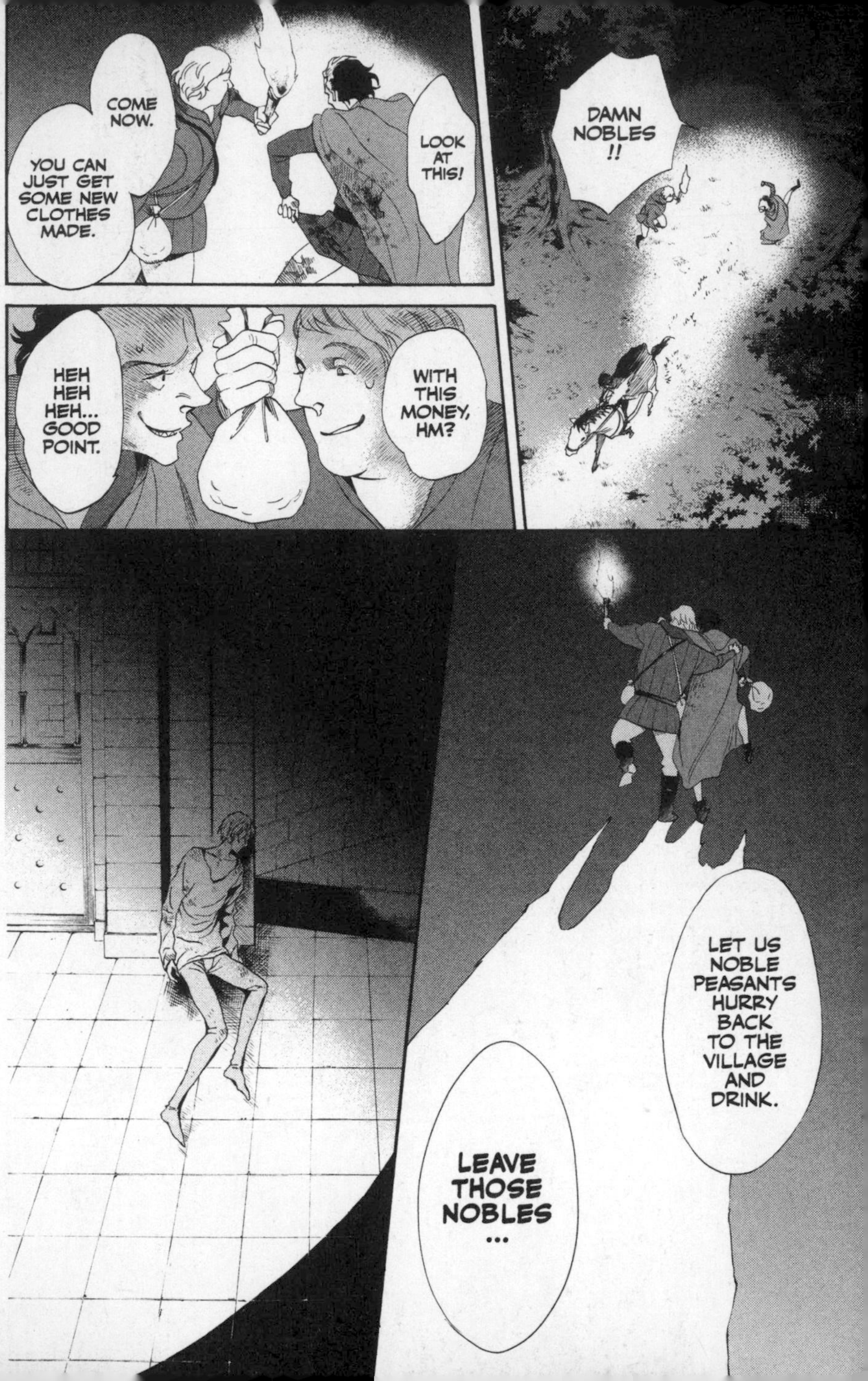
DAMN NOBLES!!
LOOK AT THIS!
COME NOW.
YOU CAN JUST GET SOME NEW CLOTHES MADE.
WITH THIS MONEY, HM?
HEH HEH HEH... GOOD POINT.
LET US NOBLE PEASANTS HURRY BACK TO THE VILLAGE AND DRINK.
LEAVE THOSE NOBLES...

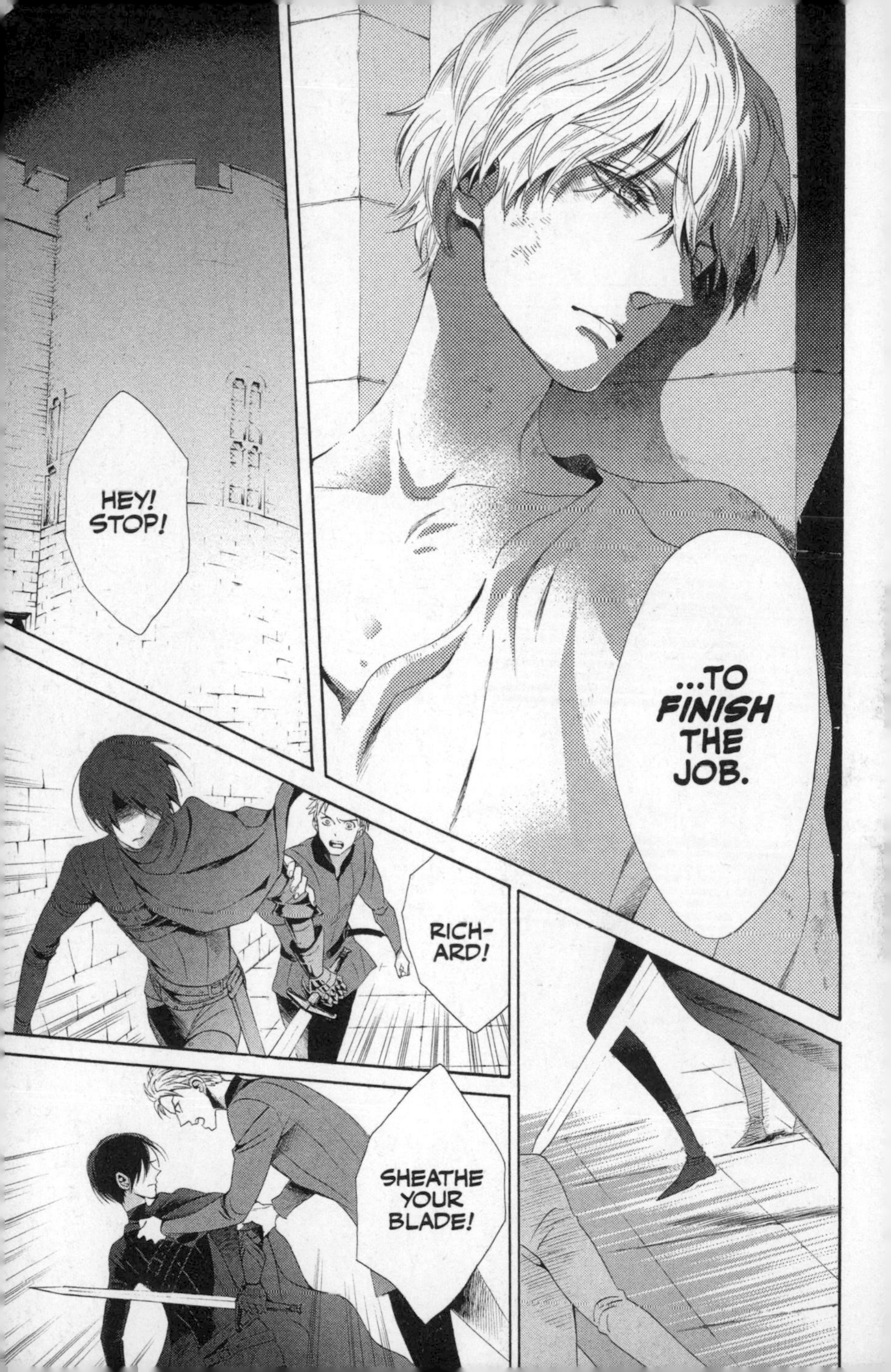
...TO *FINISH* THE JOB.
HEY! STOP!
RICH-ARD!
SHEATHE YOUR BLADE!

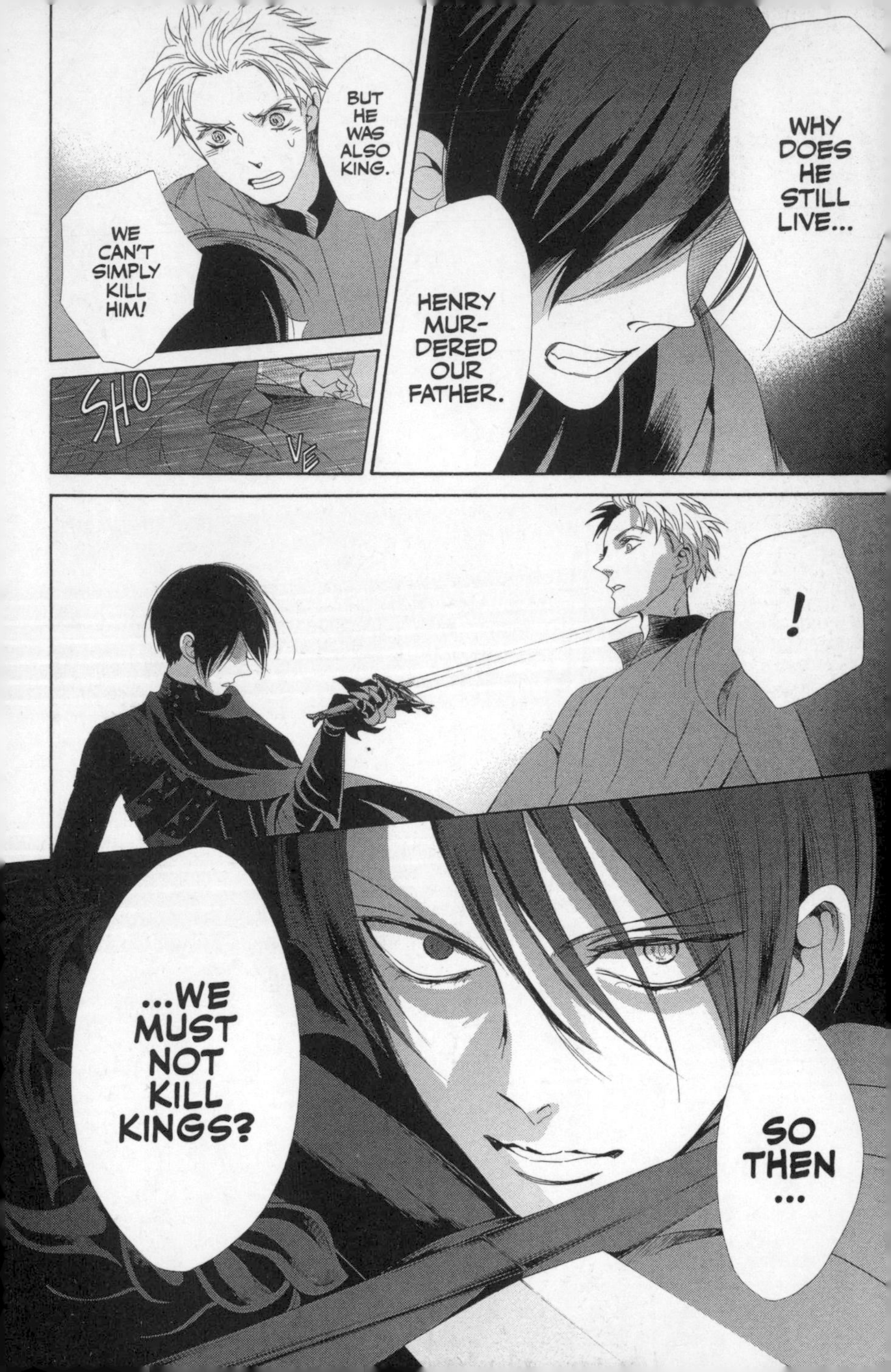

WHY DOES HE STILL LIVE...
HENRY MURDERED OUR FATHER.
BUT HE WAS ALSO KING.
WE CAN'T SIMPLY KILL HIM!
SHOVE
!
SO THEN...
...WE MUST NOT KILL KINGS?

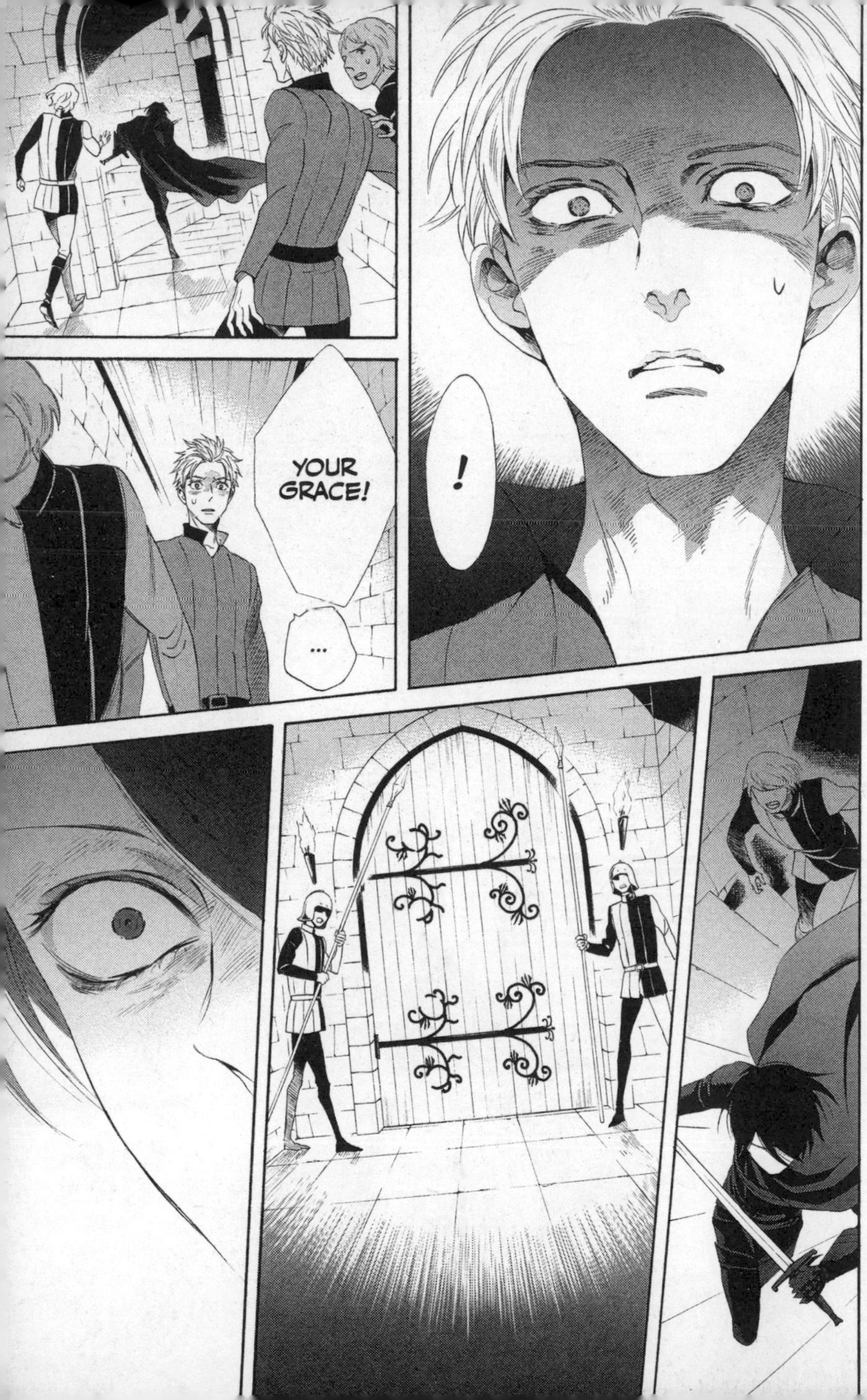
!
YOUR GRACE!
...

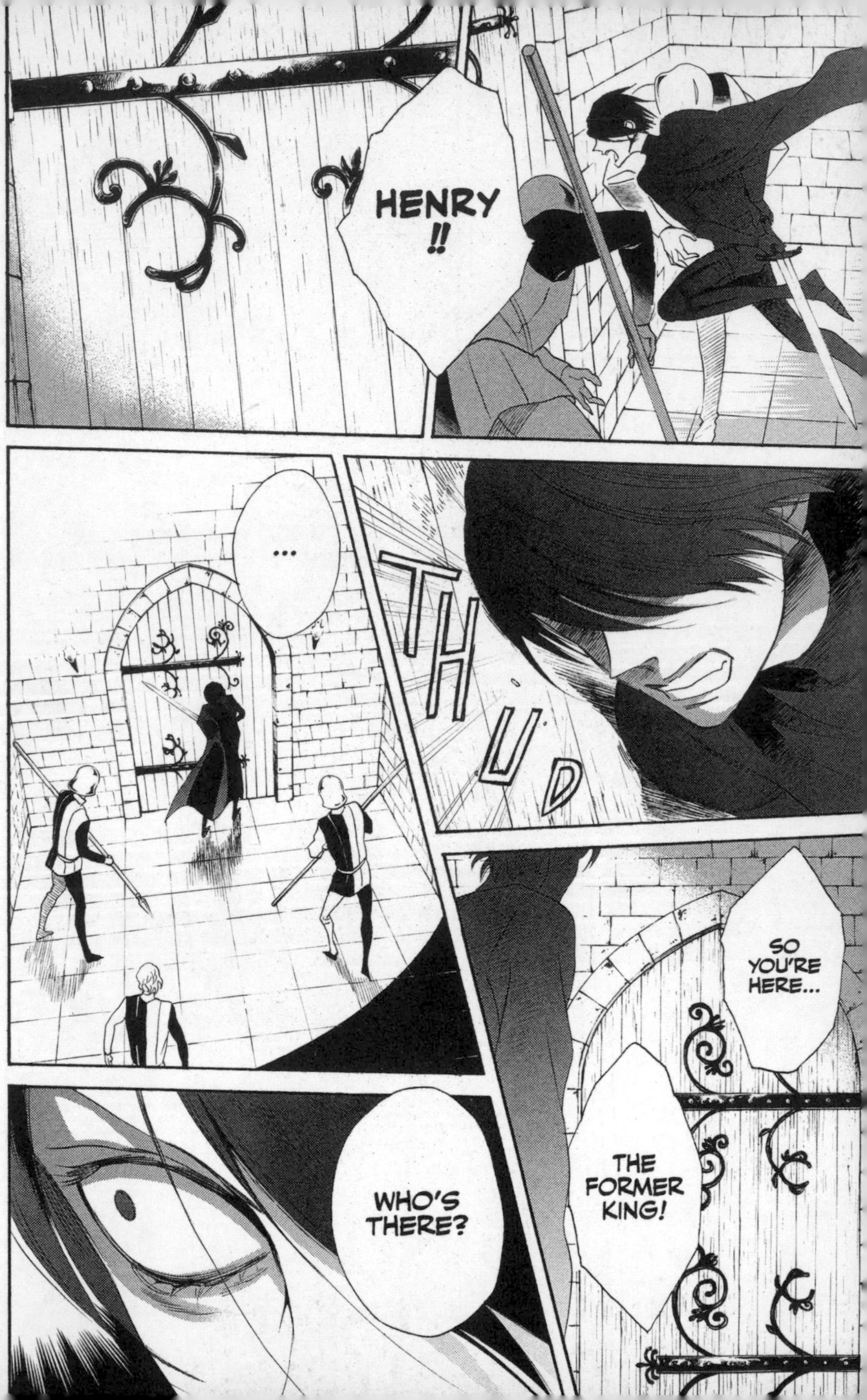
HENRY!!
THUD
...
SO YOU'RE HERE...
THE FORMER KING!
WHO'S THERE?

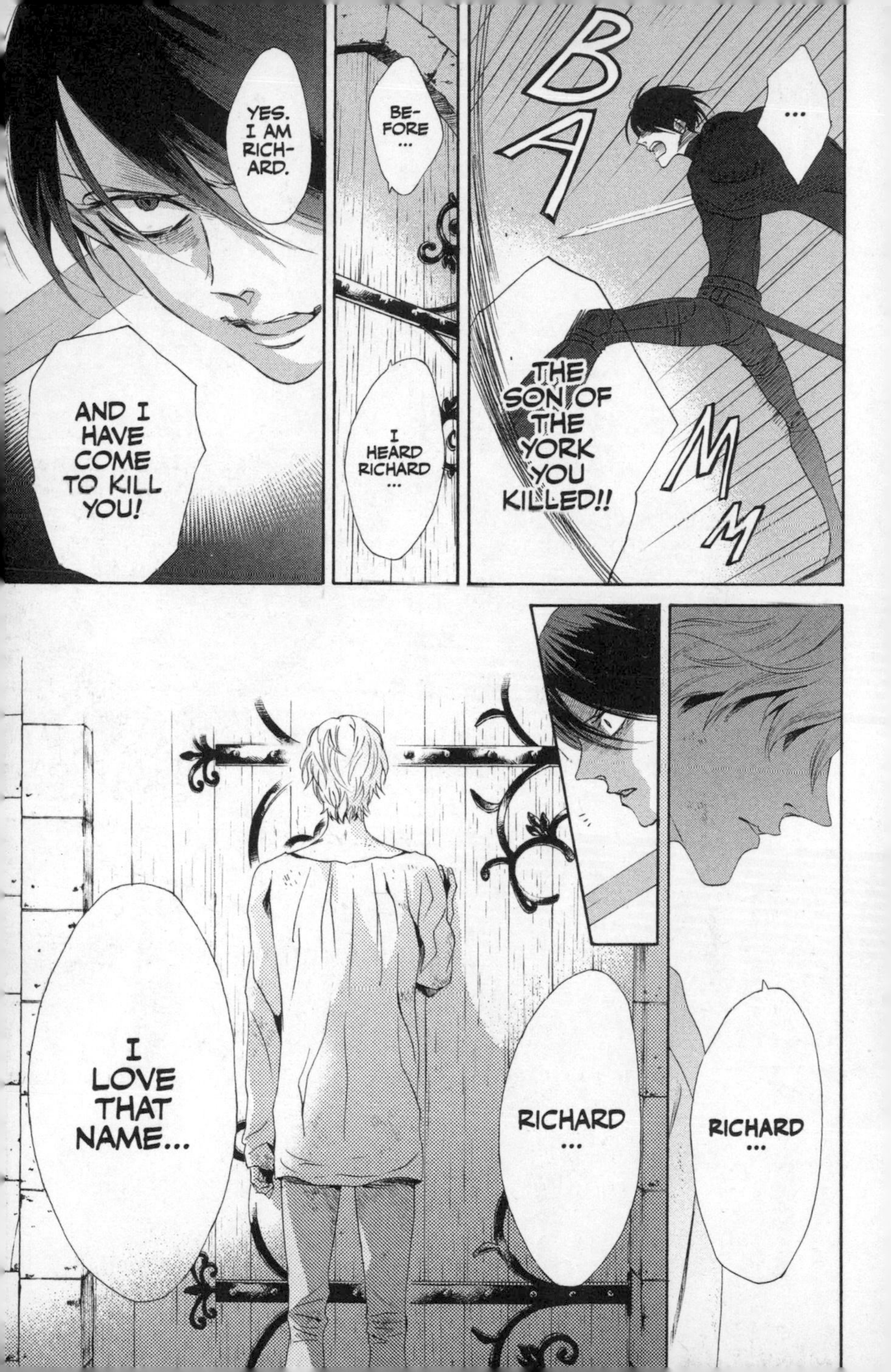
...
BAMM
THE SON OF THE YORK YOU KILLED!!
BE-FORE ...
I HEARD RICHARD ...
YES. I AM RICH-ARD.
AND I HAVE COME TO KILL YOU!
RICHARD ...
RICHARD ...
I LOVE THAT NAME...

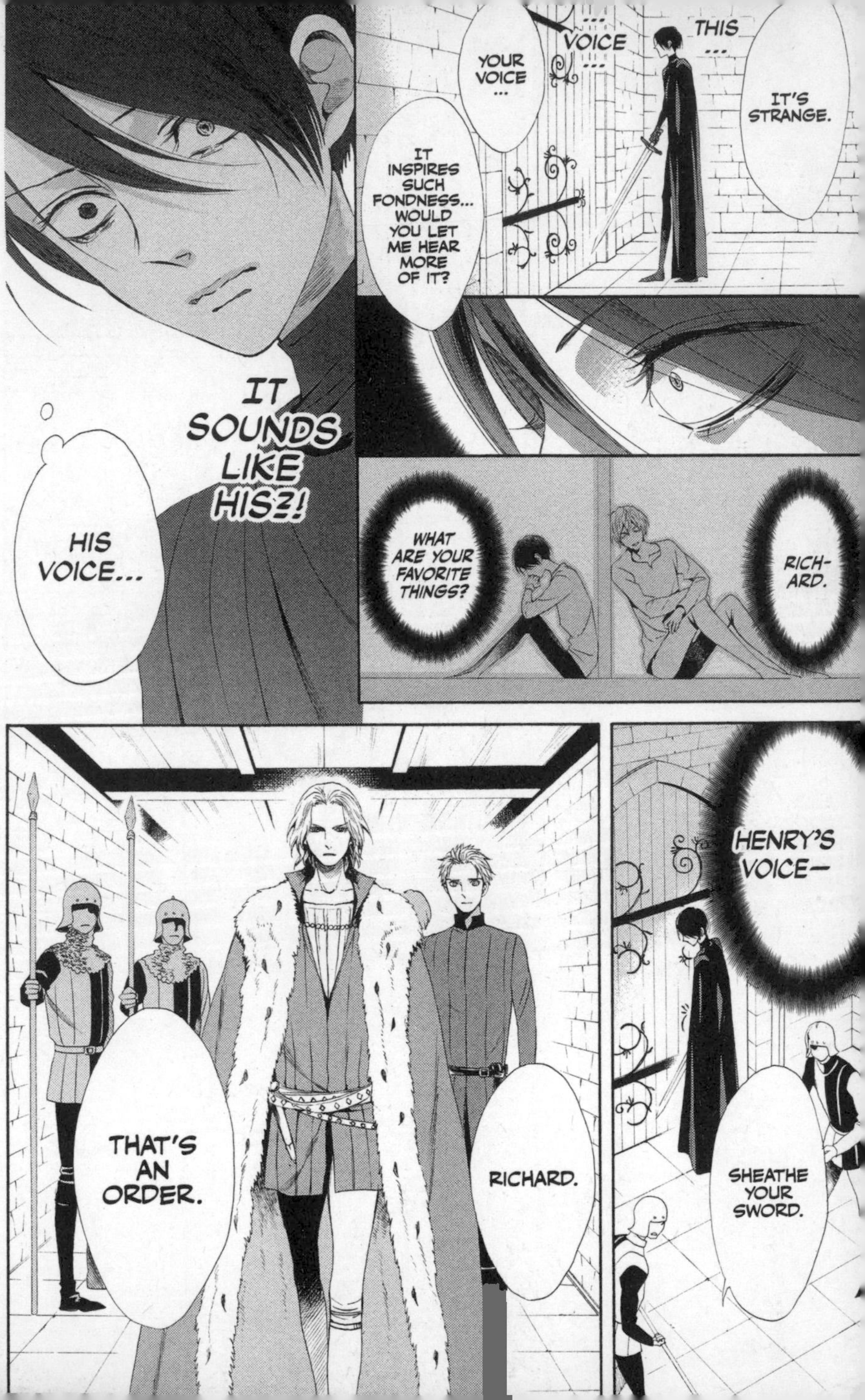
THIS...
IT'S STRANGE.
...VOICE...
YOUR VOICE...
IT INSPIRES SUCH FONDNESS... WOULD YOU LET ME HEAR MORE OF IT?
RICHARD.
WHAT ARE YOUR FAVORITE THINGS?
IT SOUNDS LIKE HIS?!
HIS VOICE...
HENRY'S VOICE—
SHEATHE YOUR SWORD.
RICHARD.
THAT'S AN ORDER.

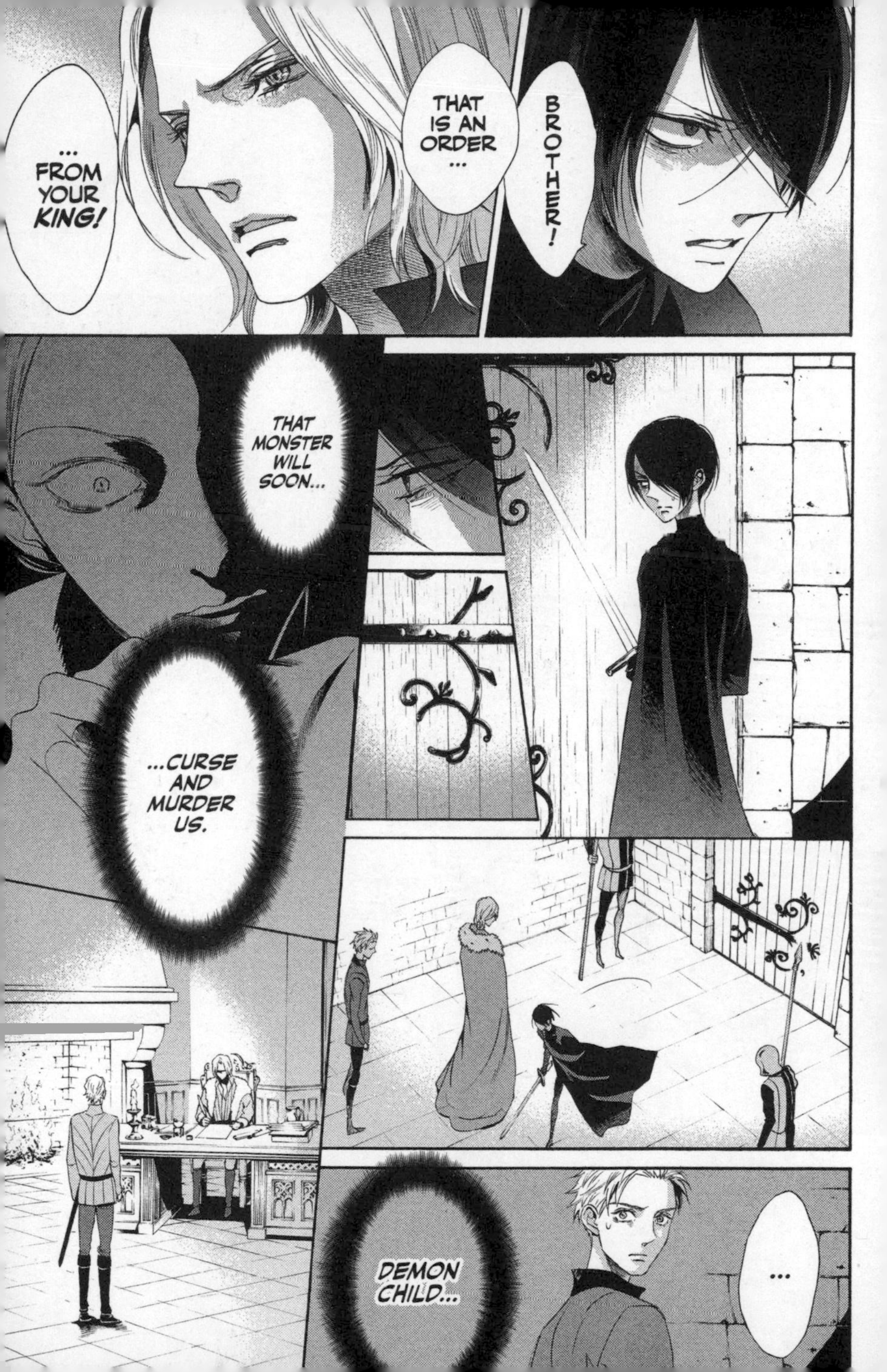
BROTHER!
THAT IS AN ORDER...
...FROM YOUR KING!
THAT MONSTER WILL SOON...
...CURSE AND MURDER US.
...
DEMON CHILD...

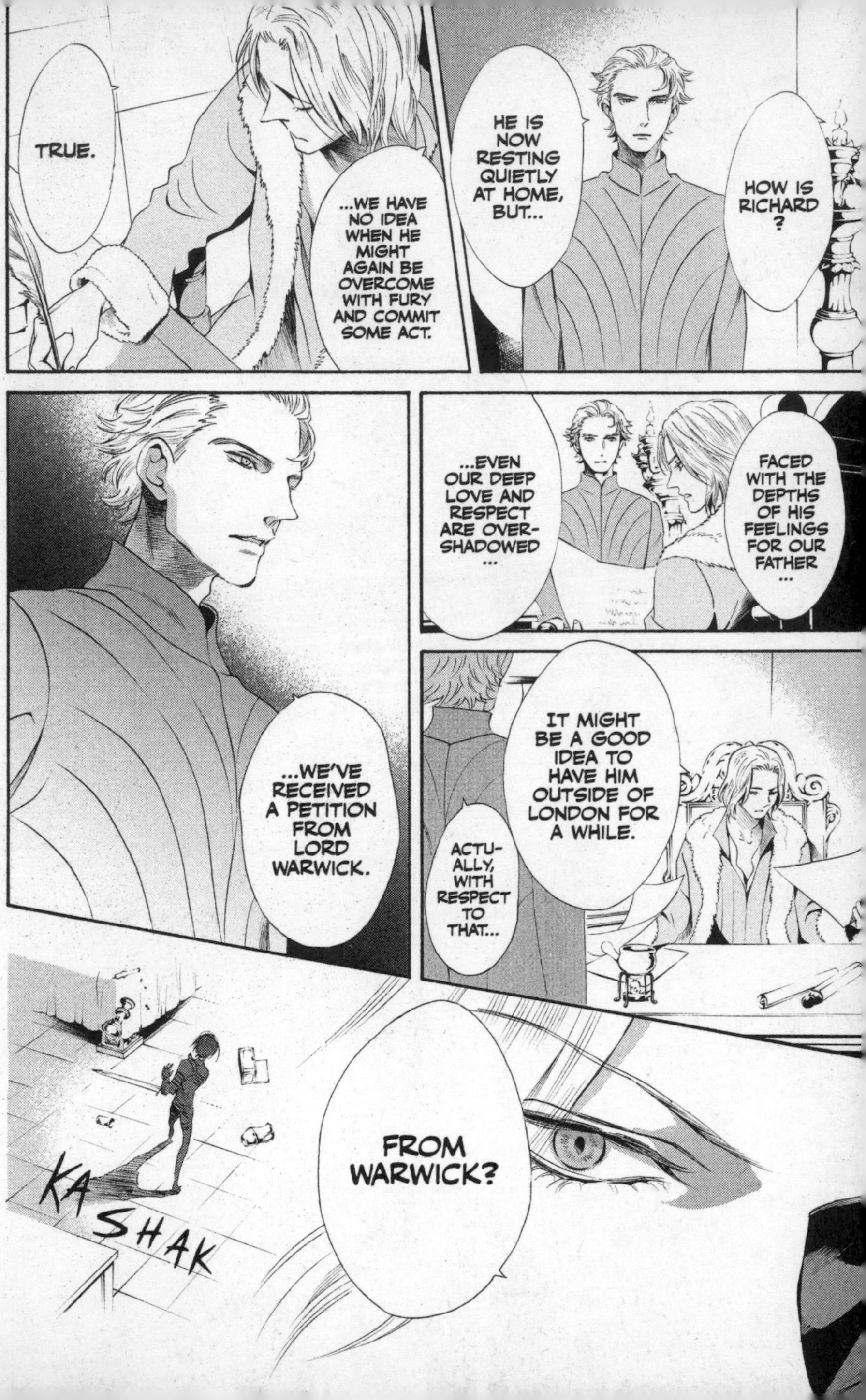
HOW IS RICHARD ?
HE IS NOW RESTING QUIETLY AT HOME, BUT...
...WE HAVE NO IDEA WHEN HE MIGHT AGAIN BE OVERCOME WITH FURY AND COMMIT SOME ACT.
TRUE.
FACED WITH THE DEPTHS OF HIS FEELINGS FOR OUR FATHER...
...EVEN OUR DEEP LOVE AND RESPECT ARE OVER-SHADOWED...
IT MIGHT BE A GOOD IDEA TO HAVE HIM OUTSIDE OF LONDON FOR A WHILE.
ACTU-ALLY, WITH RESPECT TO THAT...
...WE'VE RECEIVED A PETITION FROM LORD WARWICK.
FROM WARWICK?
KA SHAK

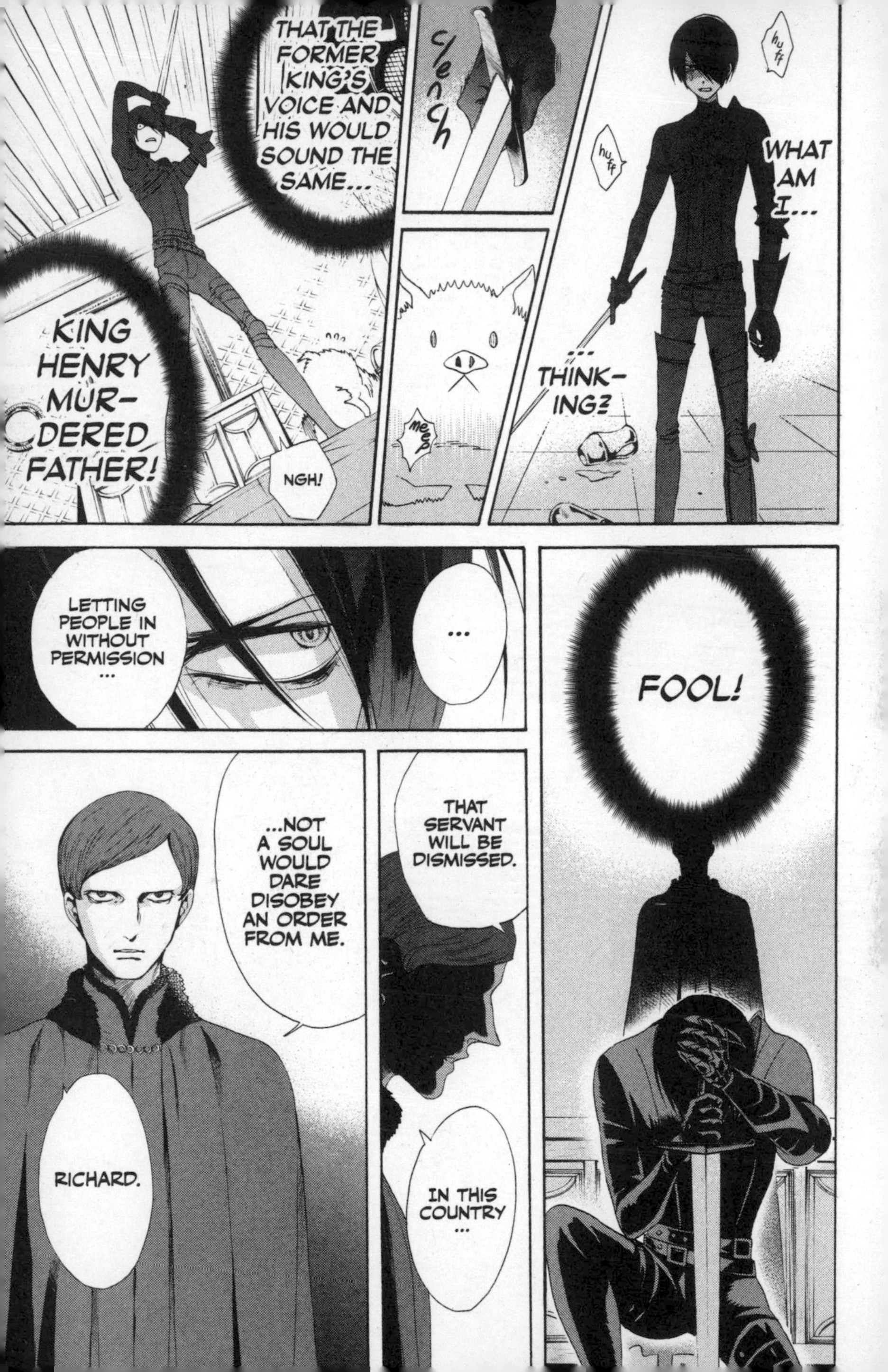
huff
huff
WHAT AM I...
...THINKING?
clench
meep
THAT THE FORMER KING'S VOICE AND HIS WOULD SOUND THE SAME...
KING HENRY MURDERED FATHER!
NGH!
FOOL!
...
LETTING PEOPLE IN WITHOUT PERMISSION ...
THAT SERVANT WILL BE DISMISSED.
IN THIS COUNTRY ...
...NOT A SOUL WOULD DARE DISOBEY AN ORDER FROM ME.
RICHARD.

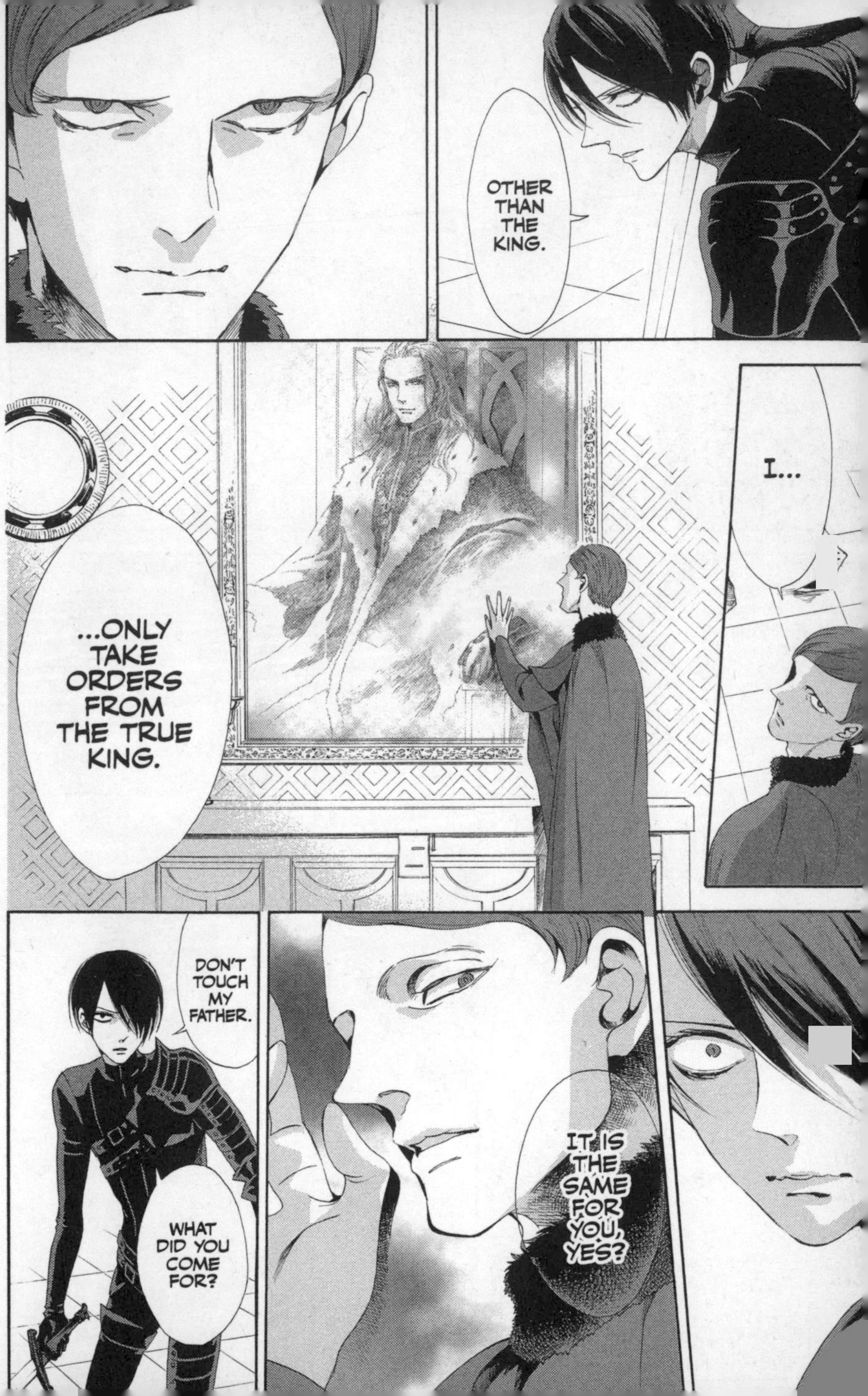
OTHER THAN THE KING.
I...
...ONLY TAKE ORDERS FROM THE TRUE KING.
IT IS THE SAME FOR YOU, YES?
DON'T TOUCH MY FATHER.
WHAT DID YOU COME FOR?

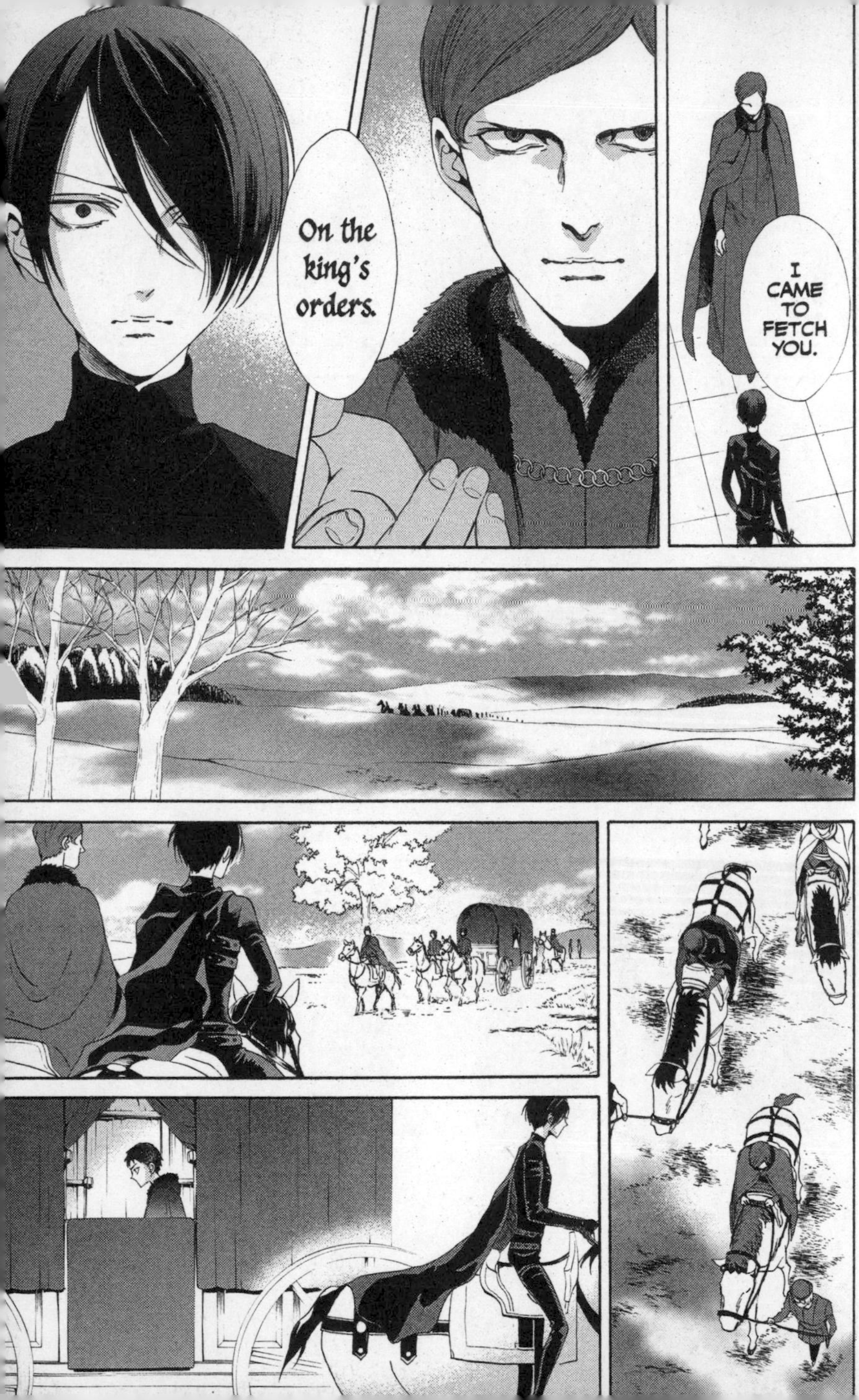
I CAME TO FETCH YOU.
On the king's orders.

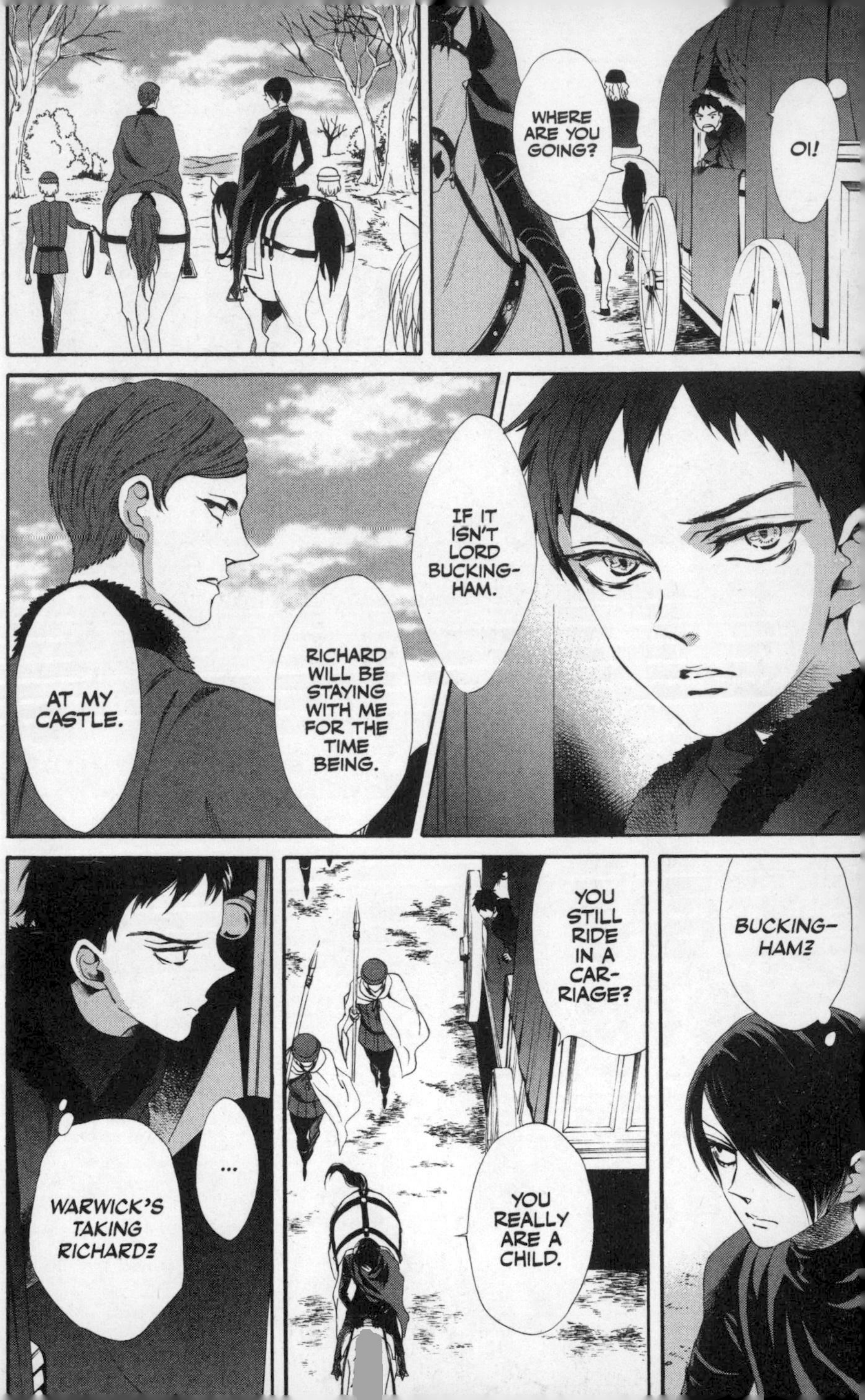

OI!
WHERE ARE YOU GOING?
IF IT ISN'T LORD BUCKING-HAM.
RICHARD WILL BE STAYING WITH ME FOR THE TIME BEING.
AT MY CASTLE.
BUCKING-HAM?
YOU STILL RIDE IN A CAR-RIAGE?
YOU REALLY ARE A CHILD.
...
WARWICK'S TAKING RICHARD?

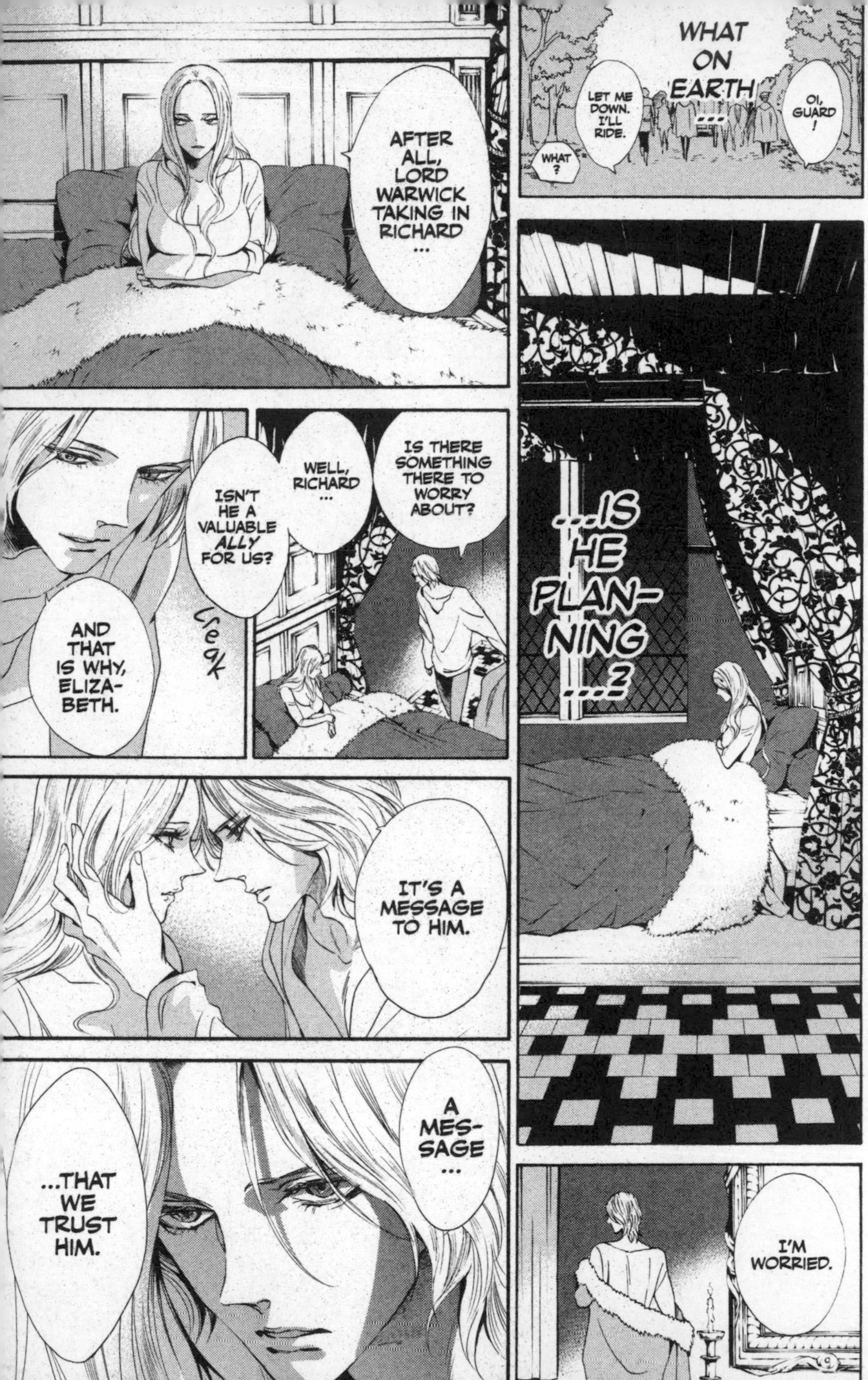
WHAT ON EARTH...
OI, GUARD!
LET ME DOWN. I'LL RIDE.
WHAT?
...IS HE PLANNING...?
I'M WORRIED.
AFTER ALL, LORD WARWICK TAKING IN RICHARD...
IS THERE SOMETHING THERE TO WORRY ABOUT?
WELL, RICHARD...
ISN'T HE A VALUABLE *ALLY* FOR US?
Creak
AND THAT IS WHY, ELIZABETH.
IT'S A MESSAGE TO HIM.
A MESSAGE...
...THAT WE TRUST HIM.

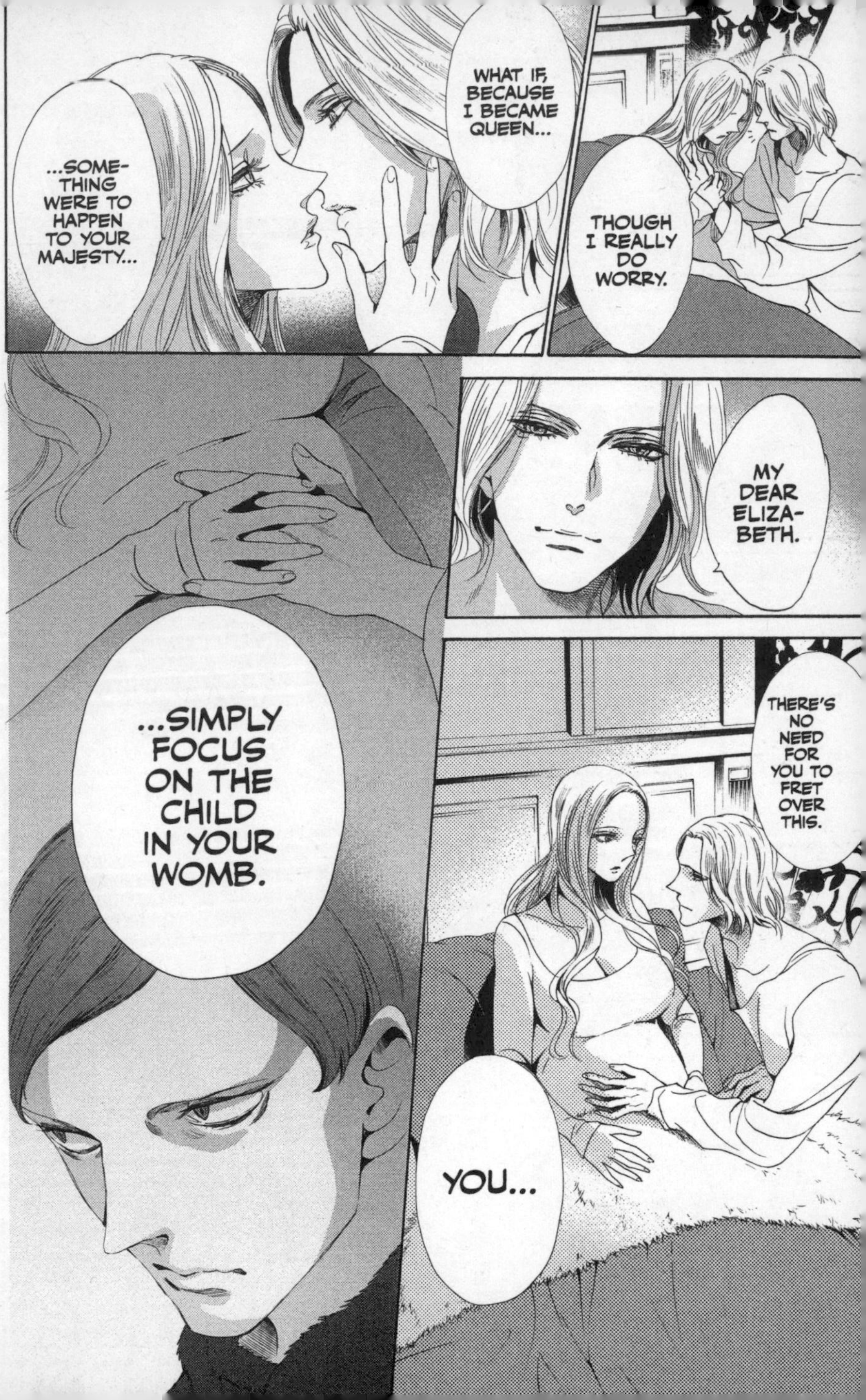
THOUGH I REALLY DO WORRY.
WHAT IF, BECAUSE I BECAME QUEEN...
...SOME-THING WERE TO HAPPEN TO YOUR MAJESTY...
MY DEAR ELIZA-BETH.
THERE'S NO NEED FOR YOU TO FRET OVER THIS.
YOU...
...SIMPLY FOCUS ON THE CHILD IN YOUR WOMB.

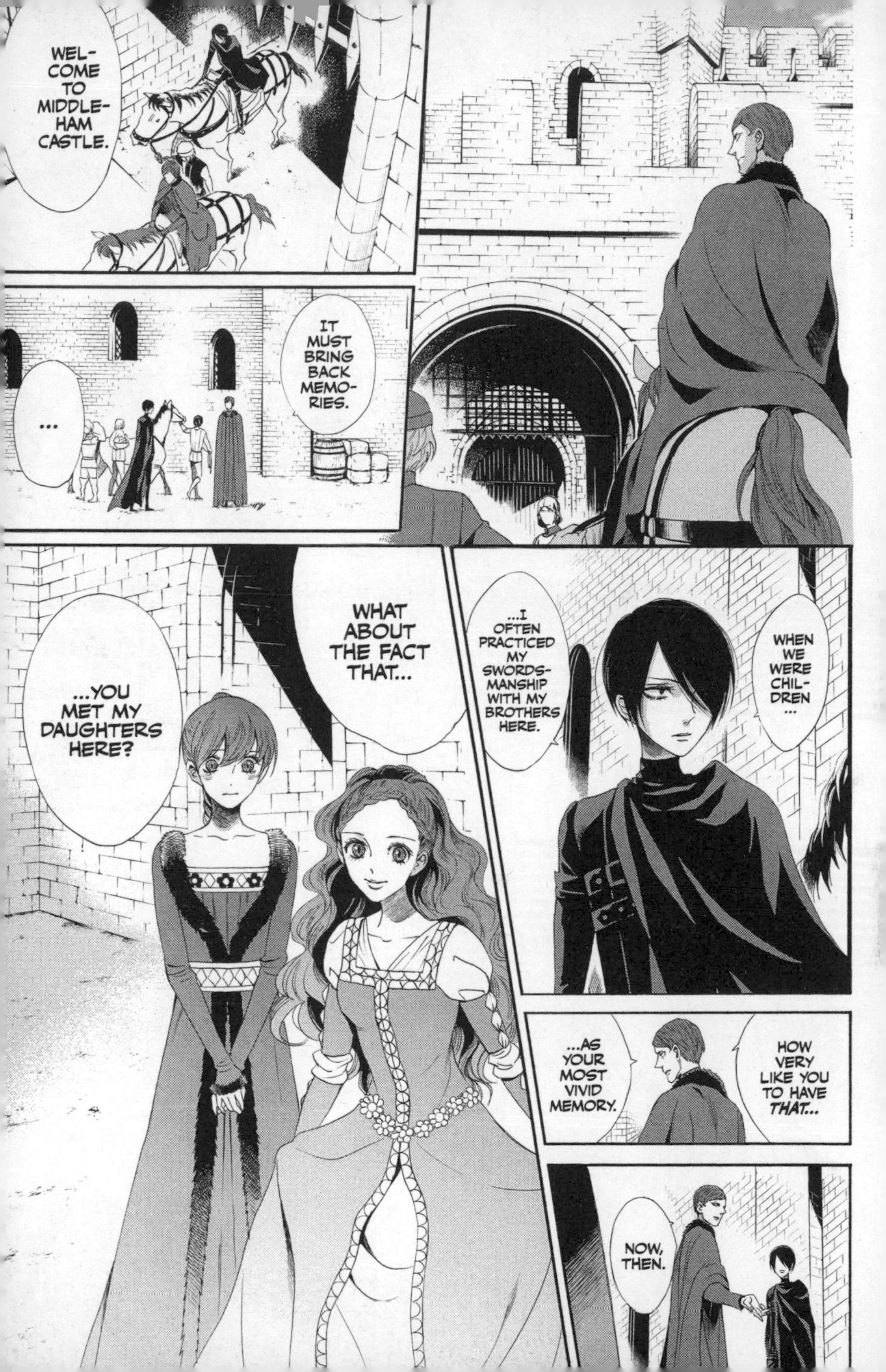
WEL-COME TO MIDDLE-HAM CASTLE.
IT MUST BRING BACK MEMO-RIES.
...
WHEN WE WERE CHIL-DREN...
...I OFTEN PRACTICED MY SWORDS-MANSHIP WITH MY BROTHERS HERE.
HOW VERY LIKE YOU TO HAVE *THAT*...
...AS YOUR MOST VIVID MEMORY.
NOW, THEN.
WHAT ABOUT THE FACT THAT...
...YOU MET MY DAUGHTERS HERE?

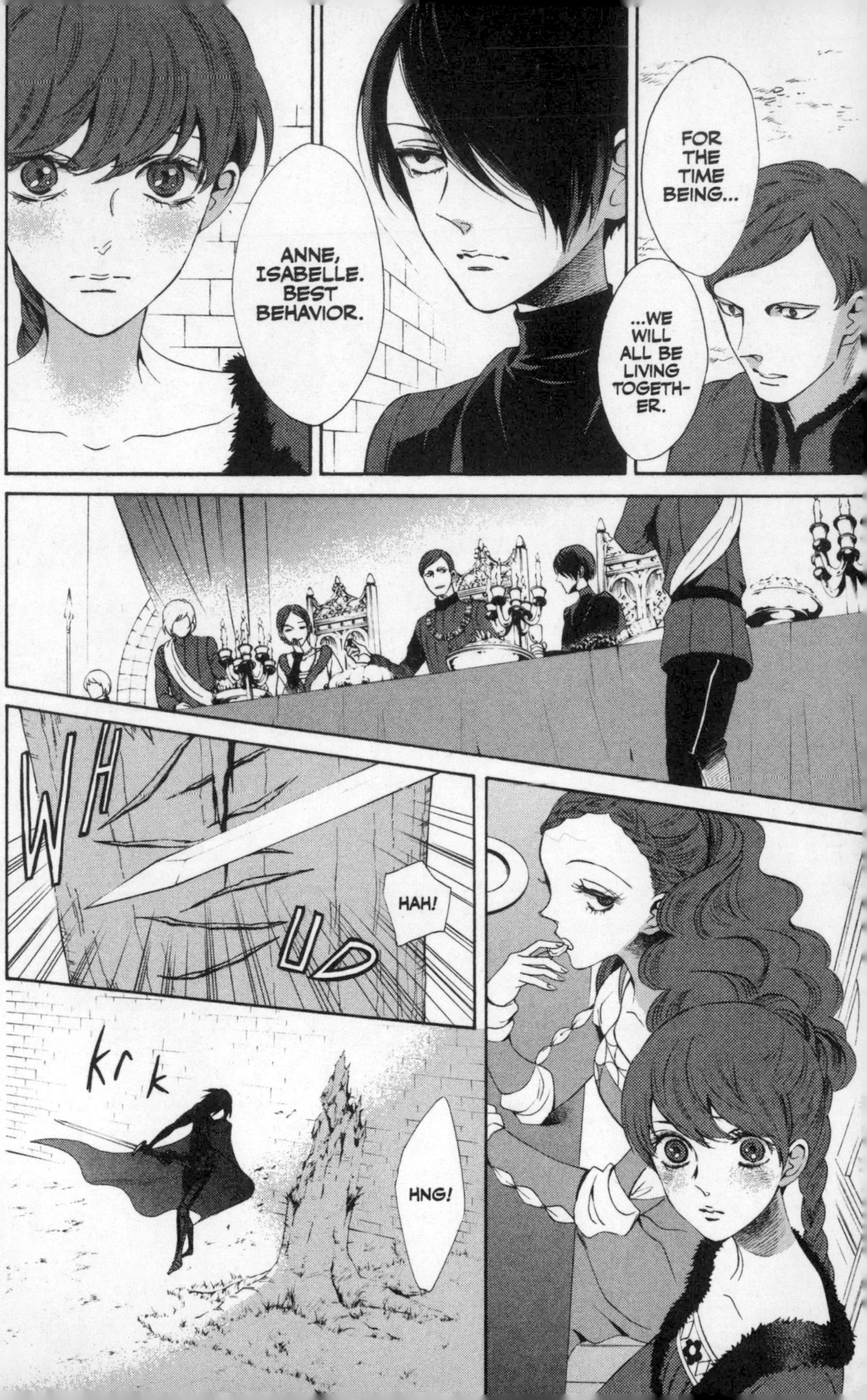
FOR THE TIME BEING...
...WE WILL ALL BE LIVING TOGETHER.
ANNE, ISABELLE. BEST BEHAVIOR.
HAH!
WHUD
krk
HNG!

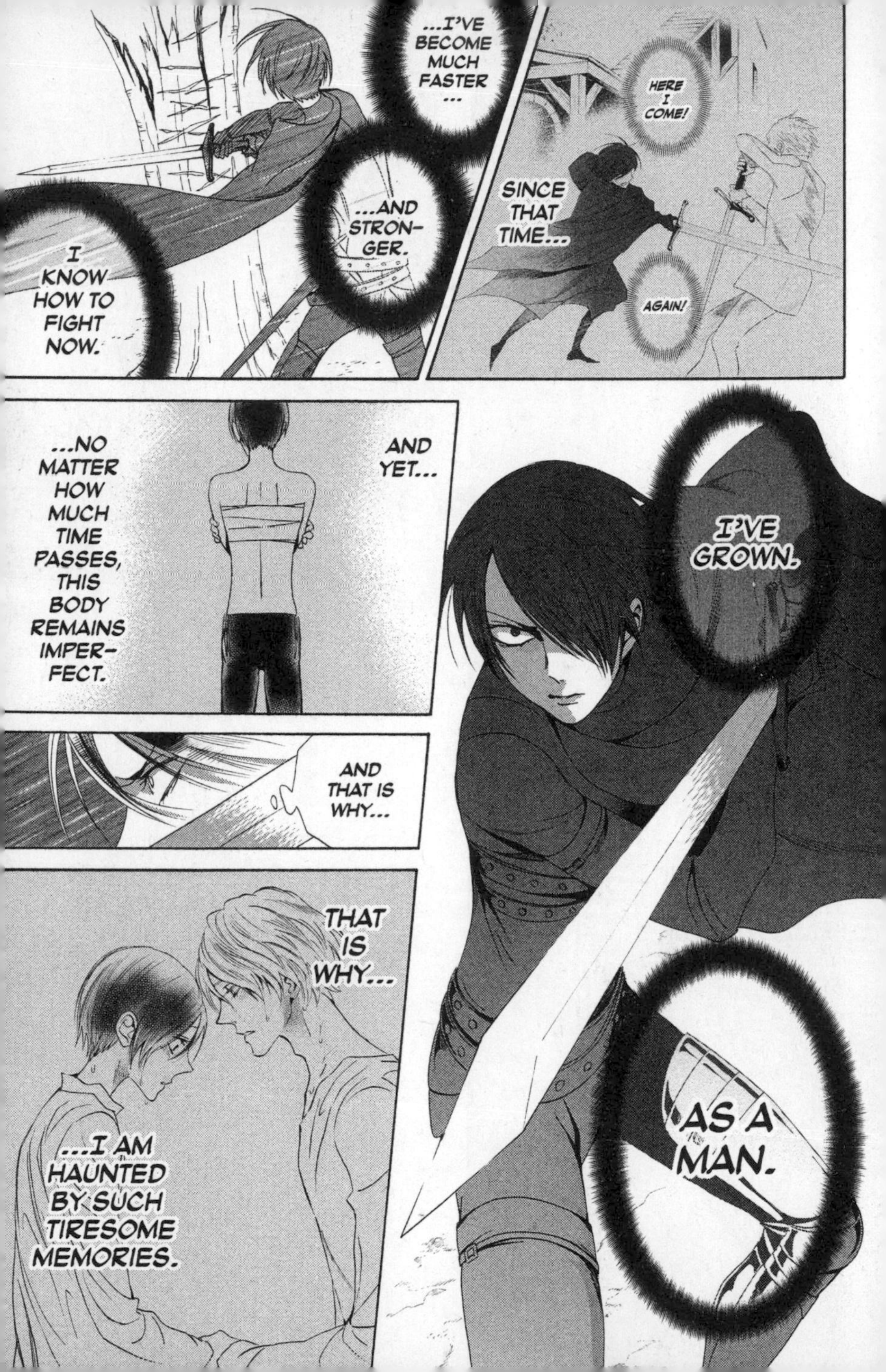
HERE I COME!
SINCE THAT TIME...
AGAIN!
...I'VE BECOME MUCH FASTER...
...AND STRONGER.
I KNOW HOW TO FIGHT NOW.
I'VE GROWN.
AS A MAN.
AND YET...
...NO MATTER HOW MUCH TIME PASSES, THIS BODY REMAINS IMPERFECT.
AND THAT IS WHY...
THAT IS WHY...
...I AM HAUNTED BY SUCH TIRESOME MEMORIES.

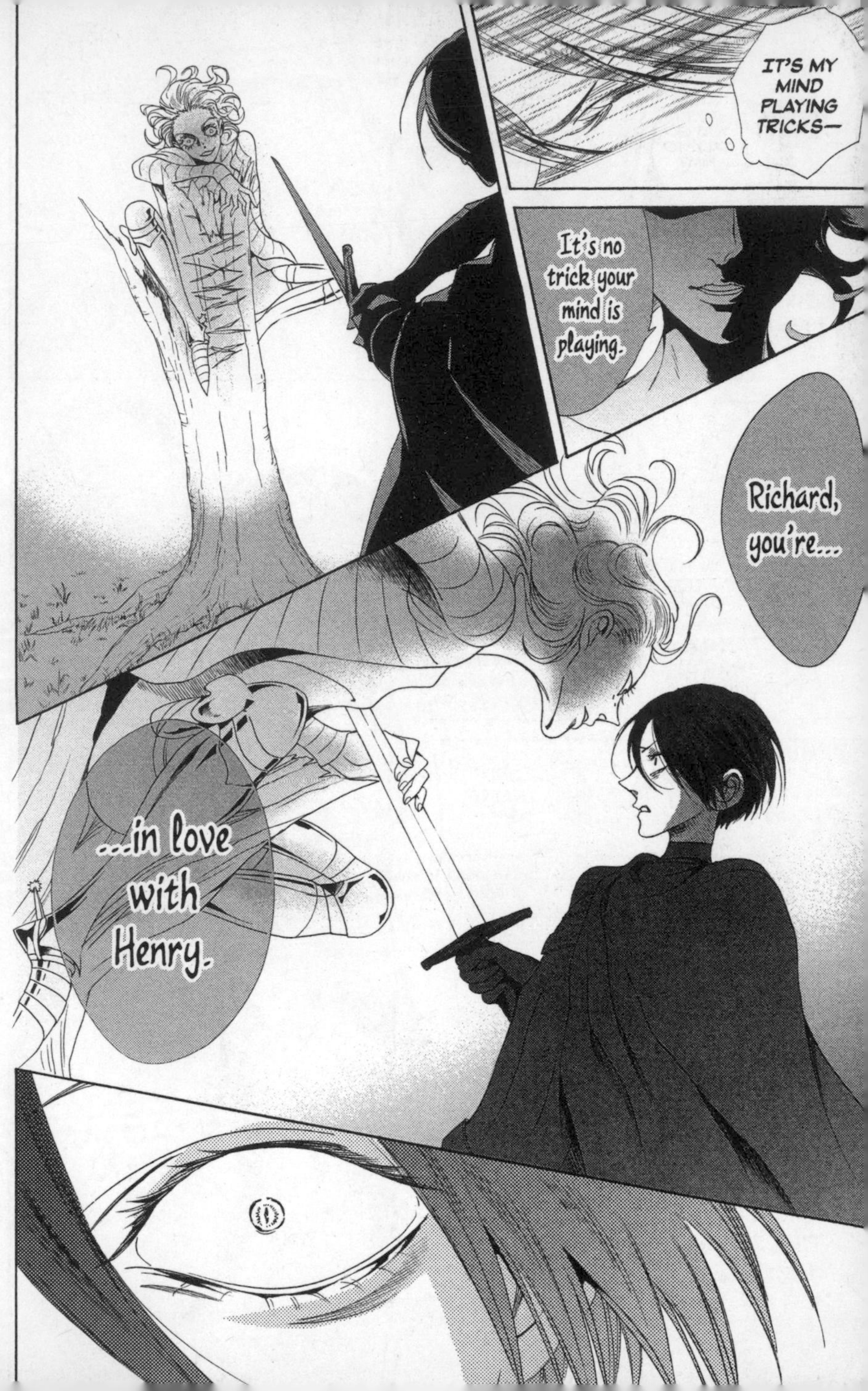
IT'S MY MIND PLAYING TRICKS—
It's no trick your mind is playing.
Richard, you're...
...in love with Henry.

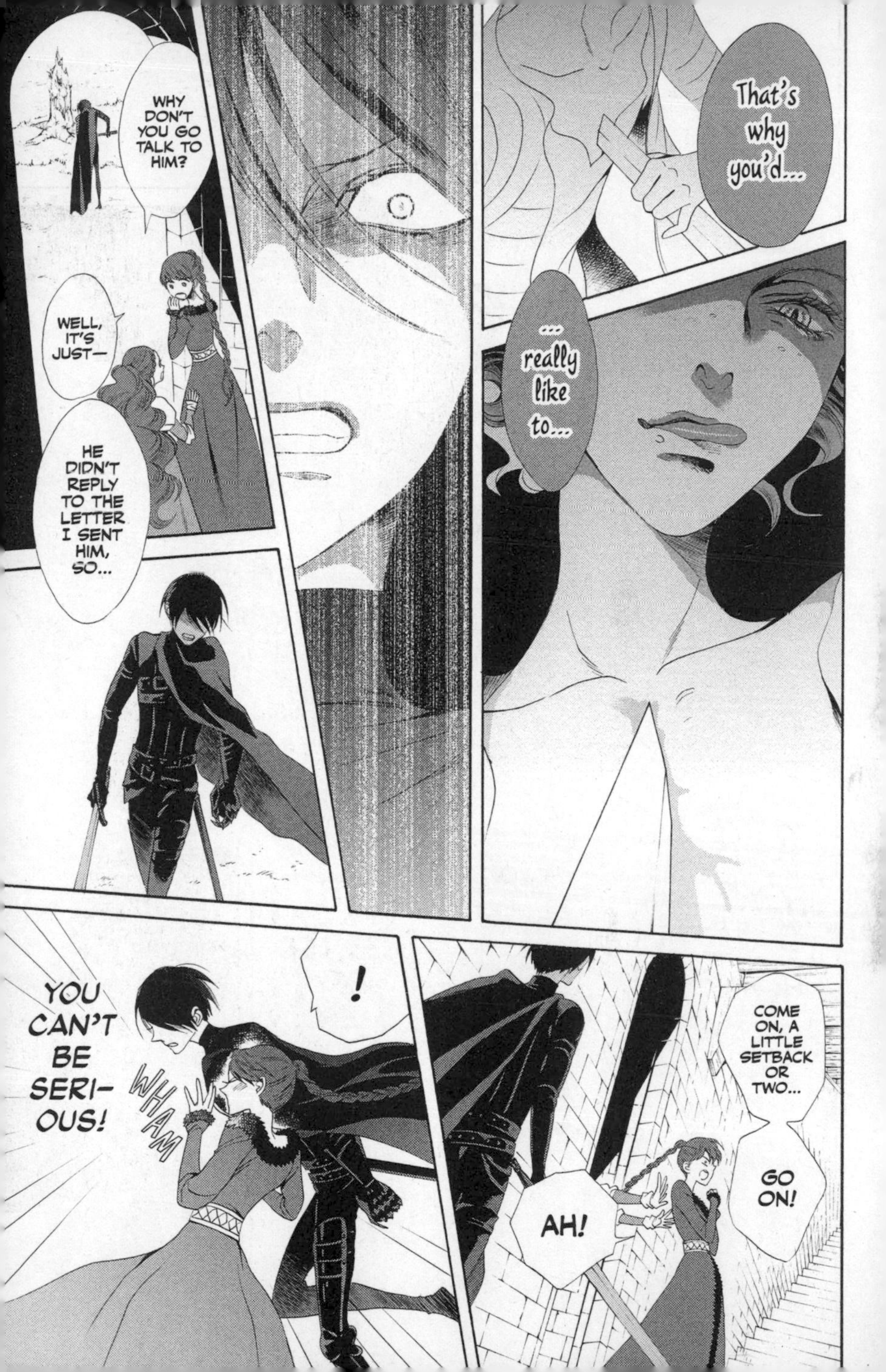
That's why you'd...
...really like to...
WHY DON'T YOU GO TALK TO HIM?
WELL, IT'S JUST—
HE DIDN'T REPLY TO THE LETTER I SENT HIM, SO...
COME ON, A LITTLE SETBACK OR TWO...
GO ON!
AH!
!
YOU CAN'T BE SERI-OUS!
WHAM

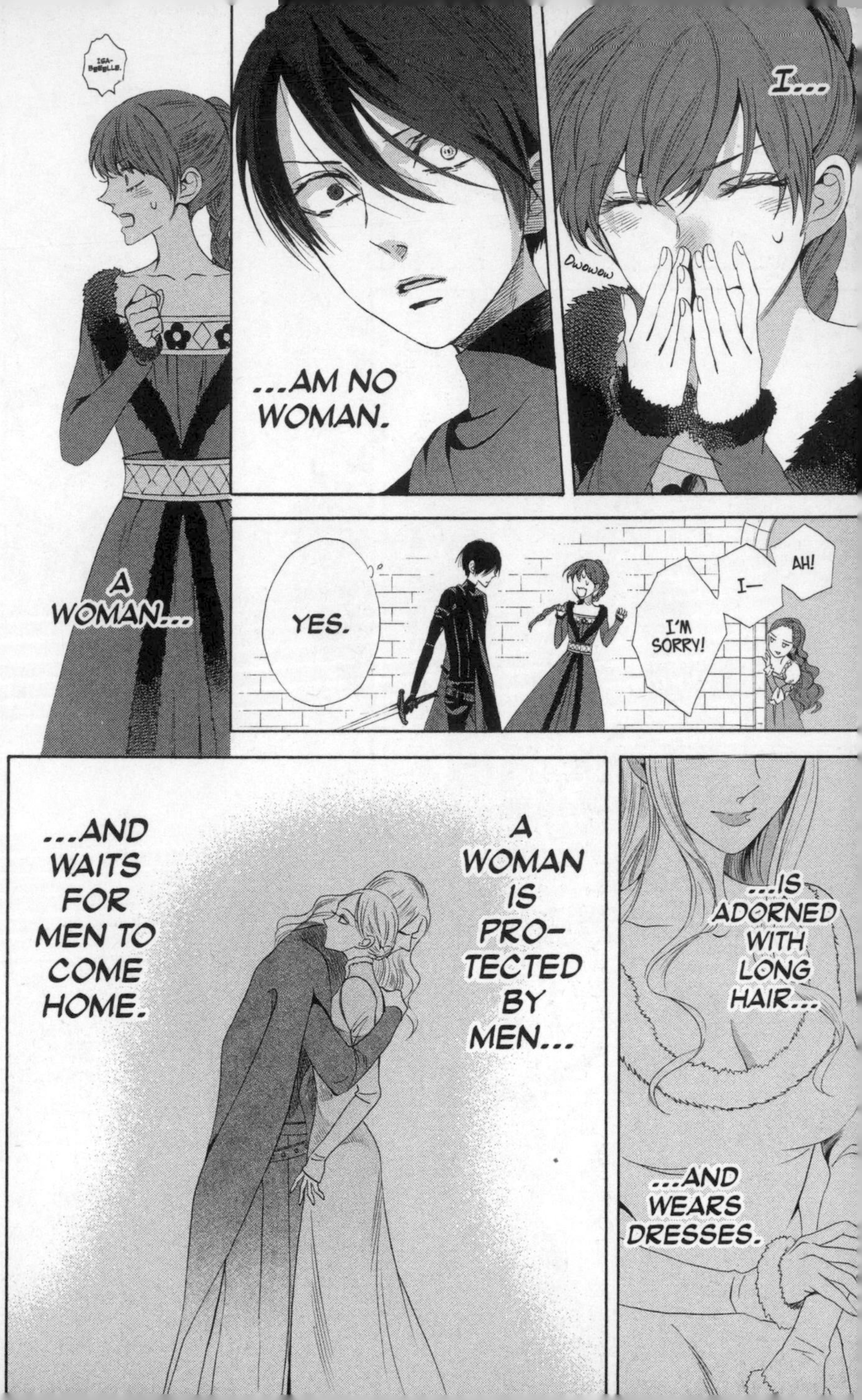

I...
Owowow
...AM NO WOMAN.
ISA-BEEELLE.
A WOMAN...
AH!
I—
I'M SORRY!
YES.
...IS ADORNED WITH LONG HAIR...
...AND WEARS DRESSES.
A WOMAN IS PRO-TECTED BY MEN...
...AND WAITS FOR MEN TO COME HOME.

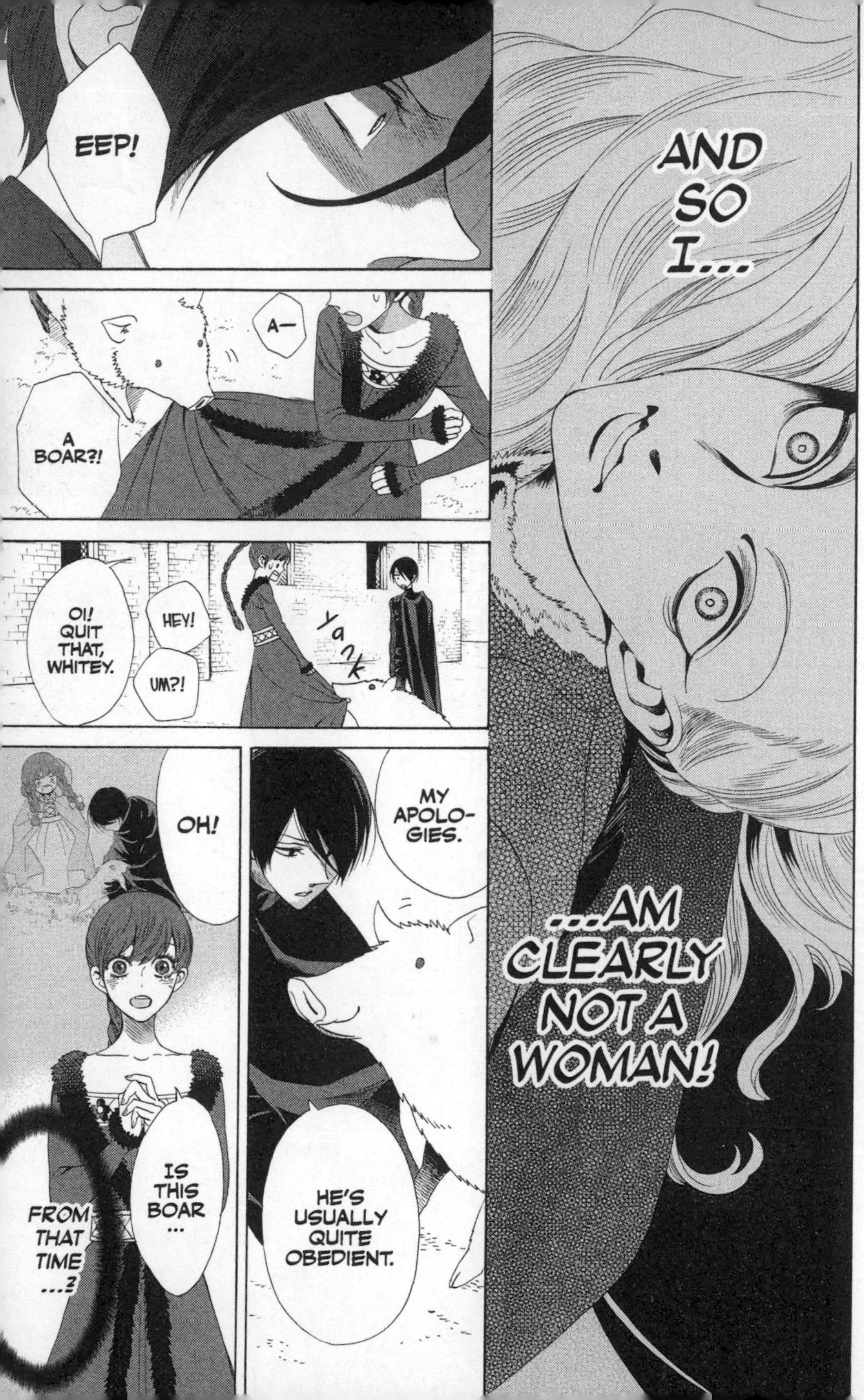
AND SO I...
...AM CLEARLY NOT A WOMAN!
EEP!
A—
A BOAR?!
yank
HEY!
UM?!
OI! QUIT THAT, WHITEY.
MY APOLO-GIES.
HE'S USUALLY QUITE OBEDIENT.
OH!
IS THIS BOAR...
FROM THAT TIME...?

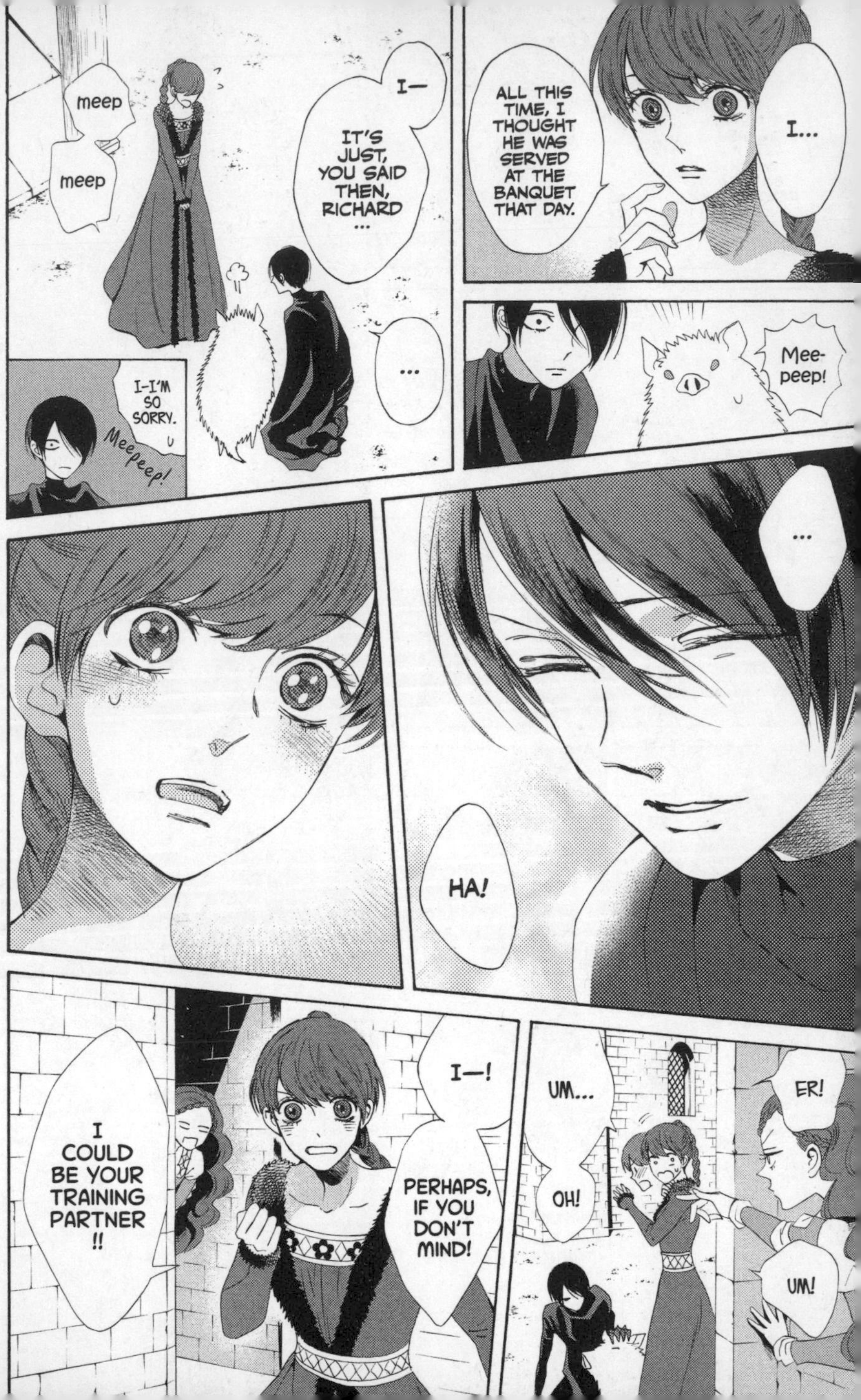
I...
ALL THIS TIME, I THOUGHT HE WAS SERVED AT THE BANQUET THAT DAY.
Mee-peep!
I—
IT'S JUST, YOU SAID THEN, RICHARD ...
meep
meep
...
I-I'M SO SORRY.
Meepeep!
...
HA!
ER!
UM...
OH!
UM!
I—!
PERHAPS, IF YOU DON'T MIND!
I COULD BE YOUR TRAINING PARTNER !!

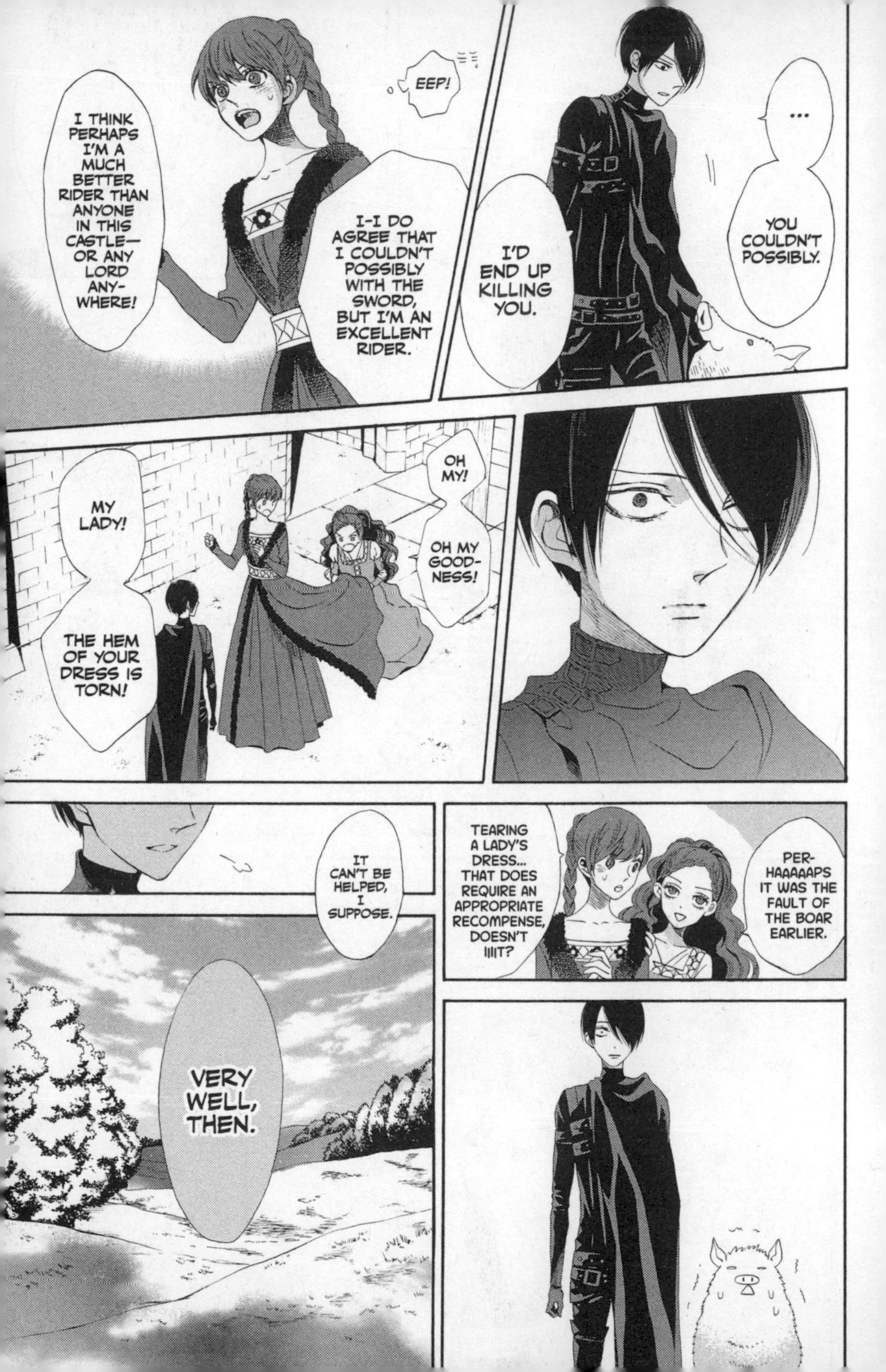
...
YOU COULDN'T POSSIBLY.
I'D END UP KILLING YOU.
EEP!
I-I DO AGREE THAT I COULDN'T POSSIBLY WITH THE SWORD, BUT I'M AN EXCELLENT RIDER.
I THINK PERHAPS I'M A MUCH BETTER RIDER THAN ANYONE IN THIS CASTLE—OR ANY LORD ANYWHERE!
OH MY!
OH MY GOODNESS!
MY LADY!
THE HEM OF YOUR DRESS IS TORN!
PER-HAAAAAPS IT WAS THE FAULT OF THE BOAR EARLIER.
TEARING A LADY'S DRESS... THAT DOES REQUIRE AN APPROPRIATE RECOMPENSE, DOESN'T IIIIT?
IT CAN'T BE HELPED, I SUPPOSE.
VERY WELL, THEN.

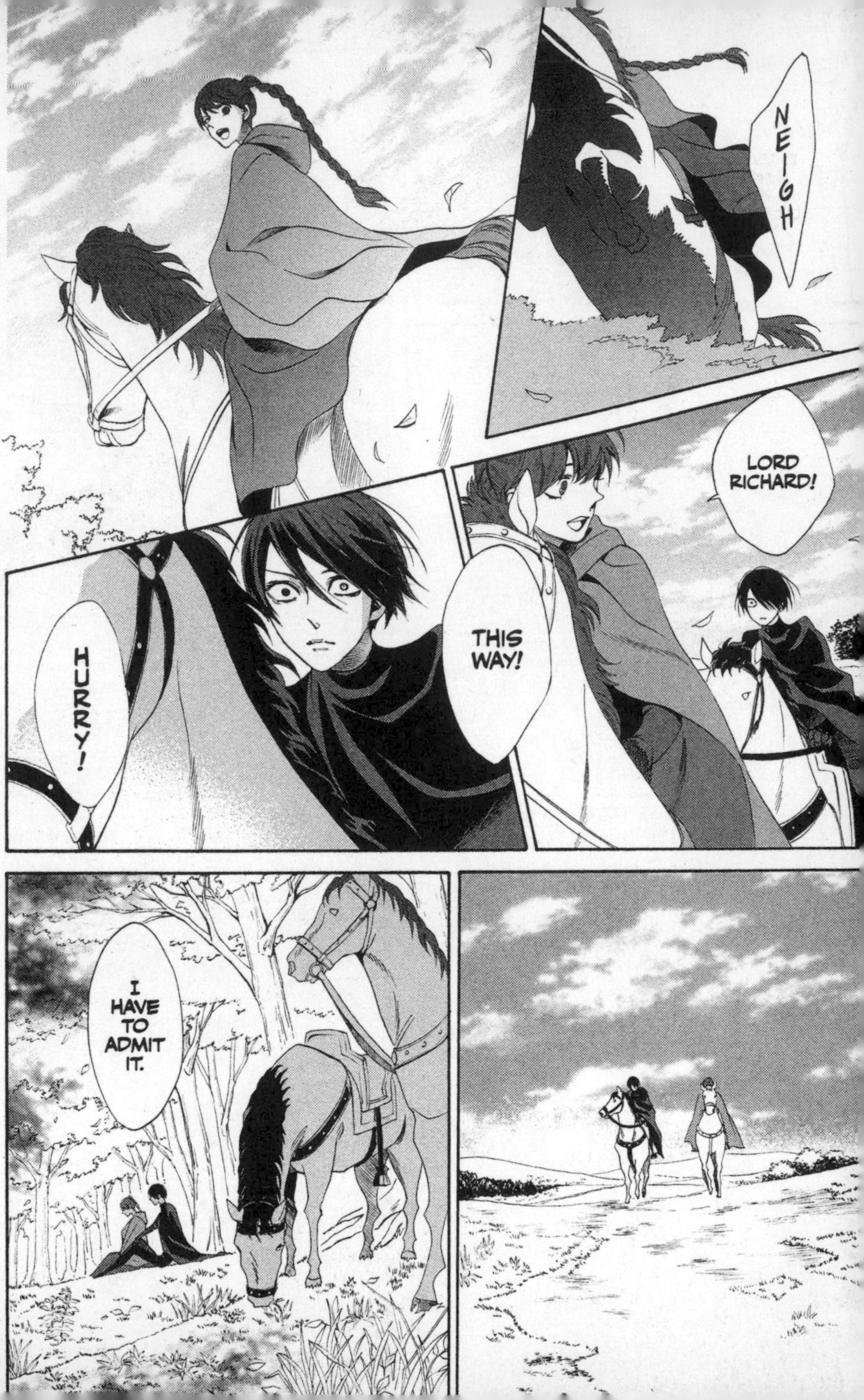
NEIGH
LORD RICHARD!
THIS WAY!
HURRY!
I HAVE TO ADMIT IT.

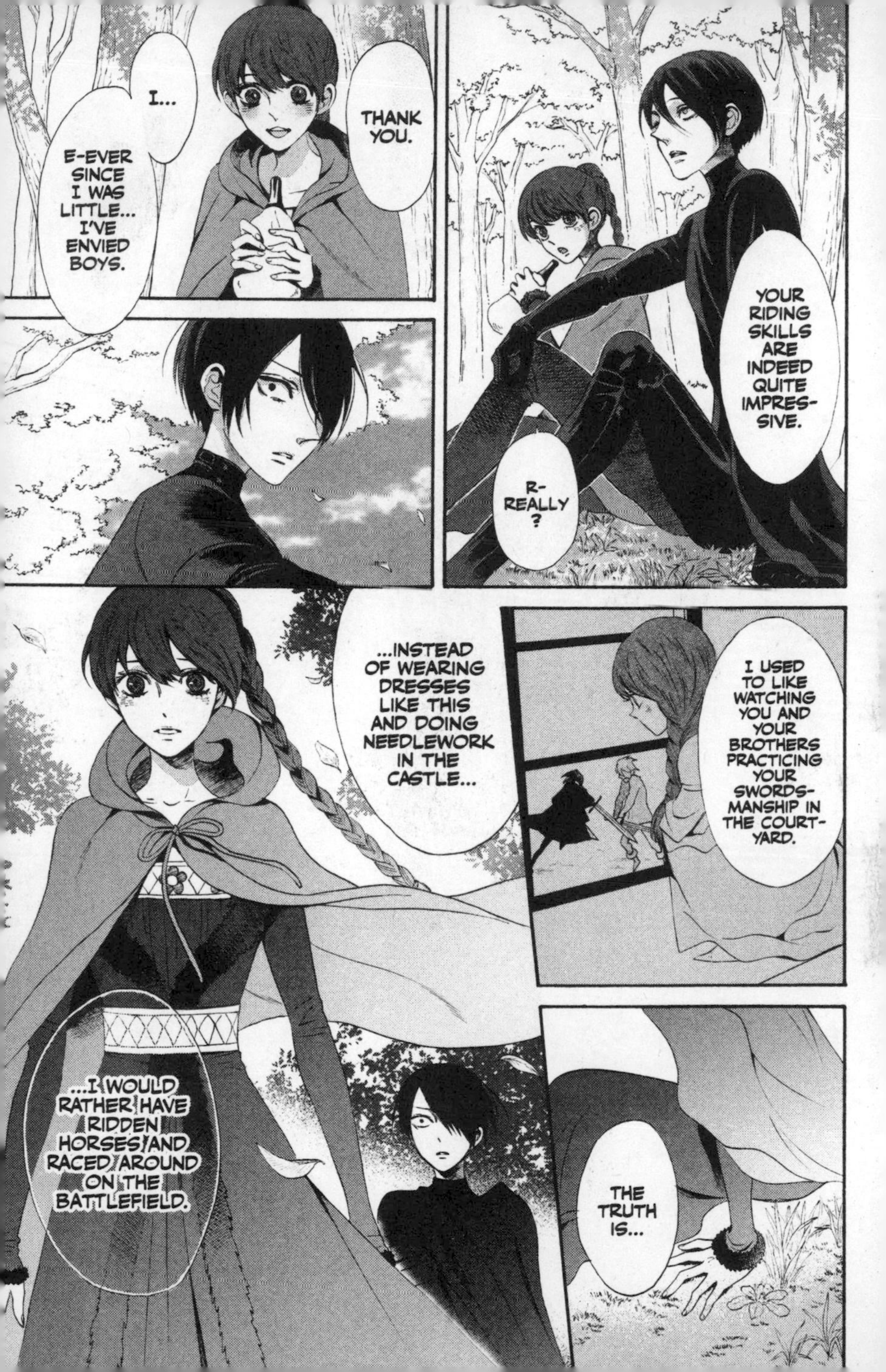
YOUR RIDING SKILLS ARE INDEED QUITE IMPRES-SIVE.
R-REALLY?
THANK YOU.
I...
E-EVER SINCE I WAS LITTLE... I'VE ENVIED BOYS.
I USED TO LIKE WATCHING YOU AND YOUR BROTHERS PRACTICING YOUR SWORDS-MANSHIP IN THE COURT-YARD.
THE TRUTH IS...
...INSTEAD OF WEARING DRESSES LIKE THIS AND DOING NEEDLEWORK IN THE CASTLE...
...I WOULD RATHER HAVE RIDDEN HORSES AND RACED AROUND ON THE BATTLEFIELD.

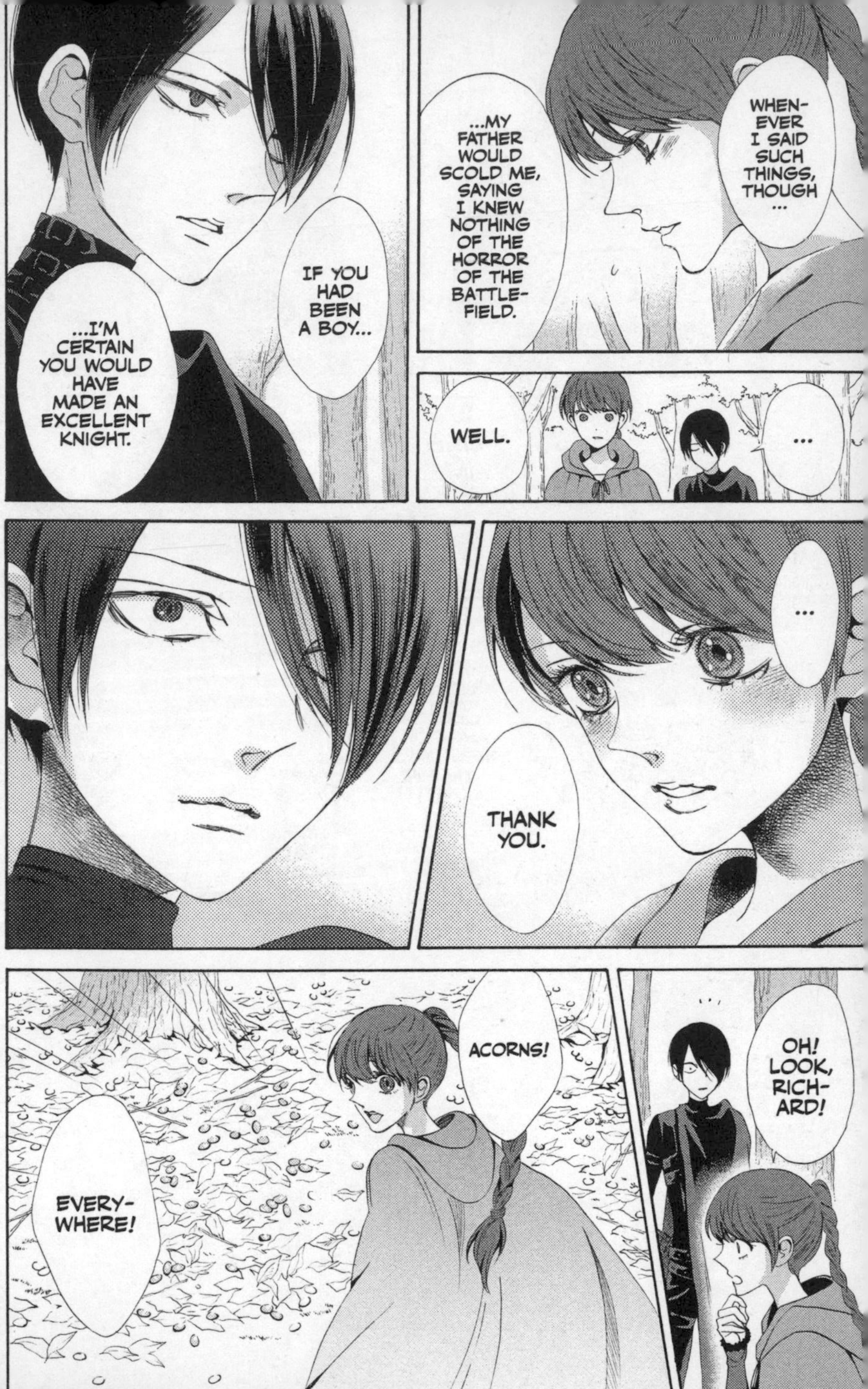
WHEN-EVER I SAID SUCH THINGS, THOUGH...
...MY FATHER WOULD SCOLD ME, SAYING I KNEW NOTHING OF THE HORROR OF THE BATTLE-FIELD.
...
WELL.
IF YOU HAD BEEN A BOY...
...I'M CERTAIN YOU WOULD HAVE MADE AN EXCELLENT KNIGHT.
...
THANK YOU.
OH! LOOK, RICH-ARD!
ACORNS!
EVERY-WHERE!

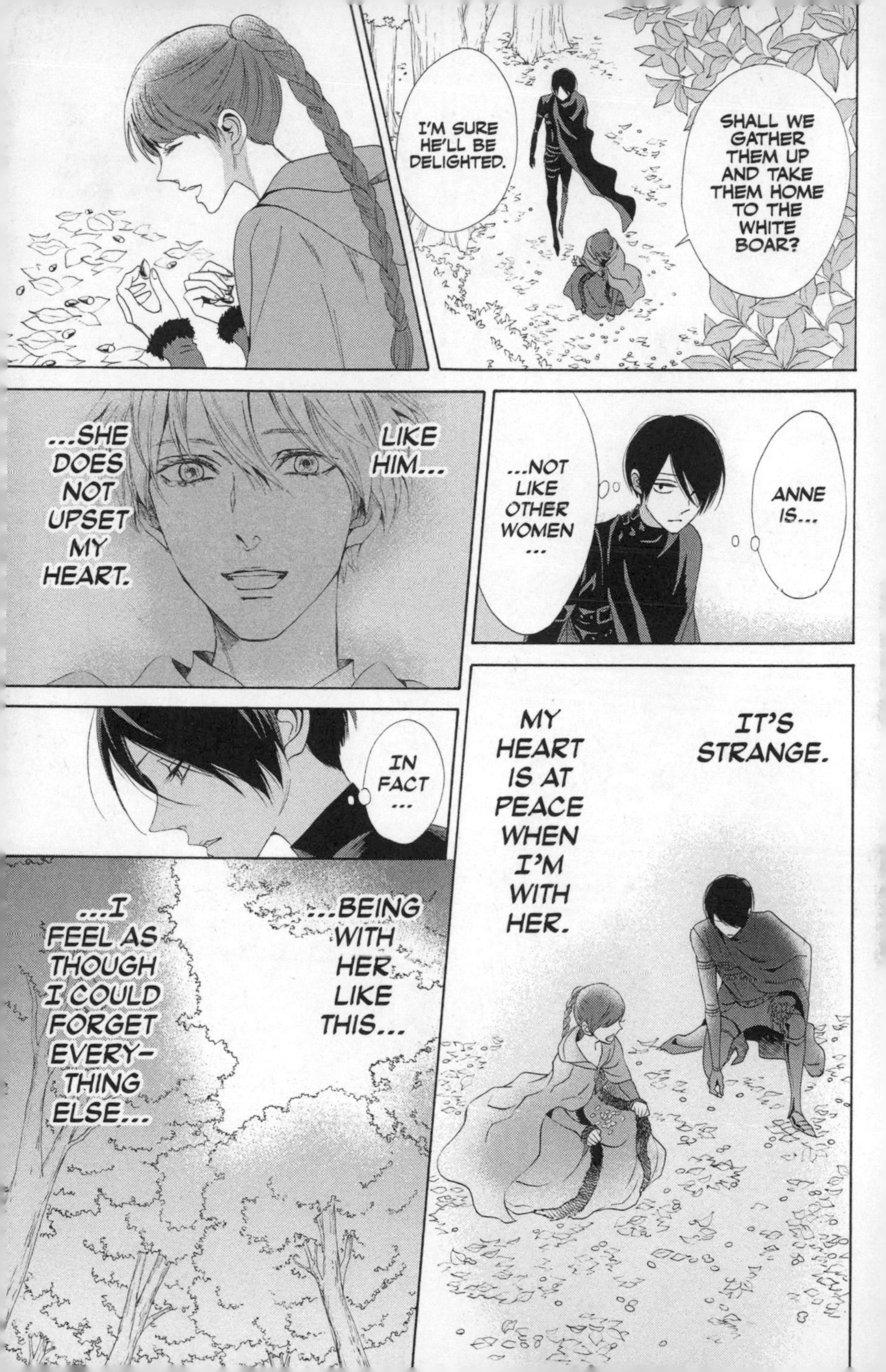
SHALL WE GATHER THEM UP AND TAKE THEM HOME TO THE WHITE BOAR?
I'M SURE HE'LL BE DELIGHTED.
ANNE IS...
...NOT LIKE OTHER WOMEN...
LIKE HIM...
...SHE DOES NOT UPSET MY HEART.
IT'S STRANGE.
MY HEART IS AT PEACE WHEN I'M WITH HER.
IN FACT...
...BEING WITH HER LIKE THIS...
...I FEEL AS THOUGH I COULD FORGET EVERY-THING ELSE...

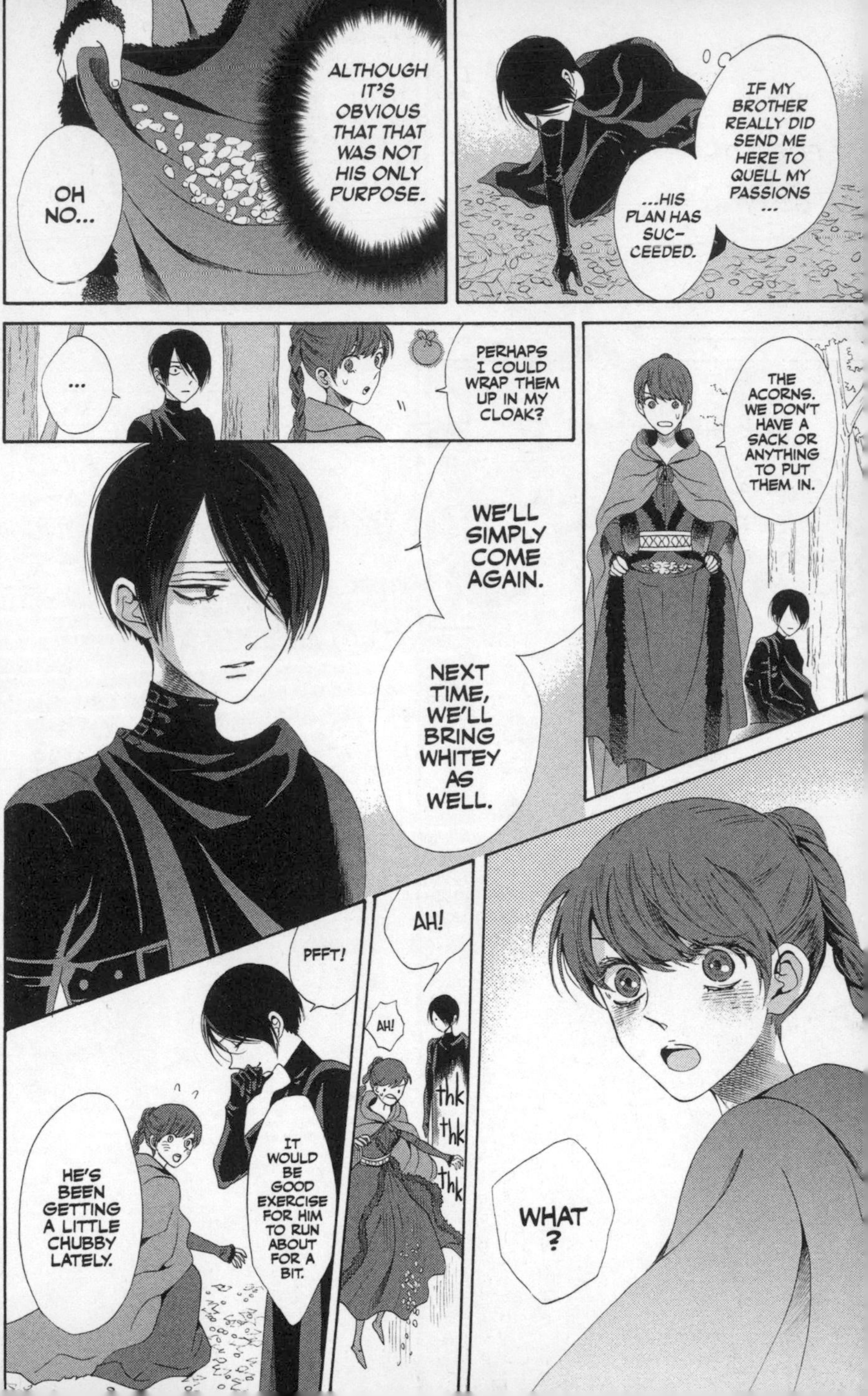
IF MY BROTHER REALLY DID SEND ME HERE TO QUELL MY PASSIONS ...
...HIS PLAN HAS SUC-CEEDED.
ALTHOUGH IT'S OBVIOUS THAT THAT WAS NOT HIS ONLY PURPOSE.
OH NO...
THE ACORNS. WE DON'T HAVE A SACK OR ANYTHING TO PUT THEM IN.
PERHAPS I COULD WRAP THEM UP IN MY CLOAK?
...
WE'LL SIMPLY COME AGAIN.
NEXT TIME, WE'LL BRING WHITEY AS WELL.
WHAT?
AH!
AH!
thk thk thk
PFFT!
IT WOULD BE GOOD EXERCISE FOR HIM TO RUN ABOUT FOR A BIT.
HE'S BEEN GETTING A LITTLE CHUBBY LATELY.

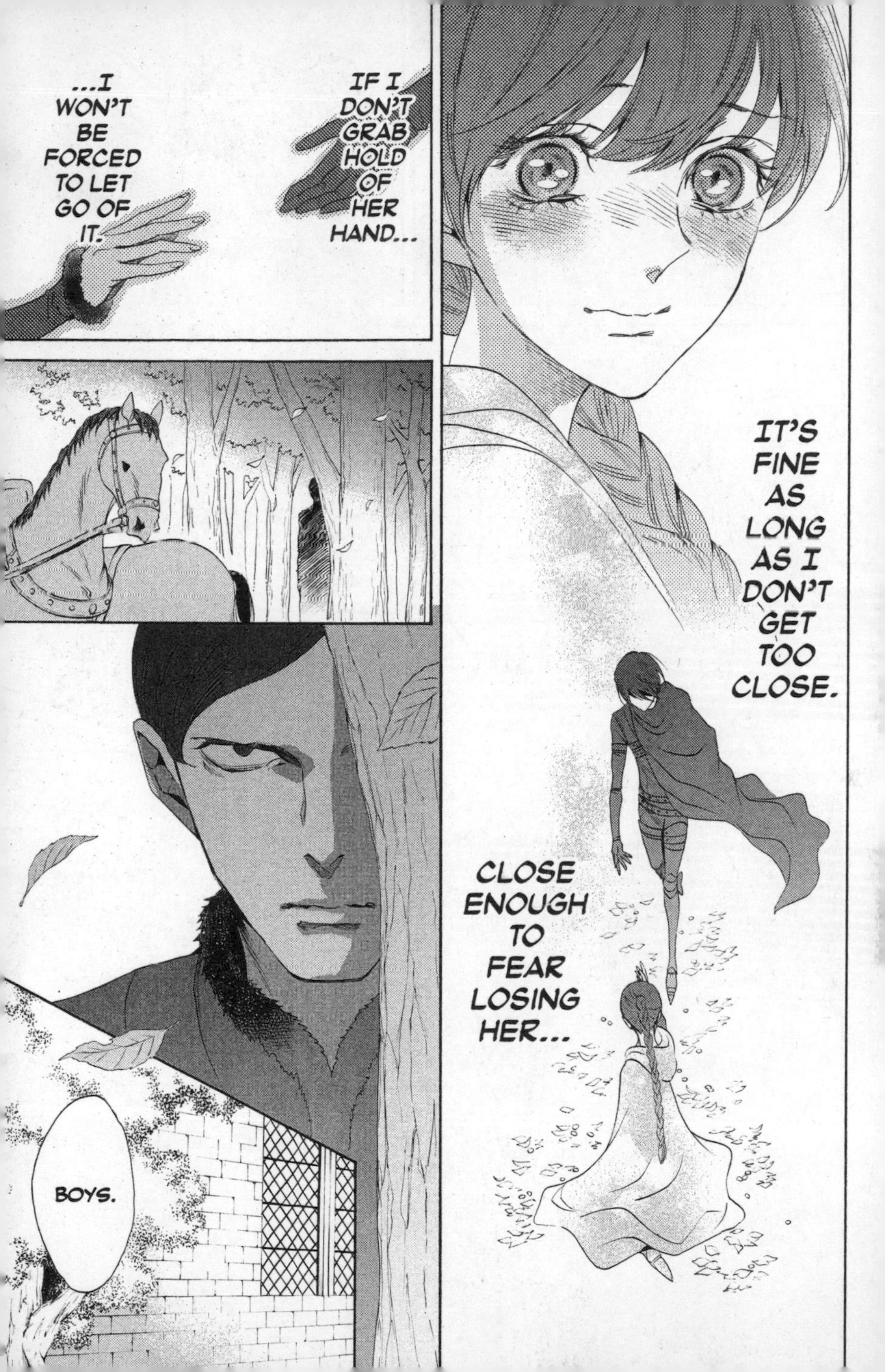

IT'S FINE AS LONG AS I DON'T GET TOO CLOSE.
CLOSE ENOUGH TO FEAR LOSING HER...
IF I DON'T GRAB HOLD OF HER HAND...
...I WON'T BE FORCED TO LET GO OF IT.
BOYS.

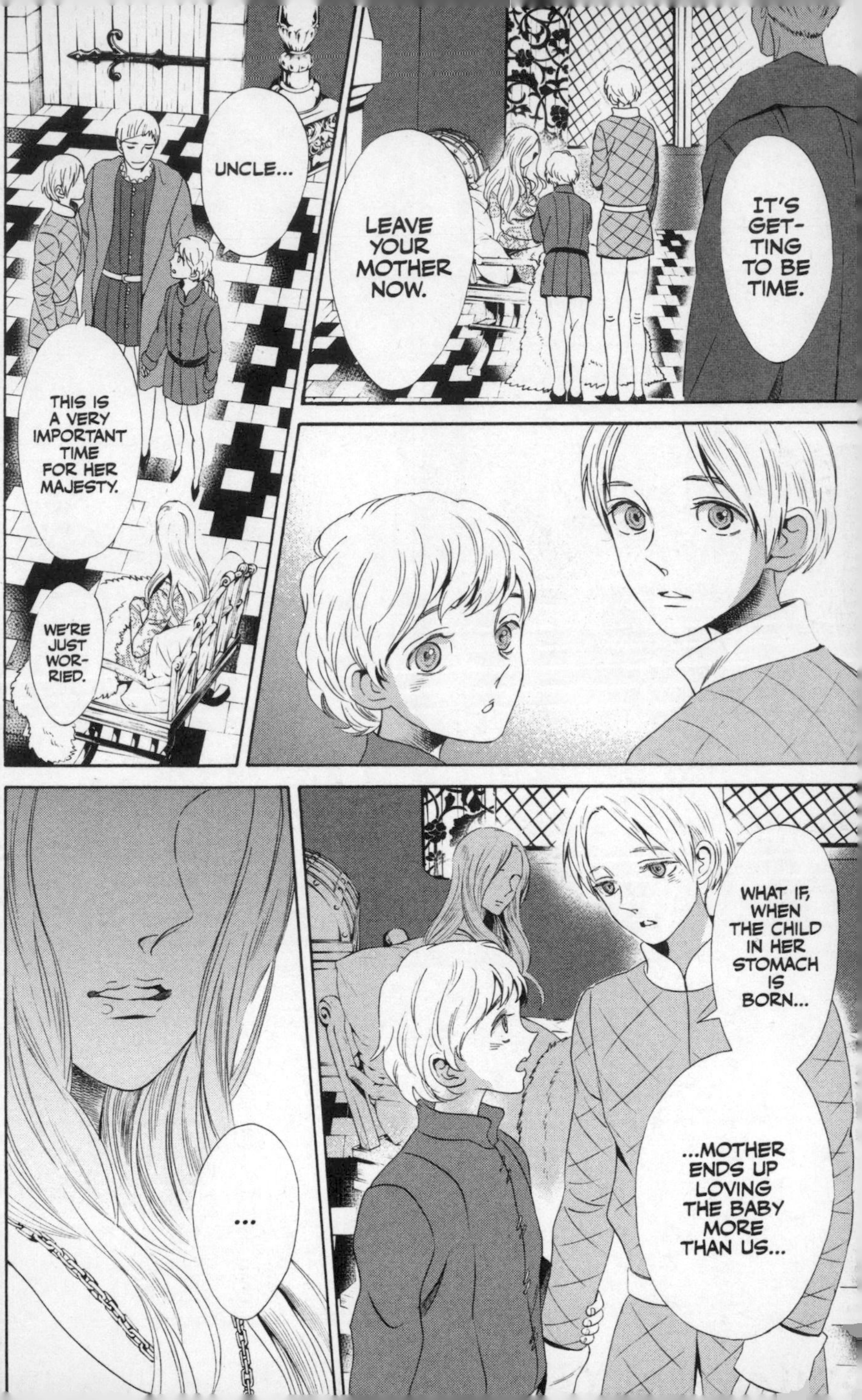
IT'S GETTING TO BE TIME.
LEAVE YOUR MOTHER NOW.
UNCLE...
THIS IS A VERY IMPORTANT TIME FOR HER MAJESTY.
WE'RE JUST WORRIED.
WHAT IF, WHEN THE CHILD IN HER STOMACH IS BORN...
...MOTHER ENDS UP LOVING THE BABY MORE THAN US...
...

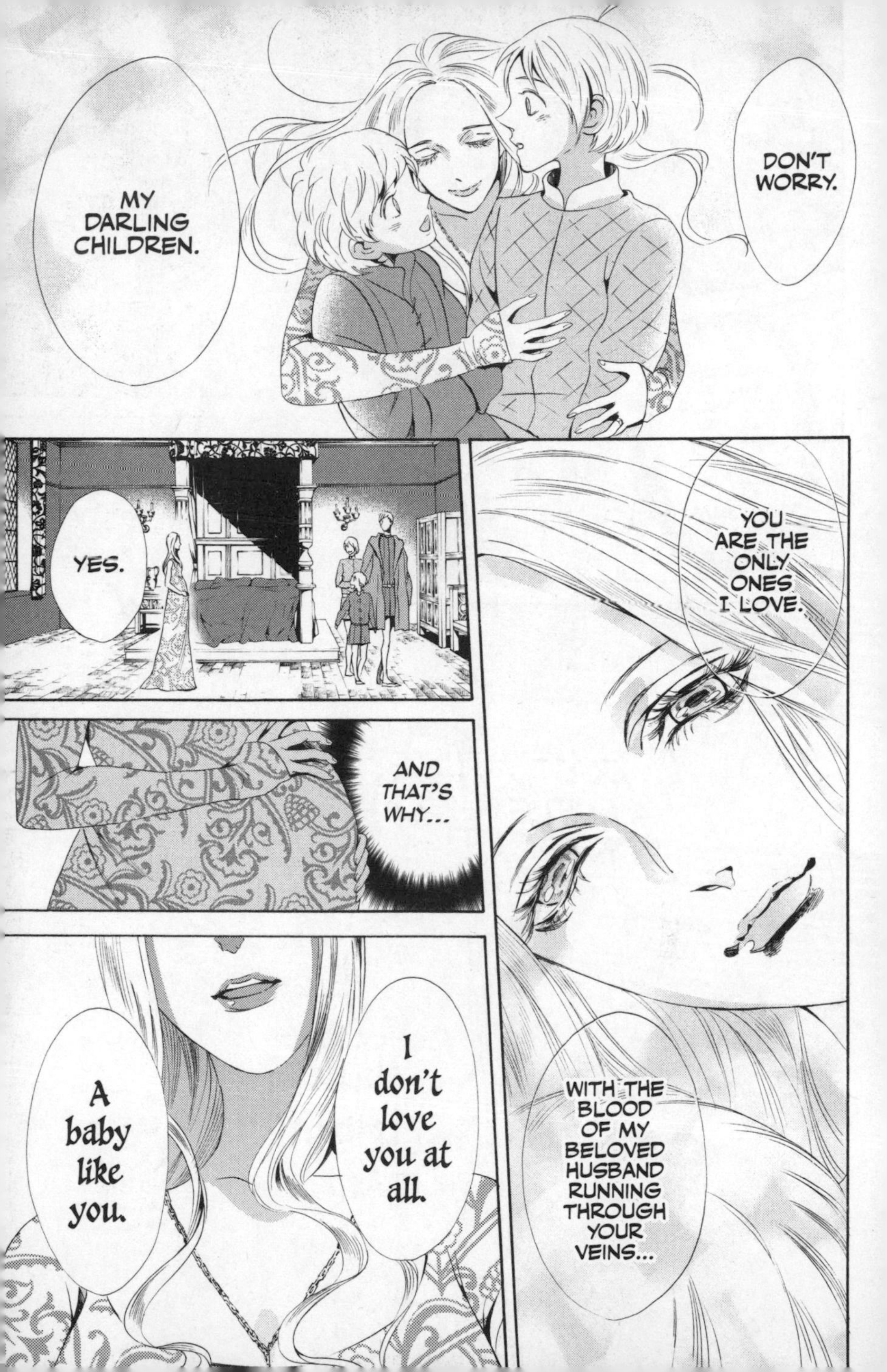
DON'T WORRY.
MY DARLING CHILDREN.
YOU ARE THE ONLY ONES I LOVE.
WITH THE BLOOD OF MY BELOVED HUSBAND RUNNING THROUGH YOUR VEINS...
YES.
AND THAT'S WHY...
I don't love you at all.
A baby like you.

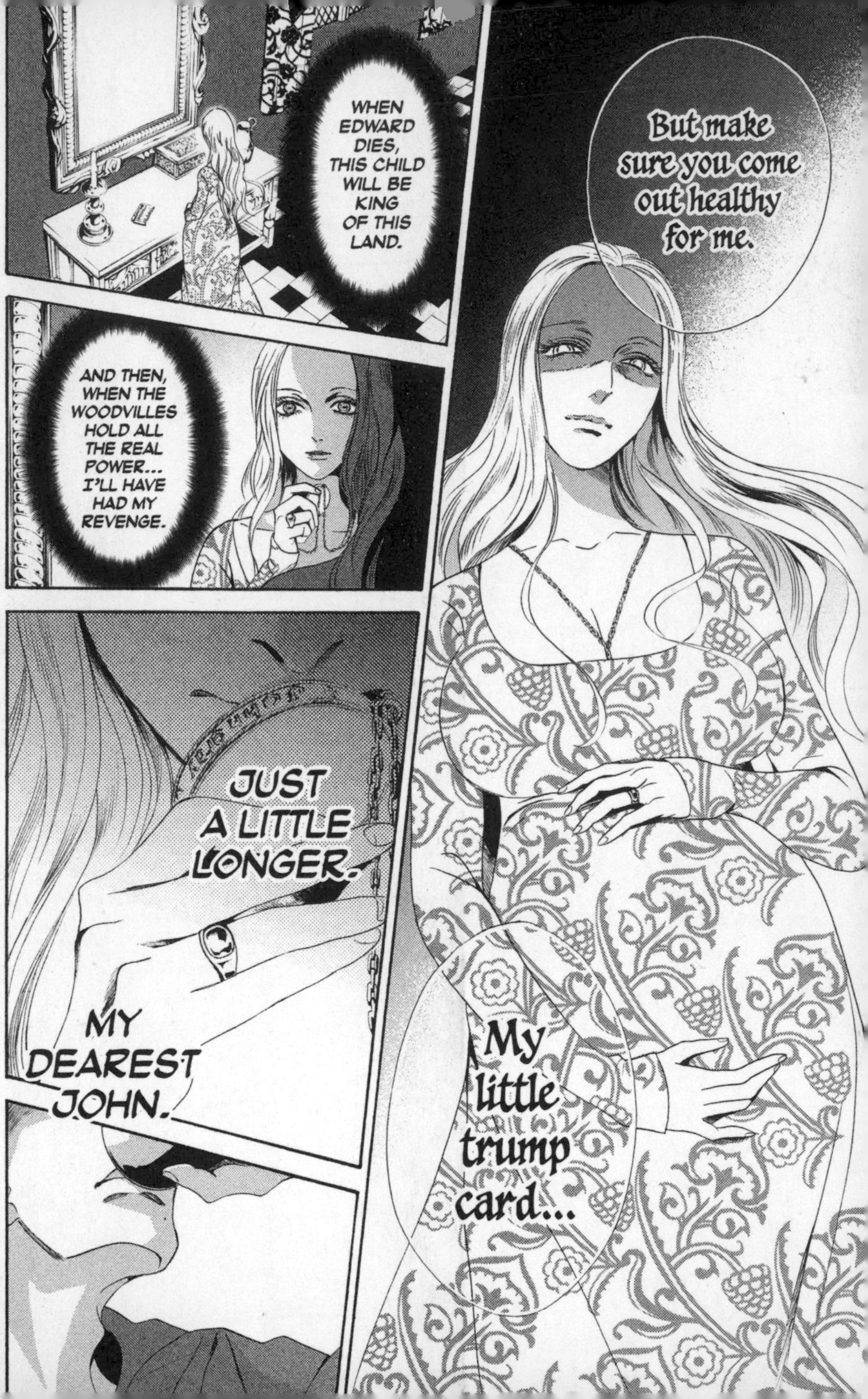
But make sure you come out healthy for me.
My little trump card...
WHEN EDWARD DIES, THIS CHILD WILL BE KING OF THIS LAND.
AND THEN, WHEN THE WOODVILLES HOLD ALL THE REAL POWER... I'LL HAVE HAD MY REVENGE.
JUST A LITTLE LONGER.
MY DEAREST JOHN.

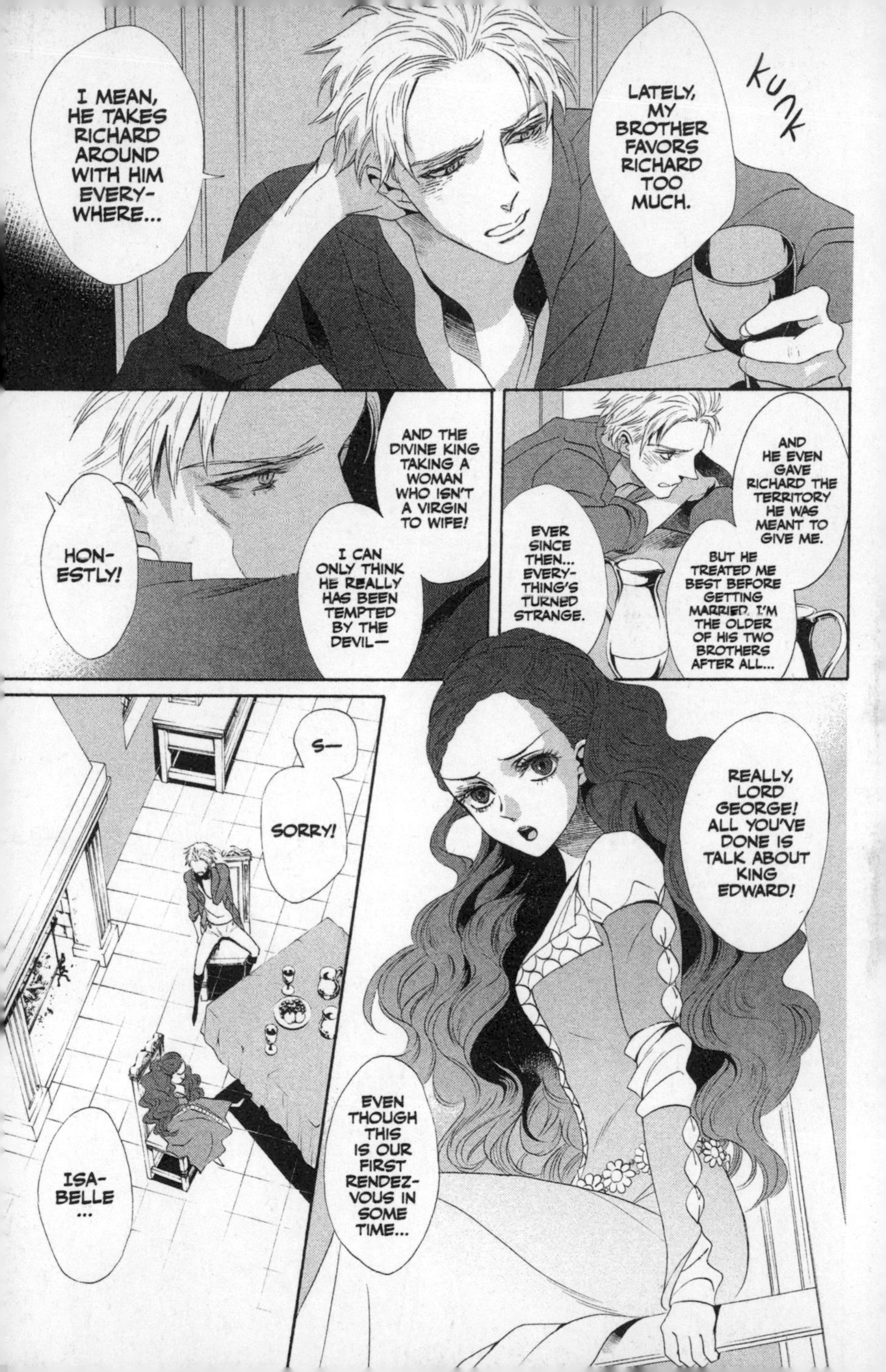
KUNK
LATELY, MY BROTHER FAVORS RICHARD TOO MUCH.
I MEAN, HE TAKES RICHARD AROUND WITH HIM EVERY-WHERE...
AND HE EVEN GAVE RICHARD THE TERRITORY HE WAS MEANT TO GIVE ME.
BUT HE TREATED ME BEST BEFORE GETTING MARRIED. I'M THE OLDER OF HIS TWO BROTHERS AFTER ALL...
EVER SINCE THEN... EVERY-THING'S TURNED STRANGE.
AND THE DIVINE KING TAKING A WOMAN WHO ISN'T A VIRGIN TO WIFE!
I CAN ONLY THINK HE REALLY HAS BEEN TEMPTED BY THE DEVIL—
HON-ESTLY!
REALLY, LORD GEORGE! ALL YOU'VE DONE IS TALK ABOUT KING EDWARD!
EVEN THOUGH THIS IS OUR FIRST RENDEZ-VOUS IN SOME TIME...
S—
SORRY!
ISA-BELLE ...

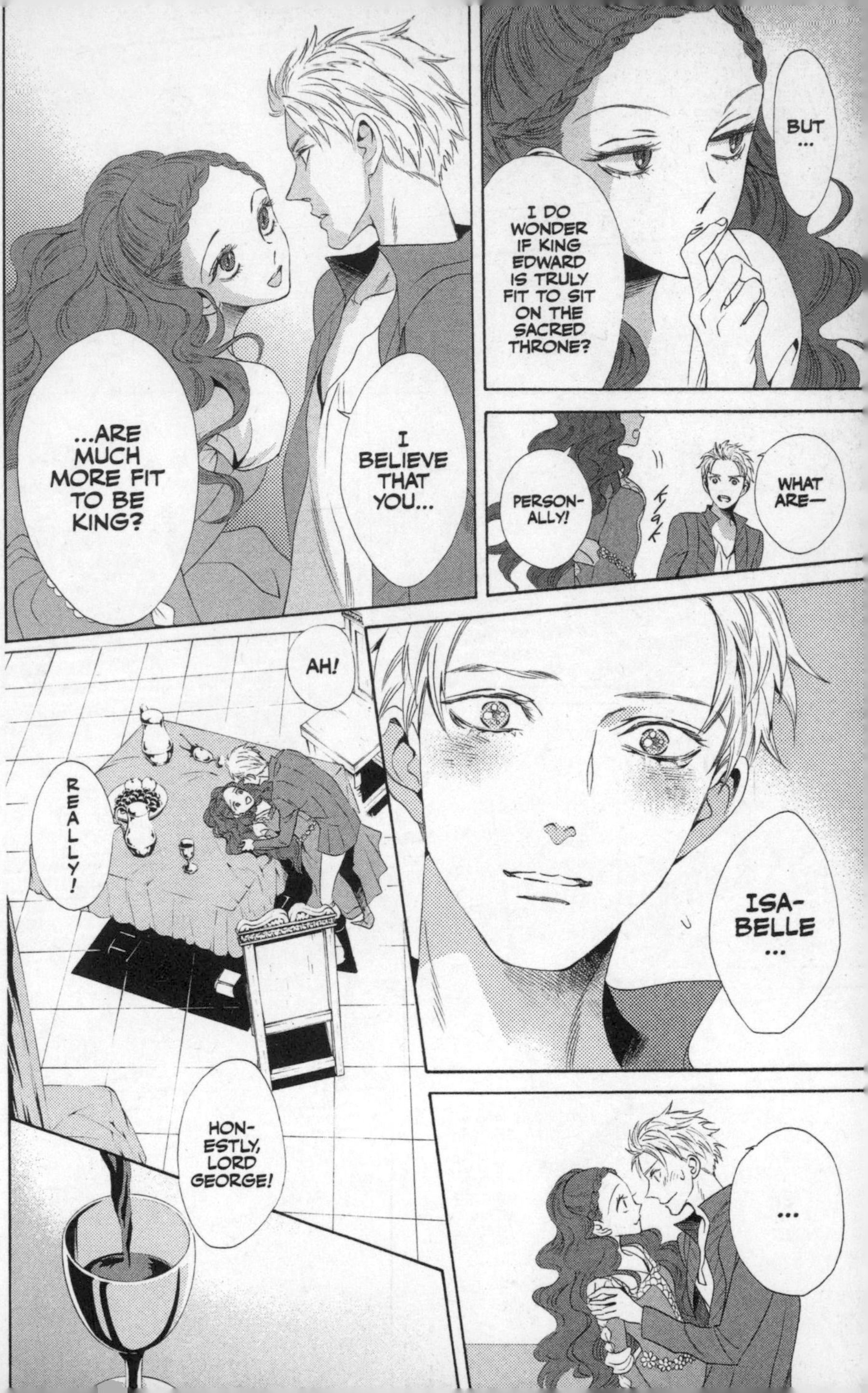
BUT...
I DO WONDER IF KING EDWARD IS TRULY FIT TO SIT ON THE SACRED THRONE?
WHAT ARE—
klak
PERSON-ALLY!
I BELIEVE THAT YOU...
...ARE MUCH MORE FIT TO BE KING?
ISA-BELLE...
AH!
REALLY!
...
HON-ESTLY, LORD GEORGE!

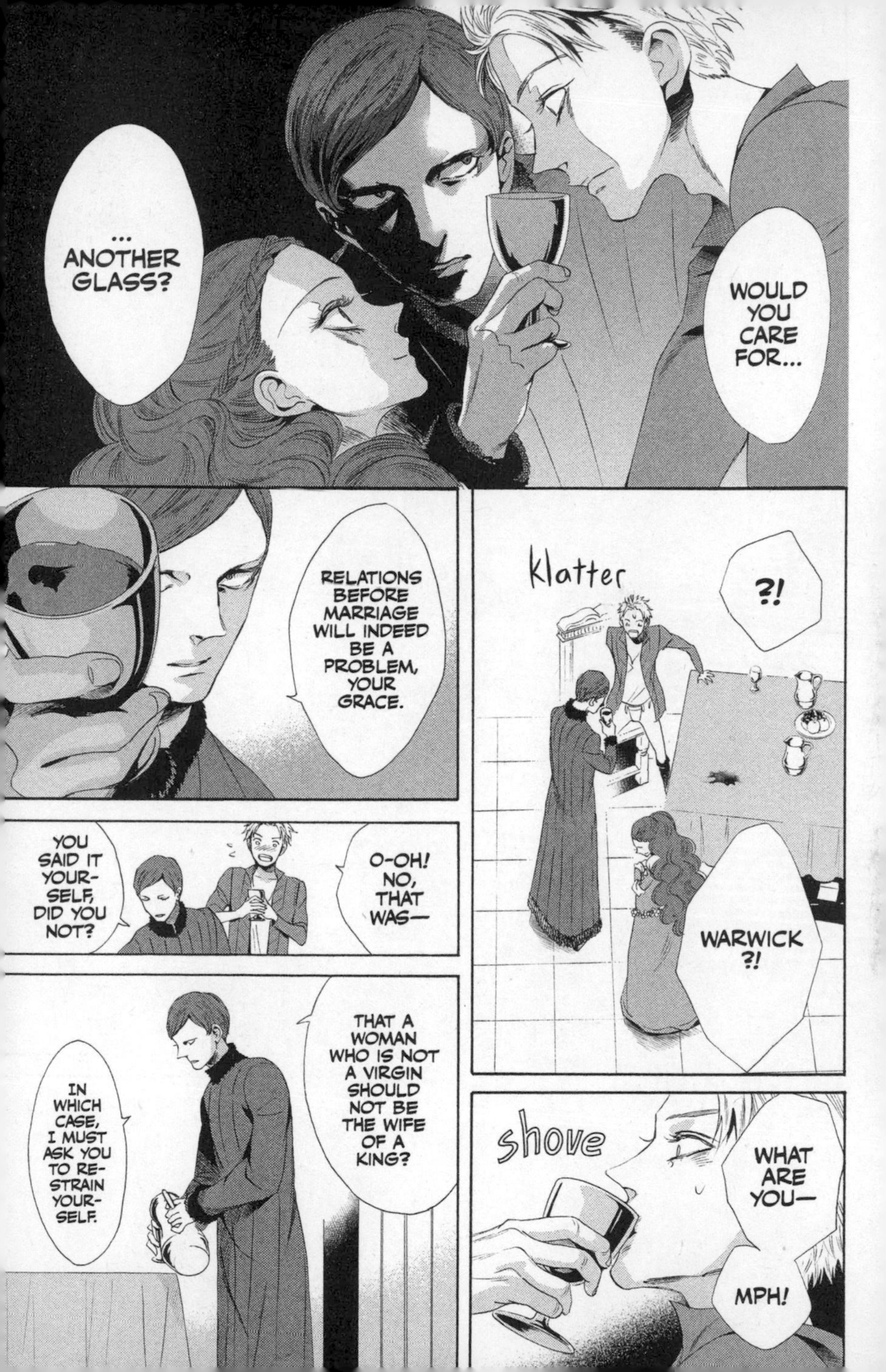
WOULD YOU CARE FOR...
... ANOTHER GLASS?
RELATIONS BEFORE MARRIAGE WILL INDEED BE A PROBLEM, YOUR GRACE.
YOU SAID IT YOURSELF, DID YOU NOT?
O-OH! NO, THAT WAS—
THAT A WOMAN WHO IS NOT A VIRGIN SHOULD NOT BE THE WIFE OF A KING?
IN WHICH CASE, I MUST ASK YOU TO RESTRAIN YOURSELF.
shove
WHAT ARE YOU—
MPH!
klatter
?!
WARWICK ?!

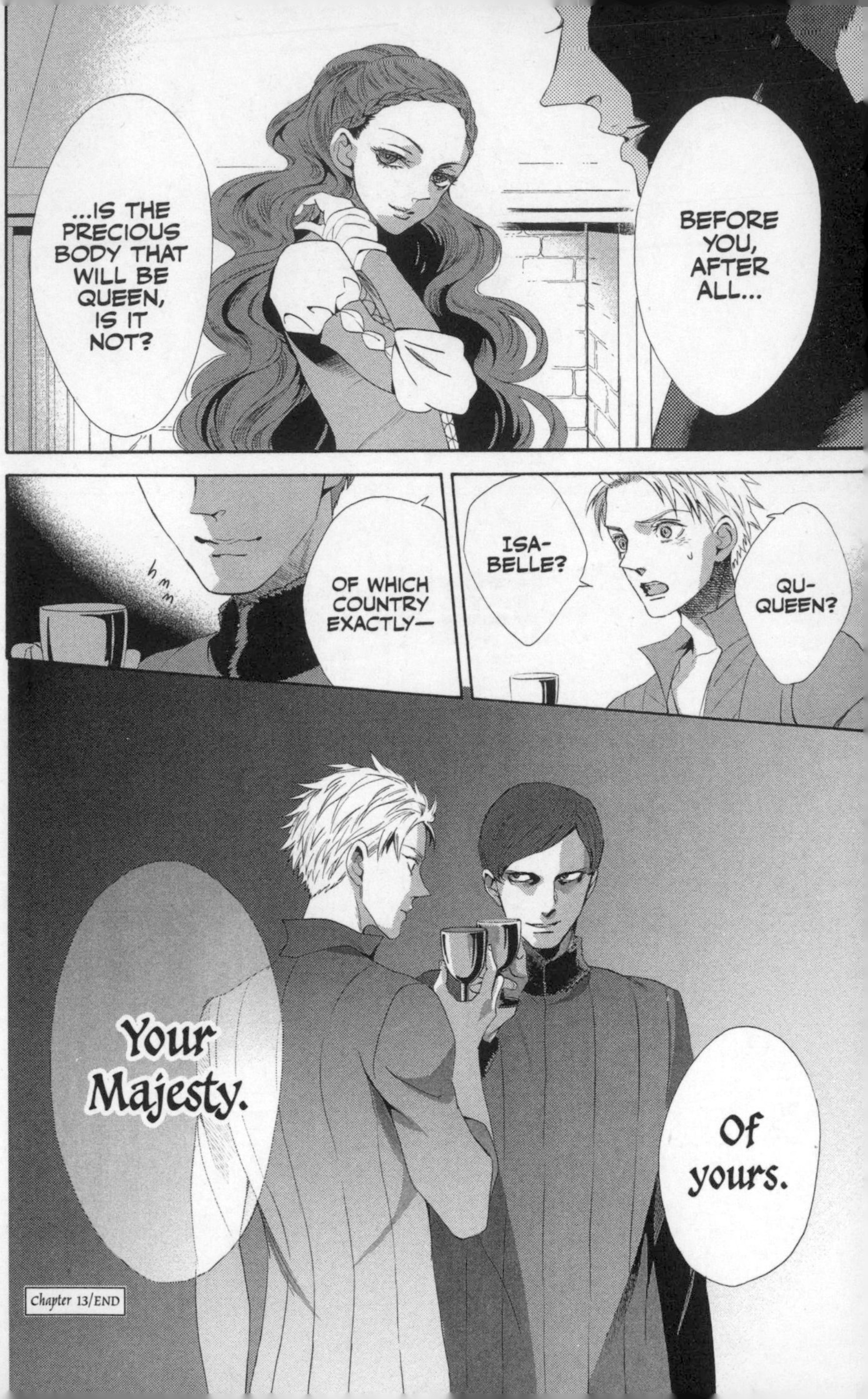
BEFORE YOU, AFTER ALL...
...IS THE PRECIOUS BODY THAT WILL BE QUEEN, IS IT NOT?
QU-QUEEN?
ISA-BELLE?
OF WHICH COUNTRY EXACTLY—
hmm
Of yours.
Your Majesty.
Chapter 13/END

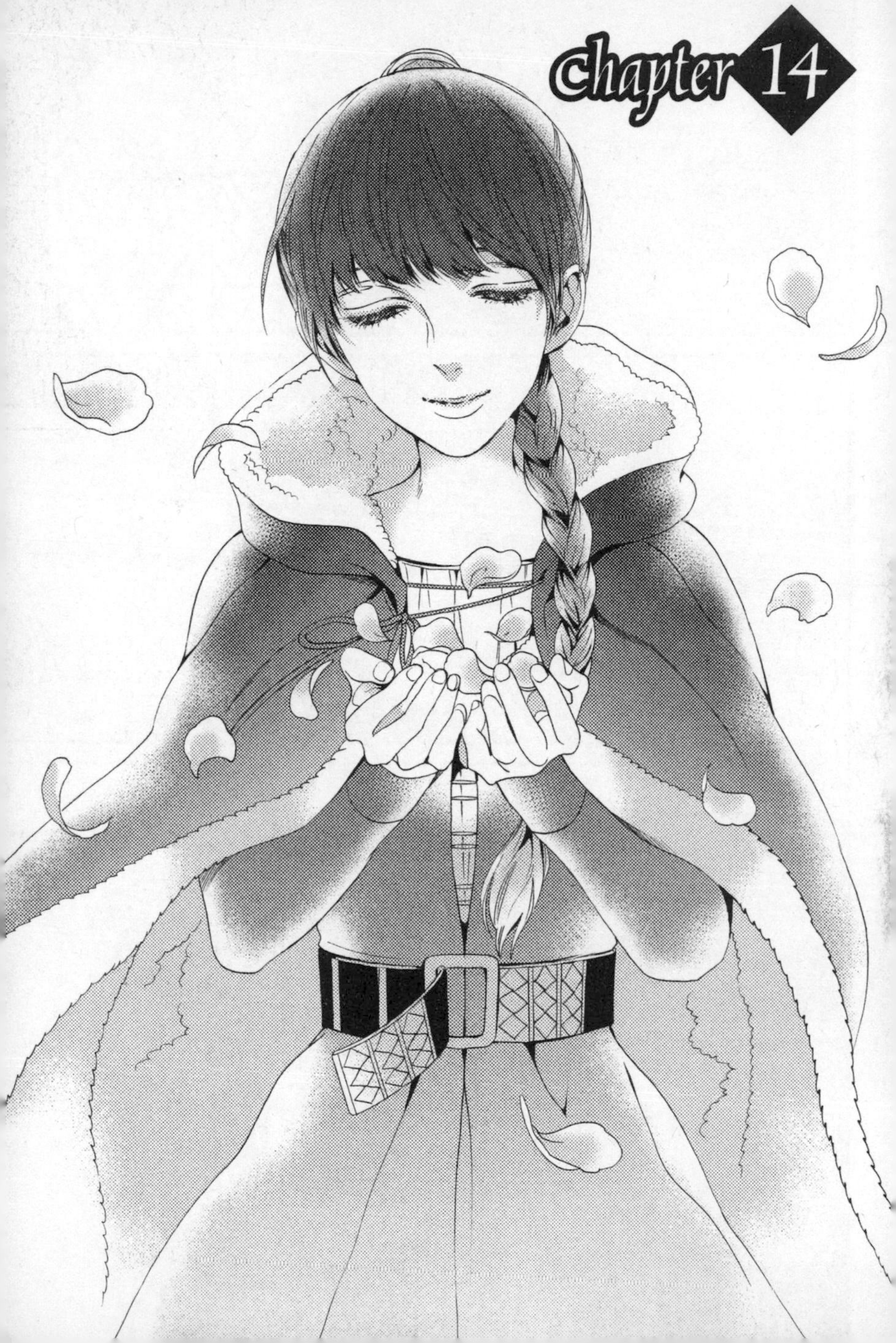
Chapter 14

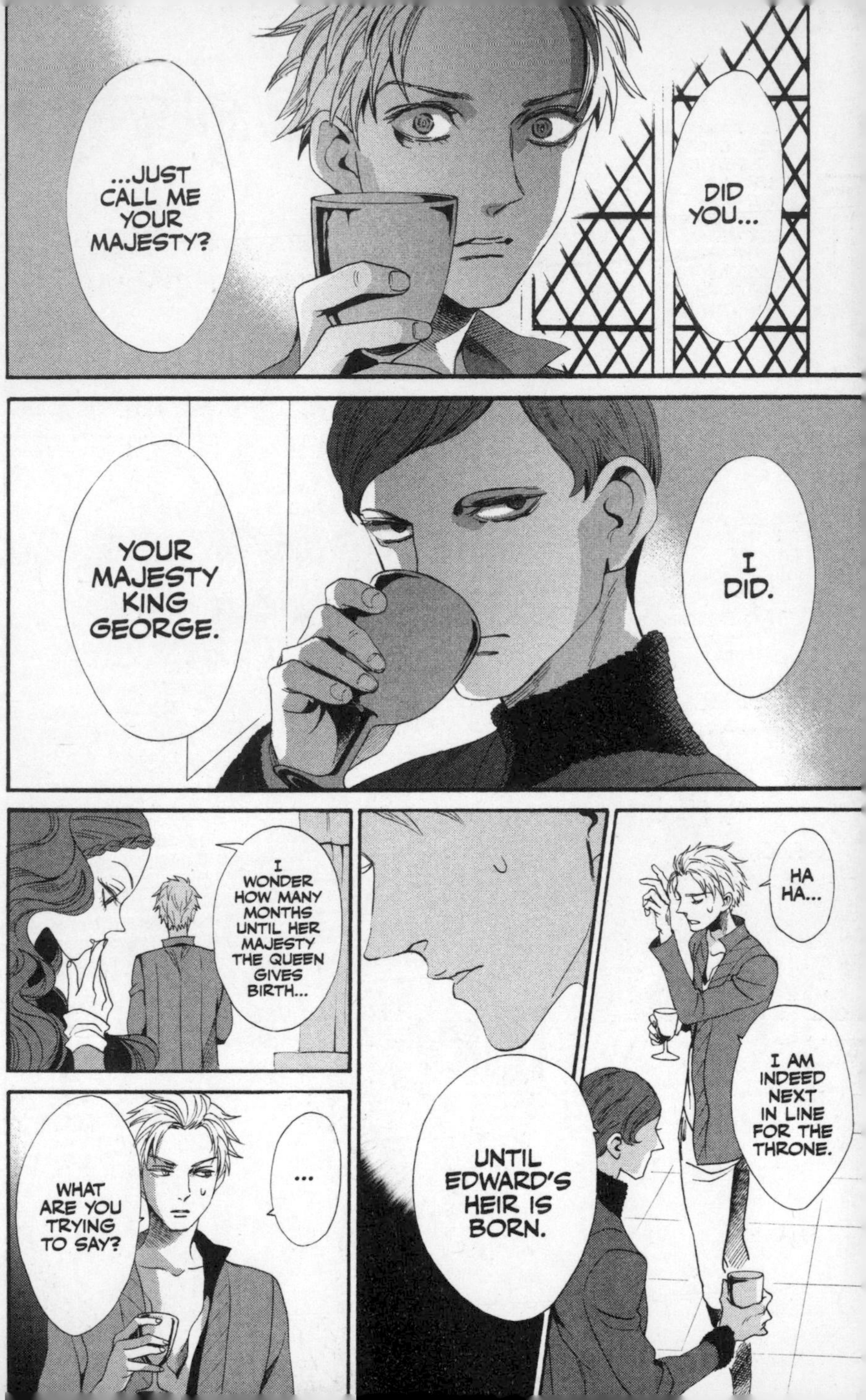
DID YOU...
...JUST CALL ME YOUR MAJESTY?
I DID.
YOUR MAJESTY KING GEORGE.
HA HA...
I AM INDEED NEXT IN LINE FOR THE THRONE.
UNTIL EDWARD'S HEIR IS BORN.
I WONDER HOW MANY MONTHS UNTIL HER MAJESTY THE QUEEN GIVES BIRTH...
...
WHAT ARE YOU TRYING TO SAY?

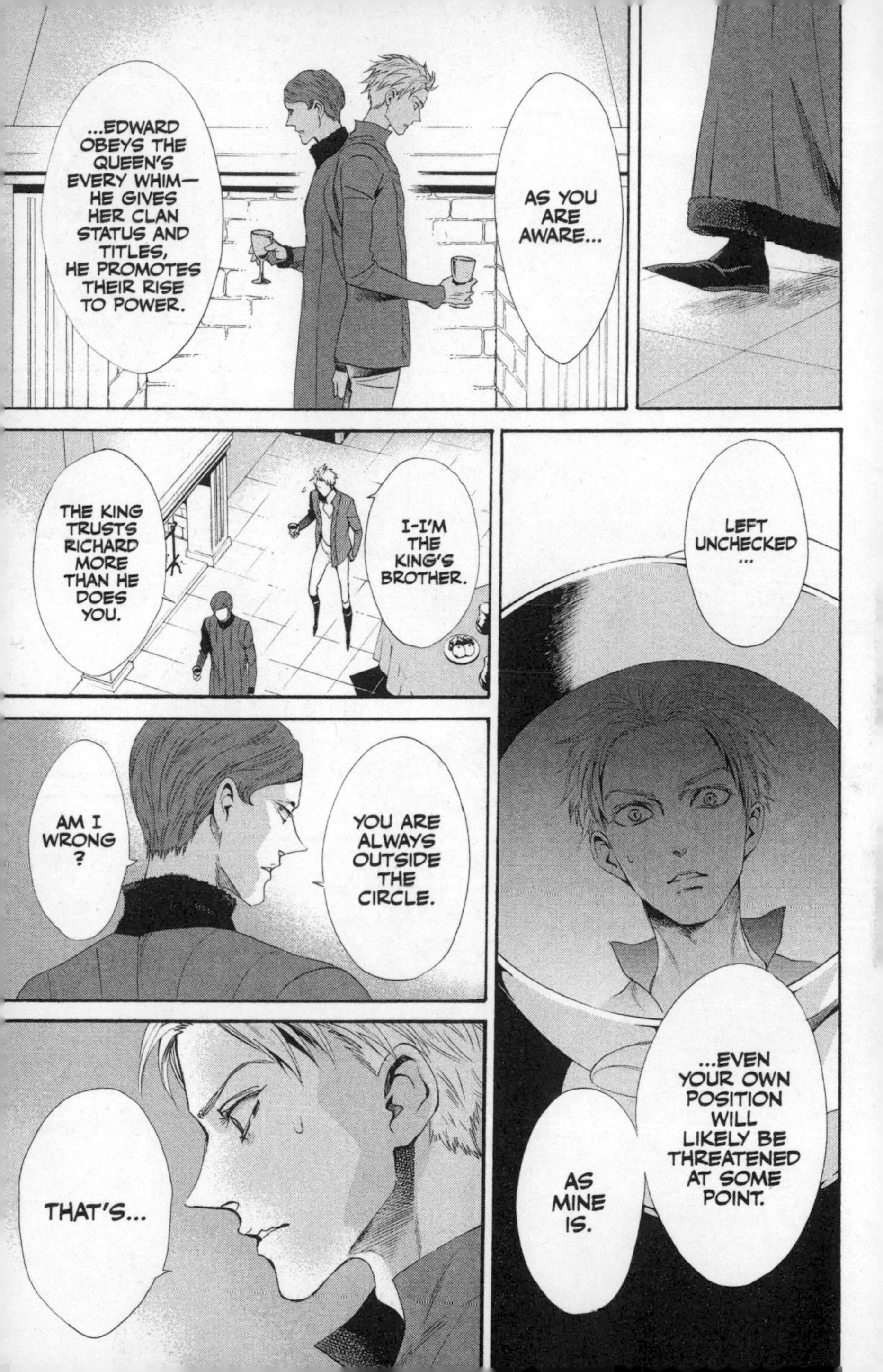
AS YOU ARE AWARE...
...EDWARD OBEYS THE QUEEN'S EVERY WHIM—HE GIVES HER CLAN STATUS AND TITLES, HE PROMOTES THEIR RISE TO POWER.
LEFT UNCHECKED ...
...EVEN YOUR OWN POSITION WILL LIKELY BE THREATENED AT SOME POINT.
AS MINE IS.
I-I'M THE KING'S BROTHER.
THE KING TRUSTS RICHARD MORE THAN HE DOES YOU.
YOU ARE ALWAYS OUTSIDE THE CIRCLE.
AM I WRONG ?
THAT'S...

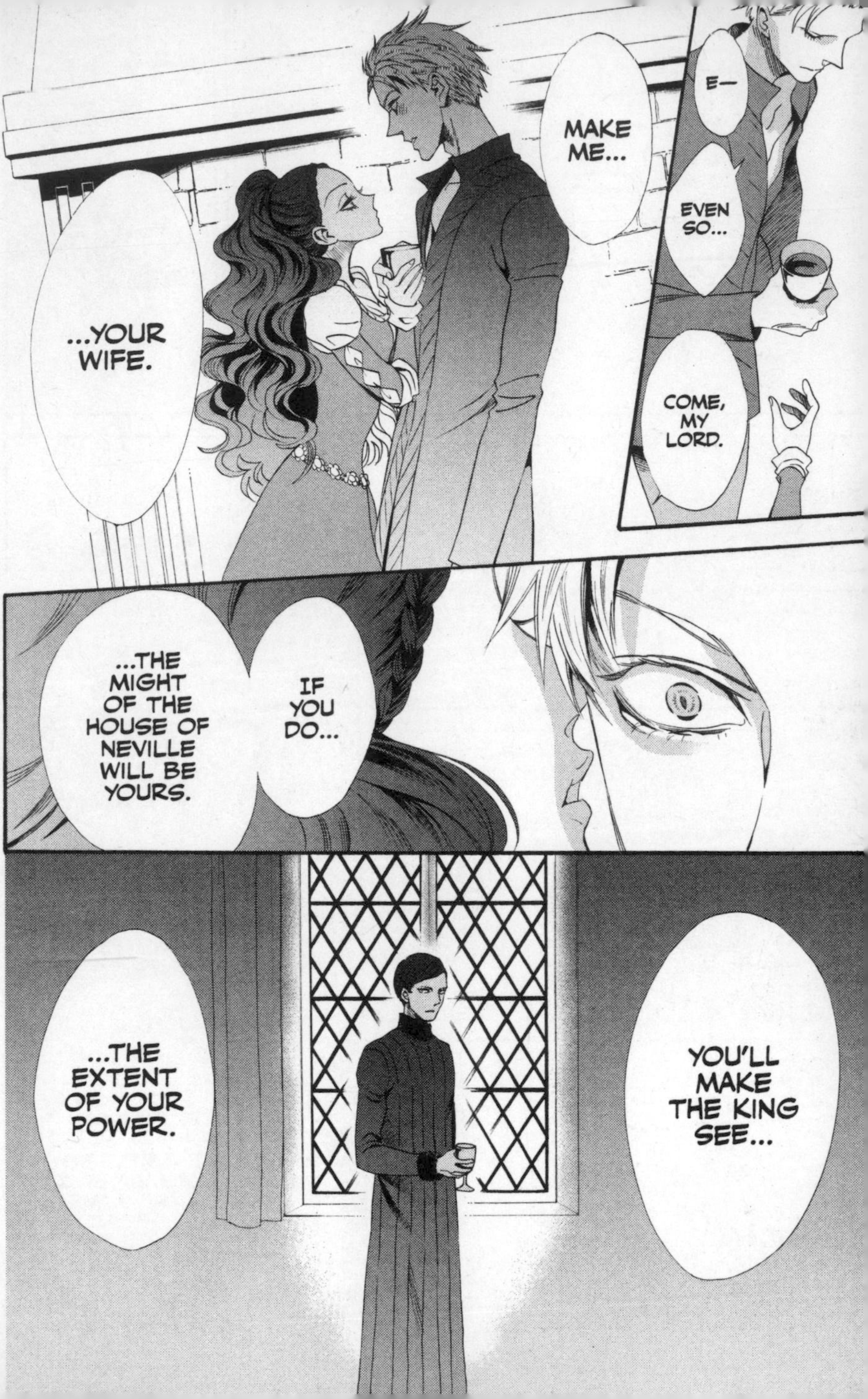
E—
EVEN SO...
COME, MY LORD.
MAKE ME...
...YOUR WIFE.
IF YOU DO...
...THE MIGHT OF THE HOUSE OF NEVILLE WILL BE YOURS.
YOU'LL MAKE THE KING SEE...
...THE EXTENT OF YOUR POWER.

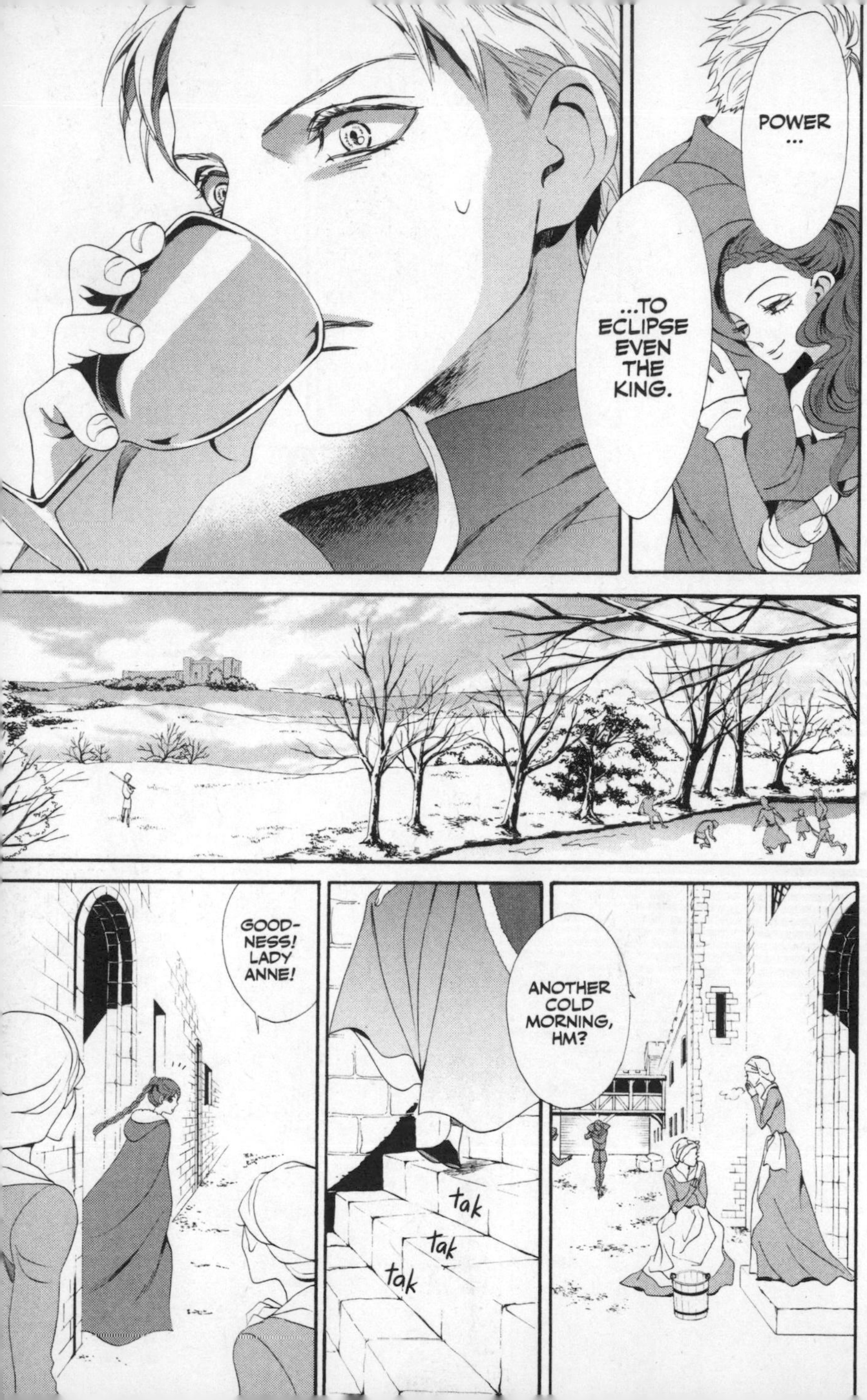
POWER ...
...TO ECLIPSE EVEN THE KING.
ANOTHER COLD MORNING, HM?
tak
tak
tak
GOOD-NESS! LADY ANNE!

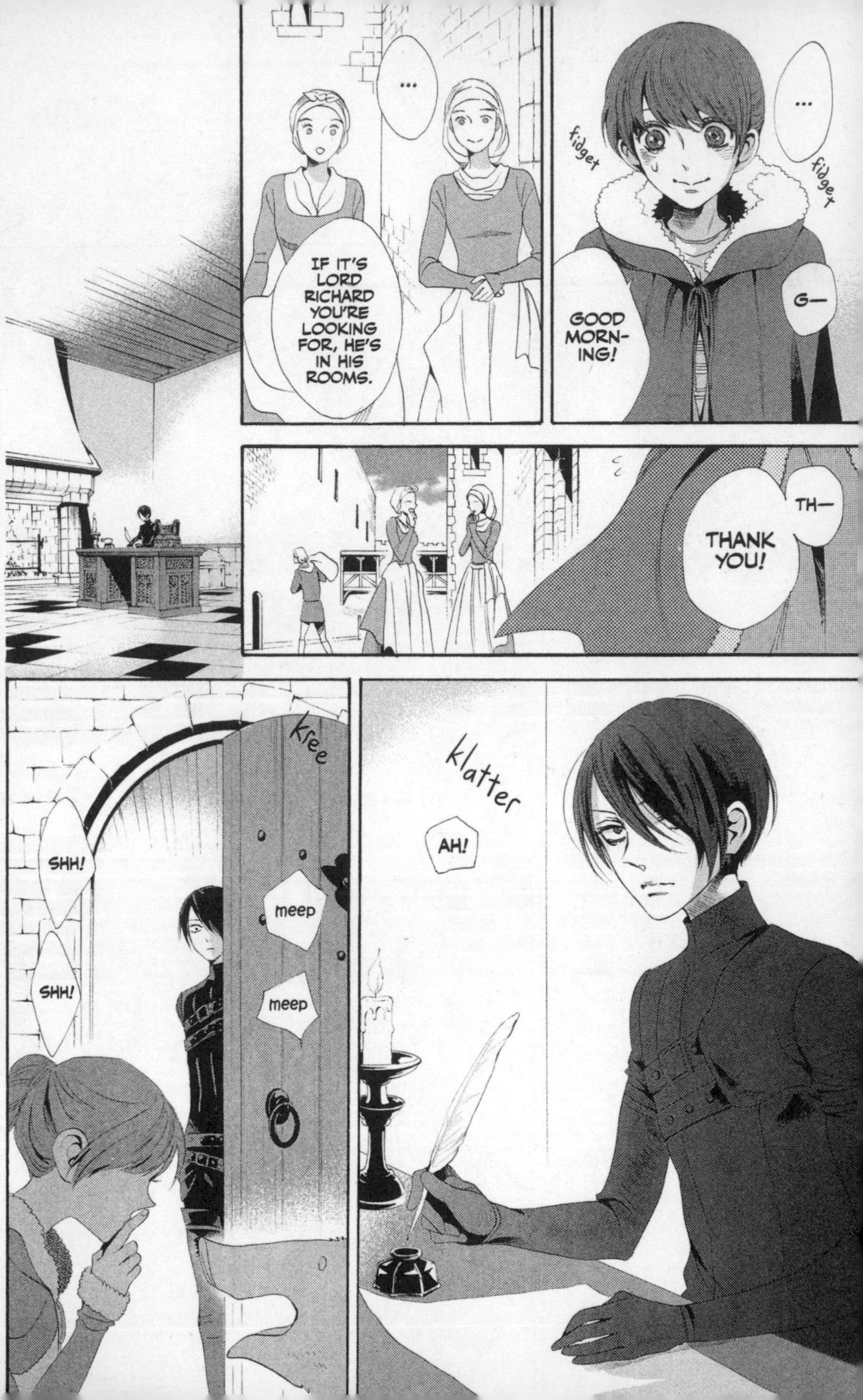
...
fidget
fidget
G—
GOOD MORNING!
...
IF IT'S LORD RICHARD YOU'RE LOOKING FOR, HE'S IN HIS ROOMS.
TH—
THANK YOU!
klatter
AH!
kree
SHH!
meep
SHH!
meep

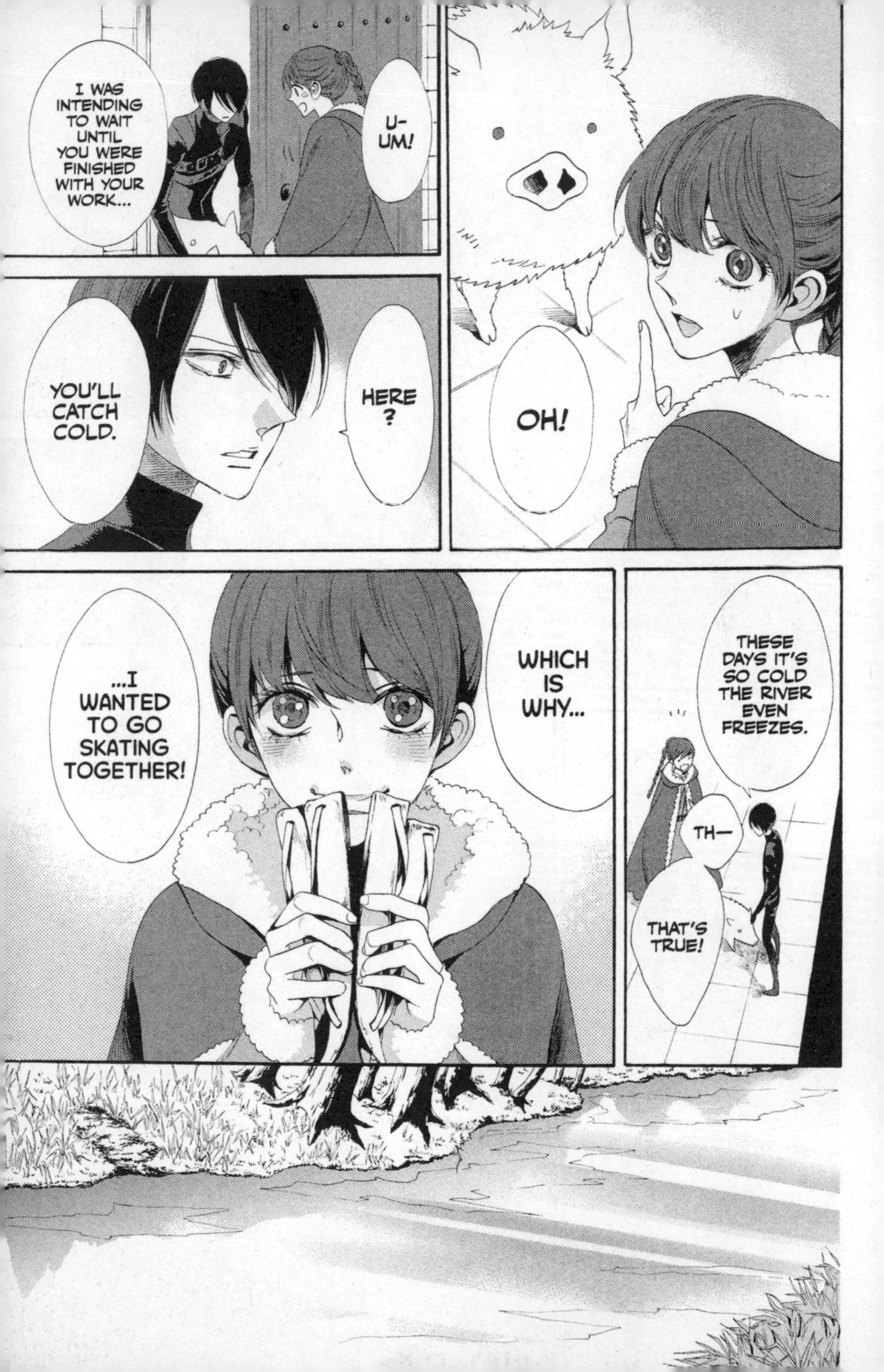
OH!
U-UM!
I WAS INTENDING TO WAIT UNTIL YOU WERE FINISHED WITH YOUR WORK...
HERE?
YOU'LL CATCH COLD.
THESE DAYS IT'S SO COLD THE RIVER EVEN FREEZES.
TH—
THAT'S TRUE!
WHICH IS WHY...
...I WANTED TO GO SKATING TOGETHER!

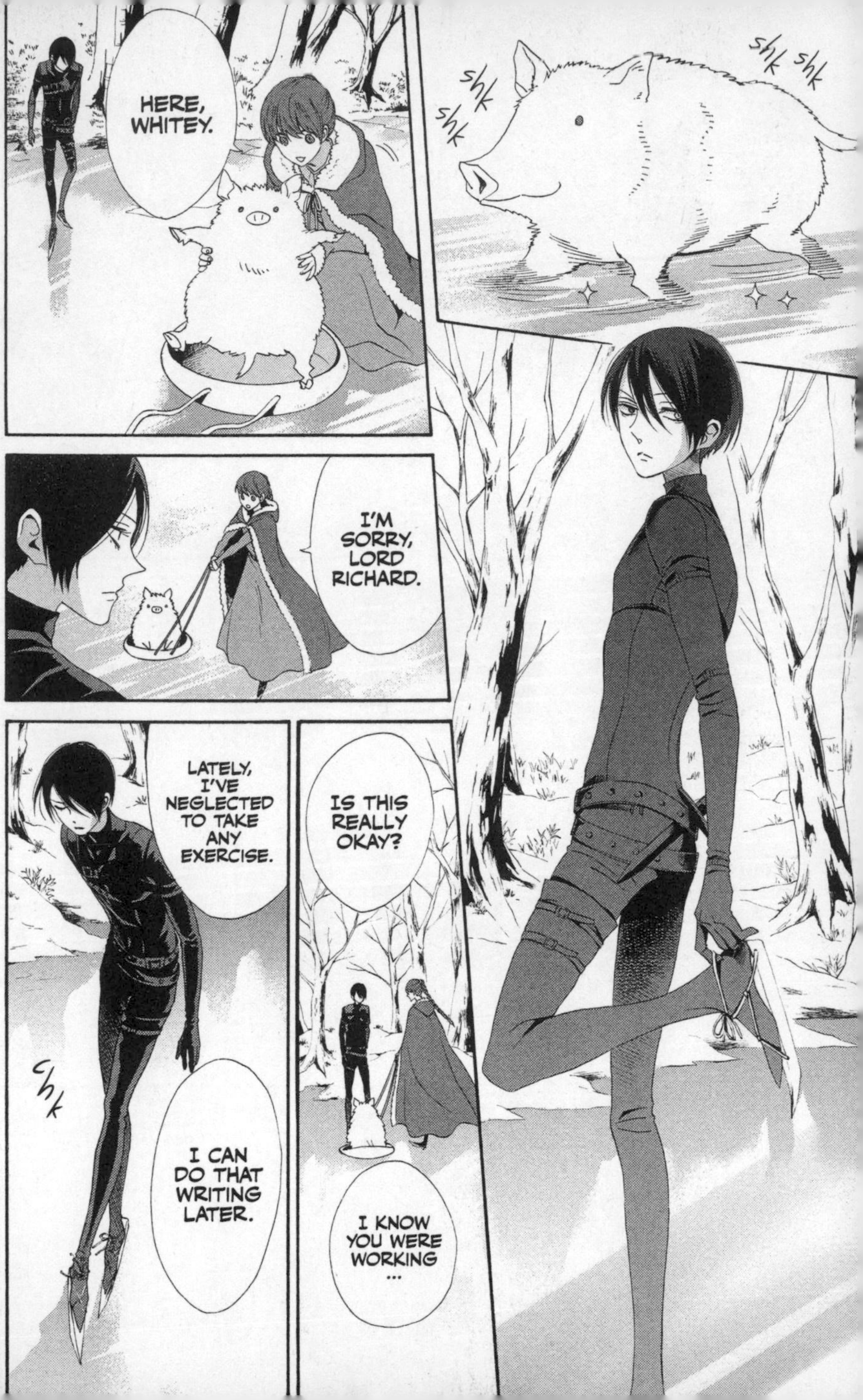
shk shk
shk
shk
HERE, WHITEY.
I'M SORRY, LORD RICHARD.
IS THIS REALLY OKAY?
I KNOW YOU WERE WORKING...
LATELY, I'VE NEGLECTED TO TAKE ANY EXERCISE.
I CAN DO THAT WRITING LATER.
chk

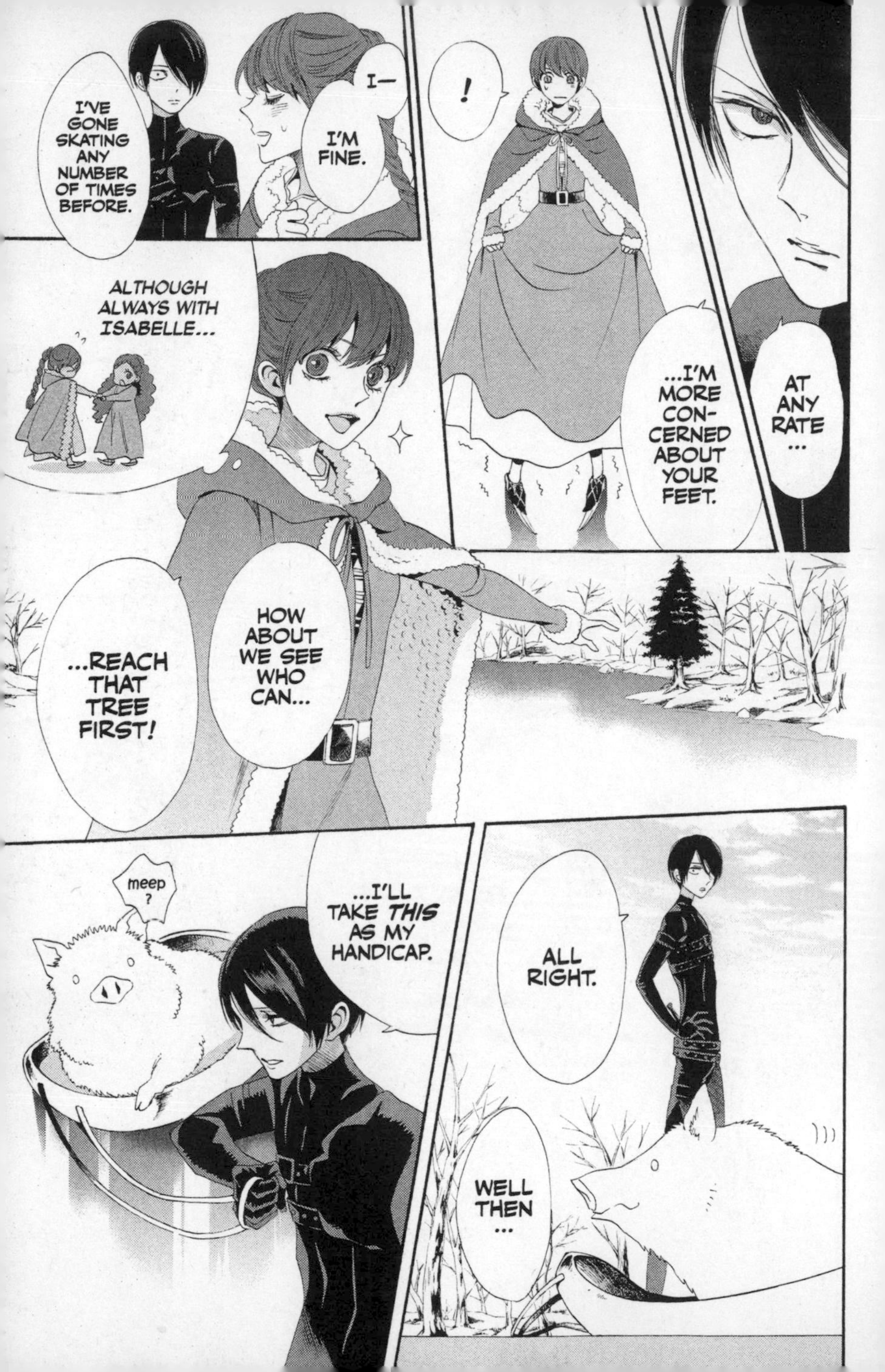
AT ANY RATE...
!
...I'M MORE CONCERNED ABOUT YOUR FEET.
I—
I'M FINE.
I'VE GONE SKATING ANY NUMBER OF TIMES BEFORE.
ALTHOUGH ALWAYS WITH ISABELLE...
HOW ABOUT WE SEE WHO CAN...
...REACH THAT TREE FIRST!
ALL RIGHT.
WELL THEN...
...I'LL TAKE *THIS* AS MY HANDICAP.
meep?

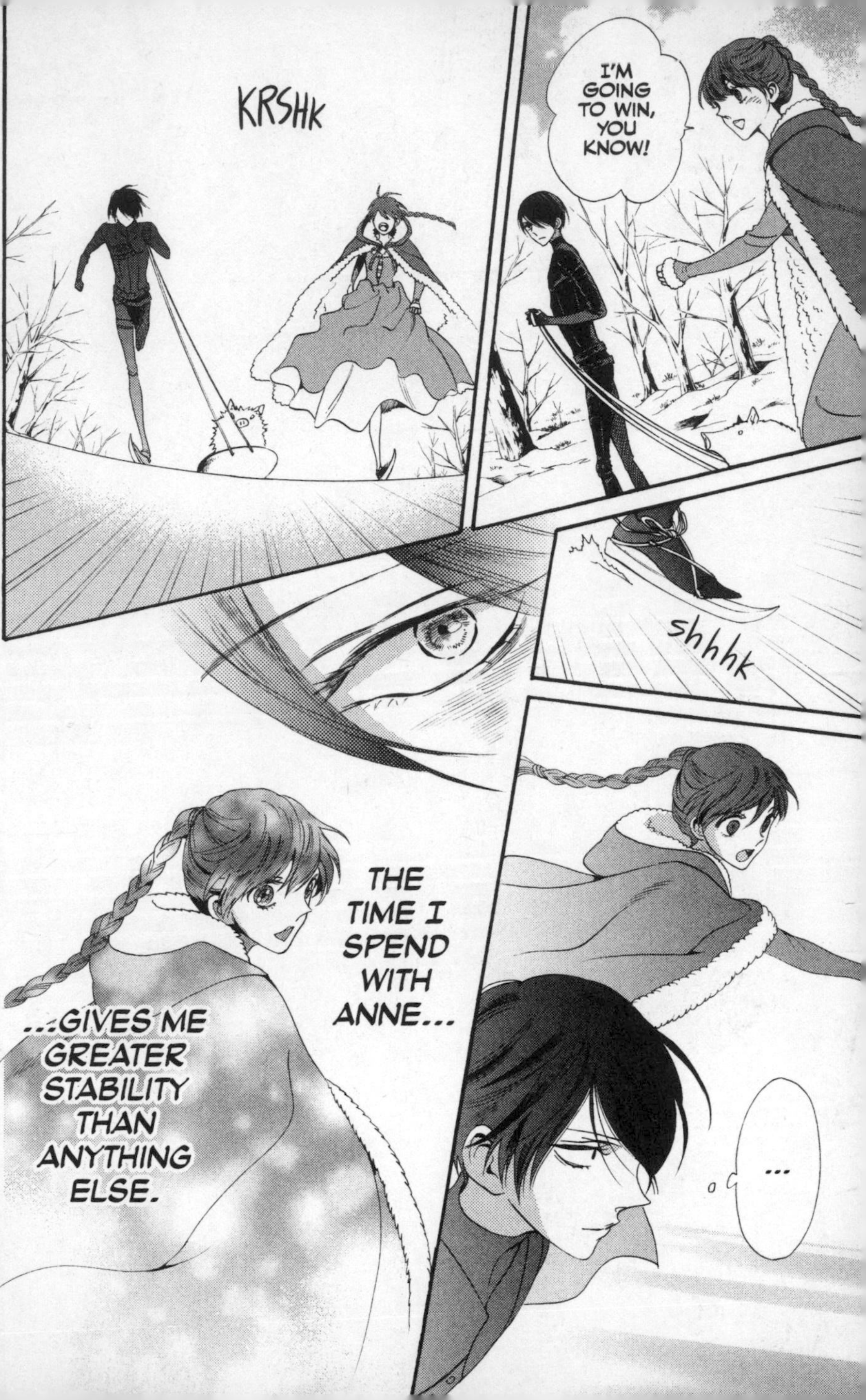
I'M GOING TO WIN, YOU KNOW!
shhhk
KRSHK
...
THE TIME I SPEND WITH ANNE...
...GIVES ME GREATER STABILITY THAN ANYTHING ELSE.

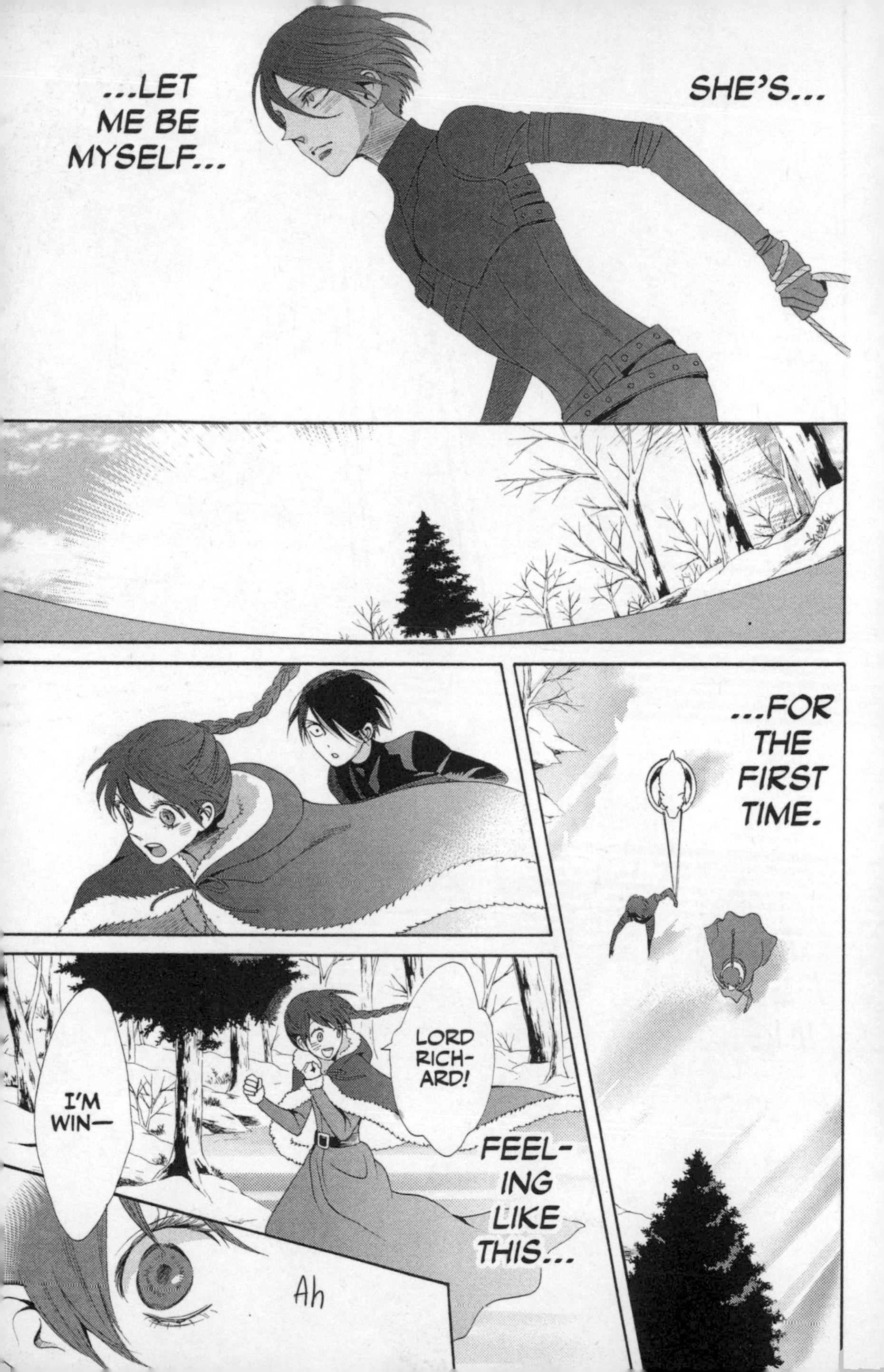
SHE'S...
...LET ME BE MYSELF...
...FOR THE FIRST TIME.
LORD RICH-ARD!
FEEL-ING LIKE THIS...
I'M WIN—
Ah

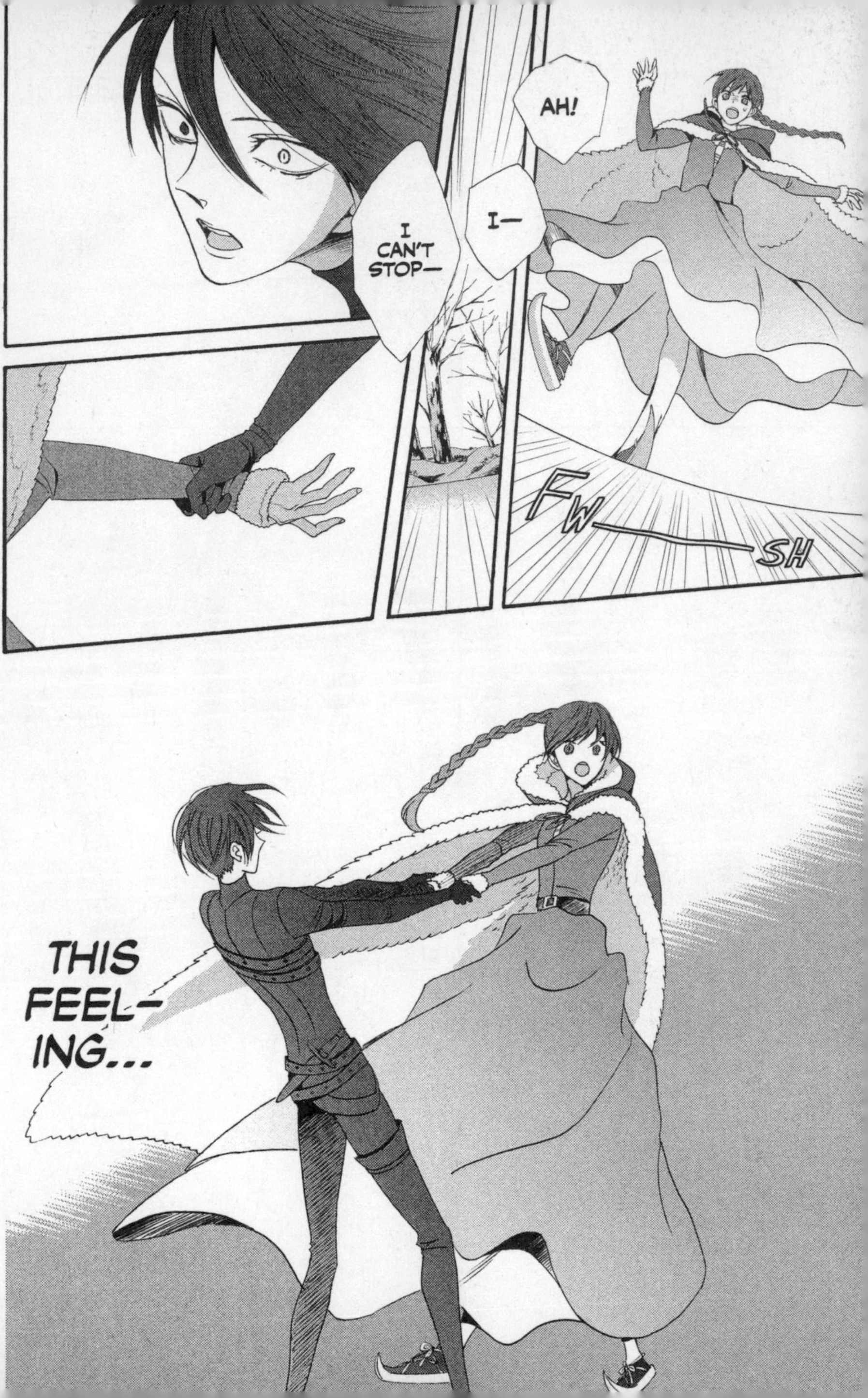
AH!
FW—SH
I—
I CAN'T STOP—
THIS FEELING...

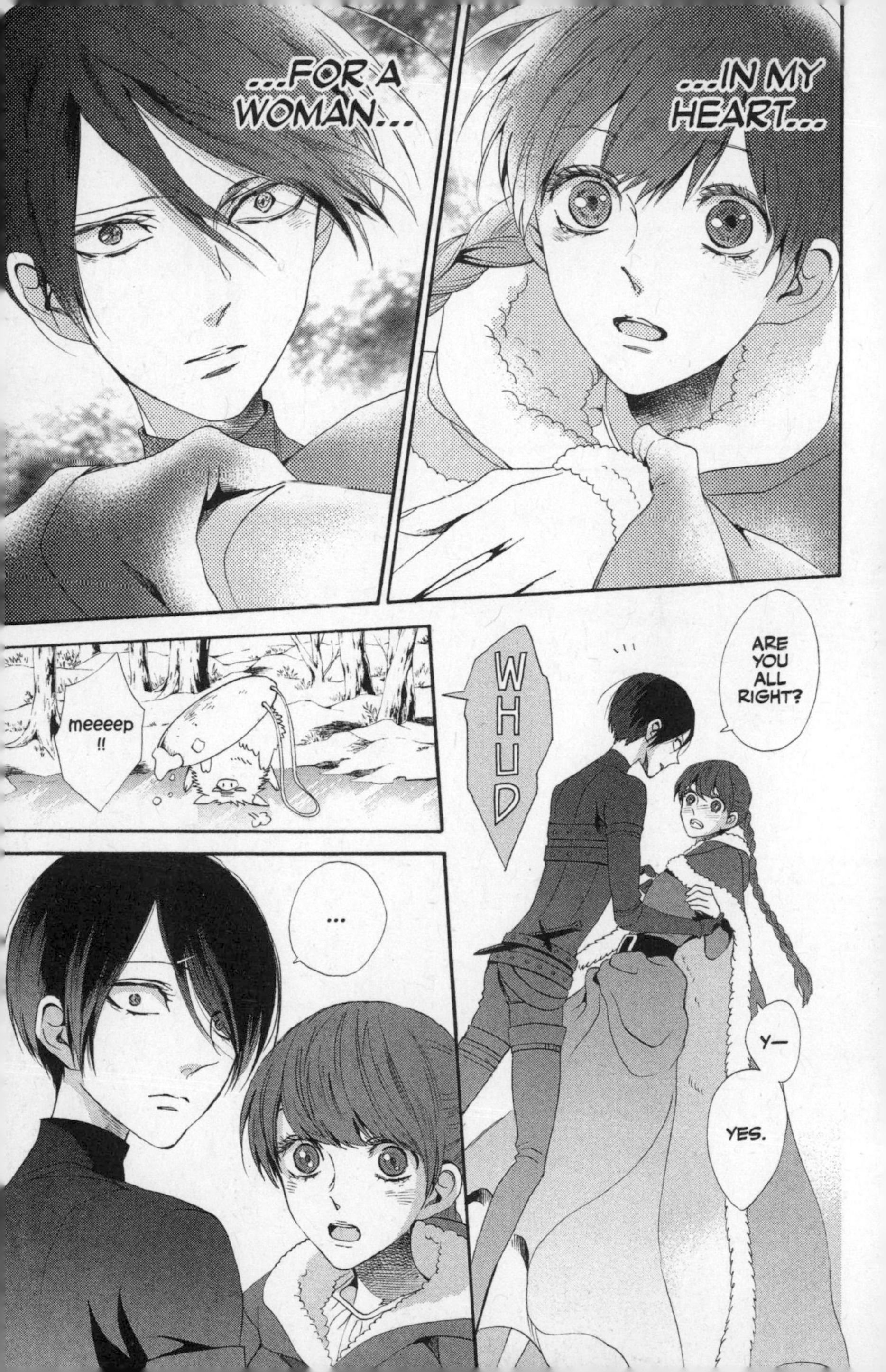
...IN MY HEART...
...FOR A WOMAN...
ARE YOU ALL RIGHT?
Y—
YES.
meeeep !!
WHUD
...

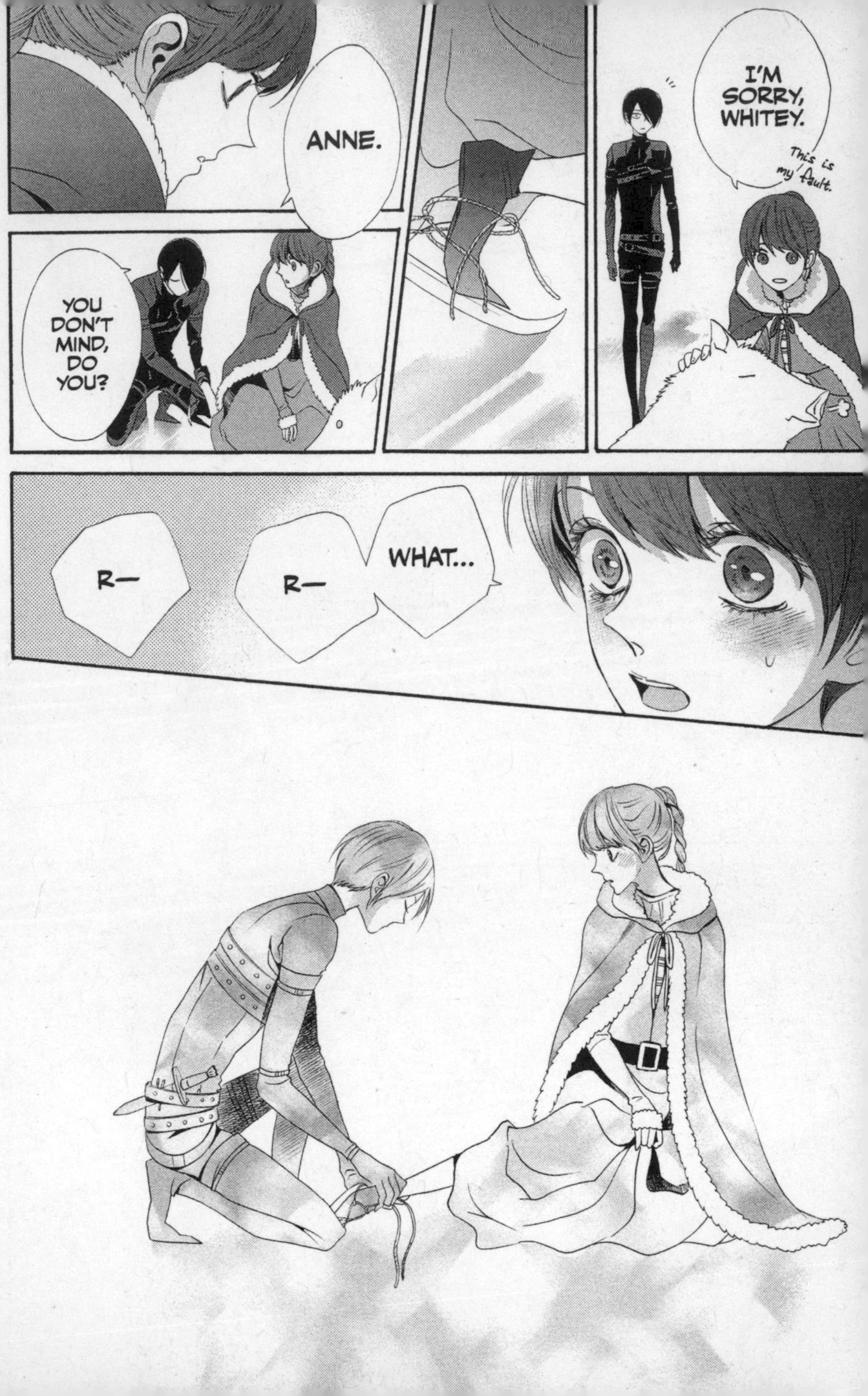
I'M SORRY, WHITEY.
This is my fault.
ANNE.
YOU DON'T MIND, DO YOU?
WHAT...
R—
R—

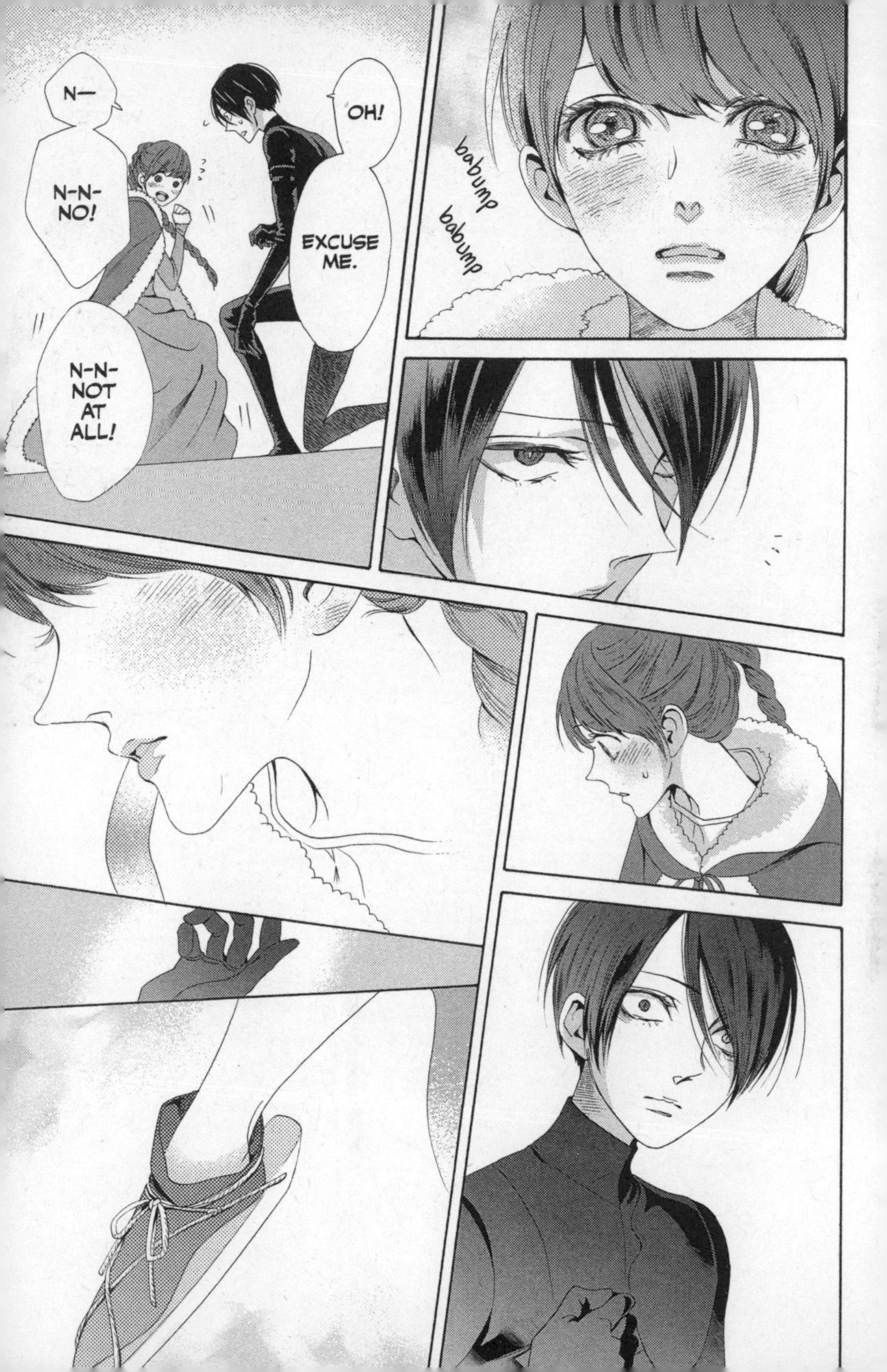
babump
babump
OH!
EXCUSE ME.
N—
N-N-NO!
N-N-NOT AT ALL!

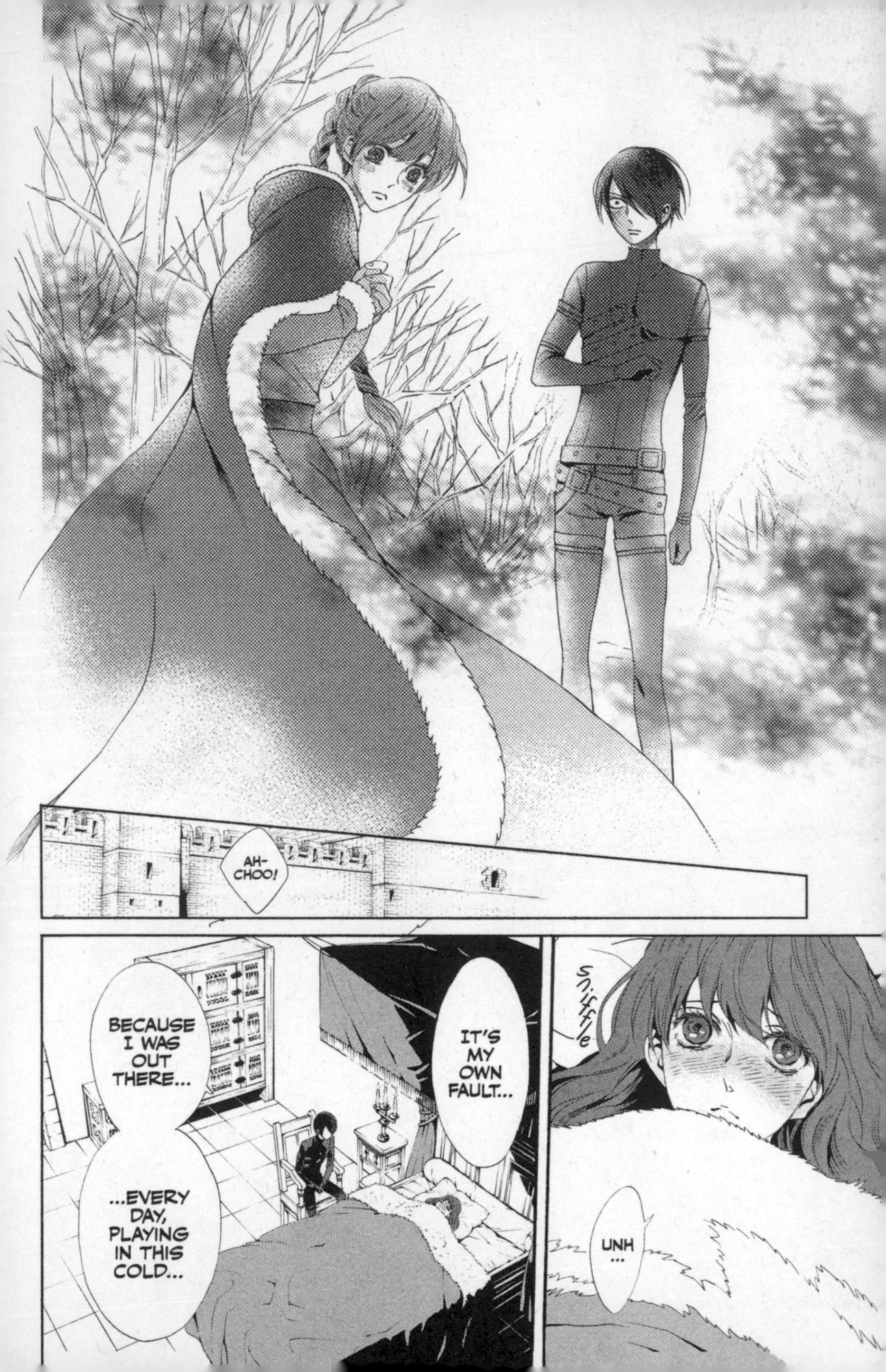
AH-CHOO!
sniffle
UNH...
IT'S MY OWN FAULT...
BECAUSE I WAS OUT THERE...
...EVERY DAY, PLAYING IN THIS COLD...

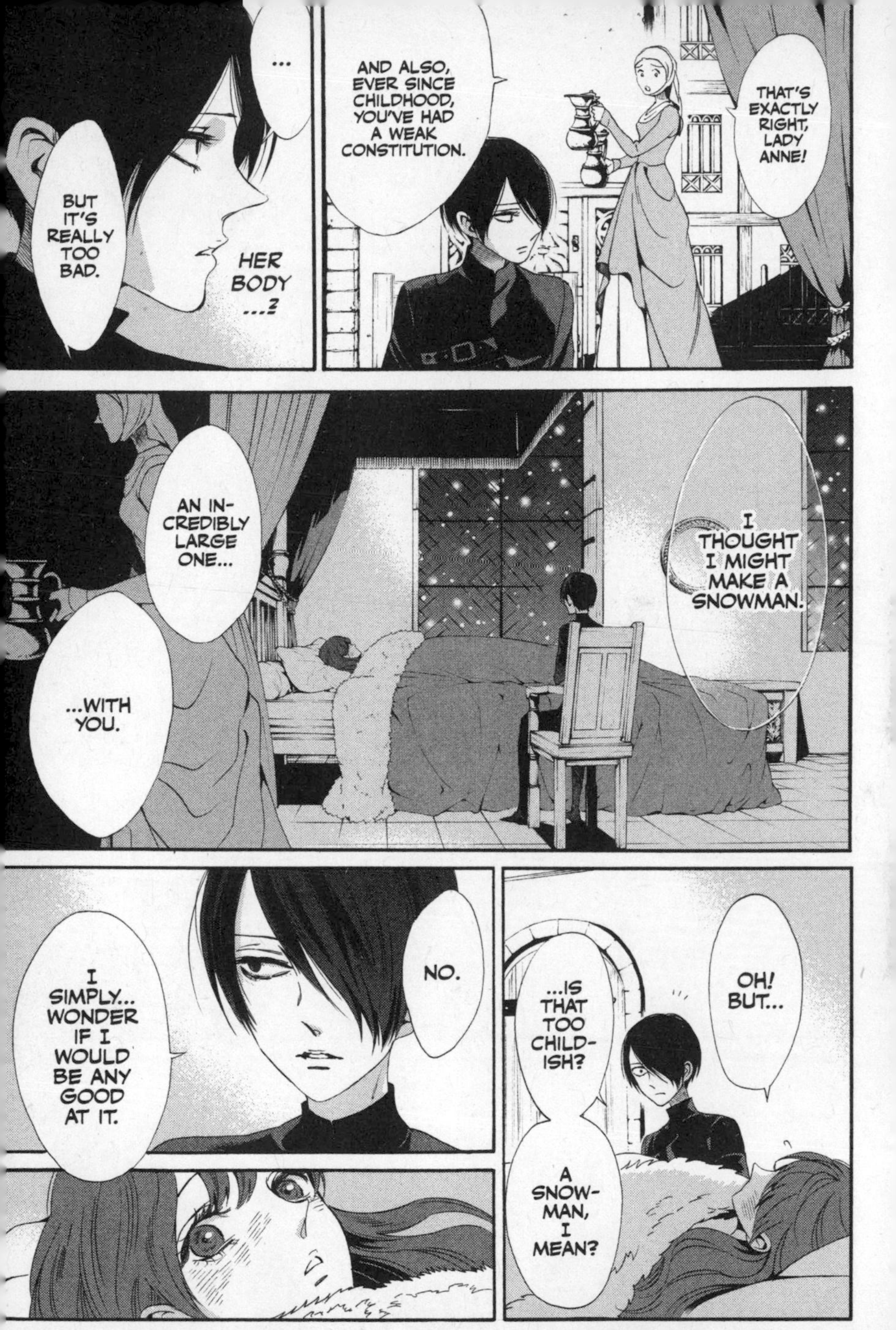
THAT'S EXACTLY RIGHT, LADY ANNE!
AND ALSO, EVER SINCE CHILDHOOD, YOU'VE HAD A WEAK CONSTITUTION.
...
HER BODY ...?
BUT IT'S REALLY TOO BAD.
I THOUGHT I MIGHT MAKE A SNOWMAN.
AN INCREDIBLY LARGE ONE...
...WITH YOU.
OH! BUT...
...IS THAT TOO CHILDISH?
A SNOWMAN, I MEAN?
NO.
I SIMPLY... WONDER IF I WOULD BE ANY GOOD AT IT.

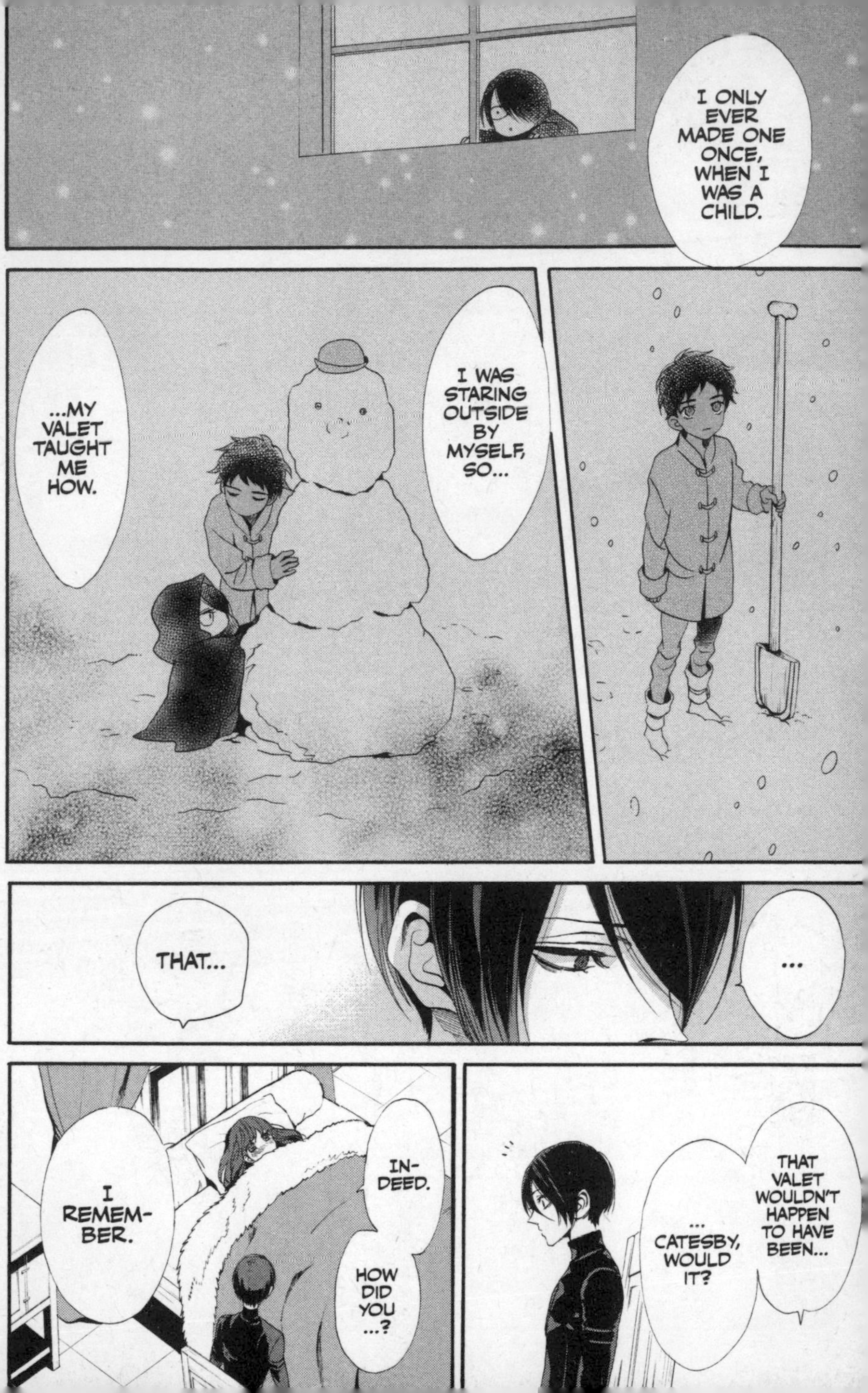
I ONLY EVER MADE ONE ONCE, WHEN I WAS A CHILD.
I WAS STARING OUTSIDE BY MYSELF, SO...
...MY VALET TAUGHT ME HOW.
...
THAT...
THAT VALET WOULDN'T HAPPEN TO HAVE BEEN...
...CATESBY, WOULD IT?
INDEED.
HOW DID YOU...?
I REMEMBER.

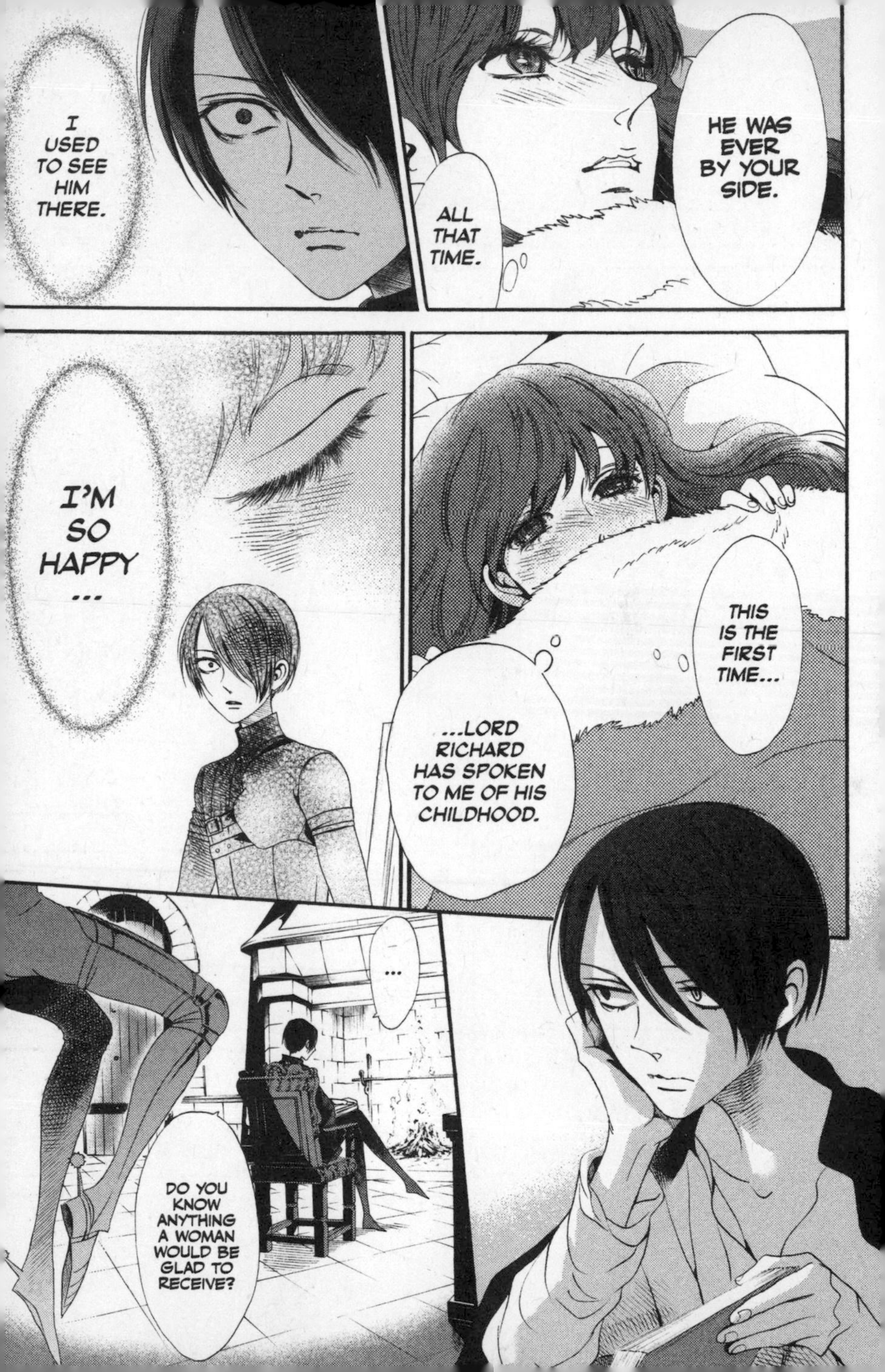
HE WAS EVER BY YOUR SIDE.
ALL THAT TIME.
I USED TO SEE HIM THERE.
THIS IS THE FIRST TIME...
...LORD RICHARD HAS SPOKEN TO ME OF HIS CHILDHOOD.
I'M SO HAPPY ...
...
DO YOU KNOW ANYTHING A WOMAN WOULD BE GLAD TO RECEIVE?

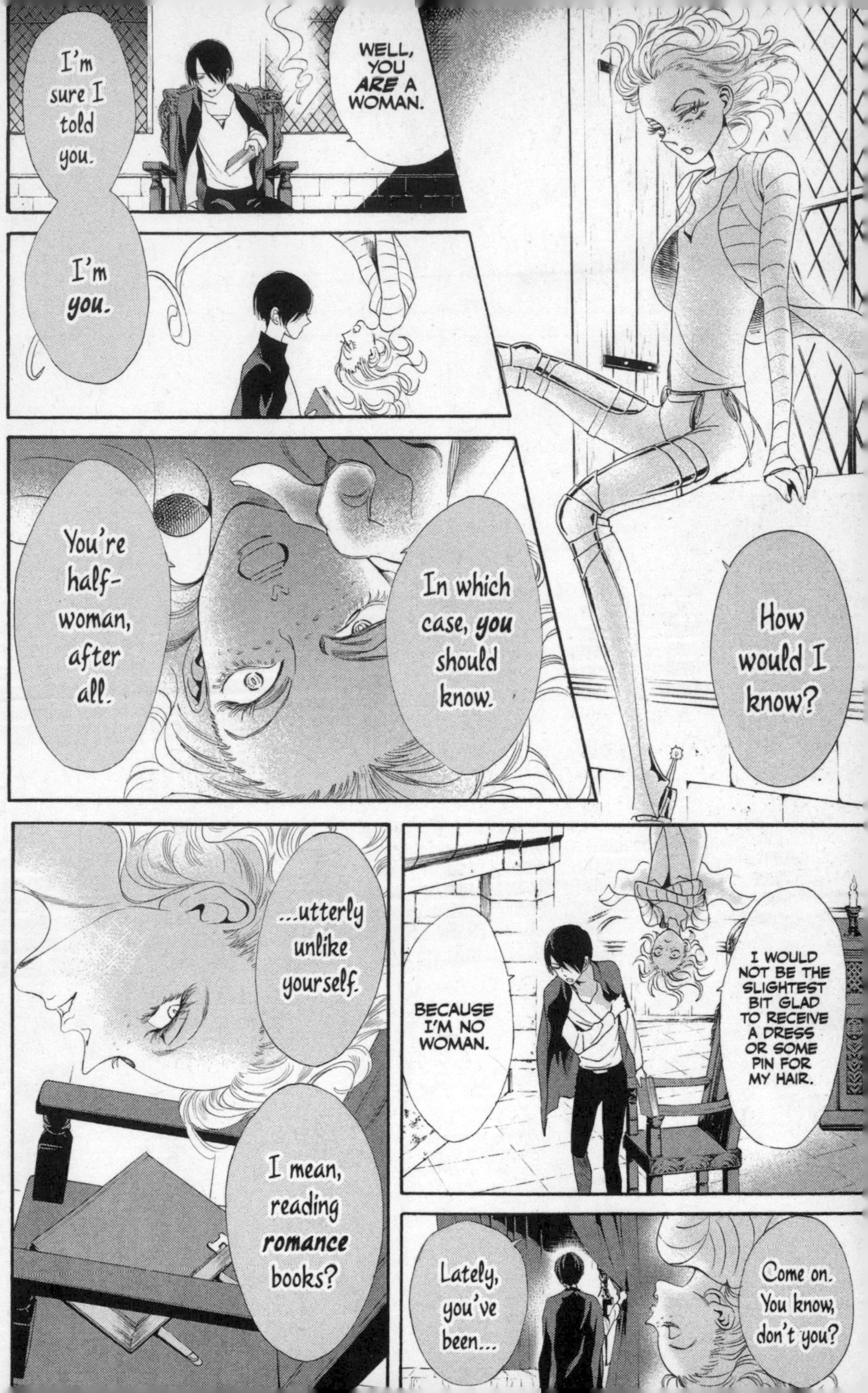
How would I know?
WELL, YOU ARE A WOMAN.
I'm sure I told you.
I'm you.
In which case, you should know.
You're half-woman, after all.
I WOULD NOT BE THE SLIGHTEST BIT GLAD TO RECEIVE A DRESS OR SOME PIN FOR MY HAIR.
BECAUSE I'M NO WOMAN.
Come on. You know, don't you?
Lately, you've been...
...utterly unlike yourself.
I mean, reading romance books?

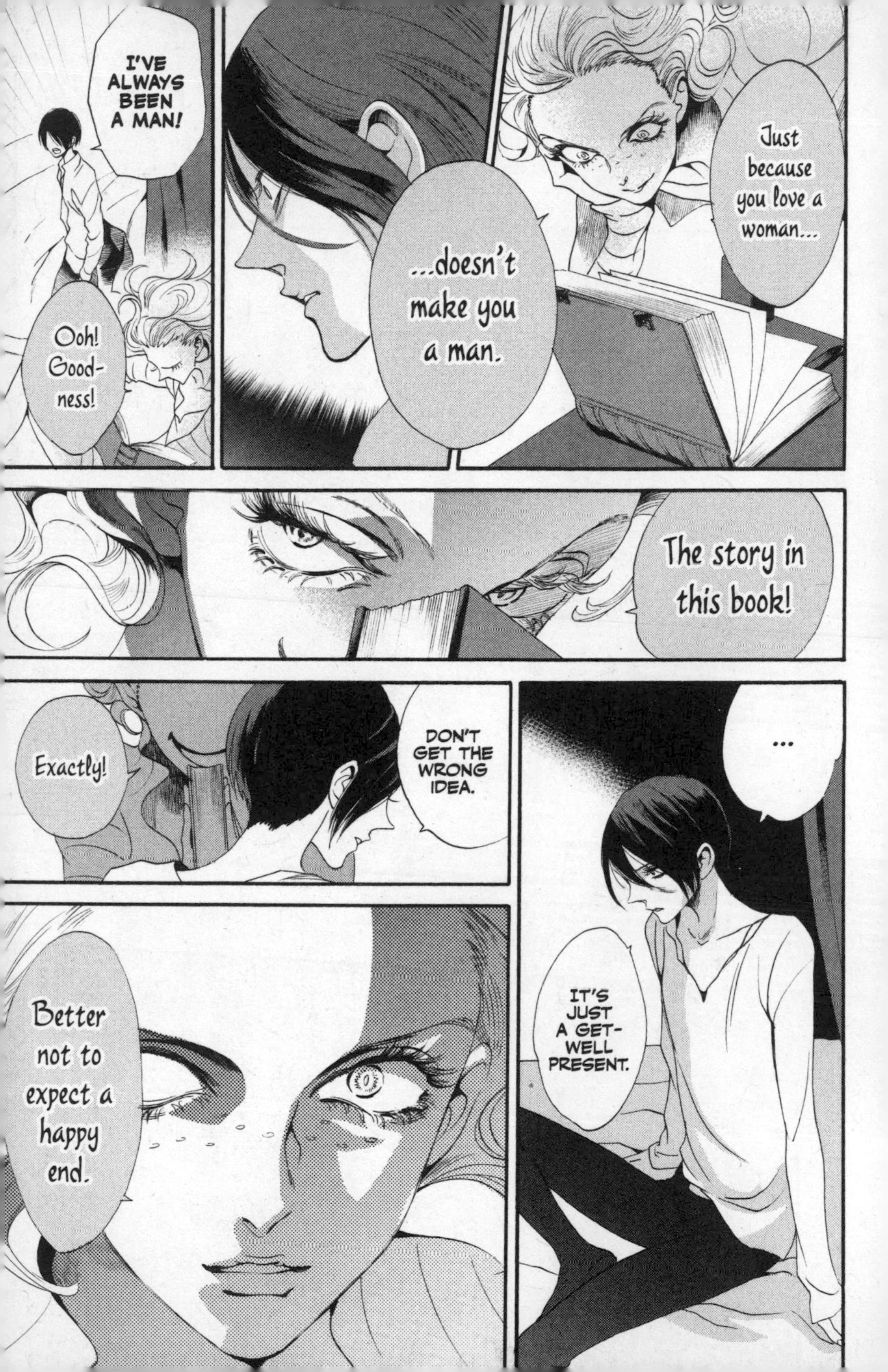
Just because you love a woman...
...doesn't make you a man.
I'VE ALWAYS BEEN A MAN!
Ooh! Goodness!
The story in this book!
...
IT'S JUST A GET-WELL PRESENT.
DON'T GET THE WRONG IDEA.
Exactly!
Better not to expect a happy end.

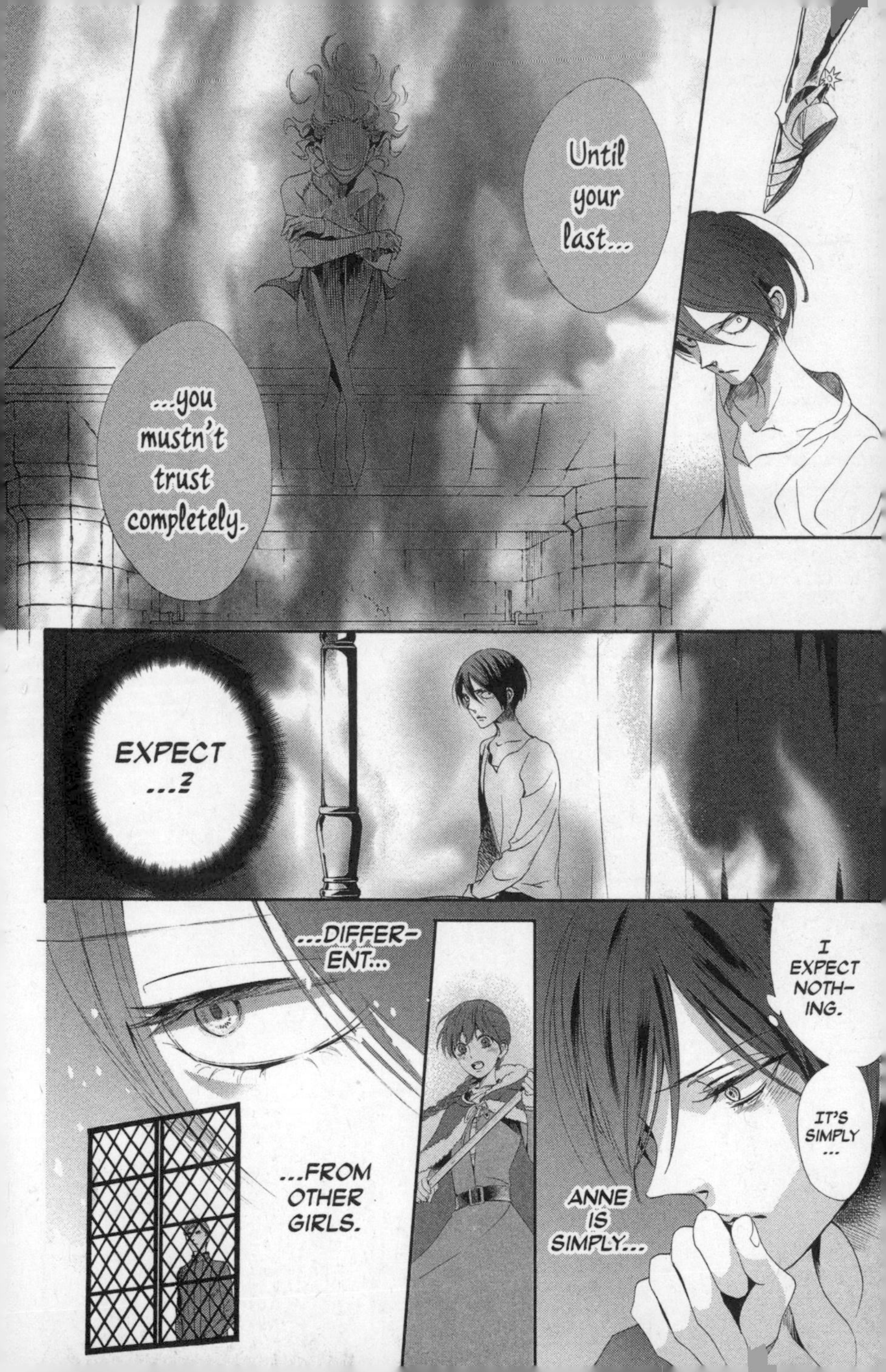
Until your last...
...you mustn't trust completely.
EXPECT ...?
I EXPECT NOTHING.
IT'S SIMPLY ...
ANNE IS SIMPLY...
...DIFFERENT...
...FROM OTHER GIRLS.

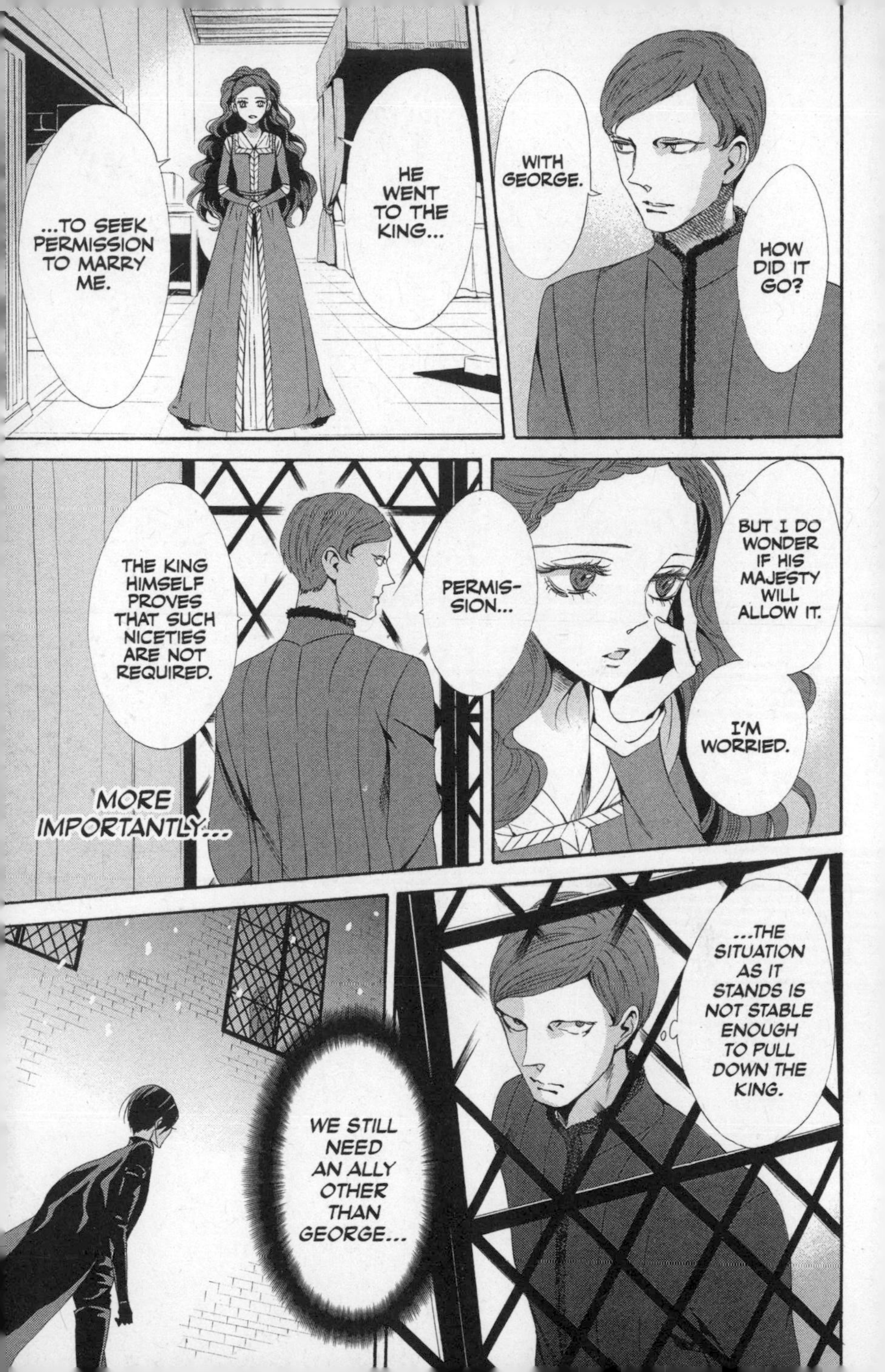
WITH GEORGE.
HOW DID IT GO?
HE WENT TO THE KING...
...TO SEEK PERMISSION TO MARRY ME.
BUT I DO WONDER IF HIS MAJESTY WILL ALLOW IT.
I'M WORRIED.
PERMIS-SION...
THE KING HIMSELF PROVES THAT SUCH NICETIES ARE NOT REQUIRED.
MORE IMPORTANTLY...
...THE SITUATION AS IT STANDS IS NOT STABLE ENOUGH TO PULL DOWN THE KING.
WE STILL NEED AN ALLY OTHER THAN GEORGE...

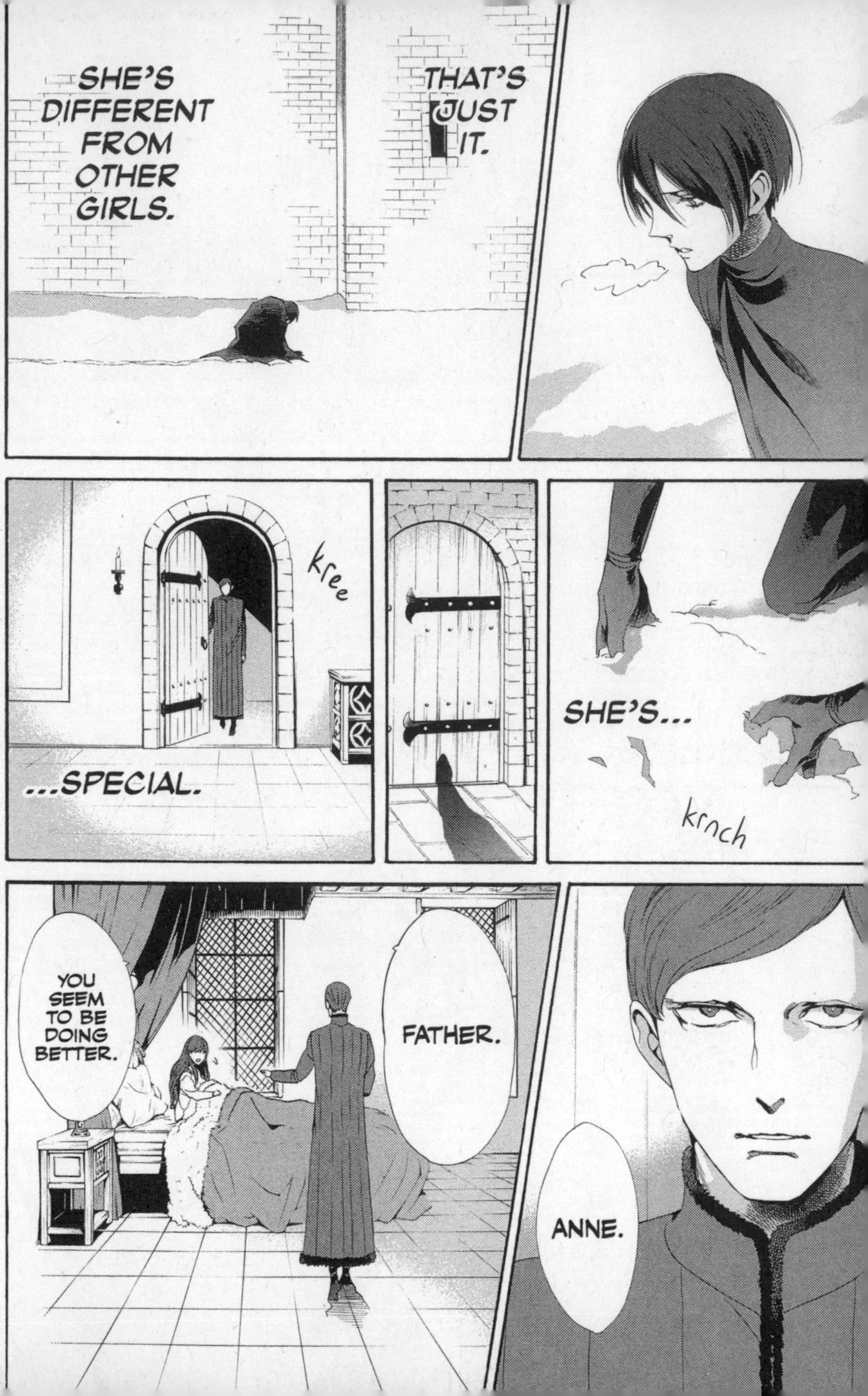
THAT'S JUST IT.
SHE'S DIFFERENT FROM OTHER GIRLS.
SHE'S...
krnch
kree
...SPECIAL.
ANNE.
FATHER.
YOU SEEM TO BE DOING BETTER.

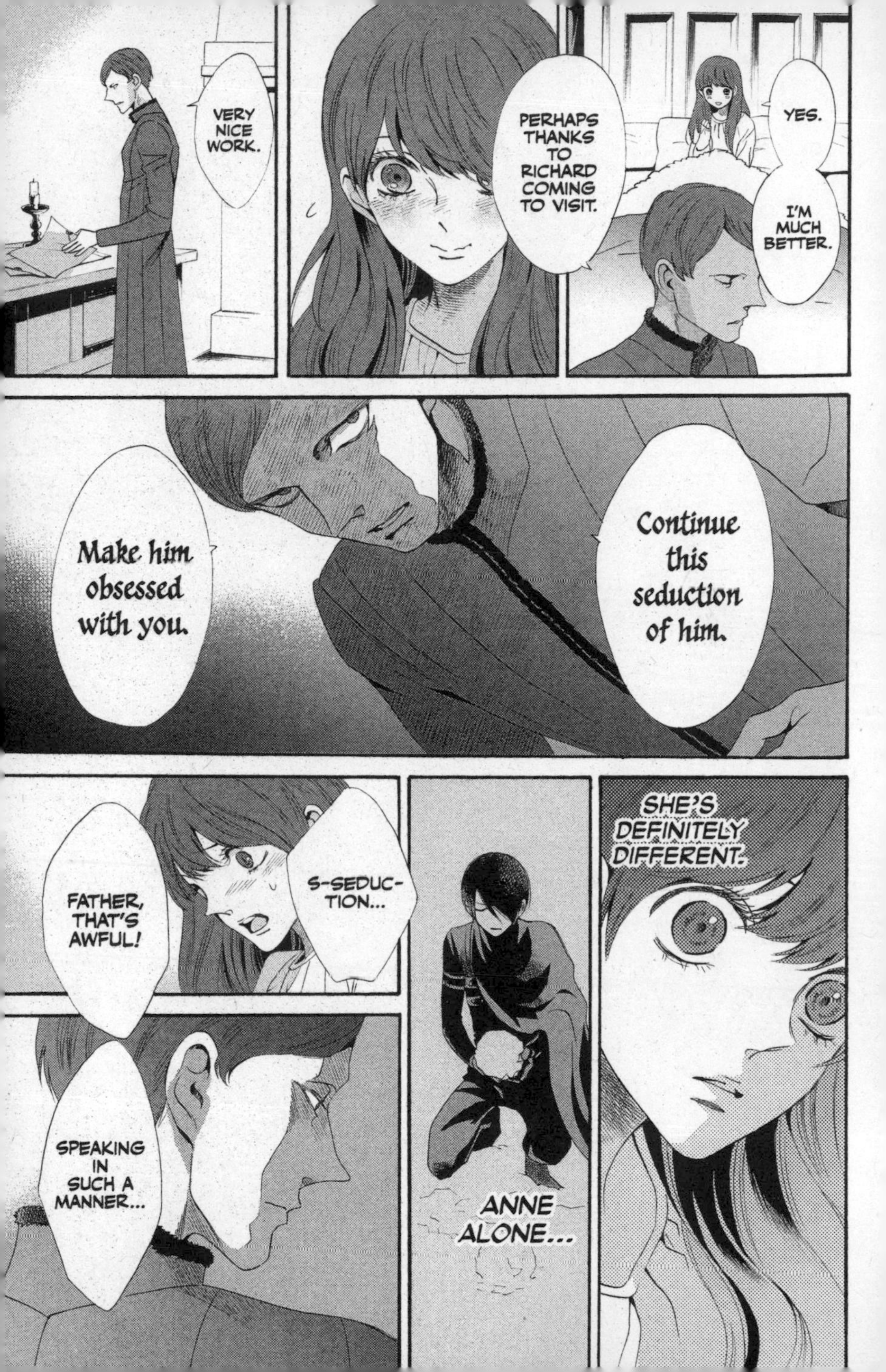
YES.
I'M MUCH BETTER.
PERHAPS THANKS TO RICHARD COMING TO VISIT.
VERY NICE WORK.
Continue this seduction of him.
Make him obsessed with you.
SHE'S DEFINITELY DIFFERENT.
ANNE ALONE...
S-SEDUC-TION...
FATHER, THAT'S AWFUL!
SPEAKING IN SUCH A MANNER...

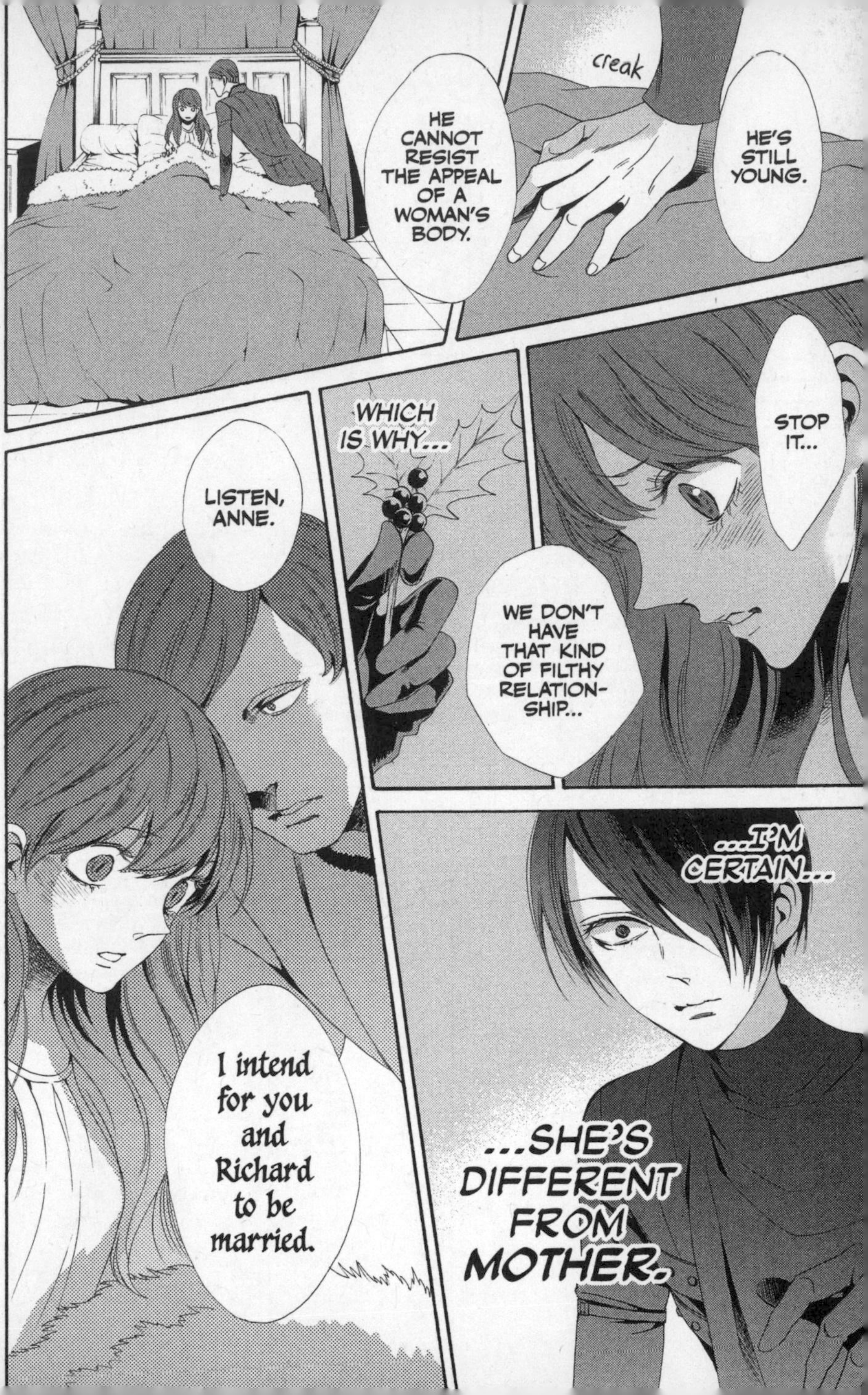
creak
HE'S STILL YOUNG.
HE CANNOT RESIST THE APPEAL OF A WOMAN'S BODY.
STOP IT...
WE DON'T HAVE THAT KIND OF FILTHY RELATION-SHIP...
WHICH IS WHY...
...I'M CERTAIN...
...SHE'S DIFFERENT FROM MOTHER.
LISTEN, ANNE.
I intend for you and Richard to be married.

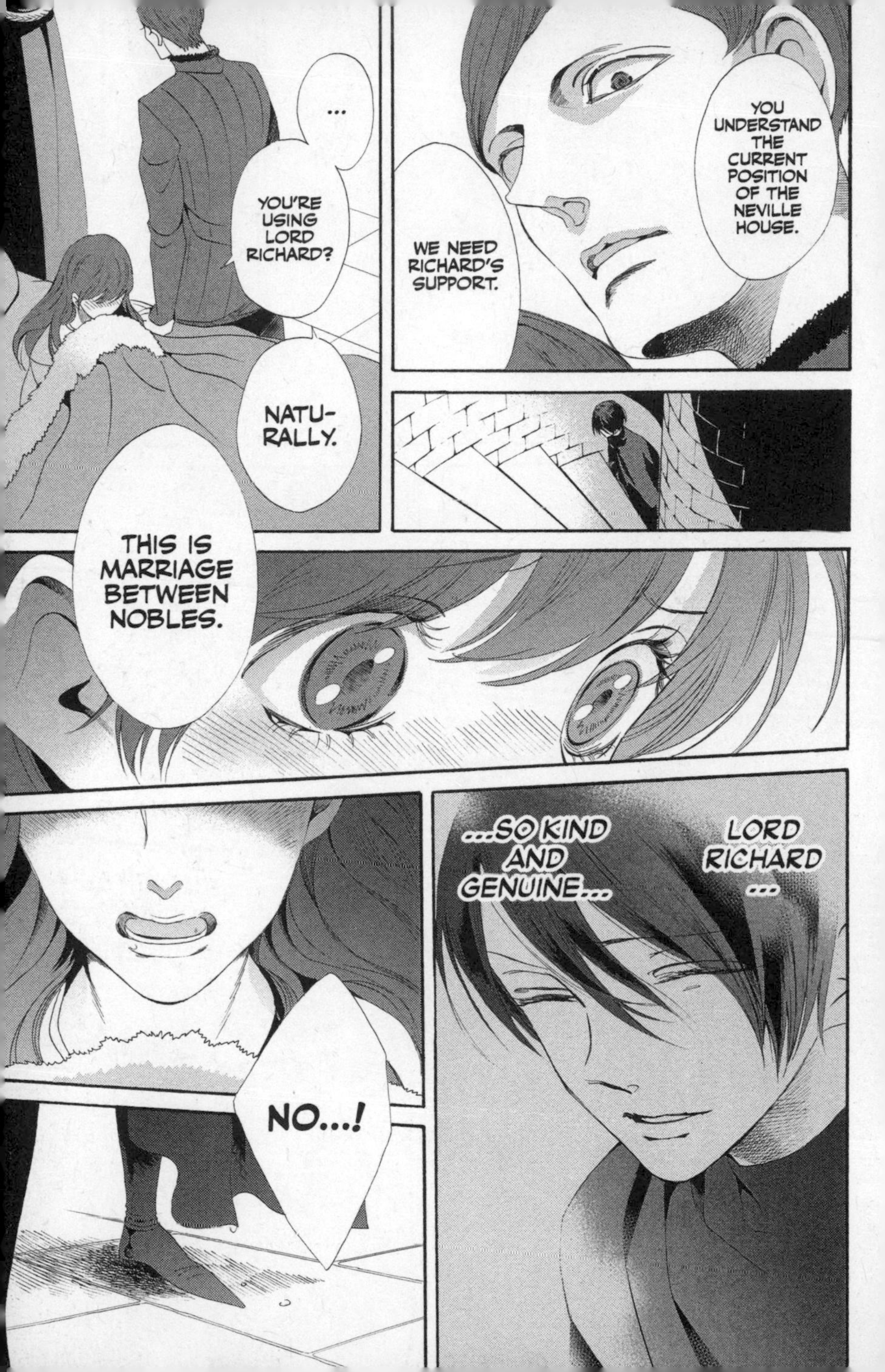
YOU UNDERSTAND THE CURRENT POSITION OF THE NEVILLE HOUSE.
WE NEED RICHARD'S SUPPORT.
...
YOU'RE USING LORD RICHARD?
NATU-RALLY.
THIS IS MARRIAGE BETWEEN NOBLES.
LORD RICHARD ...
...SO KIND AND GENUINE...
NO...!

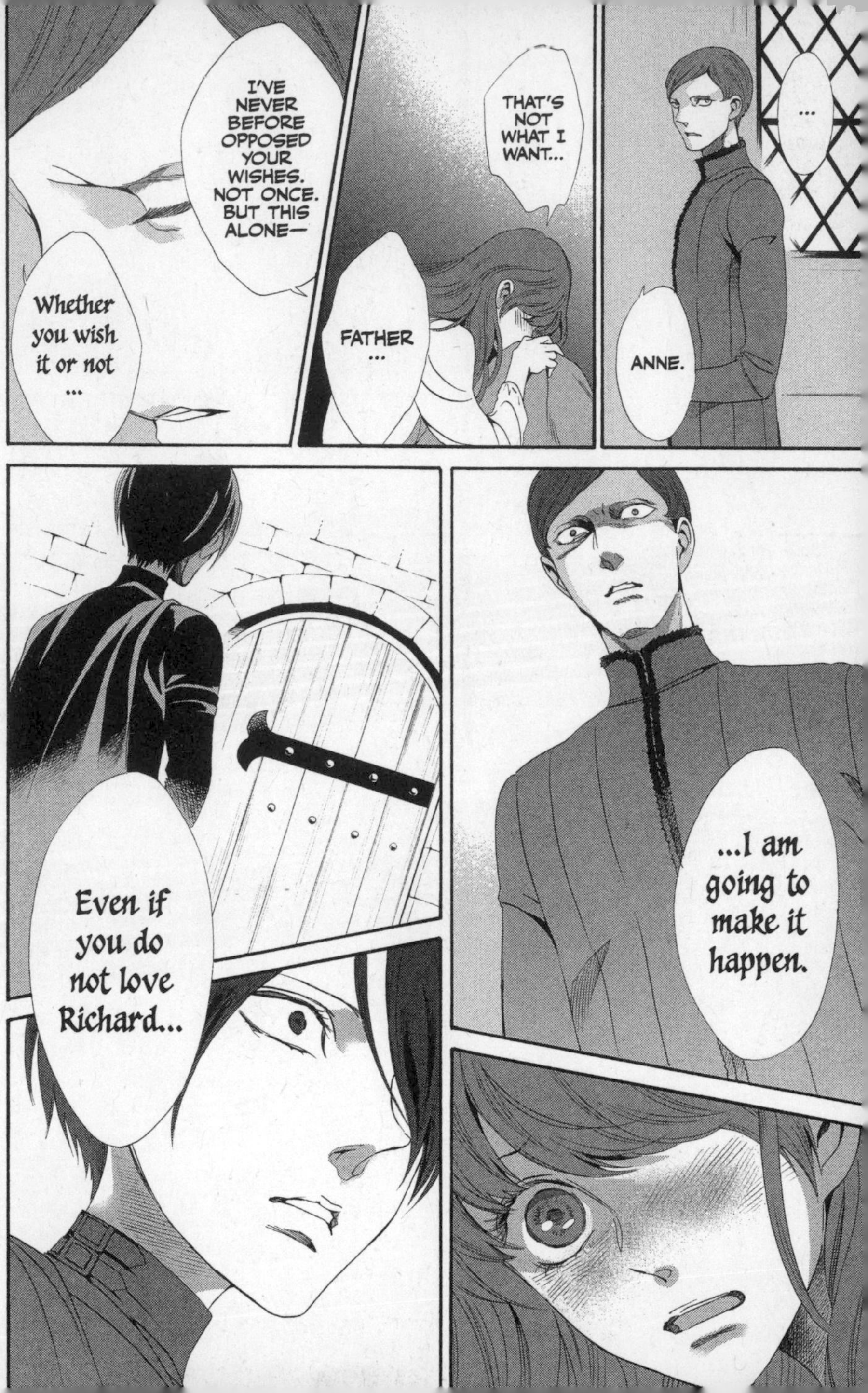
...
ANNE.
THAT'S NOT WHAT I WANT...
FATHER ...
I'VE NEVER BEFORE OPPOSED YOUR WISHES. NOT ONCE. BUT THIS ALONE—
Whether you wish it or not ...
...I am going to make it happen.
Even if you do not love Richard...

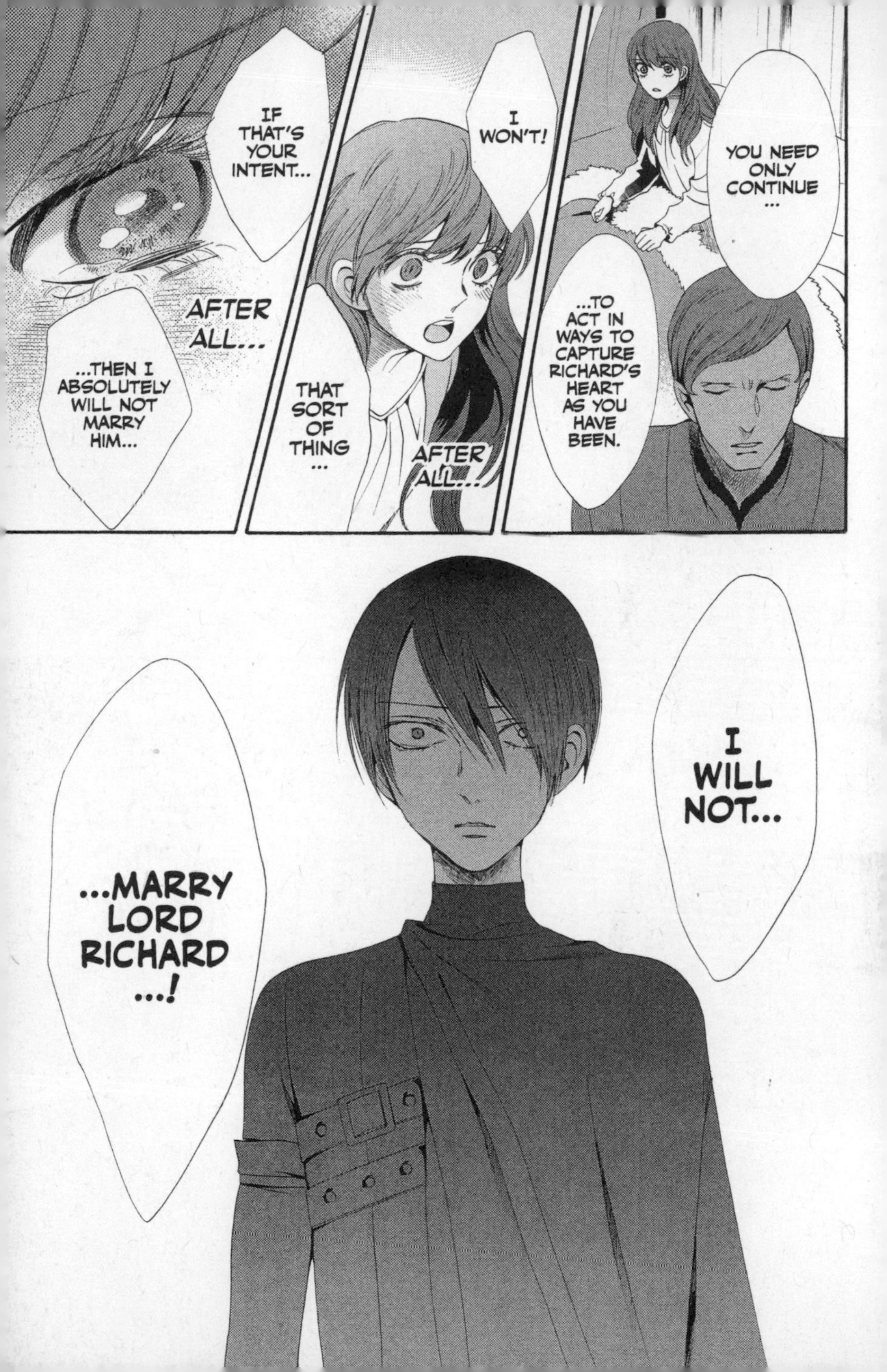
YOU NEED ONLY CONTINUE ...
...TO ACT IN WAYS TO CAPTURE RICHARD'S HEART AS YOU HAVE BEEN.
I WON'T!
THAT SORT OF THING ...
AFTER ALL...
IF THAT'S YOUR INTENT...
AFTER ALL...
...THEN I ABSOLUTELY WILL NOT MARRY HIM...
I WILL NOT...
...MARRY LORD RICHARD ...!

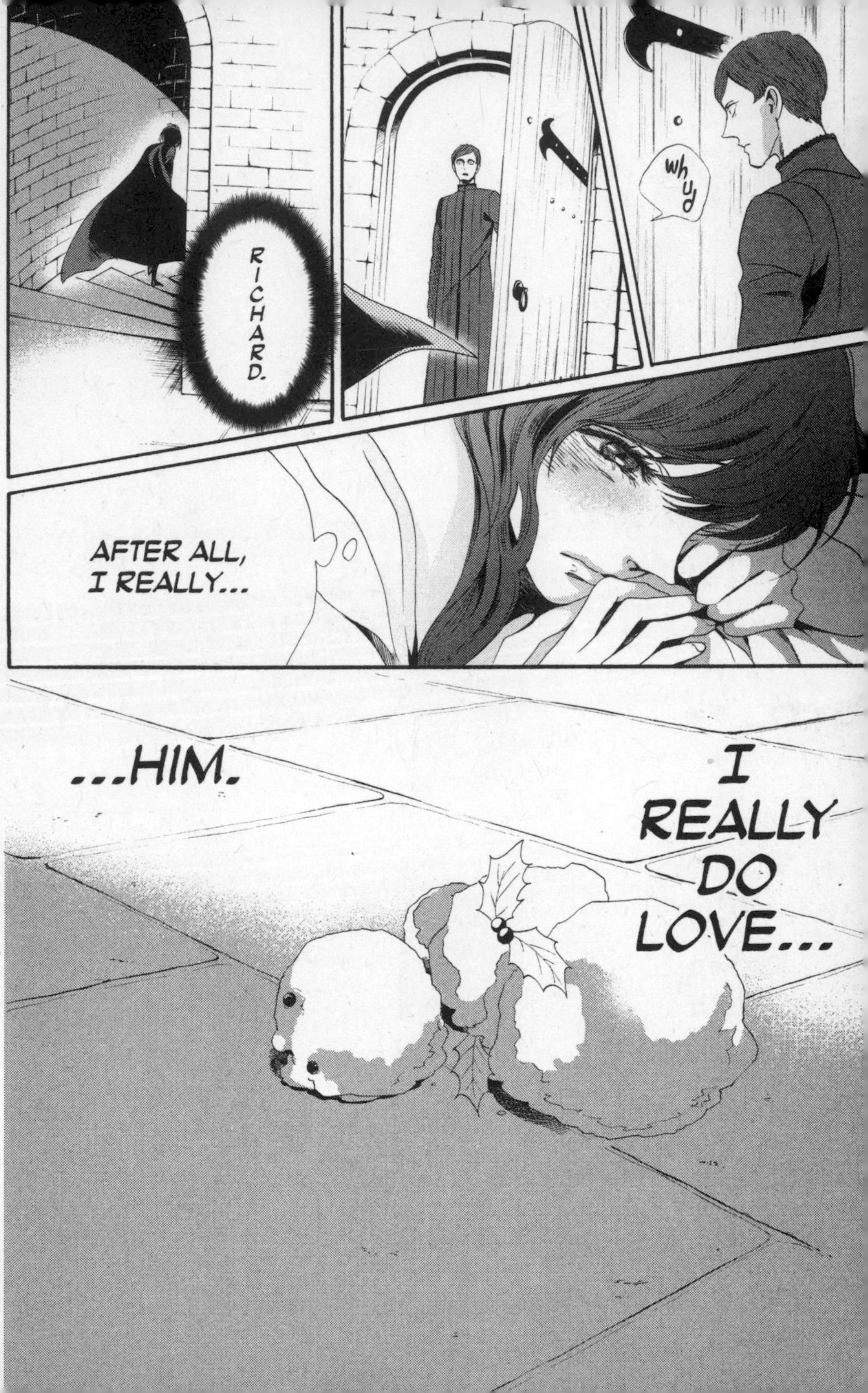
whud
RICHARD.
AFTER ALL, I REALLY...
I REALLY DO LOVE...
...HIM.

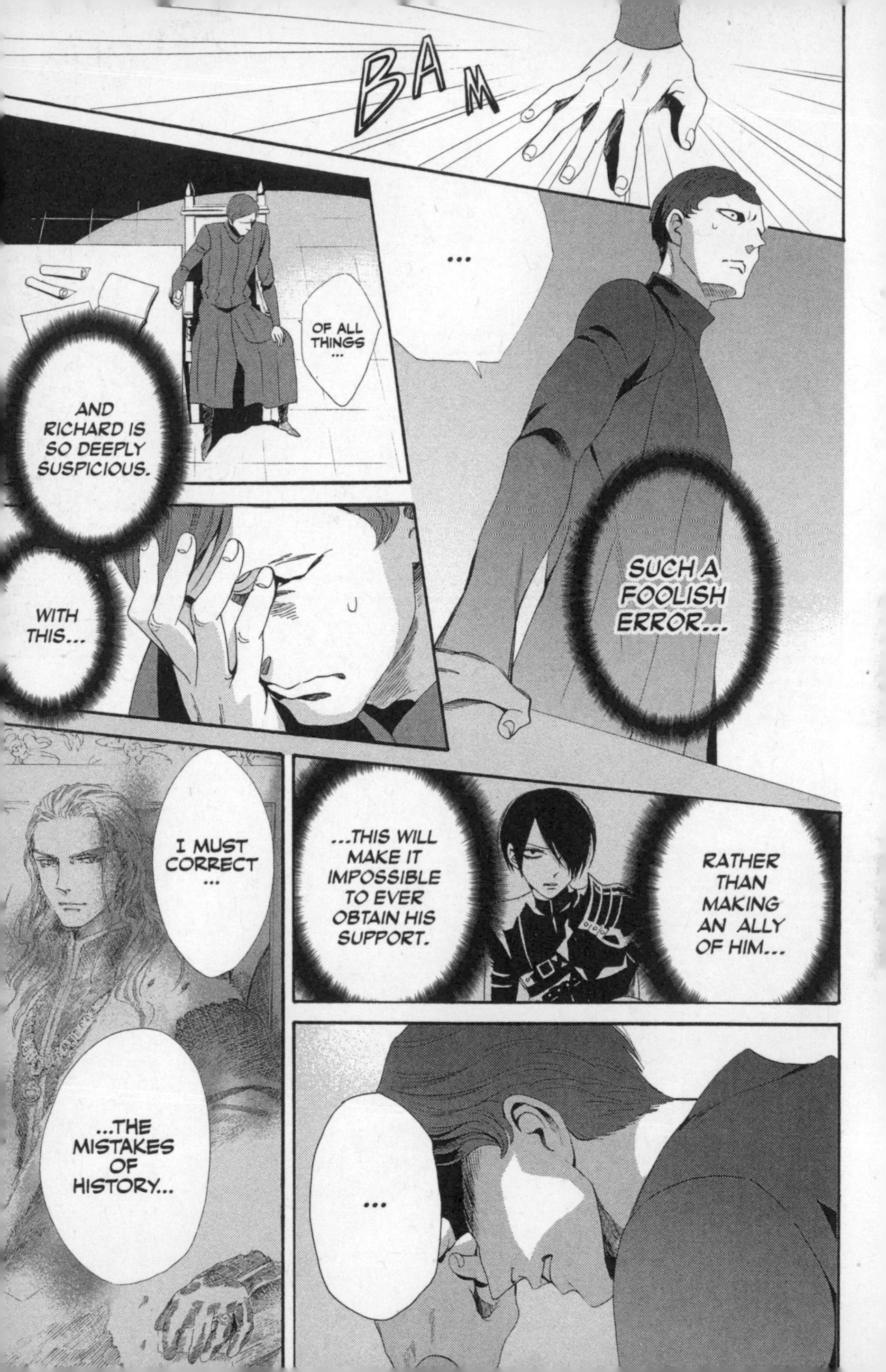
BAM
...
SUCH A FOOLISH ERROR...
OF ALL THINGS ...
AND RICHARD IS SO DEEPLY SUSPICIOUS.
WITH THIS...
RATHER THAN MAKING AN ALLY OF HIM...
...THIS WILL MAKE IT IMPOSSIBLE TO EVER OBTAIN HIS SUPPORT.
...
I MUST CORRECT ...
...THE MISTAKES OF HISTORY...

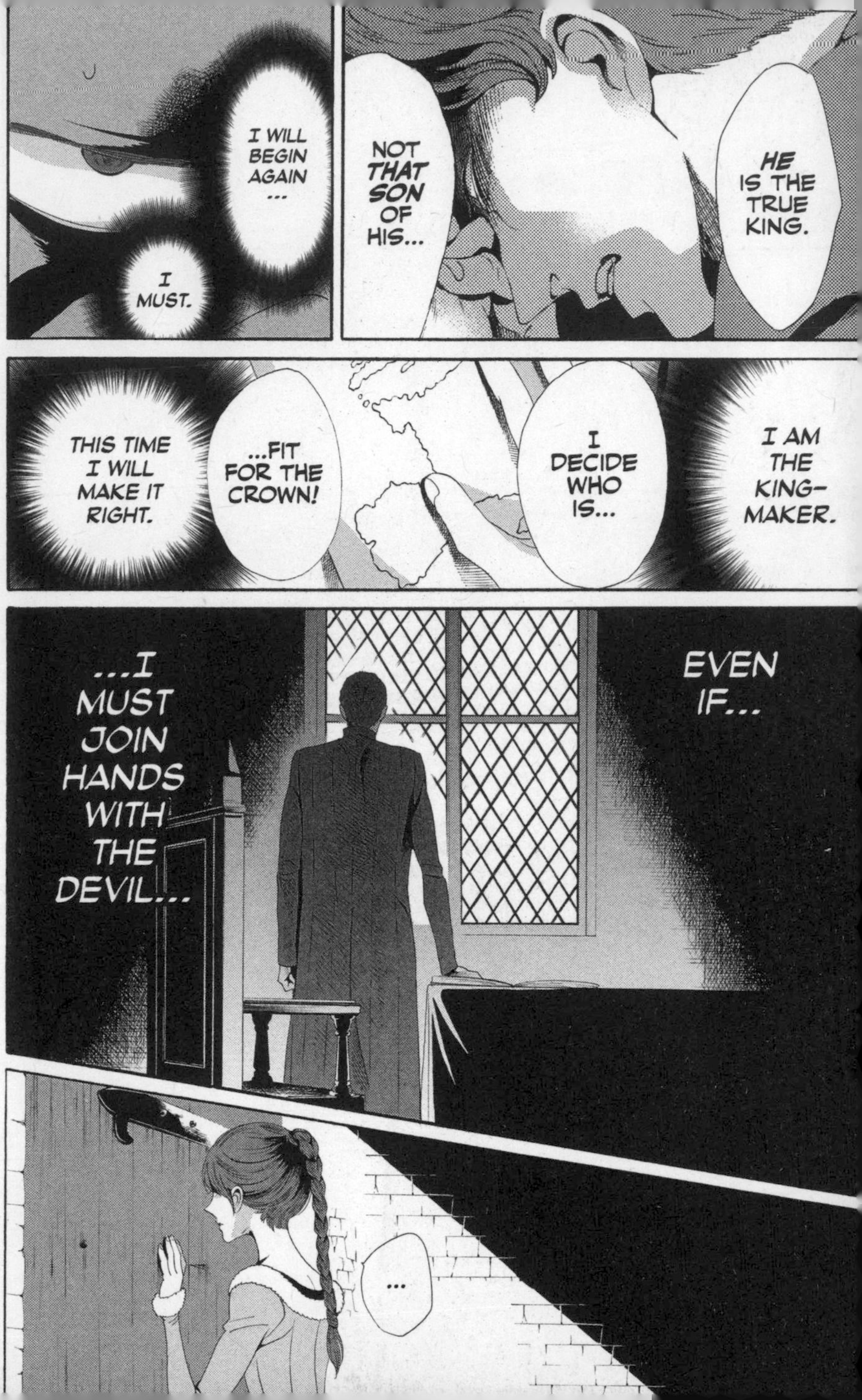
HE IS THE TRUE KING.
NOT THAT SON OF HIS...
I WILL BEGIN AGAIN ...
I MUST.
I AM THE KING-MAKER.
I DECIDE WHO IS...
...FIT FOR THE CROWN!
THIS TIME I WILL MAKE IT RIGHT.
EVEN IF...
...I MUST JOIN HANDS WITH THE DEVIL...
...

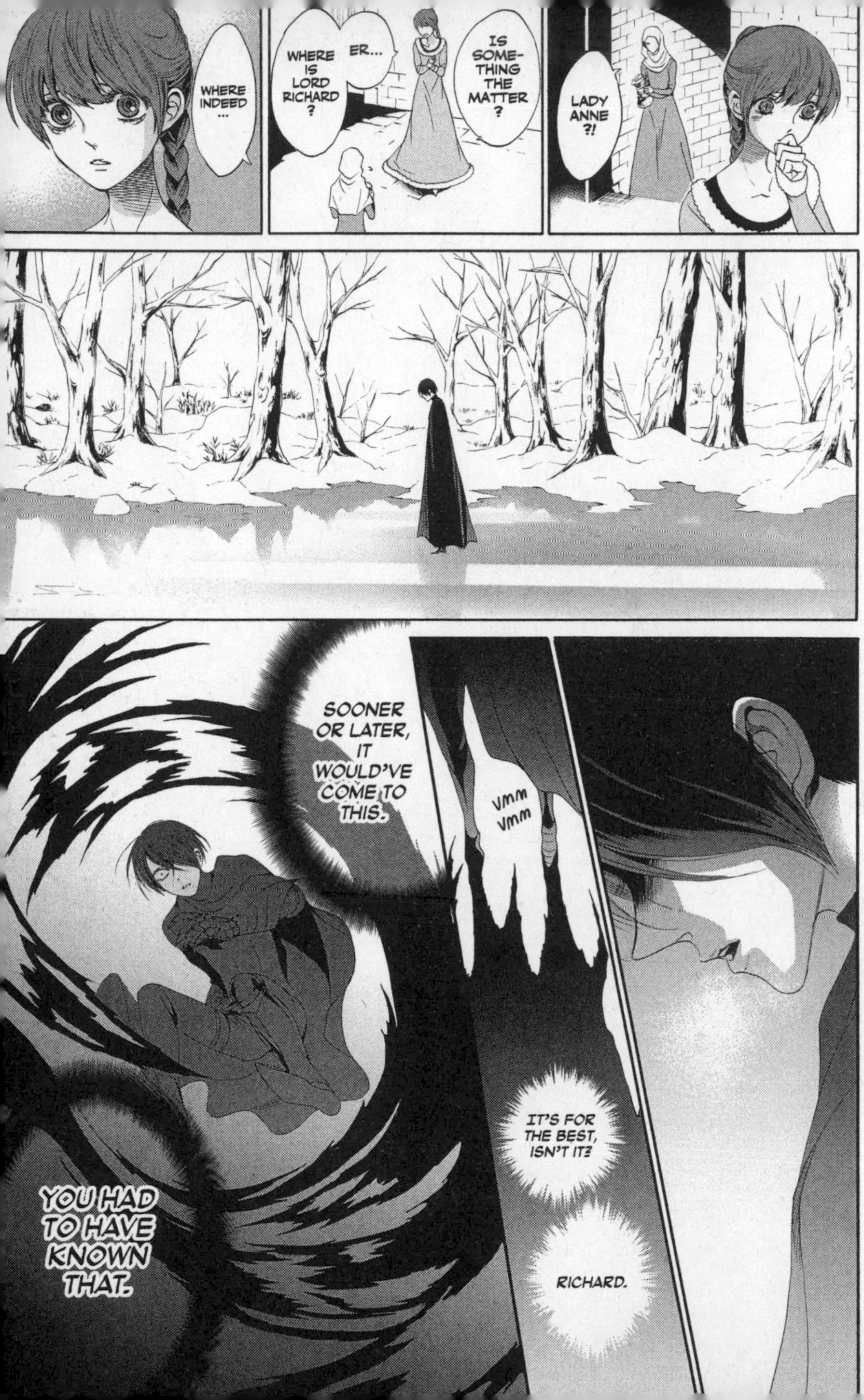
LADY ANNE ?!
IS SOMETHING THE MATTER ?
ER...
WHERE IS LORD RICHARD ?
WHERE INDEED ...
SOONER OR LATER, IT WOULD'VE COME TO THIS.
VMM VMM
IT'S FOR THE BEST, ISN'T IT?
RICHARD.
YOU HAD TO HAVE KNOWN THAT.

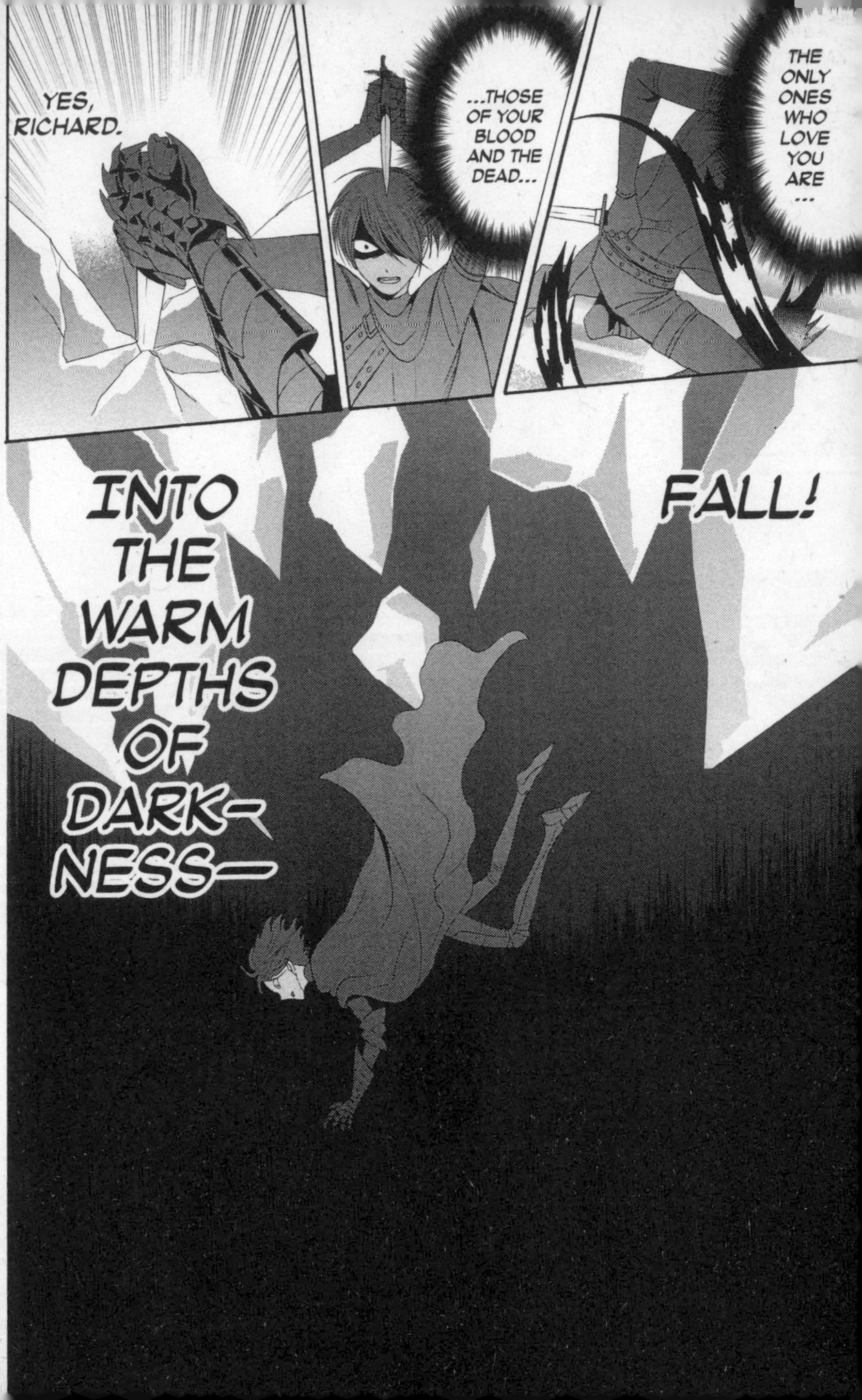
THE ONLY ONES WHO LOVE YOU ARE...
...THOSE OF YOUR BLOOD AND THE DEAD...
YES, RICHARD.
FALL!
INTO THE WARM DEPTHS OF DARK-NESS—

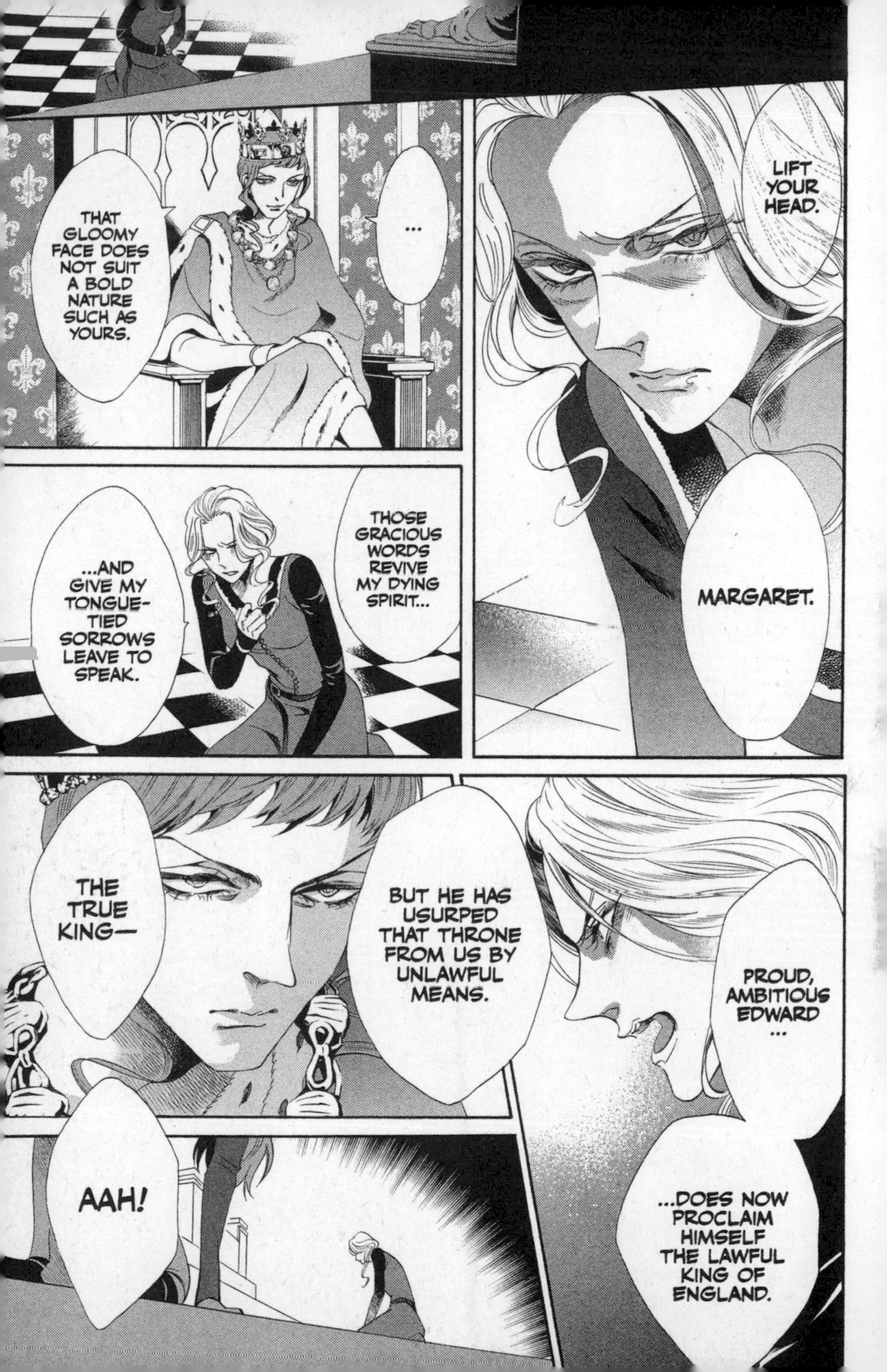
LIFT YOUR HEAD.
MARGARET.
...
THAT GLOOMY FACE DOES NOT SUIT A BOLD NATURE SUCH AS YOURS.
THOSE GRACIOUS WORDS REVIVE MY DYING SPIRIT...
...AND GIVE MY TONGUE-TIED SORROWS LEAVE TO SPEAK.
PROUD, AMBITIOUS EDWARD ...
...DOES NOW PROCLAIM HIMSELF THE LAWFUL KING OF ENGLAND.
BUT HE HAS USURPED THAT THRONE FROM US BY UNLAWFUL MEANS.
THE TRUE KING—
AAH!

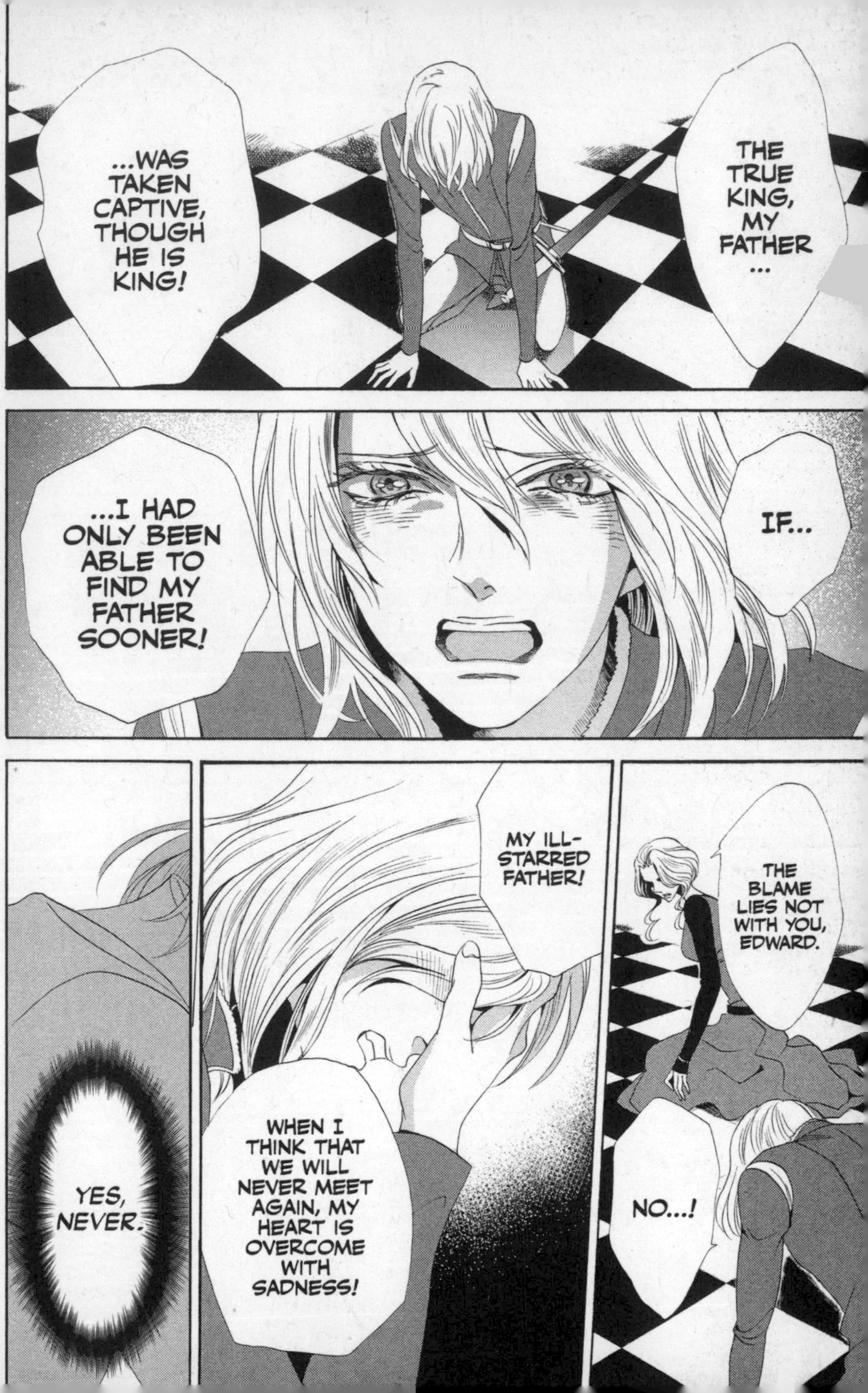
THE TRUE KING, MY FATHER...
...WAS TAKEN CAPTIVE, THOUGH HE IS KING!
IF...
...I HAD ONLY BEEN ABLE TO FIND MY FATHER SOONER!
THE BLAME LIES NOT WITH YOU, EDWARD.
NO...!
MY ILL-STARRED FATHER!
WHEN I THINK THAT WE WILL NEVER MEET AGAIN, MY HEART IS OVERCOME WITH SADNESS!
YES, NEVER.

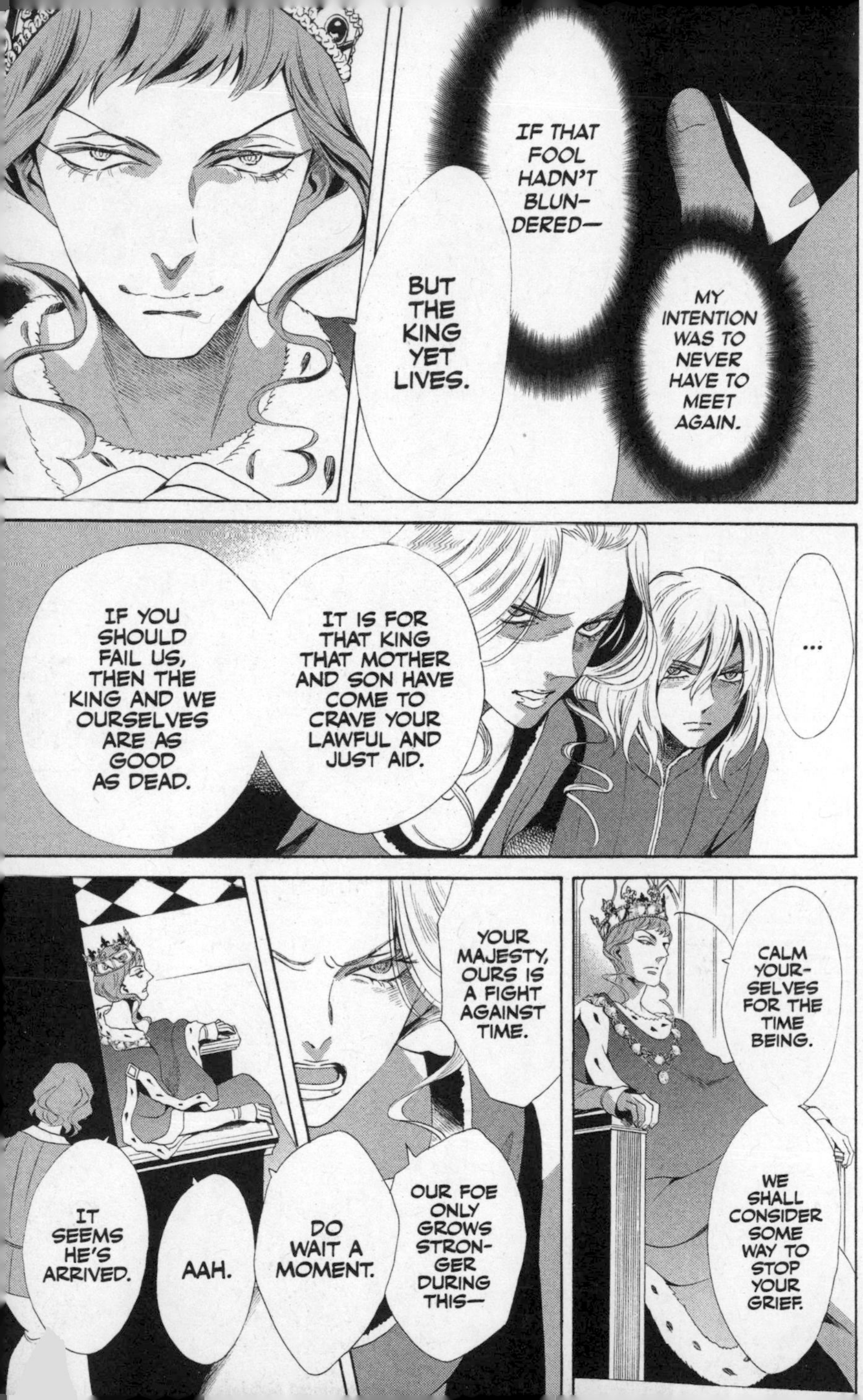
IF THAT FOOL HADN'T BLUNDERED—
MY INTENTION WAS TO NEVER HAVE TO MEET AGAIN.
BUT THE KING YET LIVES.
...
IT IS FOR THAT KING THAT MOTHER AND SON HAVE COME TO CRAVE YOUR LAWFUL AND JUST AID.
IF YOU SHOULD FAIL US, THEN THE KING AND WE OURSELVES ARE AS GOOD AS DEAD.
CALM YOUR-SELVES FOR THE TIME BEING.
WE SHALL CONSIDER SOME WAY TO STOP YOUR GRIEF.
YOUR MAJESTY, OURS IS A FIGHT AGAINST TIME.
OUR FOE ONLY GROWS STRON-GER DURING THIS—
DO WAIT A MOMENT.
AAH.
IT SEEMS HE'S ARRIVED.

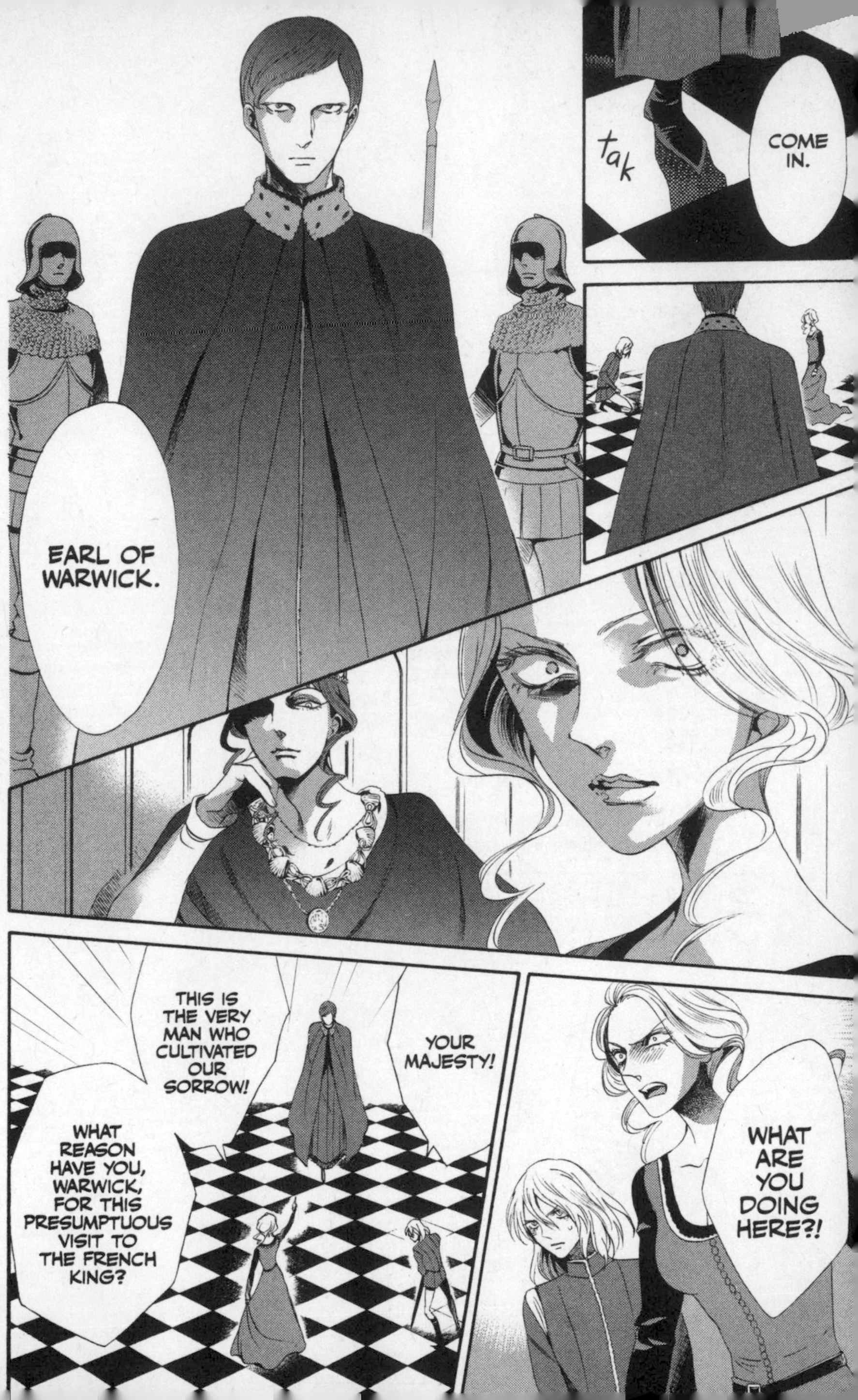
COME IN.
tak
EARL OF WARWICK.
WHAT ARE YOU DOING HERE?!
YOUR MAJESTY!
THIS IS THE VERY MAN WHO CULTIVATED OUR SORROW!
WHAT REASON HAVE YOU, WARWICK, FOR THIS PRESUMPTUOUS VISIT TO THE FRENCH KING?

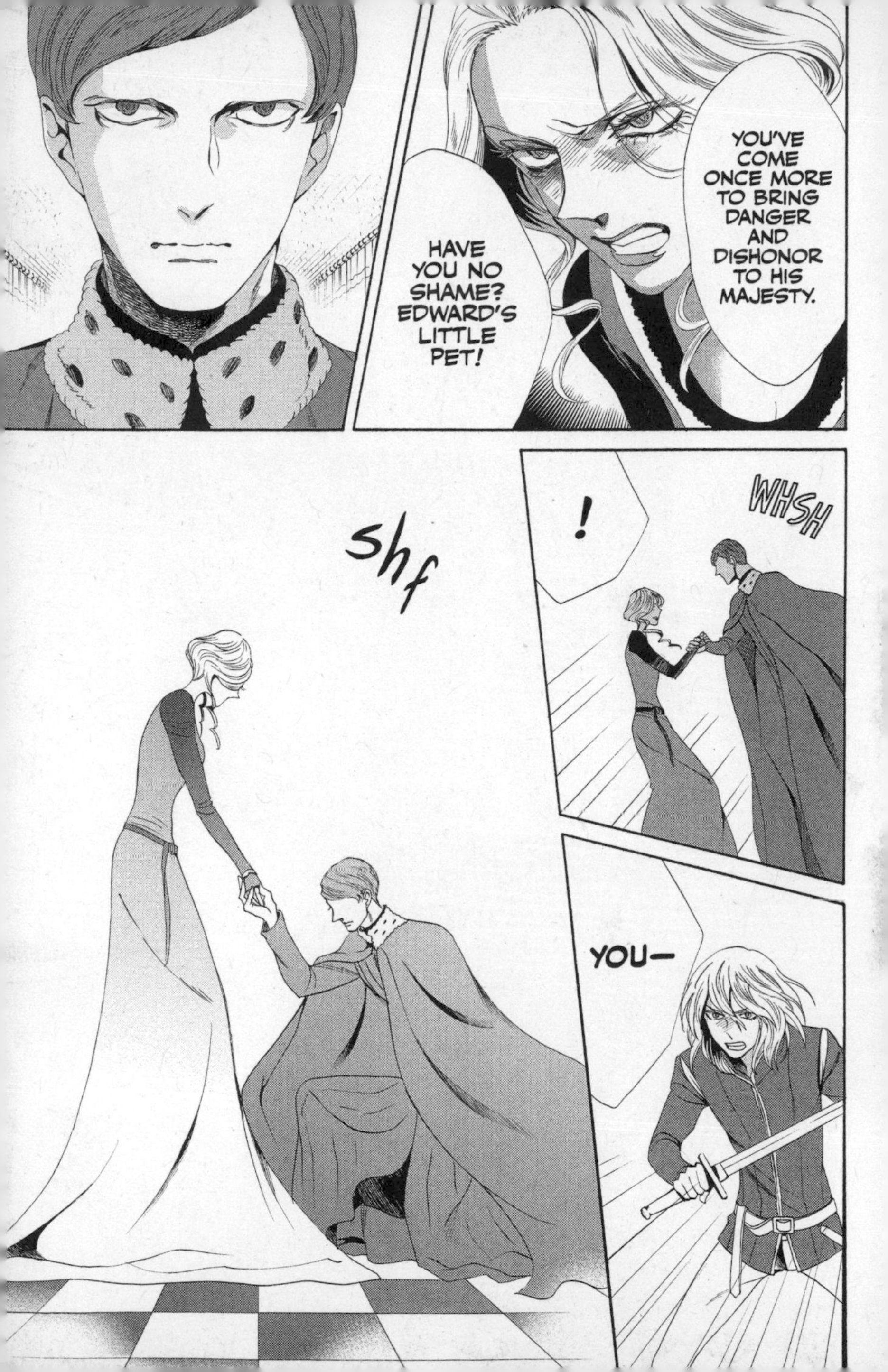
YOU'VE COME ONCE MORE TO BRING DANGER AND DISHONOR TO HIS MAJESTY.
HAVE YOU NO SHAME? EDWARD'S LITTLE PET!
WHSH
!
YOU—
shf

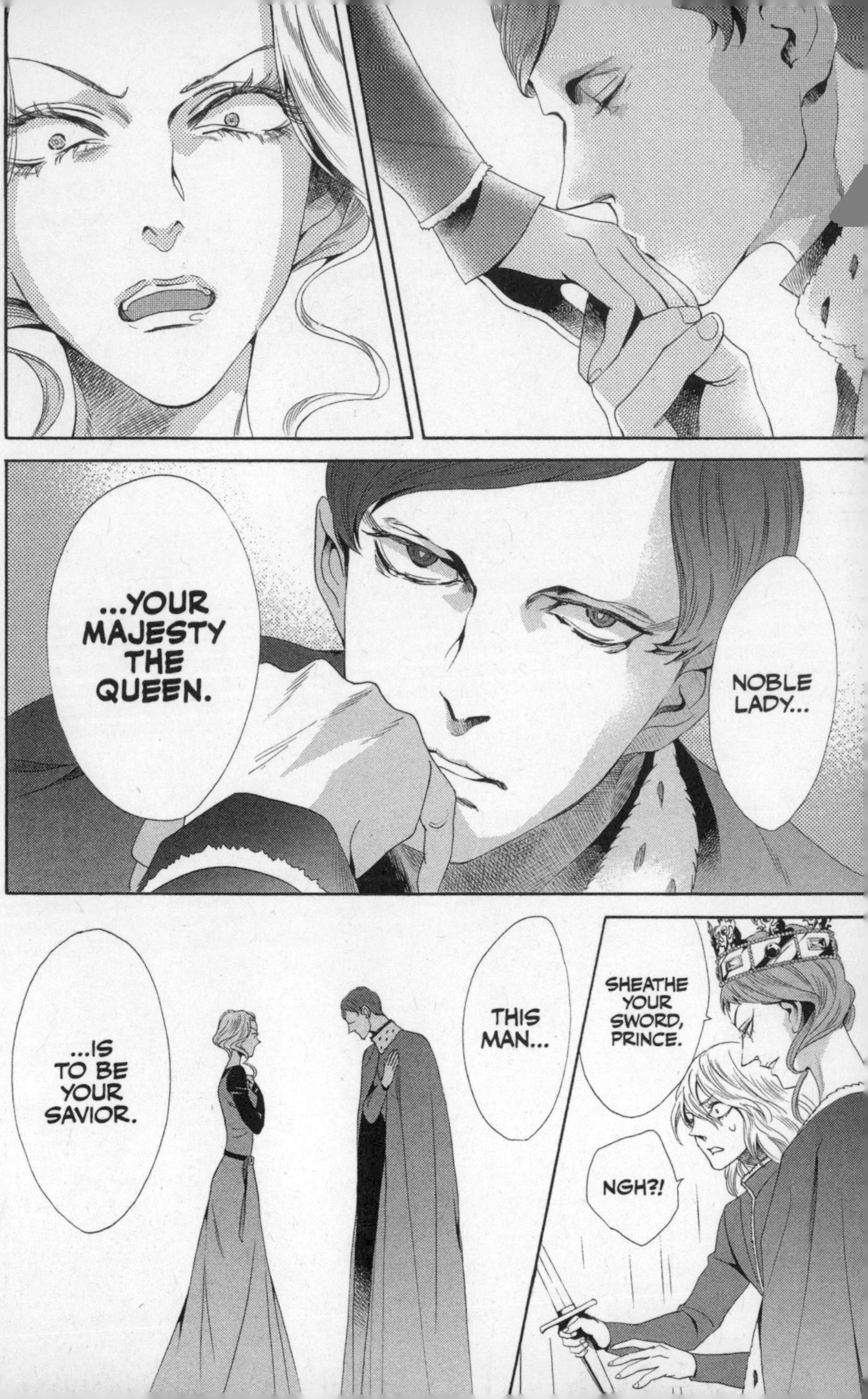
NOBLE LADY...
...YOUR MAJESTY THE QUEEN.
SHEATHE YOUR SWORD, PRINCE.
NGH?!
THIS MAN...
...IS TO BE YOUR SAVIOR.

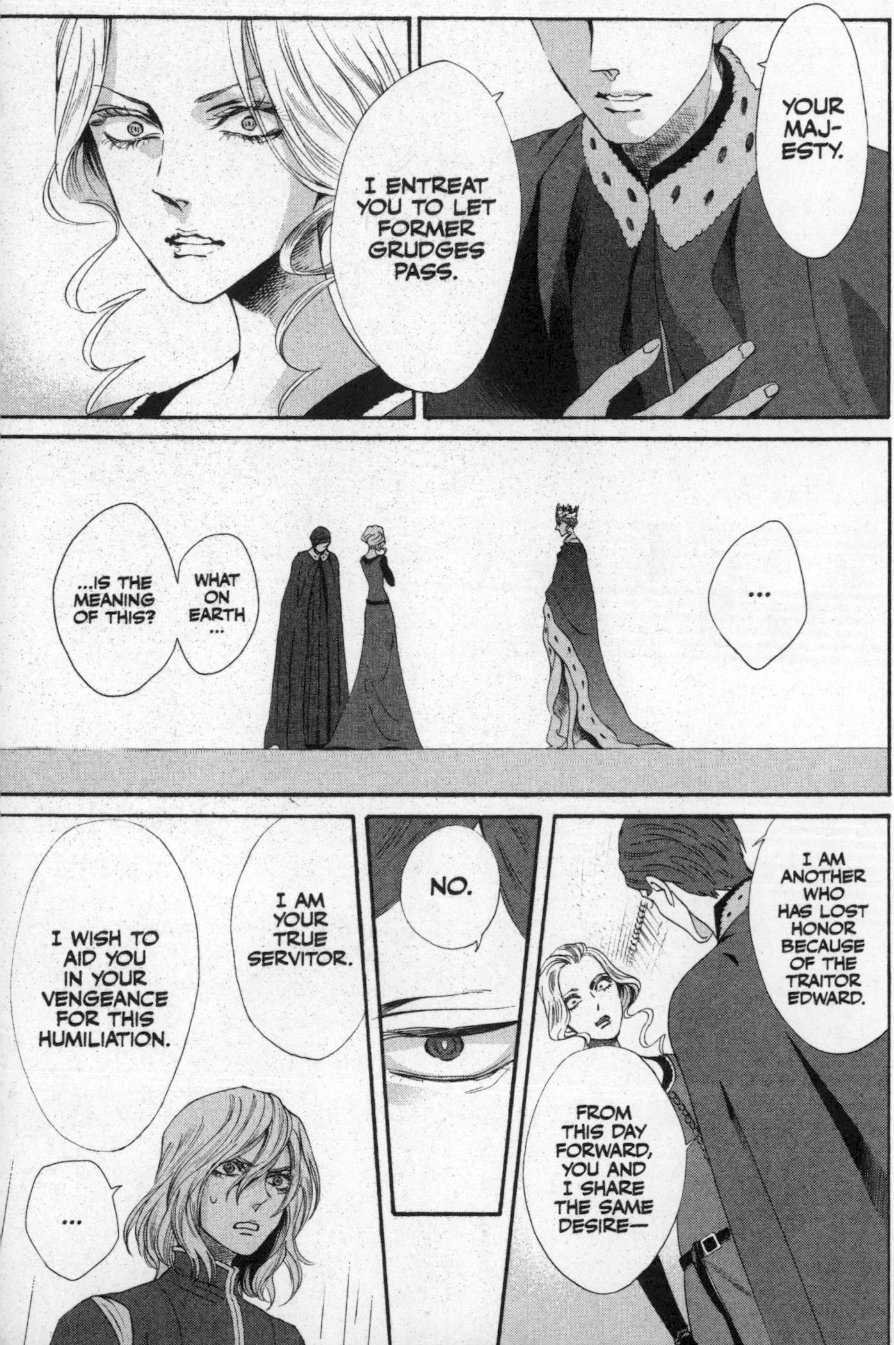
YOUR MAJ-ESTY.
I ENTREAT YOU TO LET FORMER GRUDGES PASS.
...
WHAT ON EARTH ...
...IS THE MEANING OF THIS?
I AM ANOTHER WHO HAS LOST HONOR BECAUSE OF THE TRAITOR EDWARD.
FROM THIS DAY FORWARD, YOU AND I SHARE THE SAME DESIRE—
NO.
I AM YOUR TRUE SERVITOR.
I WISH TO AID YOU IN YOUR VENGEANCE FOR THIS HUMILIATION.
...

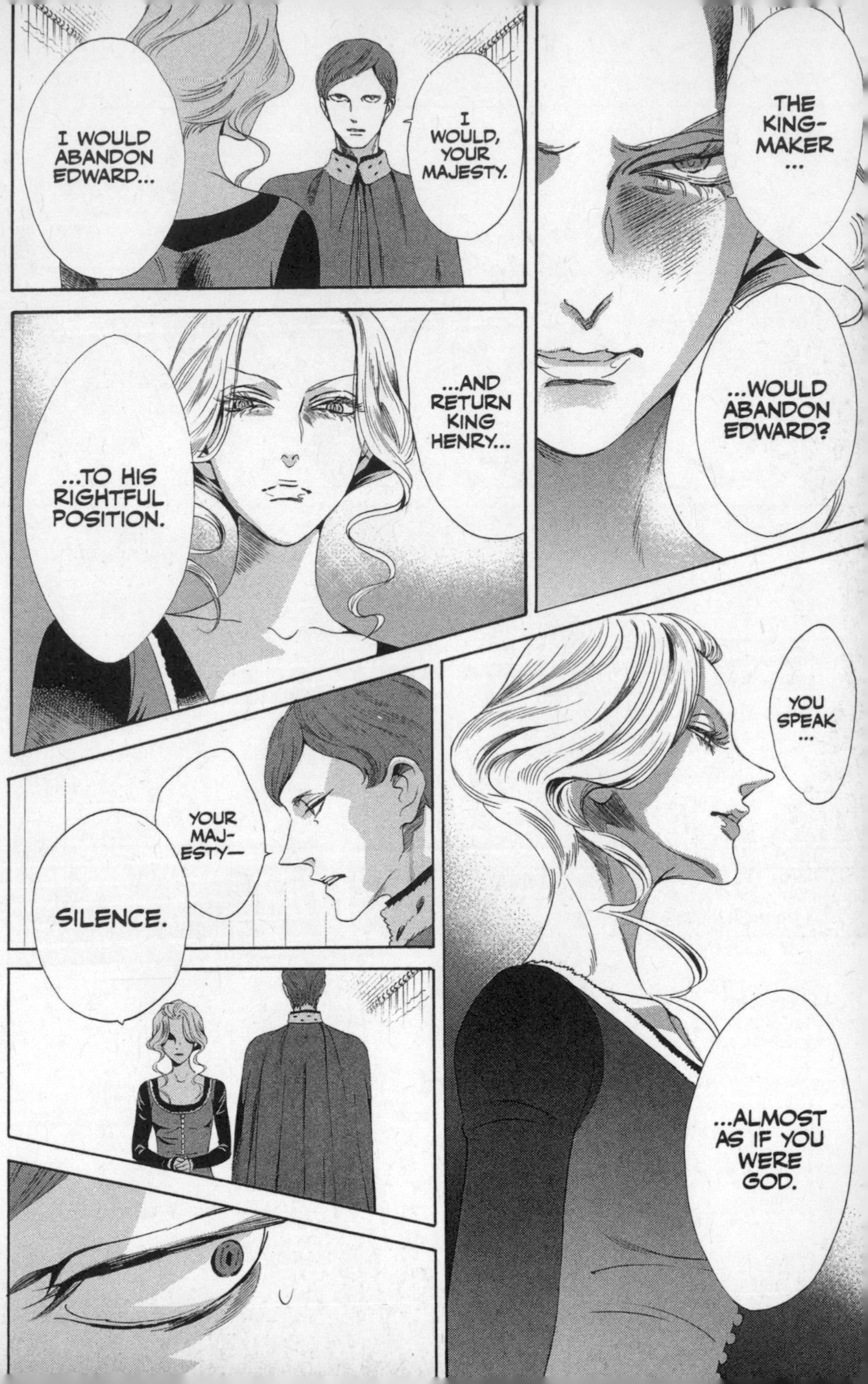
THE KING-MAKER...
...WOULD ABANDON EDWARD?
I WOULD, YOUR MAJESTY.
I WOULD ABANDON EDWARD...
...AND RETURN KING HENRY...
...TO HIS RIGHTFUL POSITION.
YOU SPEAK...
...ALMOST AS IF YOU WERE GOD.
YOUR MAJ-ESTY—
SILENCE.

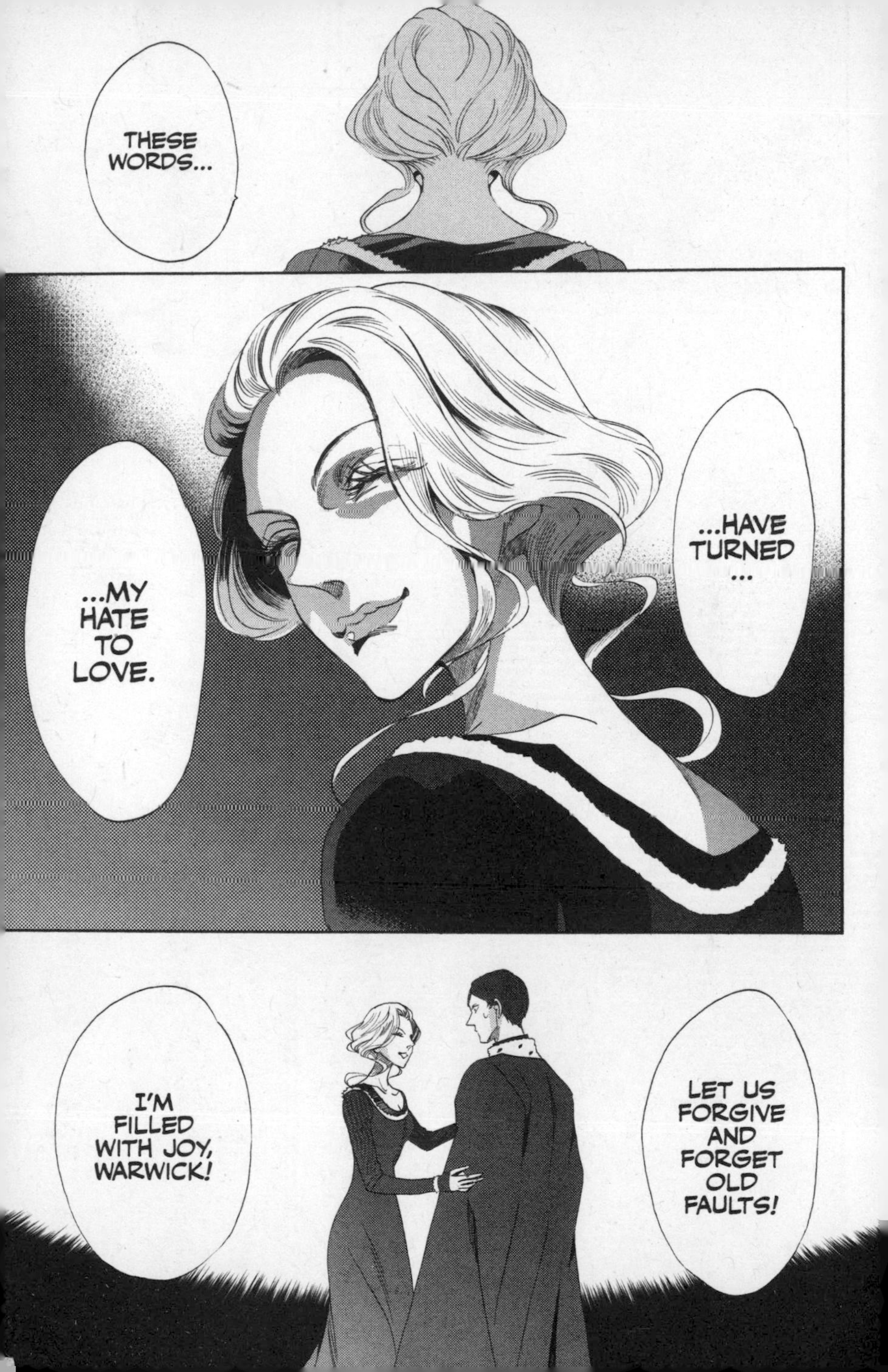
THESE WORDS...
...HAVE TURNED ...
...MY HATE TO LOVE.
LET US FORGIVE AND FORGET OLD FAULTS!
I'M FILLED WITH JOY, WARWICK!

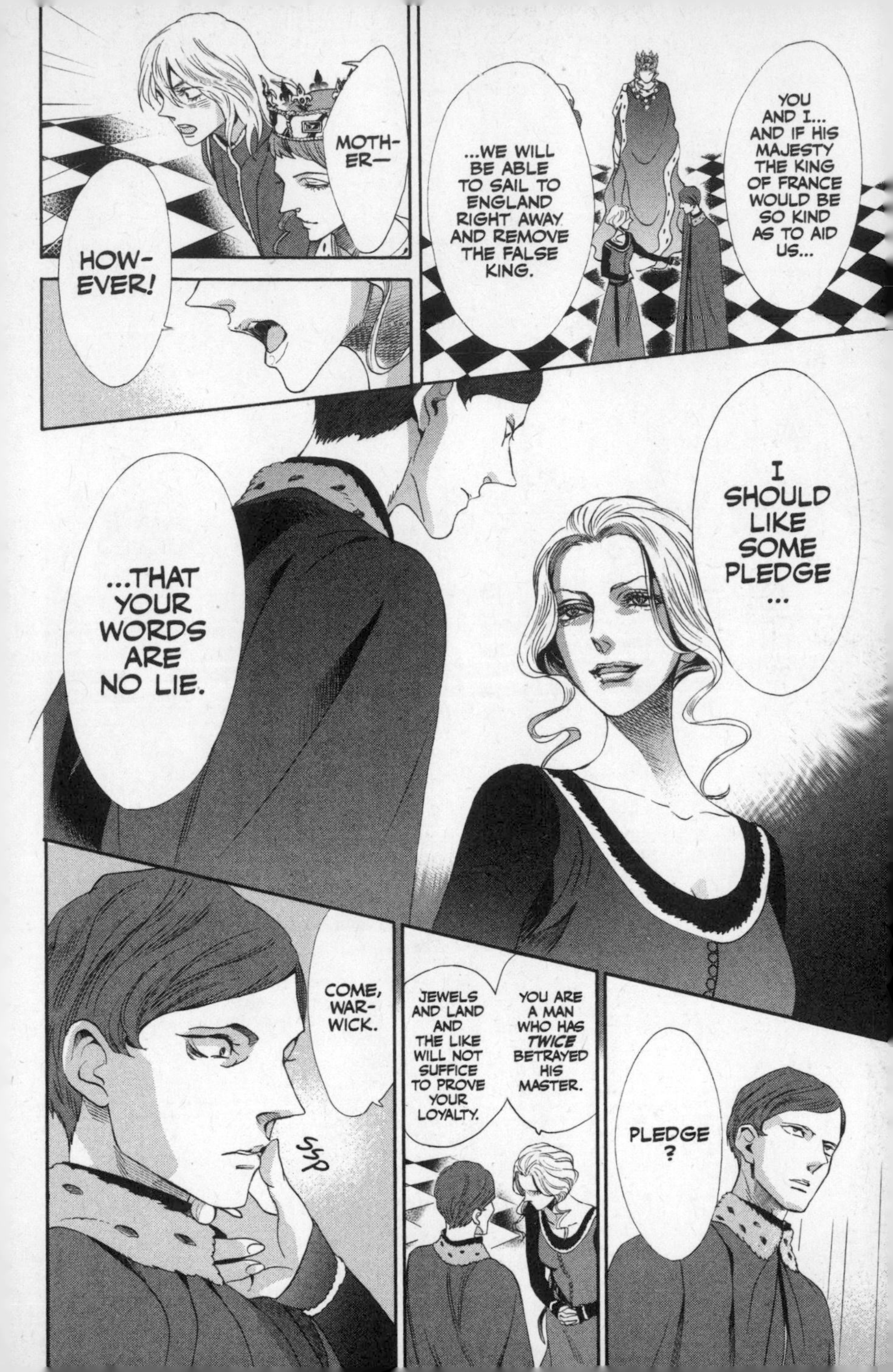

YOU AND I... AND IF HIS MAJESTY THE KING OF FRANCE WOULD BE SO KIND AS TO AID US...
...WE WILL BE ABLE TO SAIL TO ENGLAND RIGHT AWAY AND REMOVE THE FALSE KING.
MOTH-ER—
HOW-EVER!
I SHOULD LIKE SOME PLEDGE...
...THAT YOUR WORDS ARE NO LIE.
PLEDGE?
YOU ARE A MAN WHO HAS *TWICE* BETRAYED HIS MASTER.
JEWELS AND LAND AND THE LIKE WILL NOT SUFFICE TO PROVE YOUR LOYALTY.
COME, WAR-WICK.
SSP

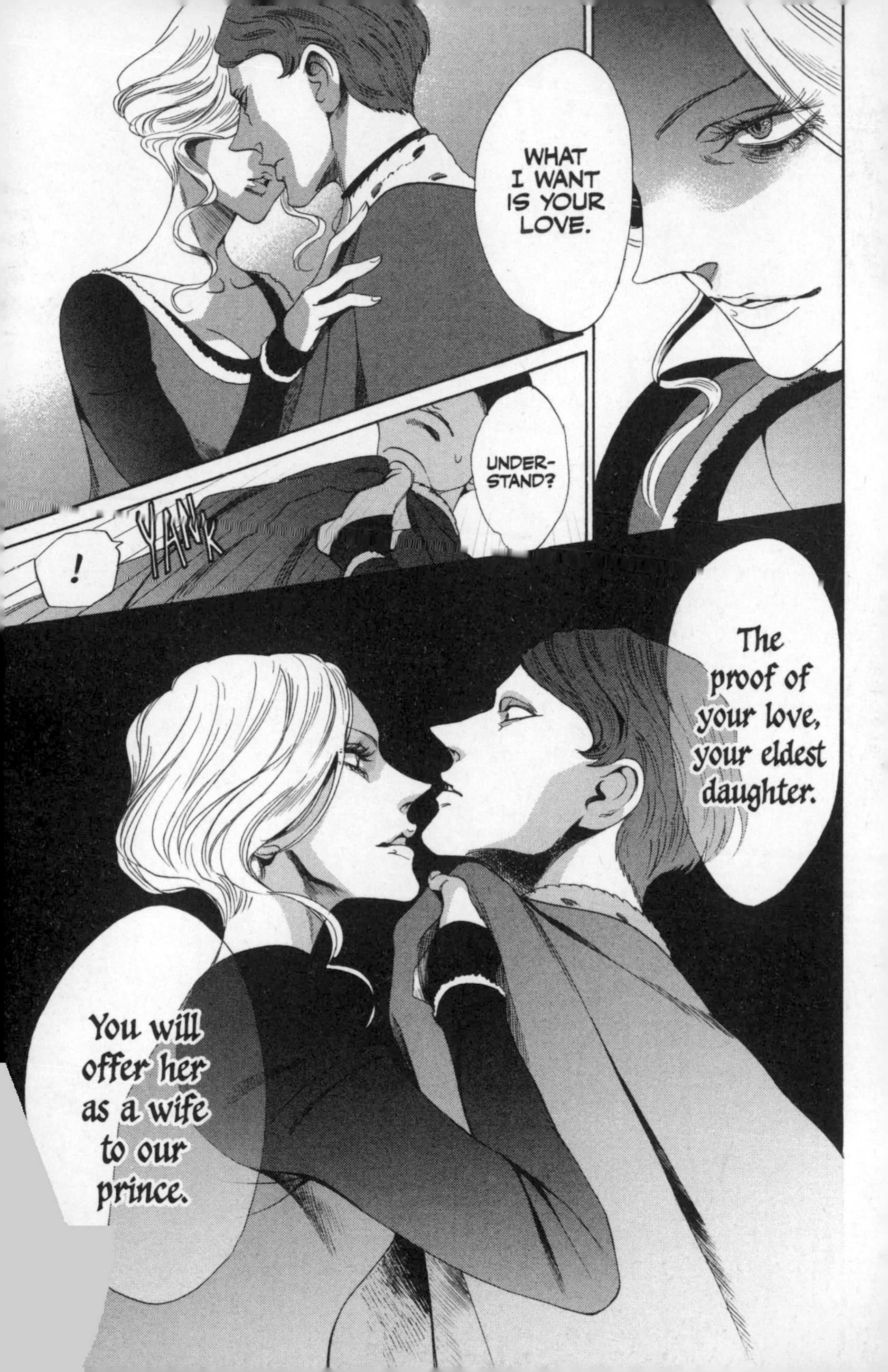
WHAT I WANT IS YOUR LOVE.
UNDER-STAND?
YANK
!
The proof of your love, your eldest daughter.
You will offer her as a wife to our prince.

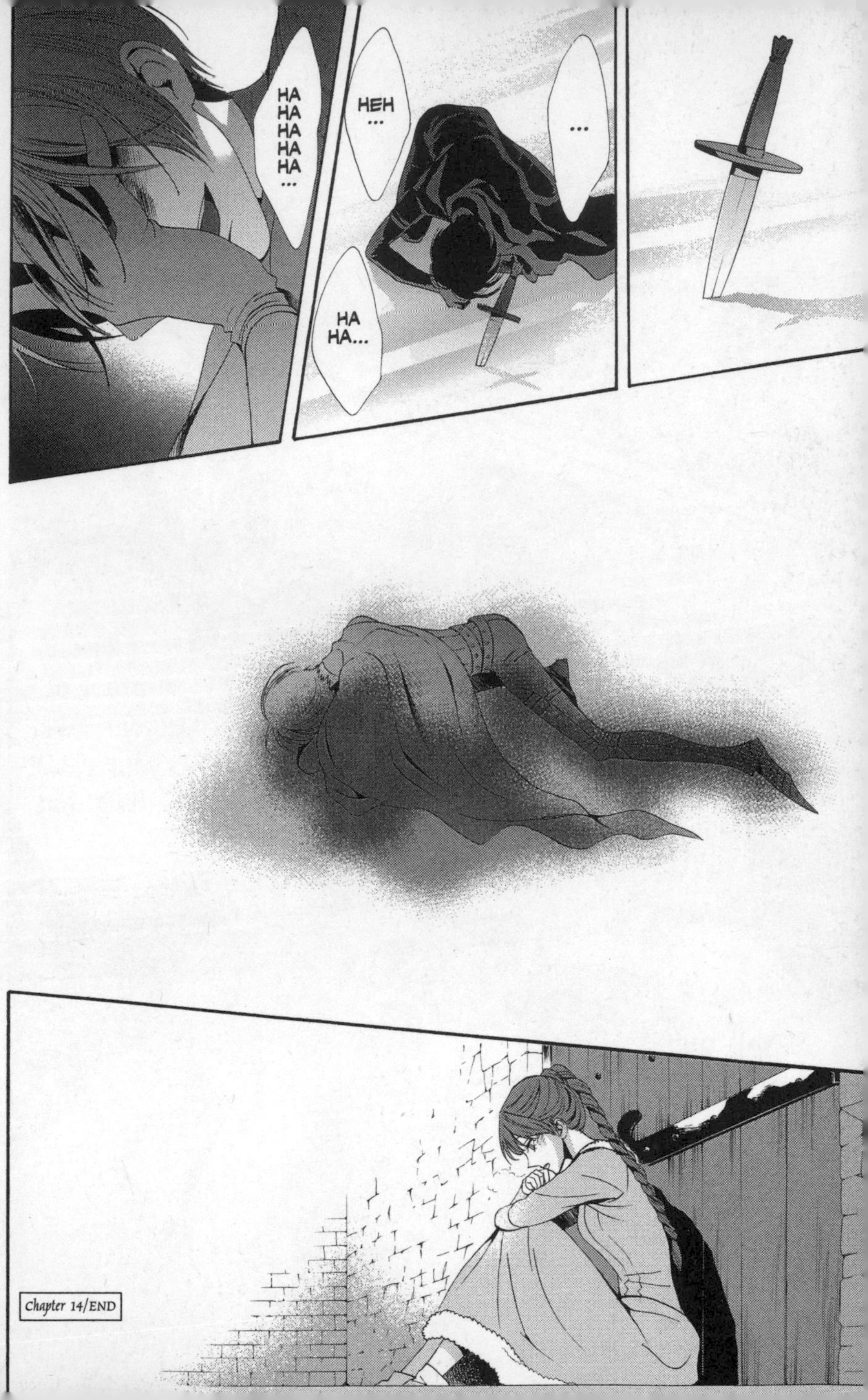
...
HEH ...
HA HA...
HA HA HA HA HA ...
Chapter 14/END

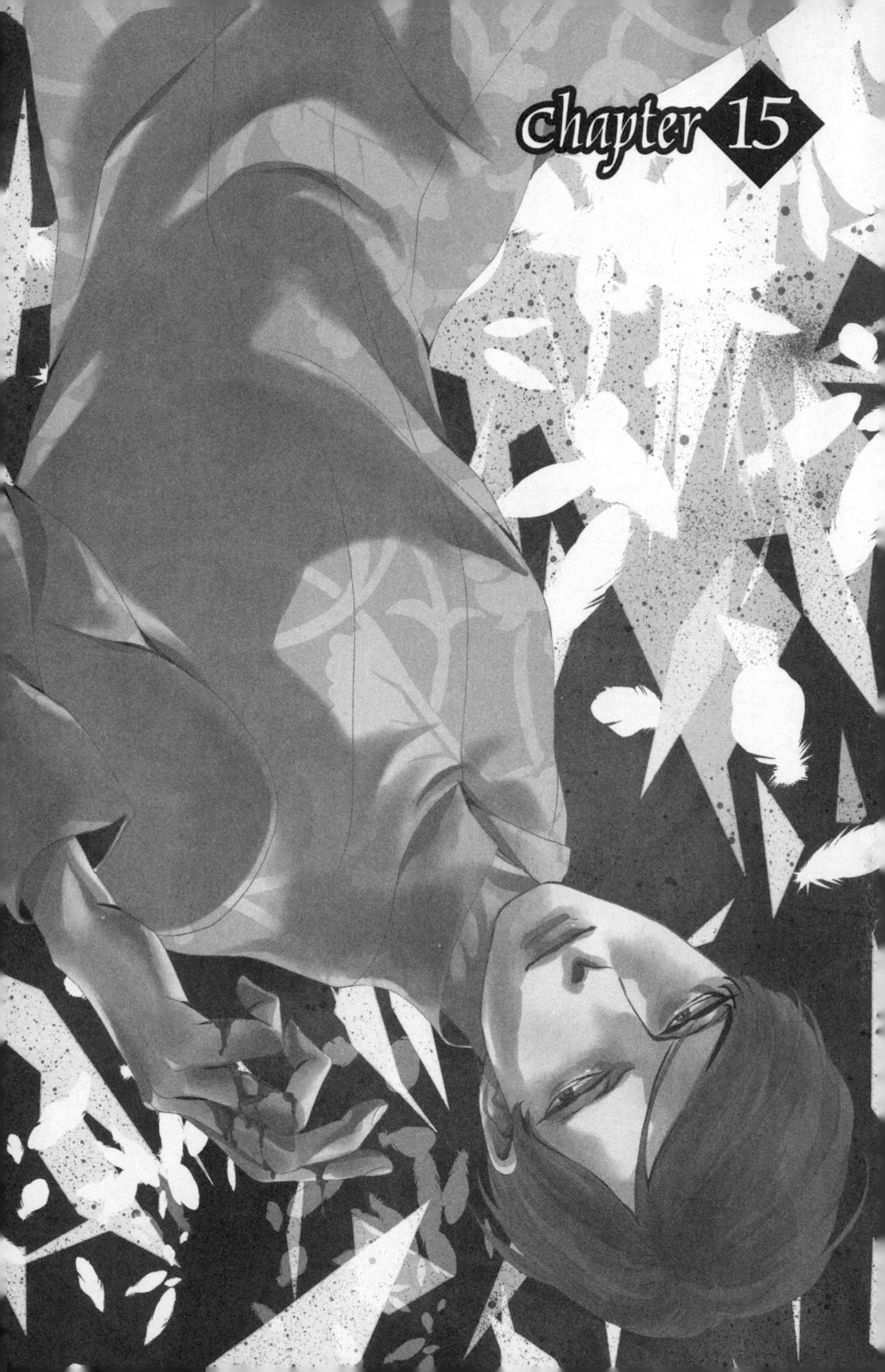
chapter 15

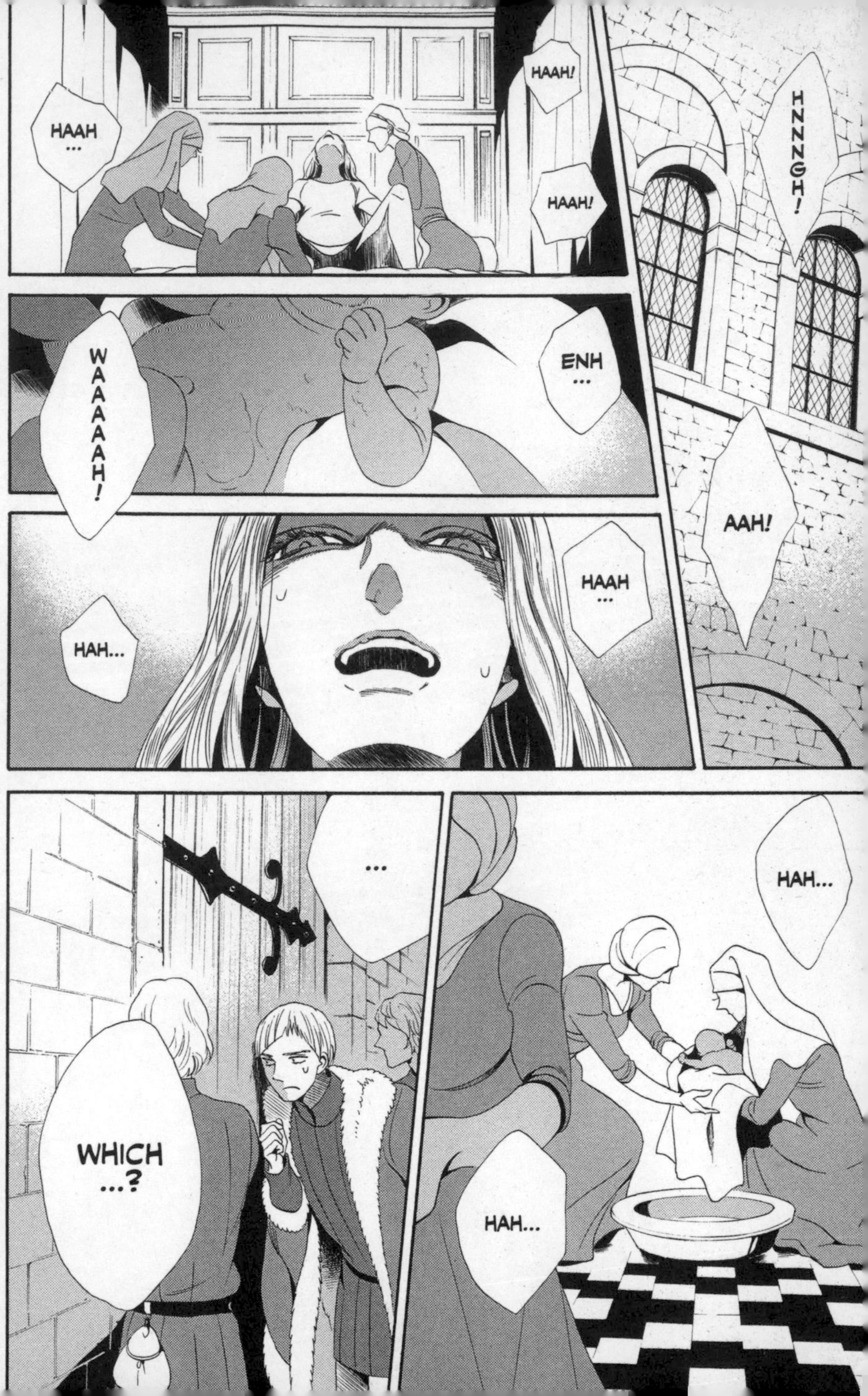
HNNNGH!
AAH!
HAAH!
HAAH!
HAAH ...
ENH ...
WAAAAAAH!
HAAH ...
HAH...
HAH...
HAH...
...
WHICH ...?

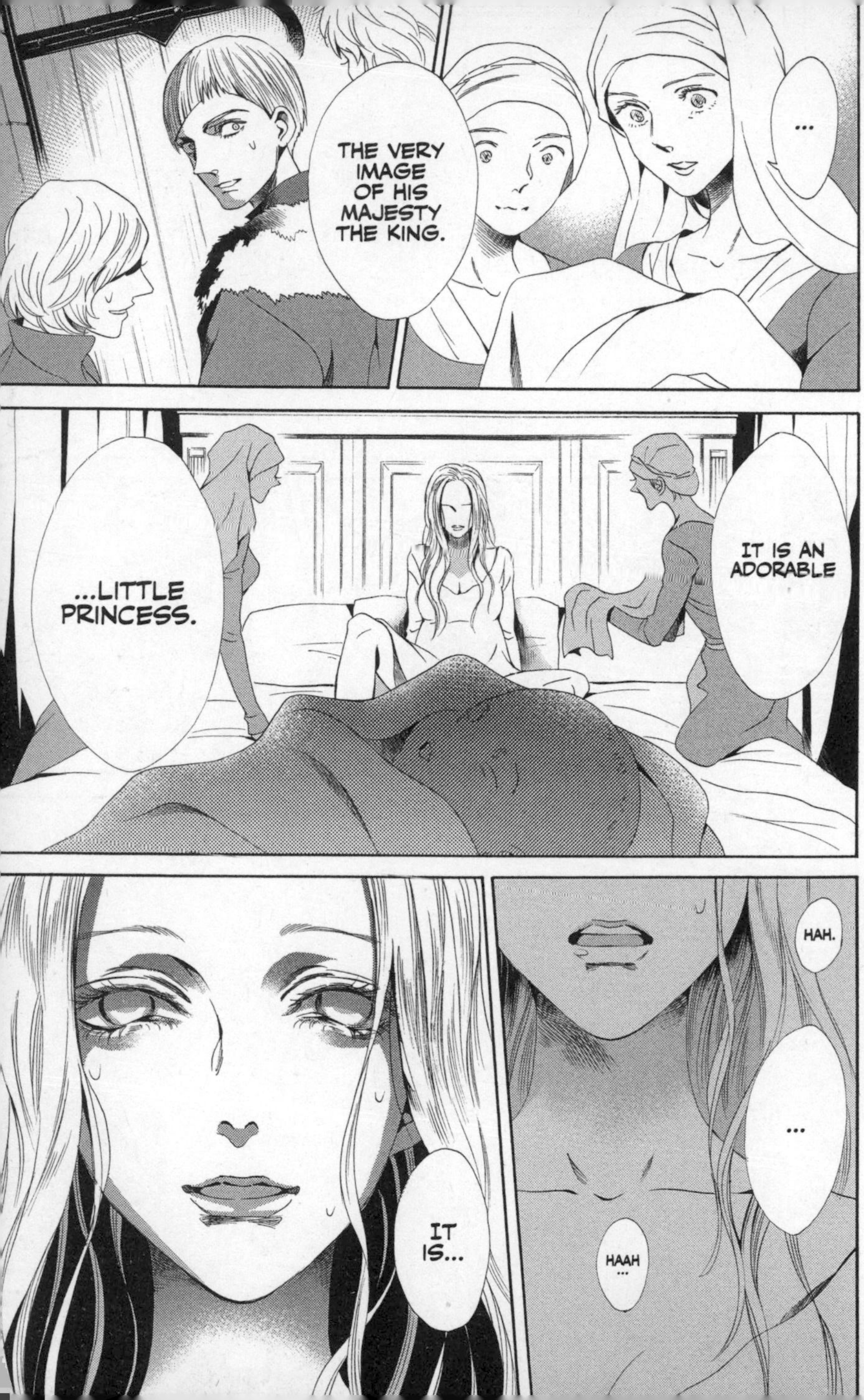
...
THE VERY IMAGE OF HIS MAJESTY THE KING.
IT IS AN ADORABLE
...LITTLE PRINCESS.
HAH.
...
HAAH ...
IT IS...

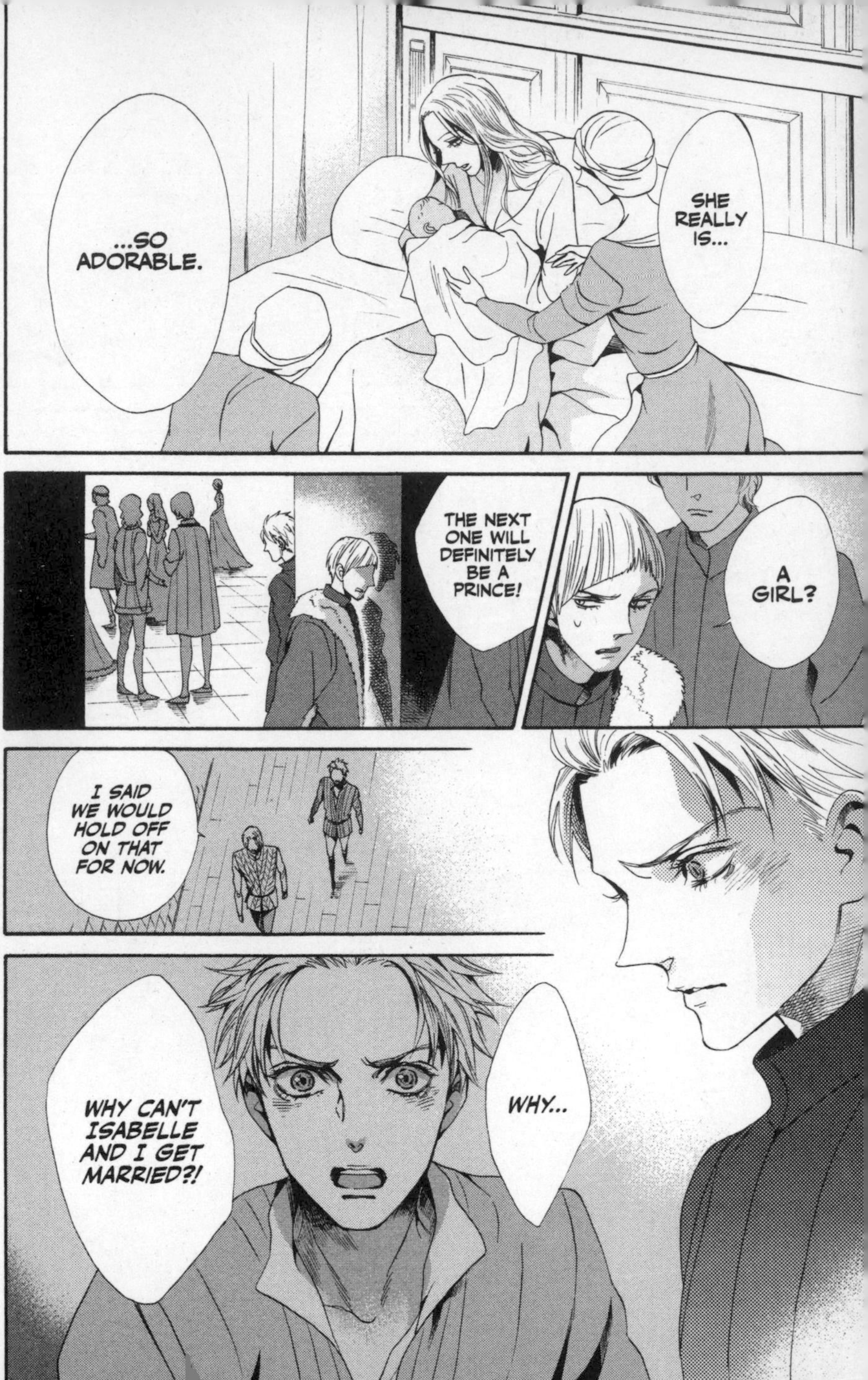
SHE REALLY IS...
...SO ADORABLE.
A GIRL?
THE NEXT ONE WILL DEFINITELY BE A PRINCE!
I SAID WE WOULD HOLD OFF ON THAT FOR NOW.
WHY...
WHY CAN'T ISABELLE AND I GET MARRIED?!

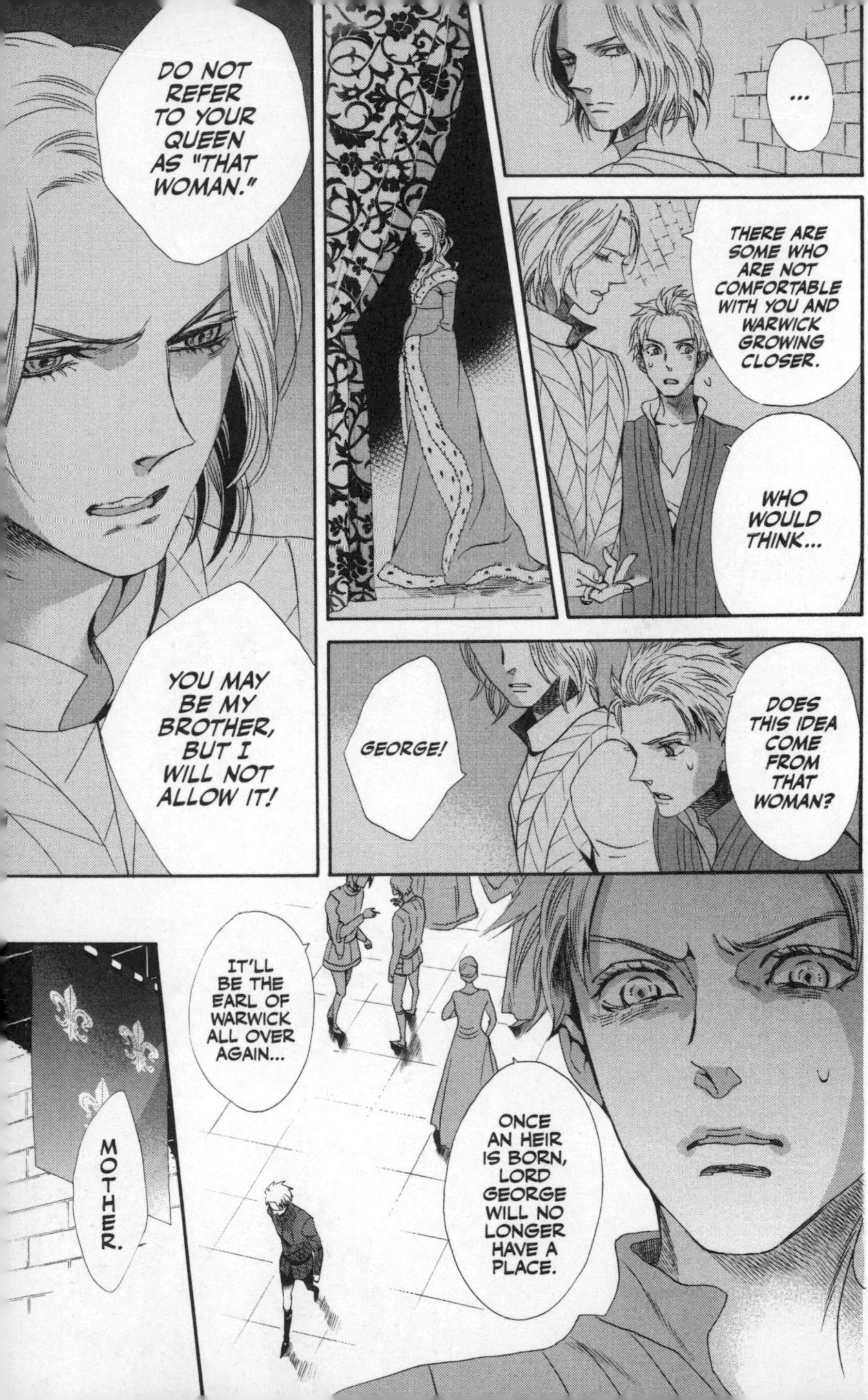
...
THERE ARE SOME WHO ARE NOT COMFORTABLE WITH YOU AND WARWICK GROWING CLOSER.
WHO WOULD THINK...
DOES THIS IDEA COME FROM THAT WOMAN?
GEORGE!
DO NOT REFER TO YOUR QUEEN AS "THAT WOMAN."
YOU MAY BE MY BROTHER, BUT I WILL NOT ALLOW IT!
ONCE AN HEIR IS BORN, LORD GEORGE WILL NO LONGER HAVE A PLACE.
IT'LL BE THE EARL OF WARWICK ALL OVER AGAIN...
MOTHER.

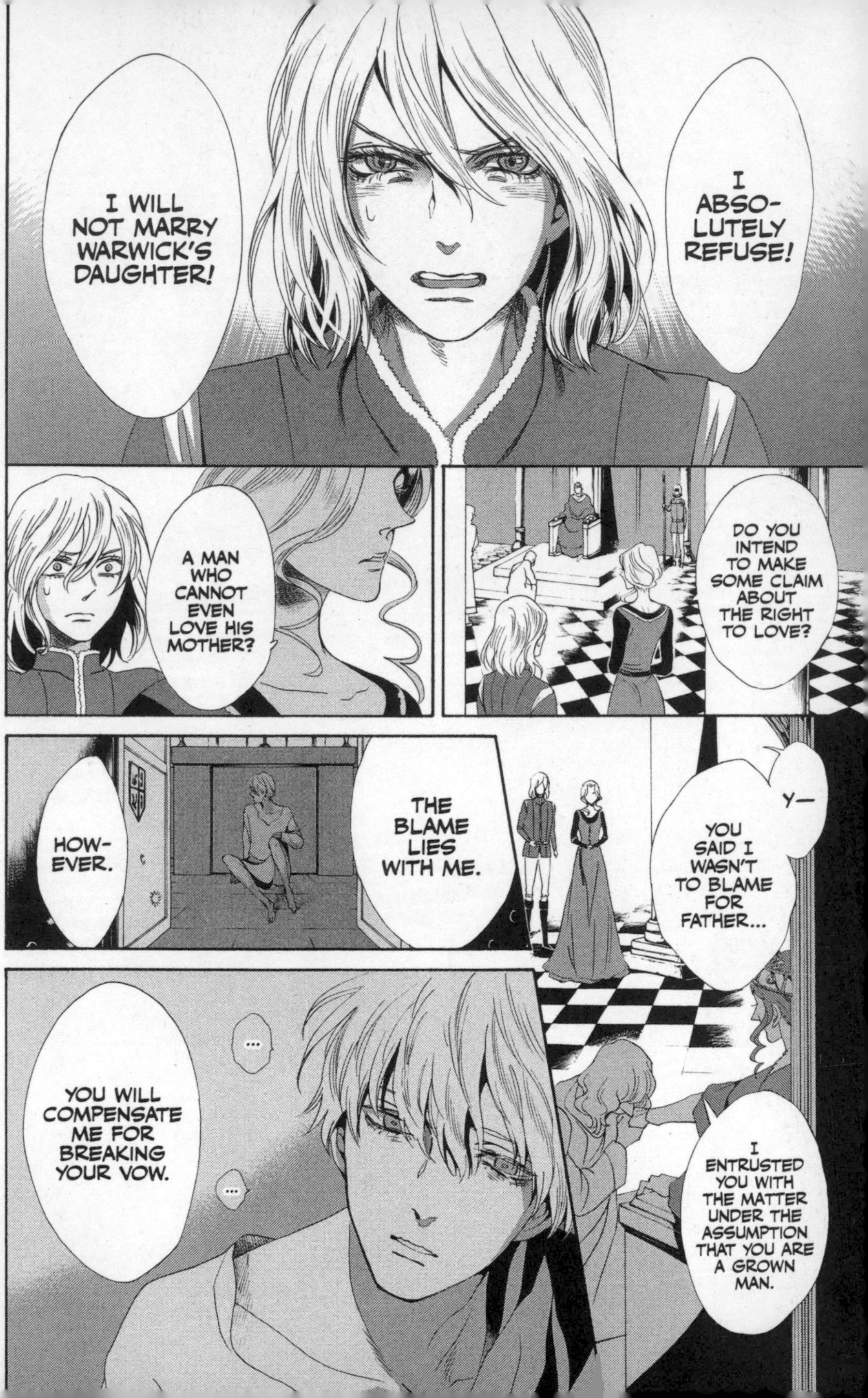
I ABSO-LUTELY REFUSE!
I WILL NOT MARRY WARWICK'S DAUGHTER!
DO YOU INTEND TO MAKE SOME CLAIM ABOUT THE RIGHT TO LOVE?
A MAN WHO CANNOT EVEN LOVE HIS MOTHER?
Y—
YOU SAID I WASN'T TO BLAME FOR FATHER...
I ENTRUSTED YOU WITH THE MATTER UNDER THE ASSUMPTION THAT YOU ARE A GROWN MAN.
THE BLAME LIES WITH ME.
HOW-EVER.
...
YOU WILL COMPENSATE ME FOR BREAKING YOUR VOW.
...

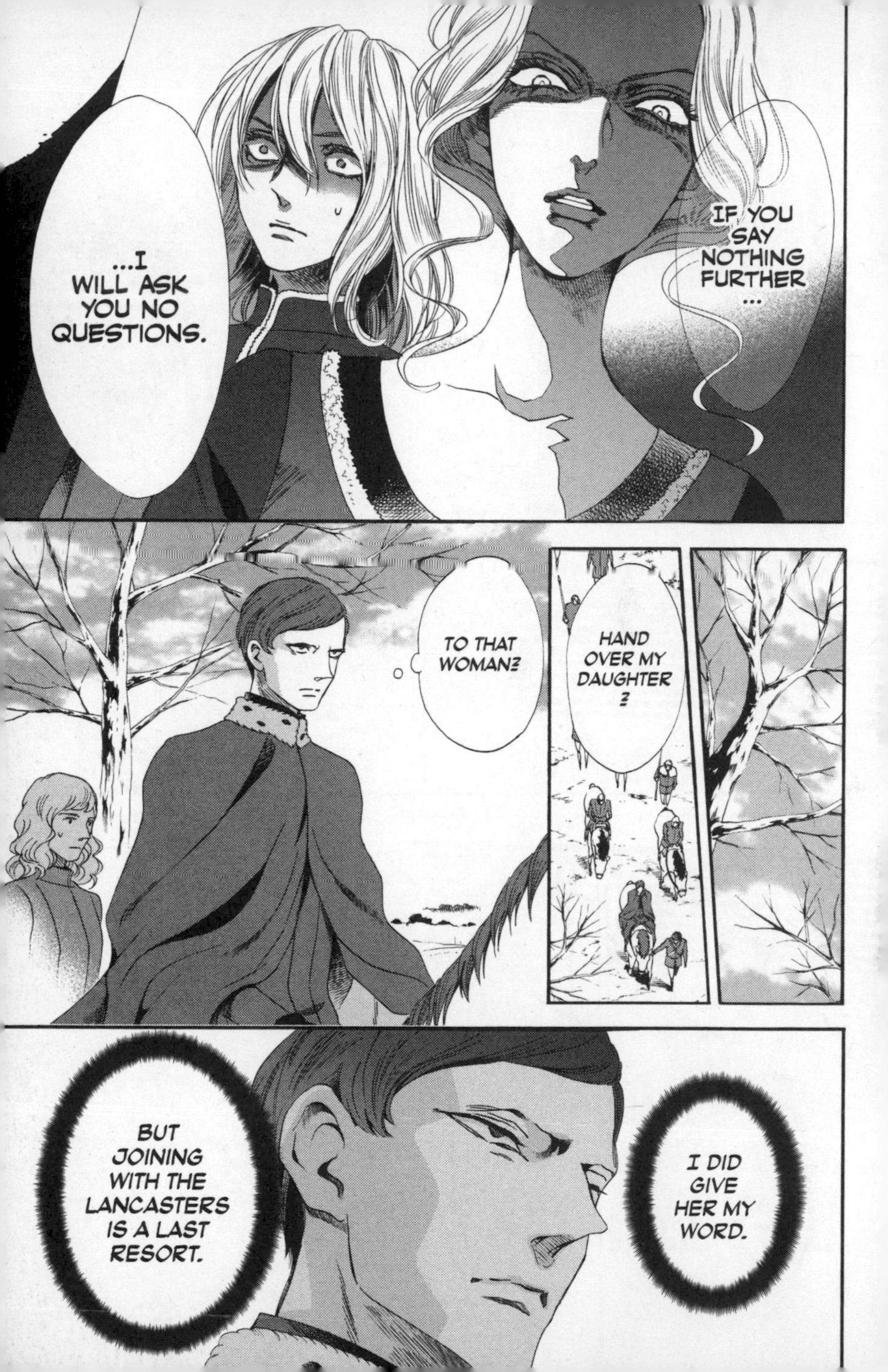
IF YOU SAY NOTHING FURTHER ...
...I WILL ASK YOU NO QUESTIONS.
HAND OVER MY DAUGHTER?
TO THAT WOMAN?
I DID GIVE HER MY WORD.
BUT JOINING WITH THE LANCASTERS IS A LAST RESORT.

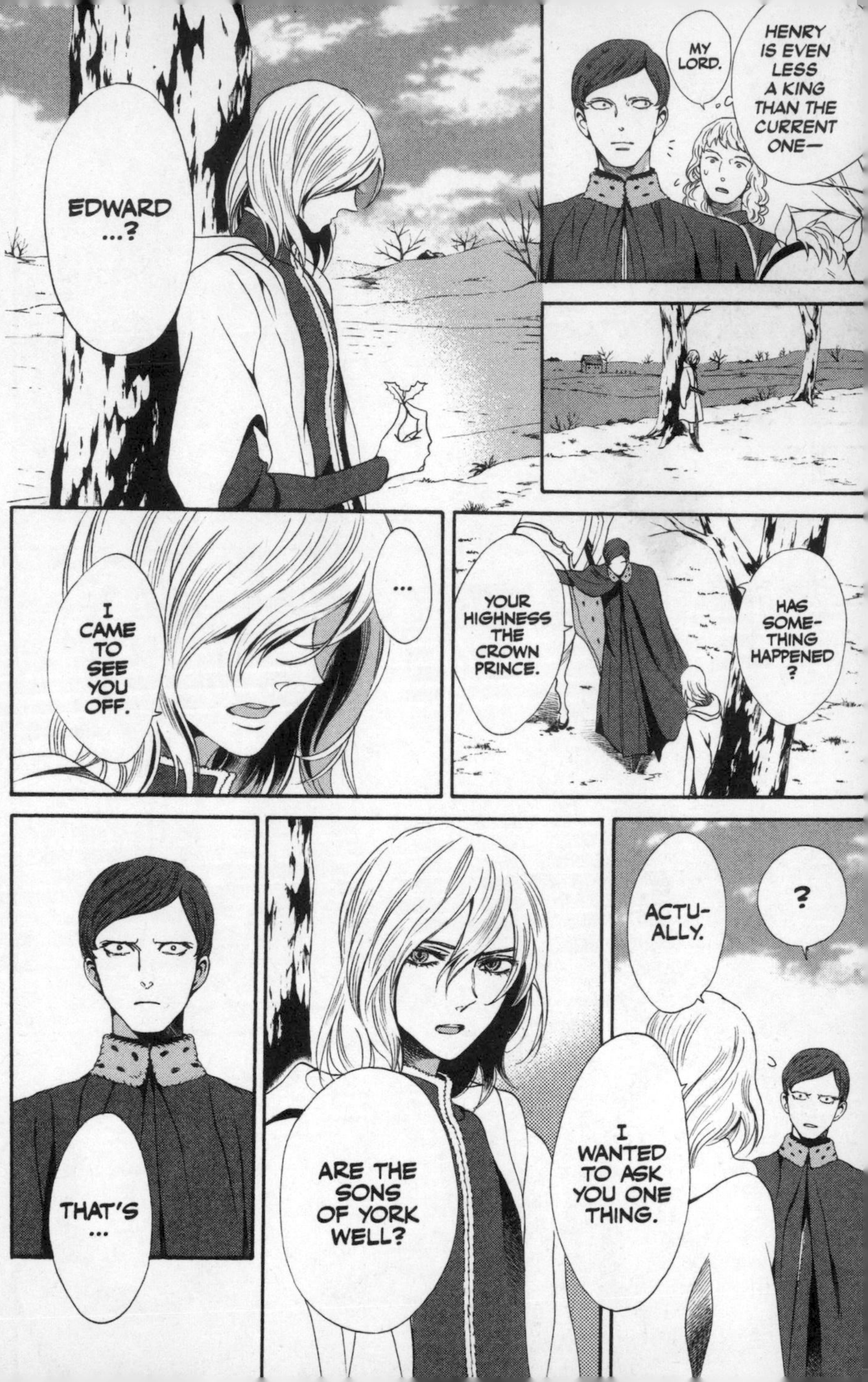
HENRY IS EVEN LESS A KING THAN THE CURRENT ONE—
MY LORD.
EDWARD ...?
HAS SOME-THING HAPPENED?
YOUR HIGHNESS THE CROWN PRINCE.
...
I CAME TO SEE YOU OFF.
?
ACTU-ALLY.
I WANTED TO ASK YOU ONE THING.
ARE THE SONS OF YORK WELL?
THAT'S ...

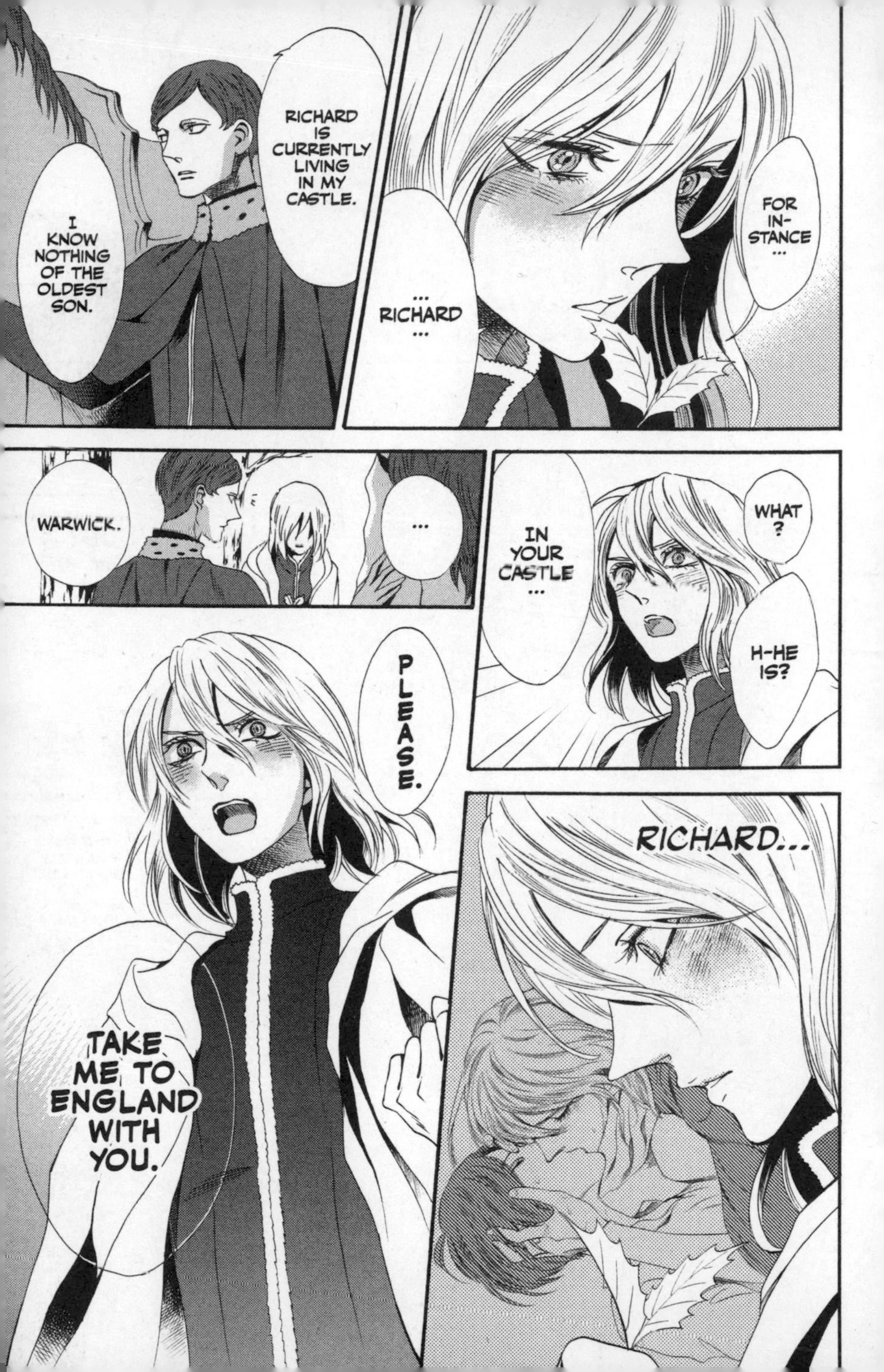
FOR IN-STANCE ...
... RICHARD ...
RICHARD IS CURRENTLY LIVING IN MY CASTLE.
I KNOW NOTHING OF THE OLDEST SON.
WHAT?
IN YOUR CASTLE ...
H-HE IS?
...
WARWICK.
PLEASE.
TAKE ME TO ENGLAND WITH YOU.
RICHARD...

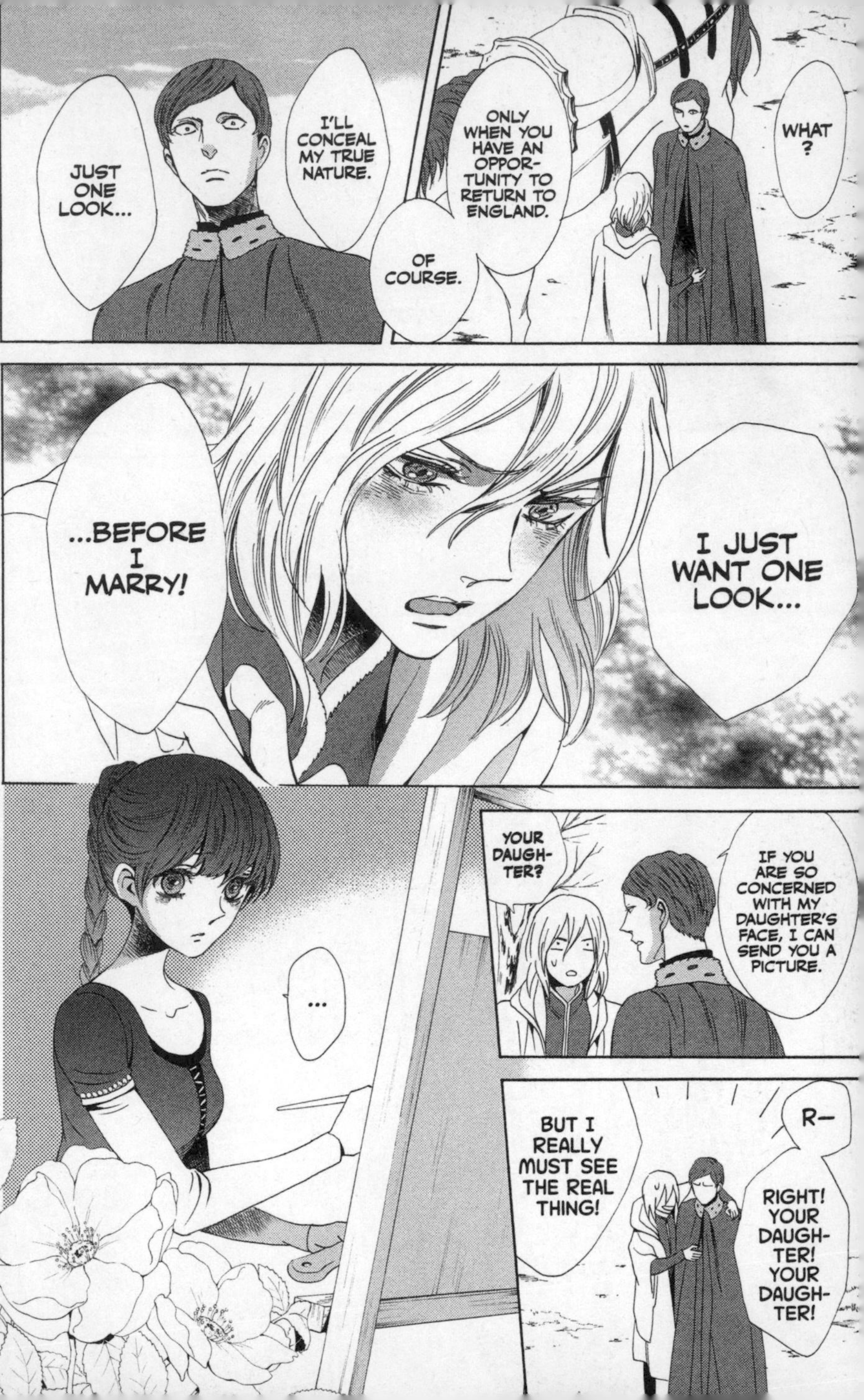
WHAT?
ONLY WHEN YOU HAVE AN OPPORTUNITY TO RETURN TO ENGLAND.
OF COURSE.
I'LL CONCEAL MY TRUE NATURE.
JUST ONE LOOK...
I JUST WANT ONE LOOK...
...BEFORE I MARRY!
IF YOU ARE SO CONCERNED WITH MY DAUGHTER'S FACE, I CAN SEND YOU A PICTURE.
YOUR DAUGHTER?
R—
RIGHT! YOUR DAUGHTER! YOUR DAUGHTER!
BUT I REALLY MUST SEE THE REAL THING!
...

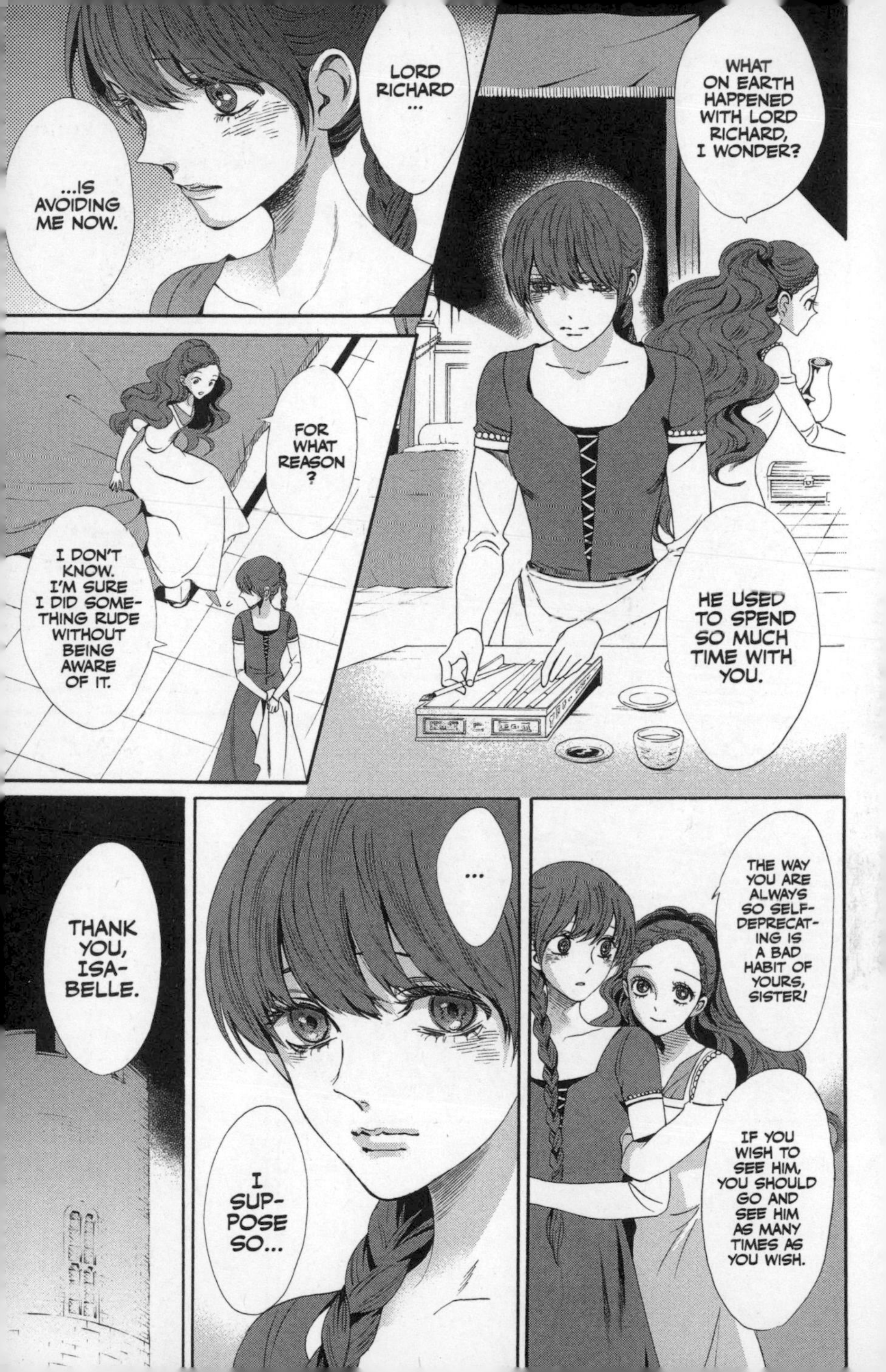
WHAT ON EARTH HAPPENED WITH LORD RICHARD, I WONDER?
HE USED TO SPEND SO MUCH TIME WITH YOU.
LORD RICHARD...
...IS AVOIDING ME NOW.
FOR WHAT REASON?
I DON'T KNOW. I'M SURE I DID SOMETHING RUDE WITHOUT BEING AWARE OF IT.
THE WAY YOU ARE ALWAYS SO SELF-DEPRECATING IS A BAD HABIT OF YOURS, SISTER!
IF YOU WISH TO SEE HIM, YOU SHOULD GO AND SEE HIM AS MANY TIMES AS YOU WISH.
...
I SUPPOSE SO...
THANK YOU, ISABELLE.

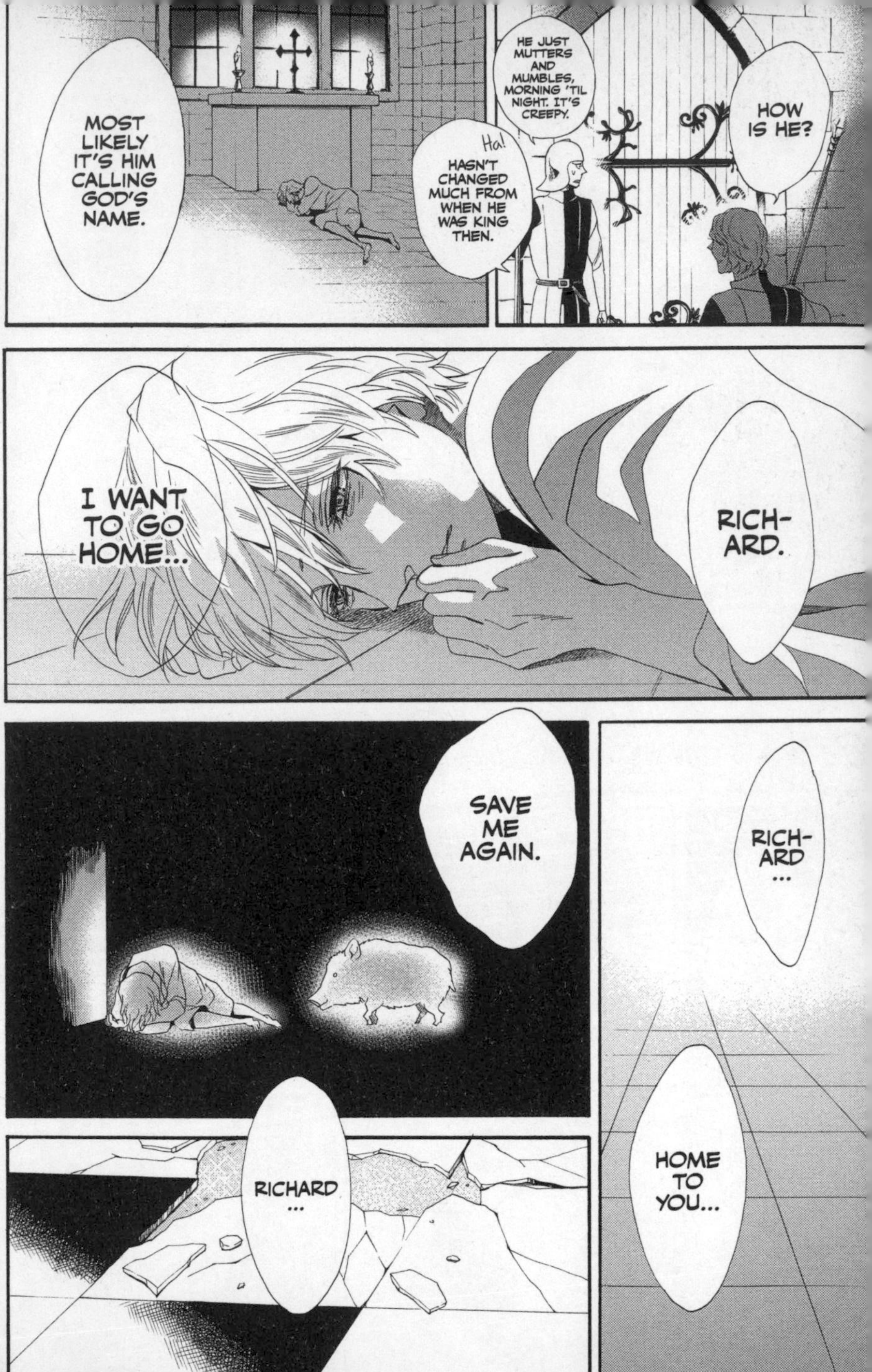
HOW IS HE?
HE JUST MUTTERS AND MUMBLES, MORNING 'TIL NIGHT. IT'S CREEPY.
Ha! HASN'T CHANGED MUCH FROM WHEN HE WAS KING THEN.
MOST LIKELY IT'S HIM CALLING GOD'S NAME.
RICH-ARD.
I WANT TO GO HOME...
RICH-ARD...
HOME TO YOU...
SAVE ME AGAIN.
RICHARD...

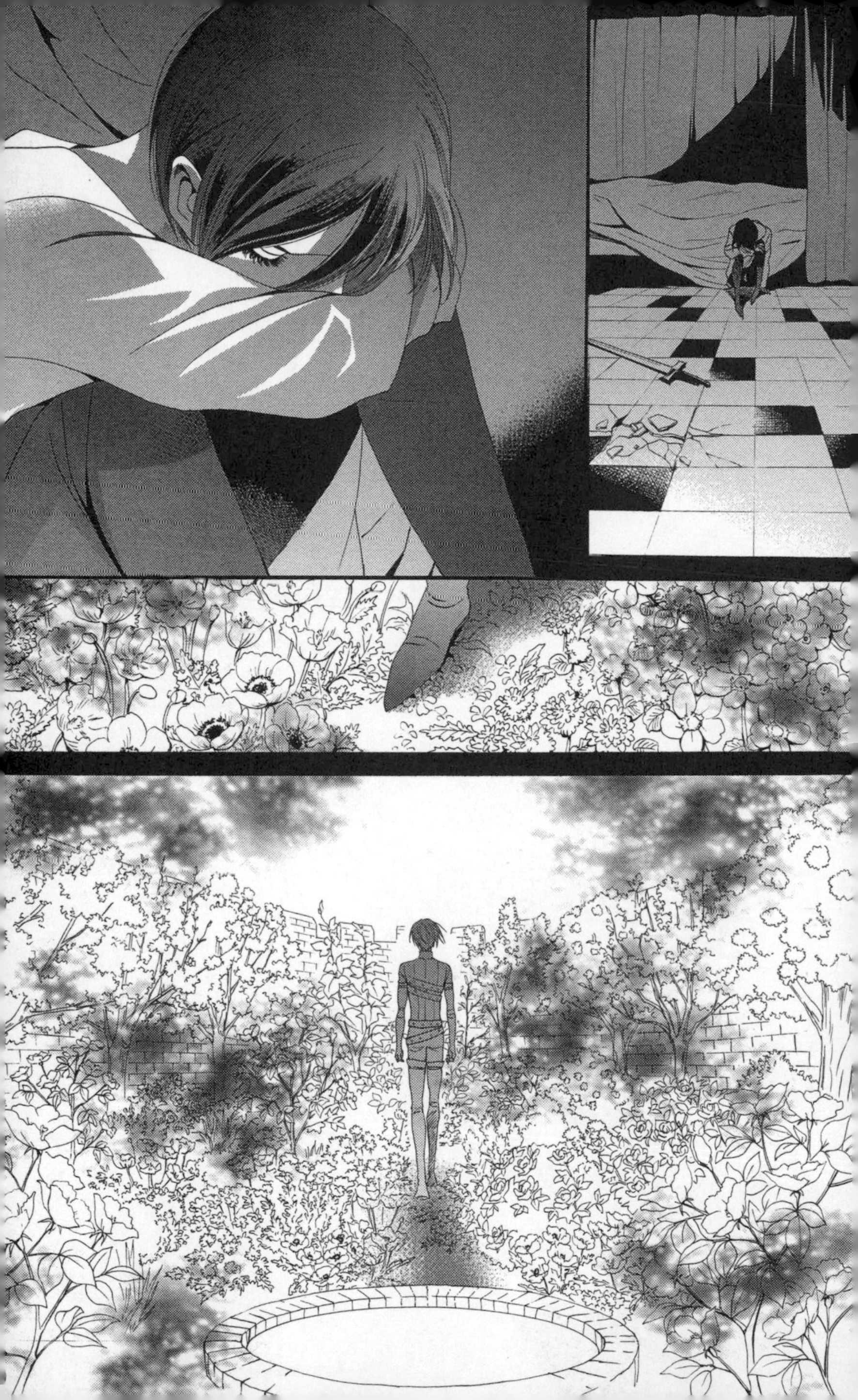

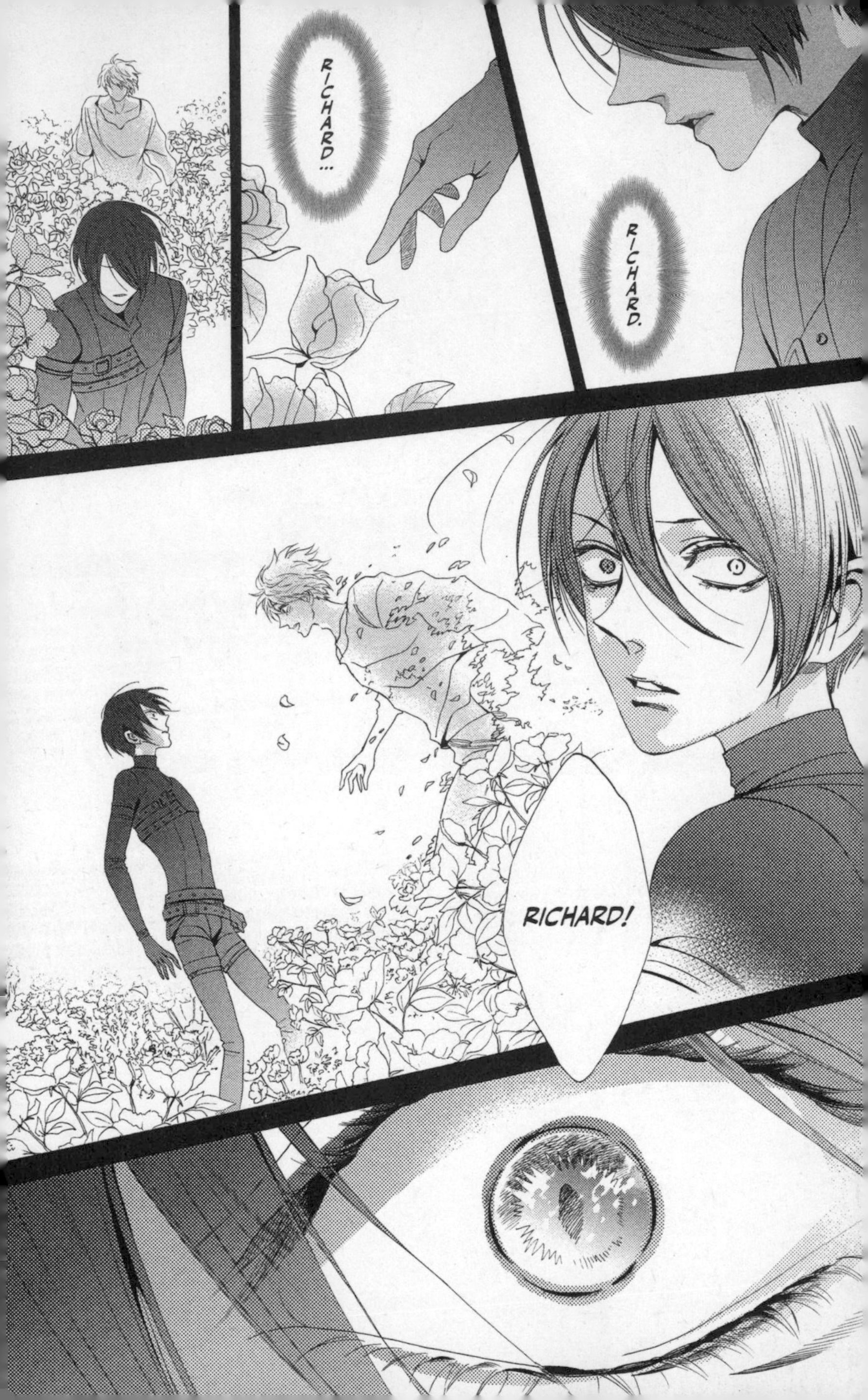
RICHARD.
RICHARD...
RICHARD!

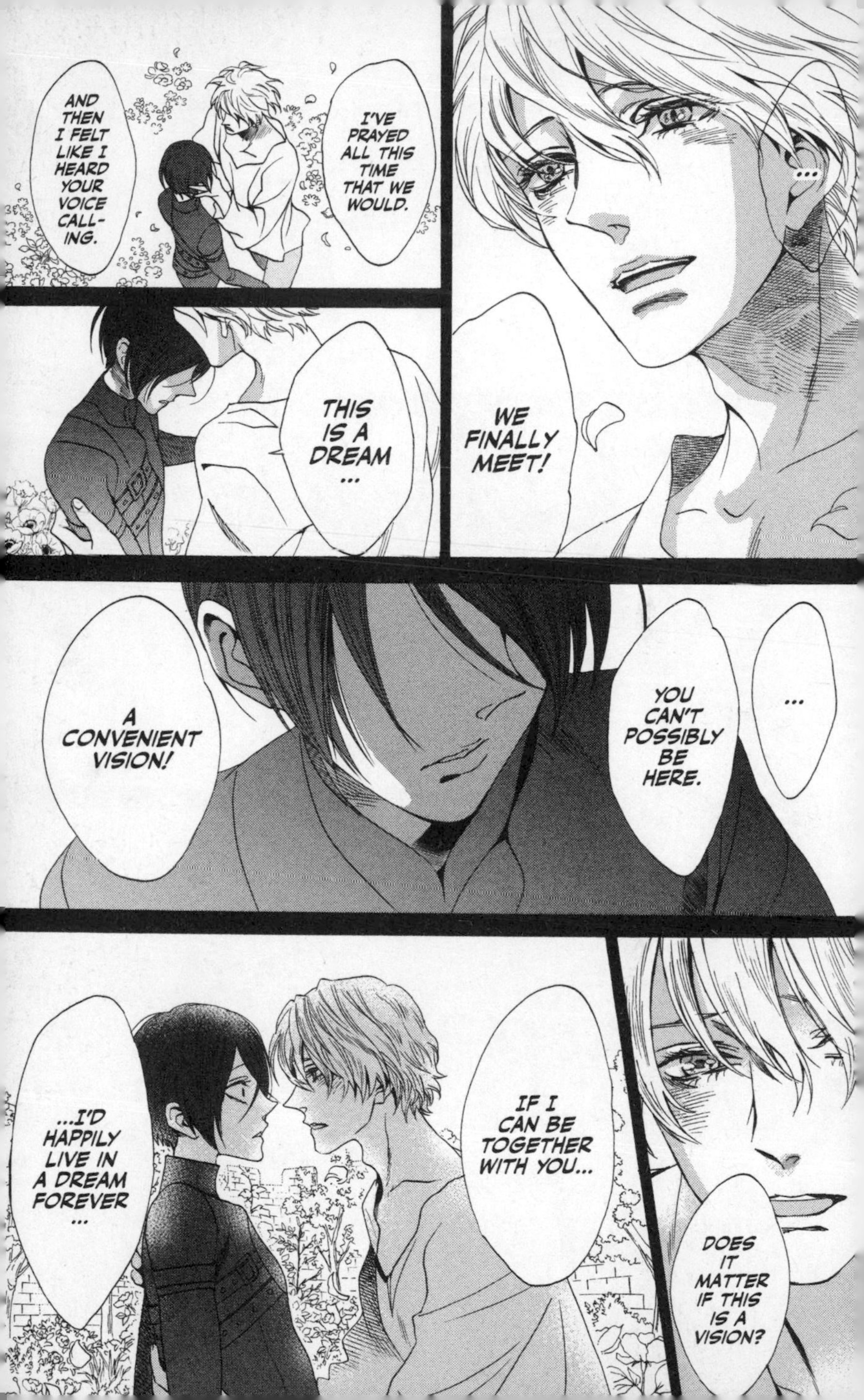
...
WE FINALLY MEET!
I'VE PRAYED ALL THIS TIME THAT WE WOULD.
AND THEN I FELT LIKE I HEARD YOUR VOICE CALLING.
THIS IS A DREAM ...
...
YOU CAN'T POSSIBLY BE HERE.
A CONVENIENT VISION!
DOES IT MATTER IF THIS IS A VISION?
IF I CAN BE TOGETHER WITH YOU...
...I'D HAPPILY LIVE IN A DREAM FOREVER ...

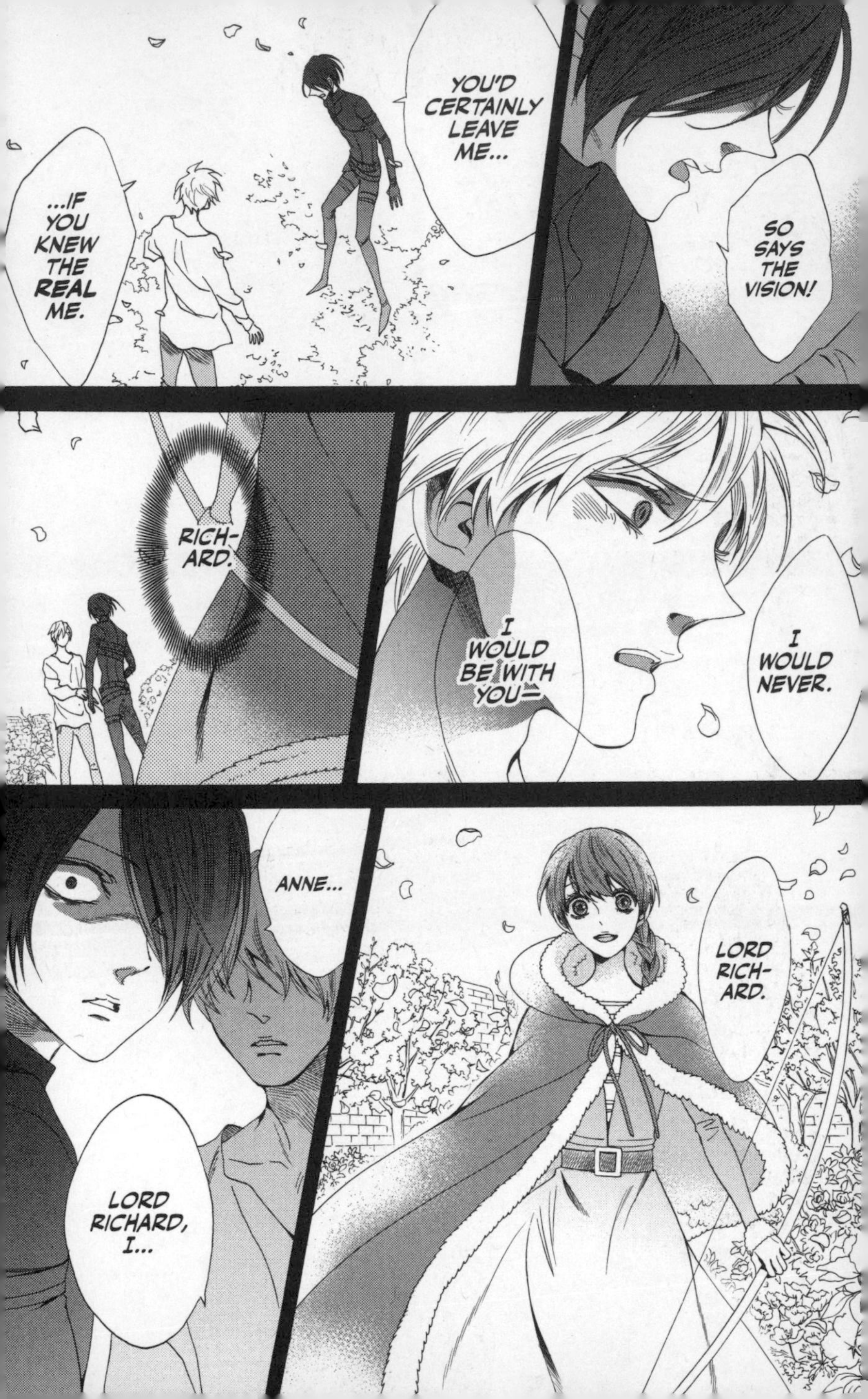
SO SAYS THE VISION!
YOU'D CERTAINLY LEAVE ME...
...IF YOU KNEW THE REAL ME.
I WOULD NEVER.
I WOULD BE WITH YOU—
RICH-ARD.
LORD RICH-ARD.
ANNE...
LORD RICHARD, I...

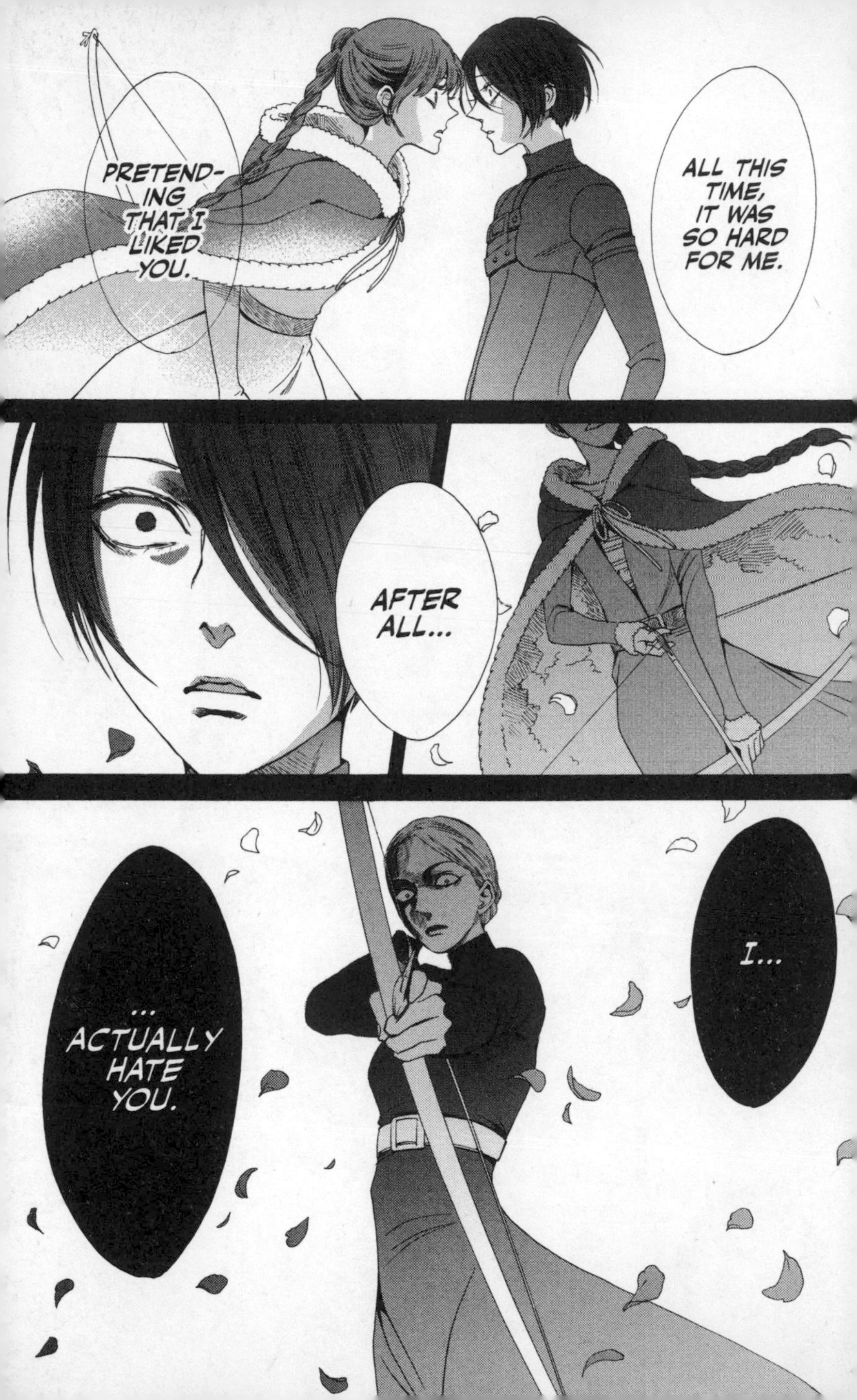
ALL THIS TIME, IT WAS SO HARD FOR ME.
PRETEND-ING THAT I LIKED YOU.
AFTER ALL...
I...
...ACTUALLY HATE YOU.

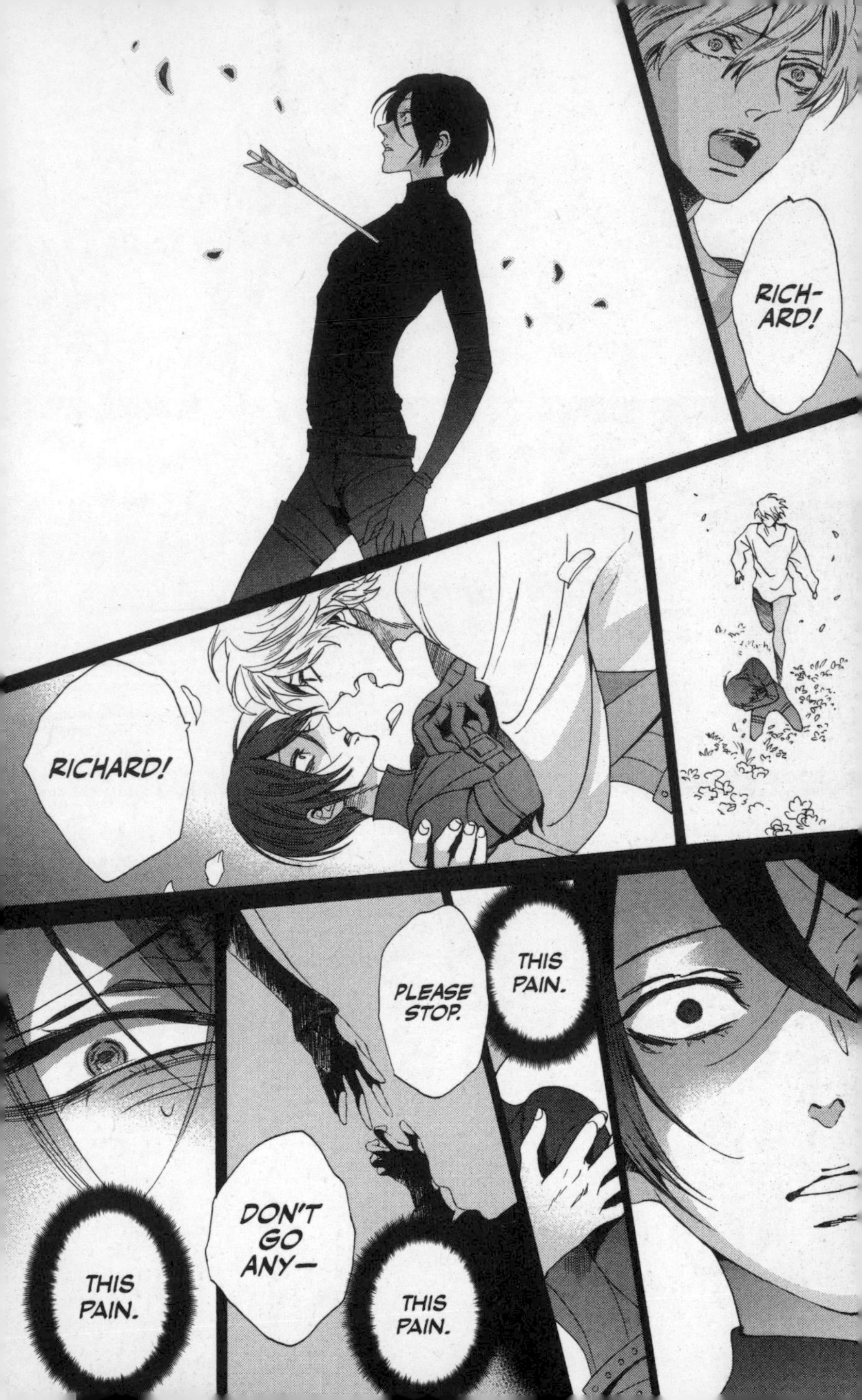
RICH-
ARD!
RICHARD!
THIS
PAIN.
PLEASE
STOP.
DON'T
GO
ANY—
THIS
PAIN.
THIS
PAIN.

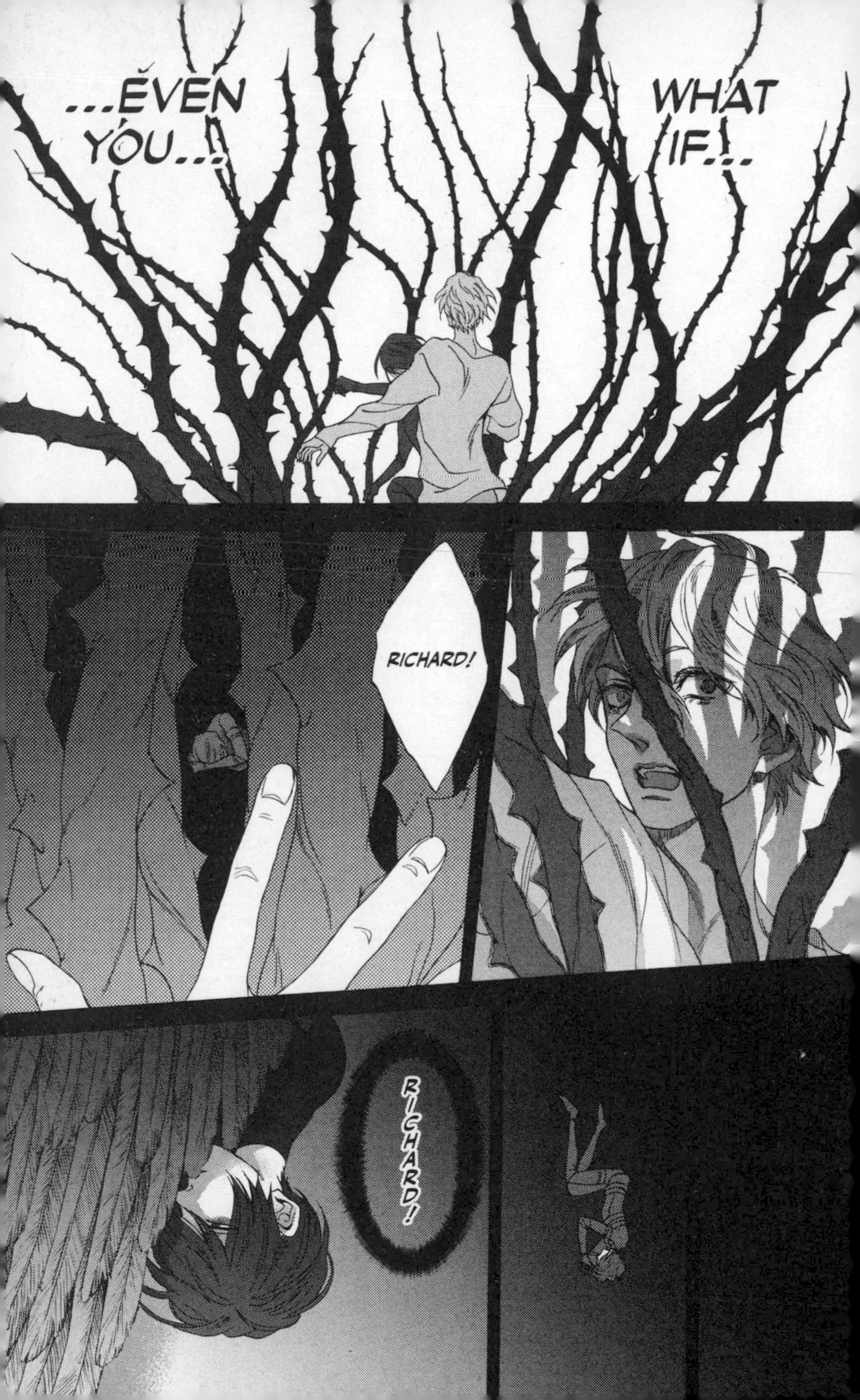
WHAT IF...
...EVEN YOU...
RICHARD!
RICHARD!

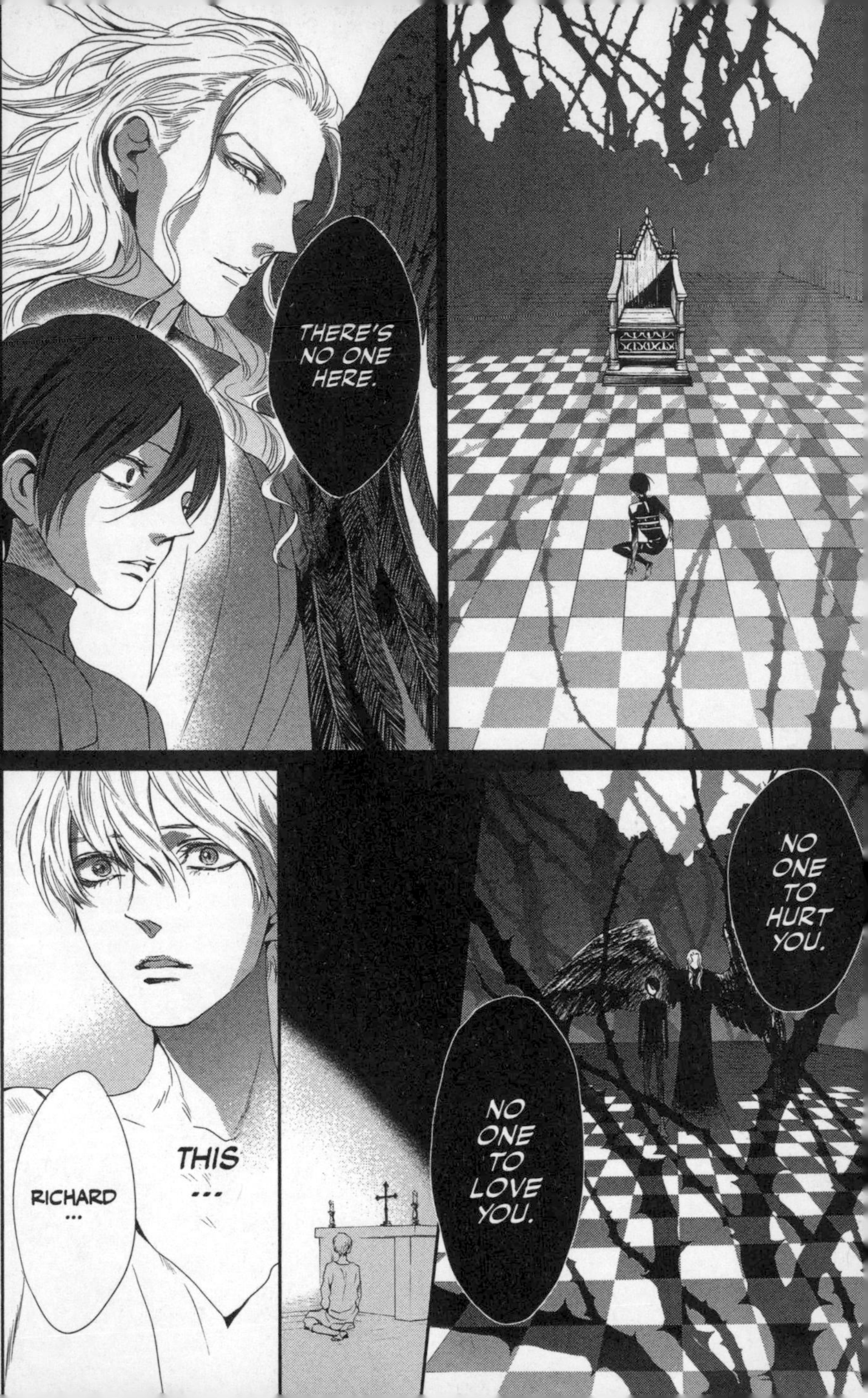
THERE'S NO ONE HERE.
NO ONE TO HURT YOU.
NO ONE TO LOVE YOU.
THIS ...
RICHARD ...

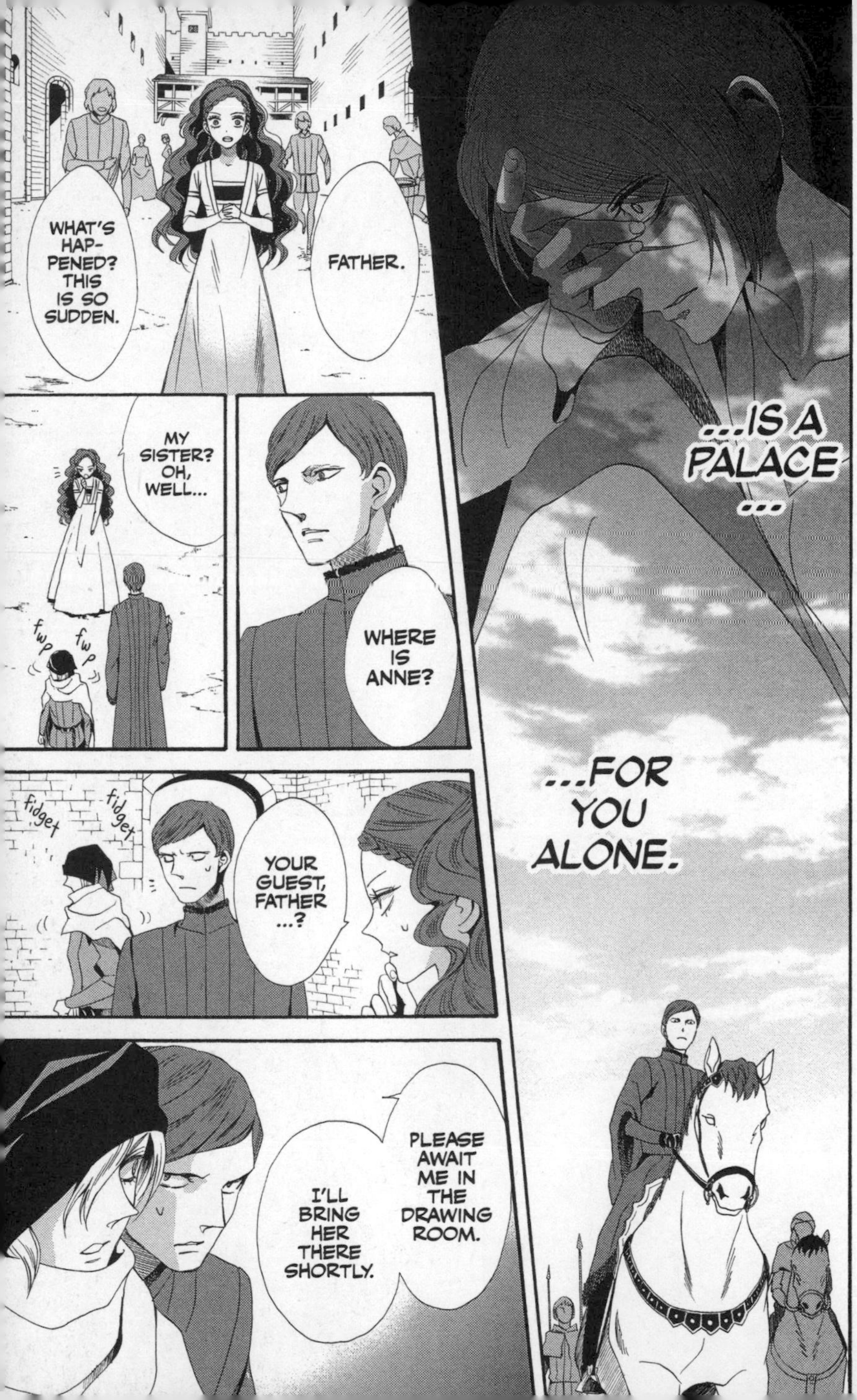
...IS A PALACE ...
...FOR YOU ALONE.
FATHER.
WHAT'S HAP-PENED? THIS IS SO SUDDEN.
WHERE IS ANNE?
MY SISTER? OH, WELL...
fwp fwp
YOUR GUEST, FATHER ...?
fidget fidget
PLEASE AWAIT ME IN THE DRAWING ROOM.
I'LL BRING HER THERE SHORTLY.

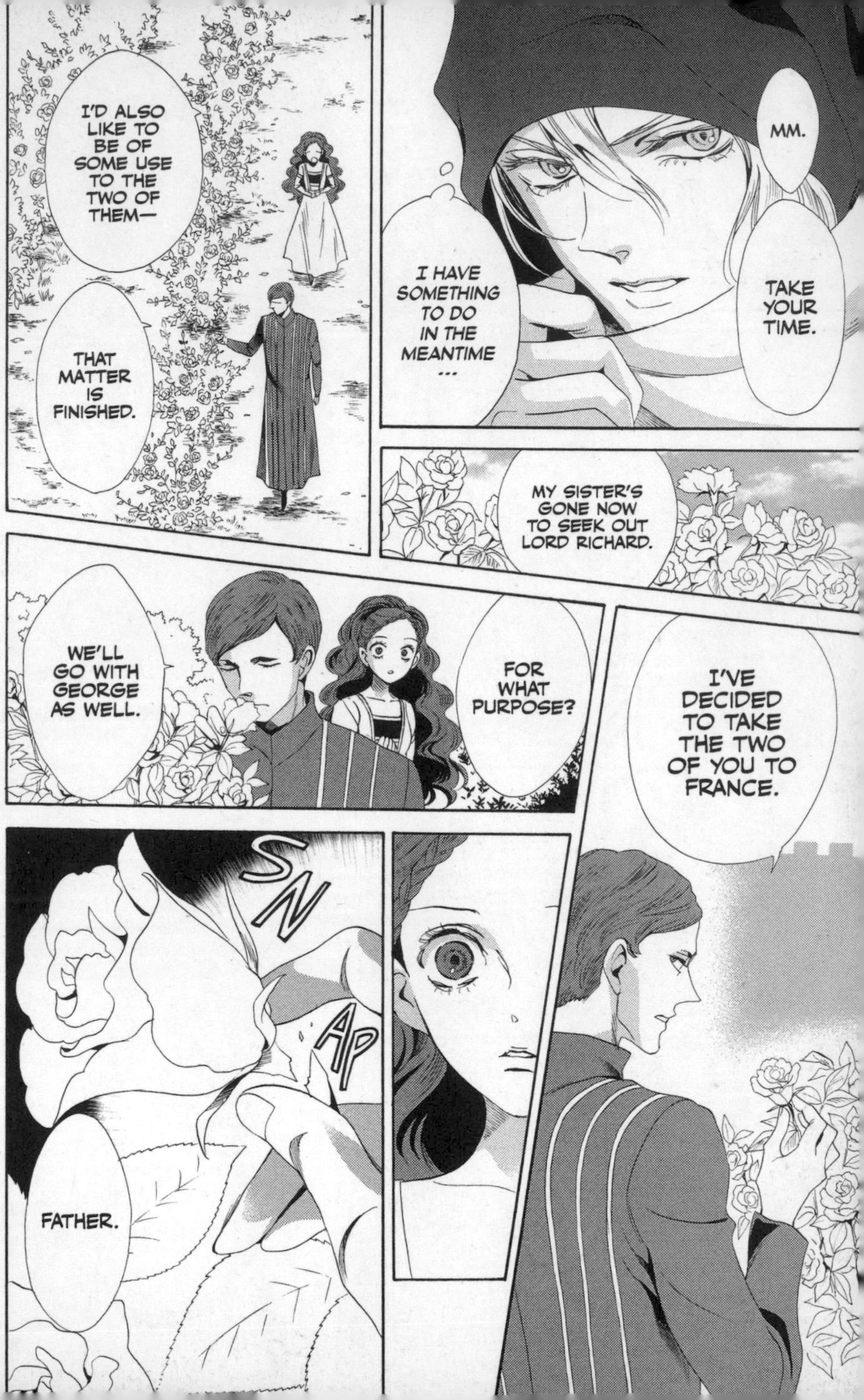
MM.
TAKE YOUR TIME.
I HAVE SOMETHING TO DO IN THE MEANTIME...
MY SISTER'S GONE NOW TO SEEK OUT LORD RICHARD.
I'D ALSO LIKE TO BE OF SOME USE TO THE TWO OF THEM—
THAT MATTER IS FINISHED.
I'VE DECIDED TO TAKE THE TWO OF YOU TO FRANCE.
FOR WHAT PURPOSE?
WE'LL GO WITH GEORGE AS WELL.
SNAP
FATHER.

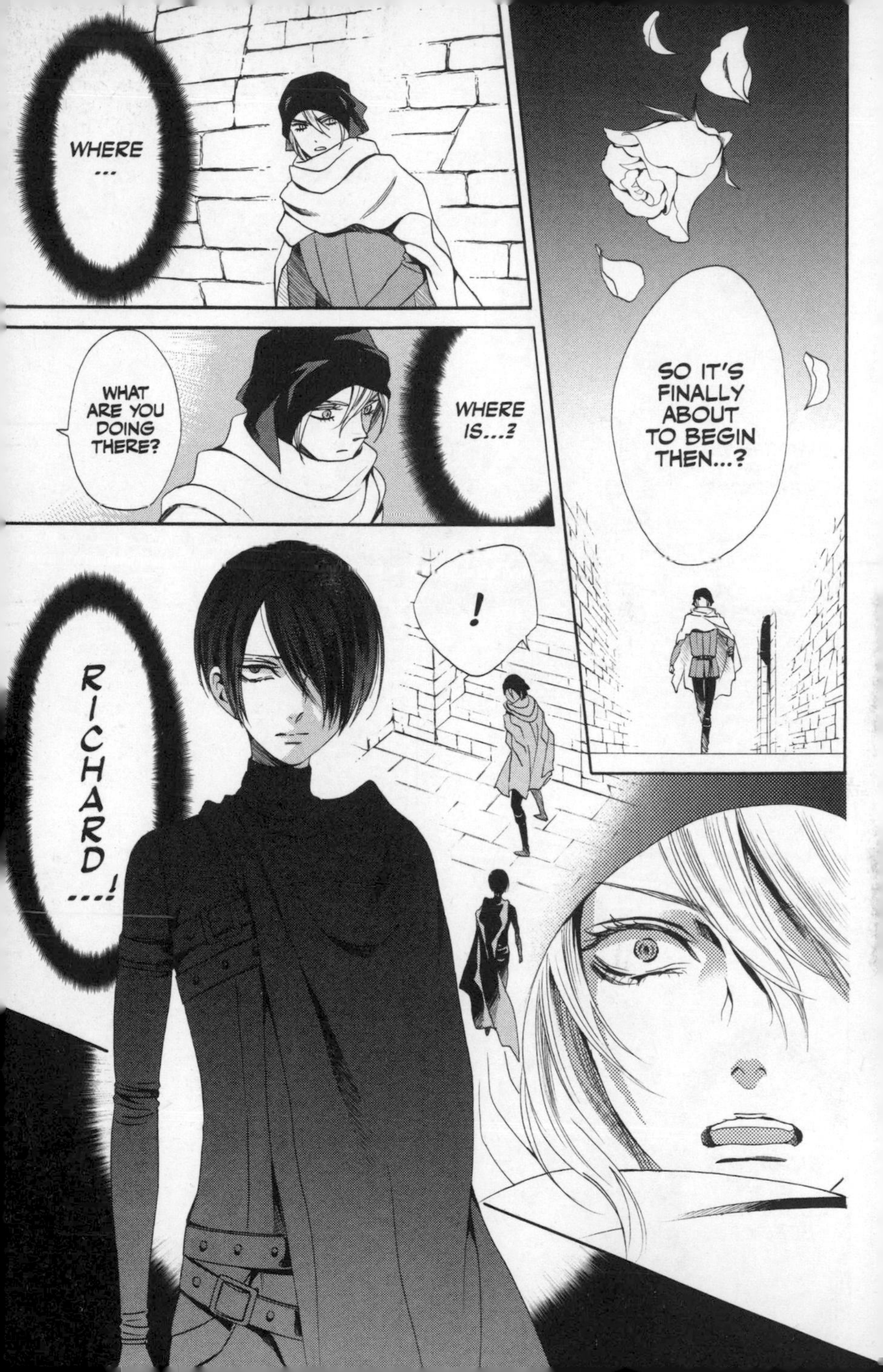
SO IT'S FINALLY ABOUT TO BEGIN THEN...?
WHERE ...
WHERE IS...?
WHAT ARE YOU DOING THERE?
!
RICHARD ...!

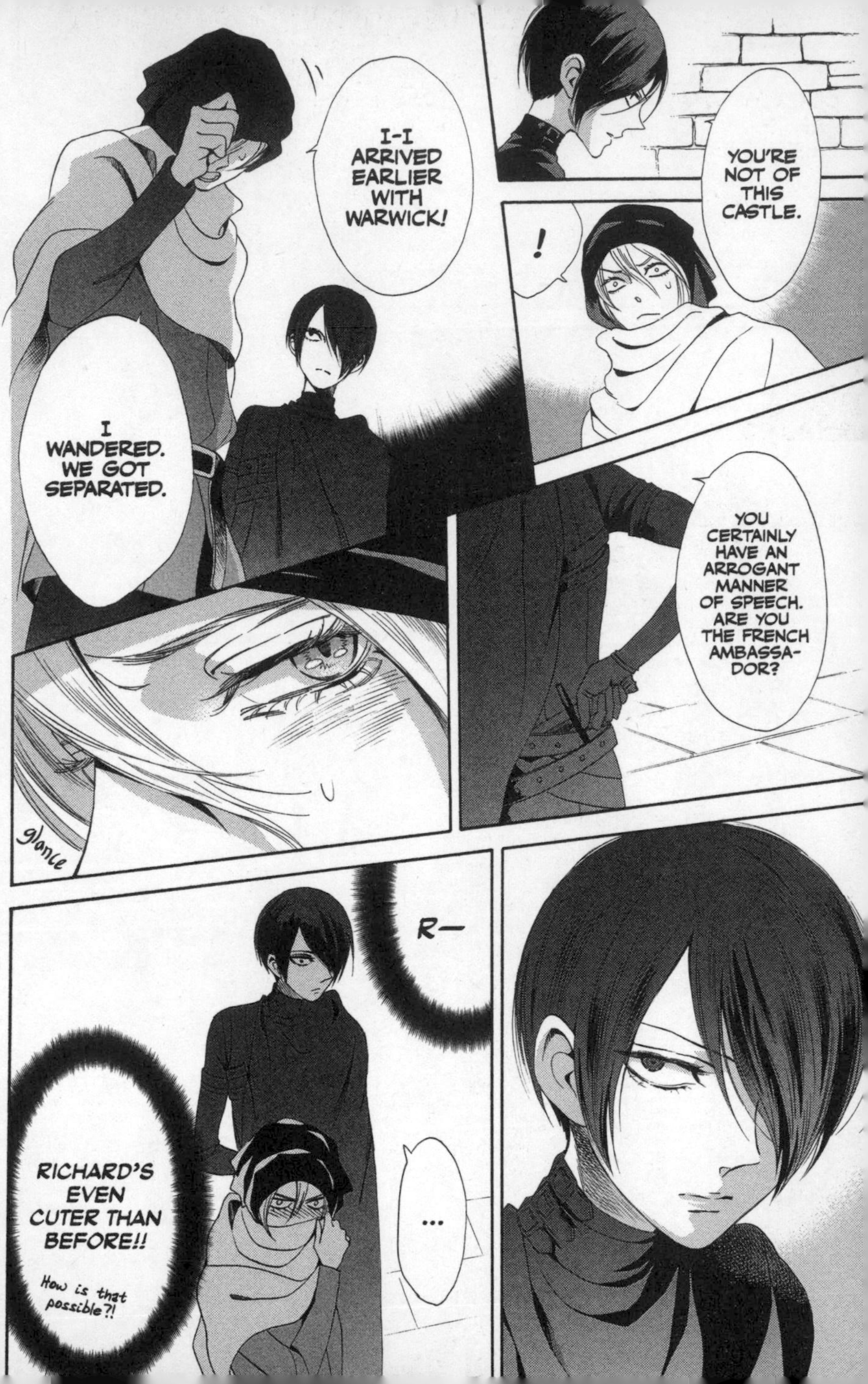
YOU'RE NOT OF THIS CASTLE.
!
I-I ARRIVED EARLIER WITH WARWICK!
I WANDERED. WE GOT SEPARATED.
YOU CERTAINLY HAVE AN ARROGANT MANNER OF SPEECH. ARE YOU THE FRENCH AMBASSA-DOR?
glance
...
R—
RICHARD'S EVEN CUTER THAN BEFORE!!
How is that possible?!

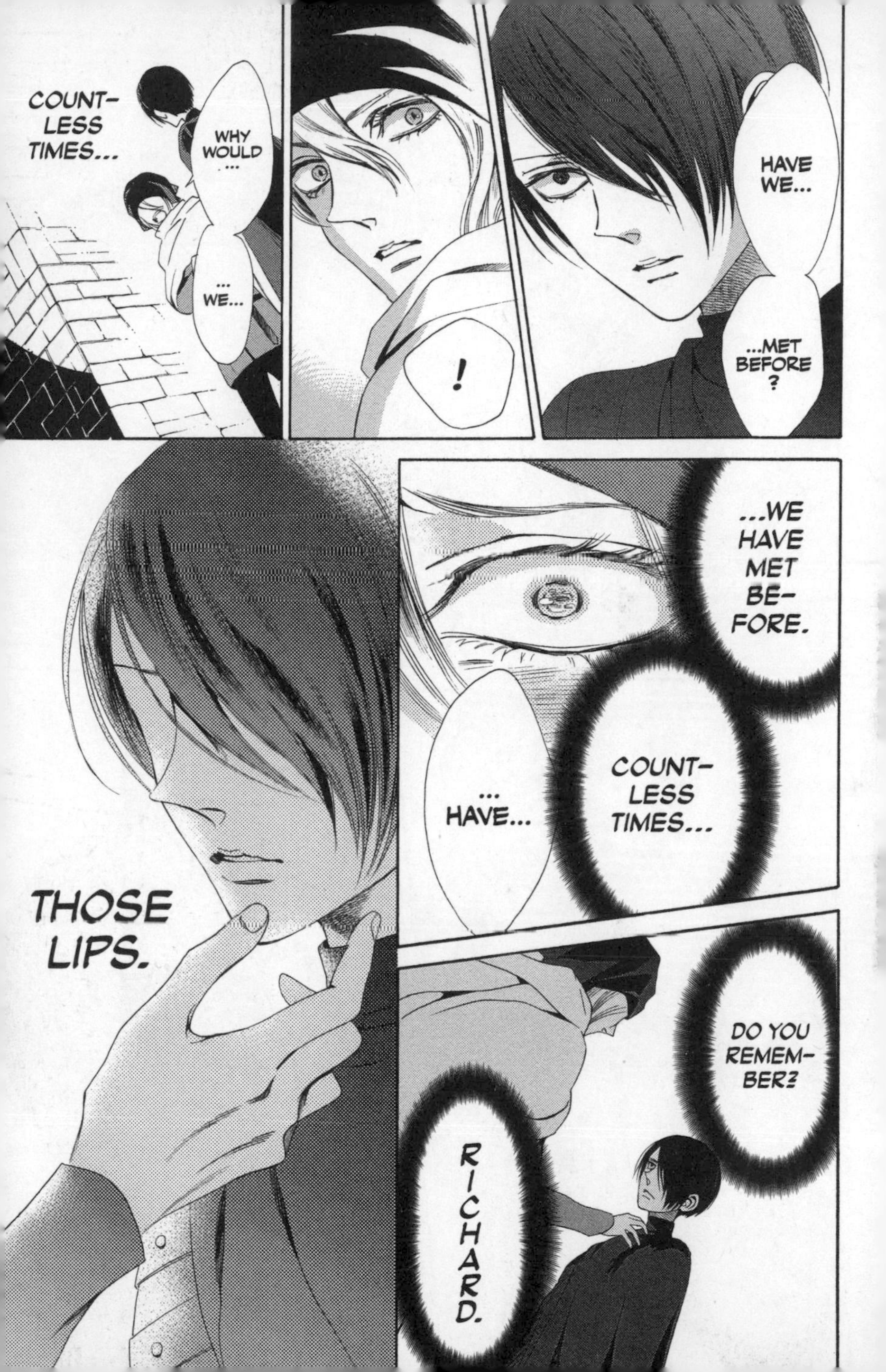
HAVE WE...
...MET BEFORE?
!
WHY WOULD ...
... WE...
COUNT-LESS TIMES...
...WE HAVE MET BE-FORE.
COUNT-LESS TIMES...
... HAVE...
DO YOU REMEM-BER?
RICHARD.
THOSE LIPS.

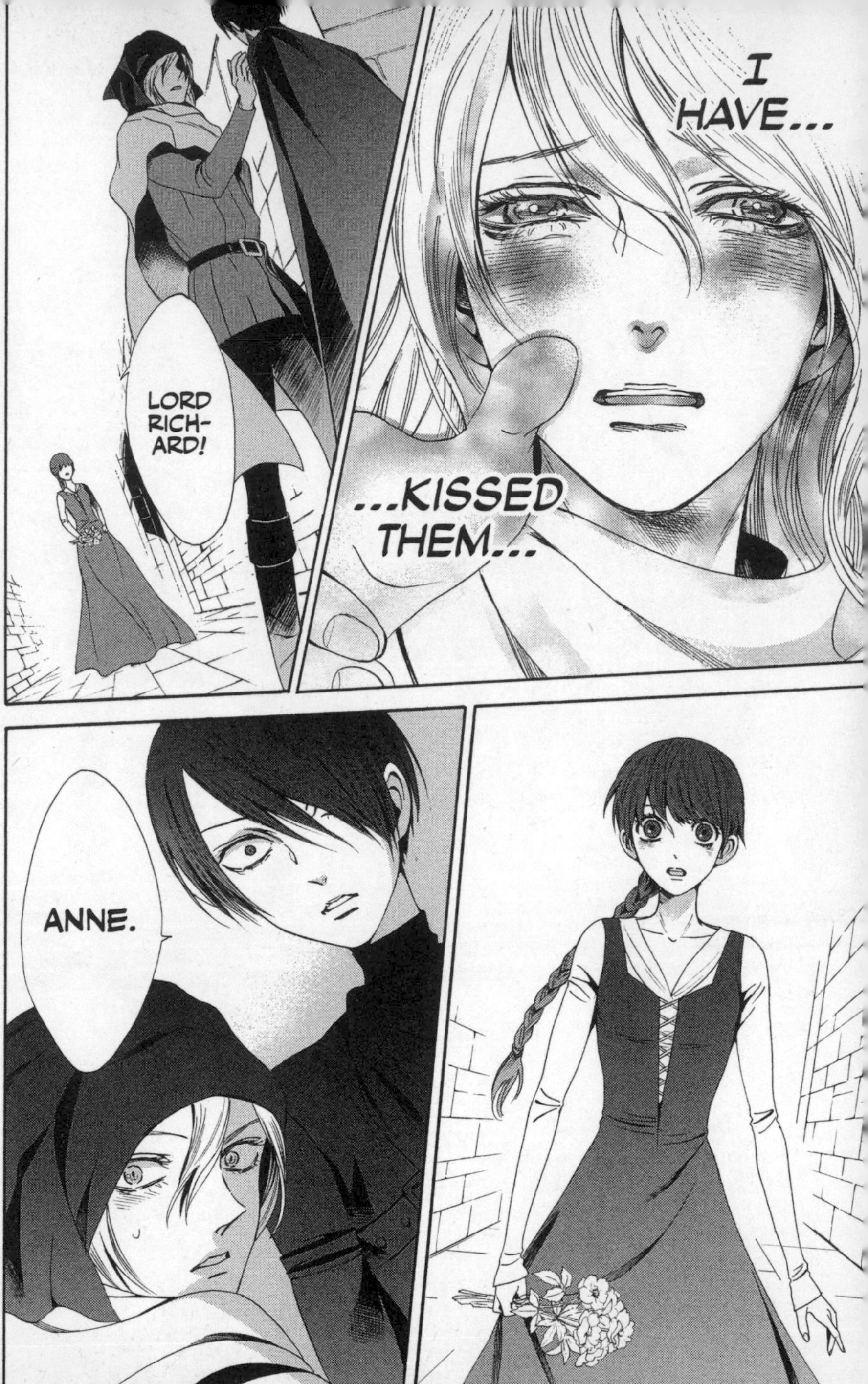
I HAVE...
...KISSED THEM...
LORD RICHARD!
ANNE.

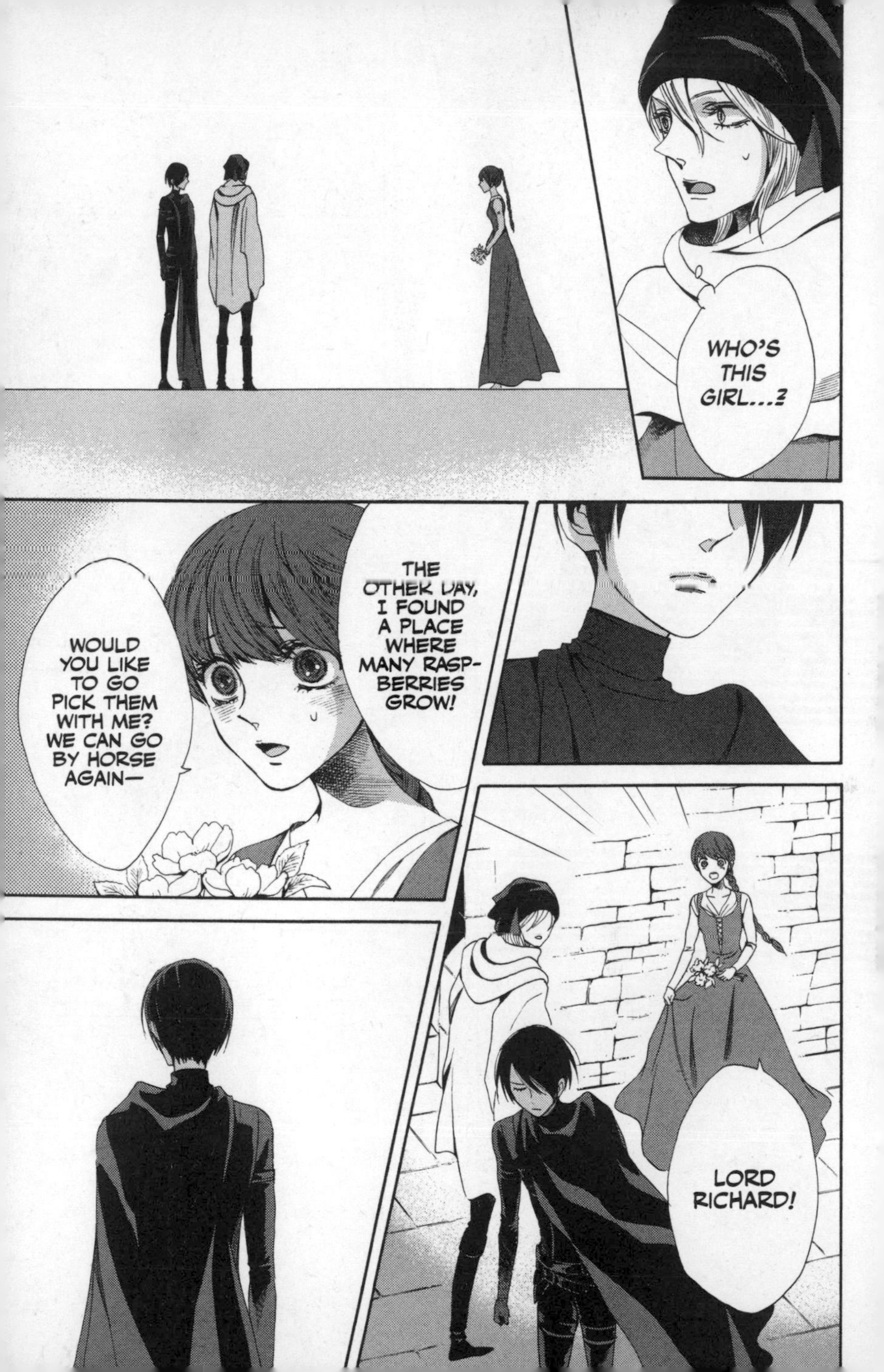
WHO'S THIS GIRL...?
THE OTHER DAY, I FOUND A PLACE WHERE MANY RASP-BERRIES GROW!
WOULD YOU LIKE TO GO PICK THEM WITH ME? WE CAN GO BY HORSE AGAIN—
LORD RICHARD!

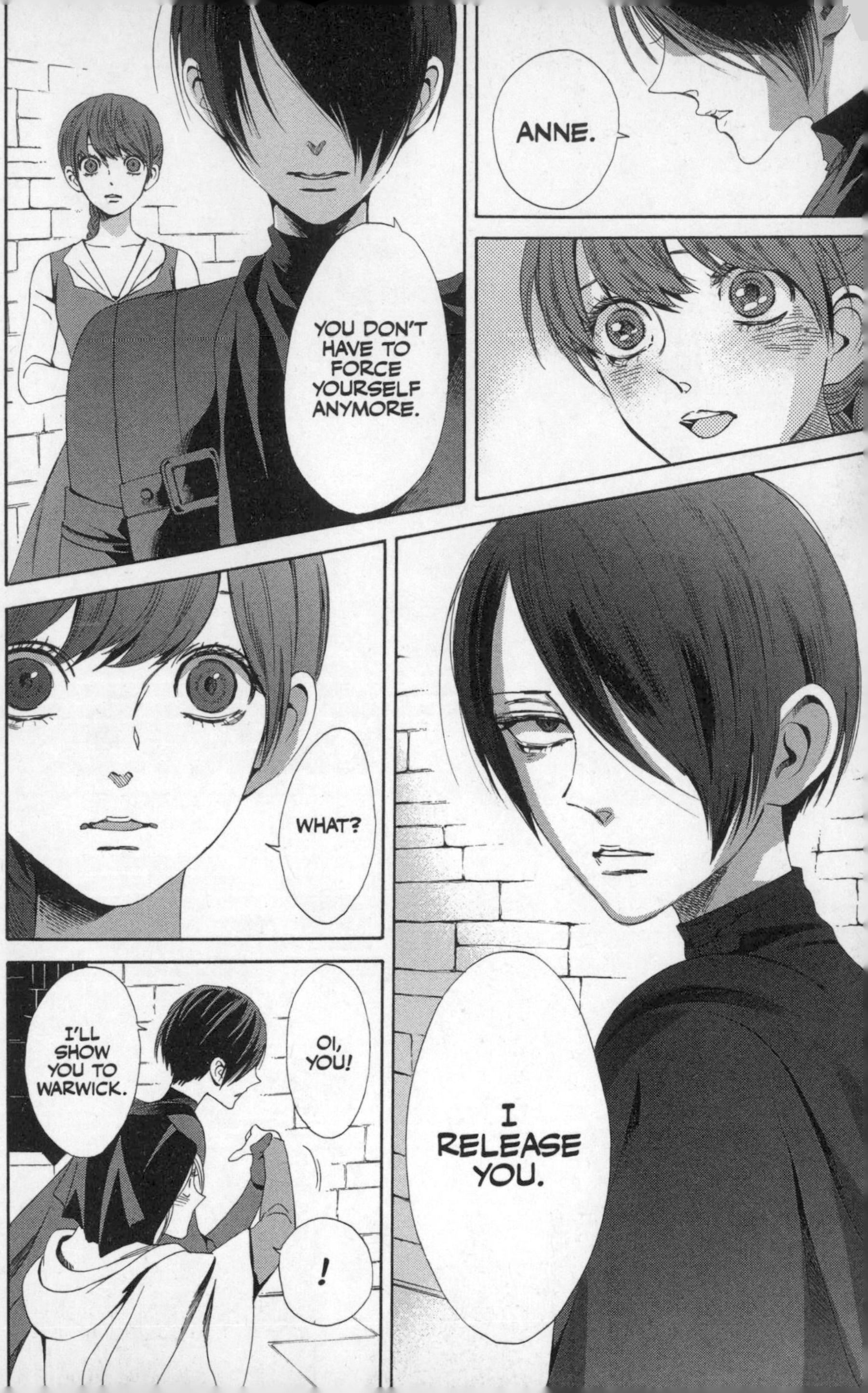
ANNE.
YOU DON'T HAVE TO FORCE YOURSELF ANYMORE.
I RELEASE YOU.
WHAT?
OI, YOU!
I'LL SHOW YOU TO WARWICK.
!

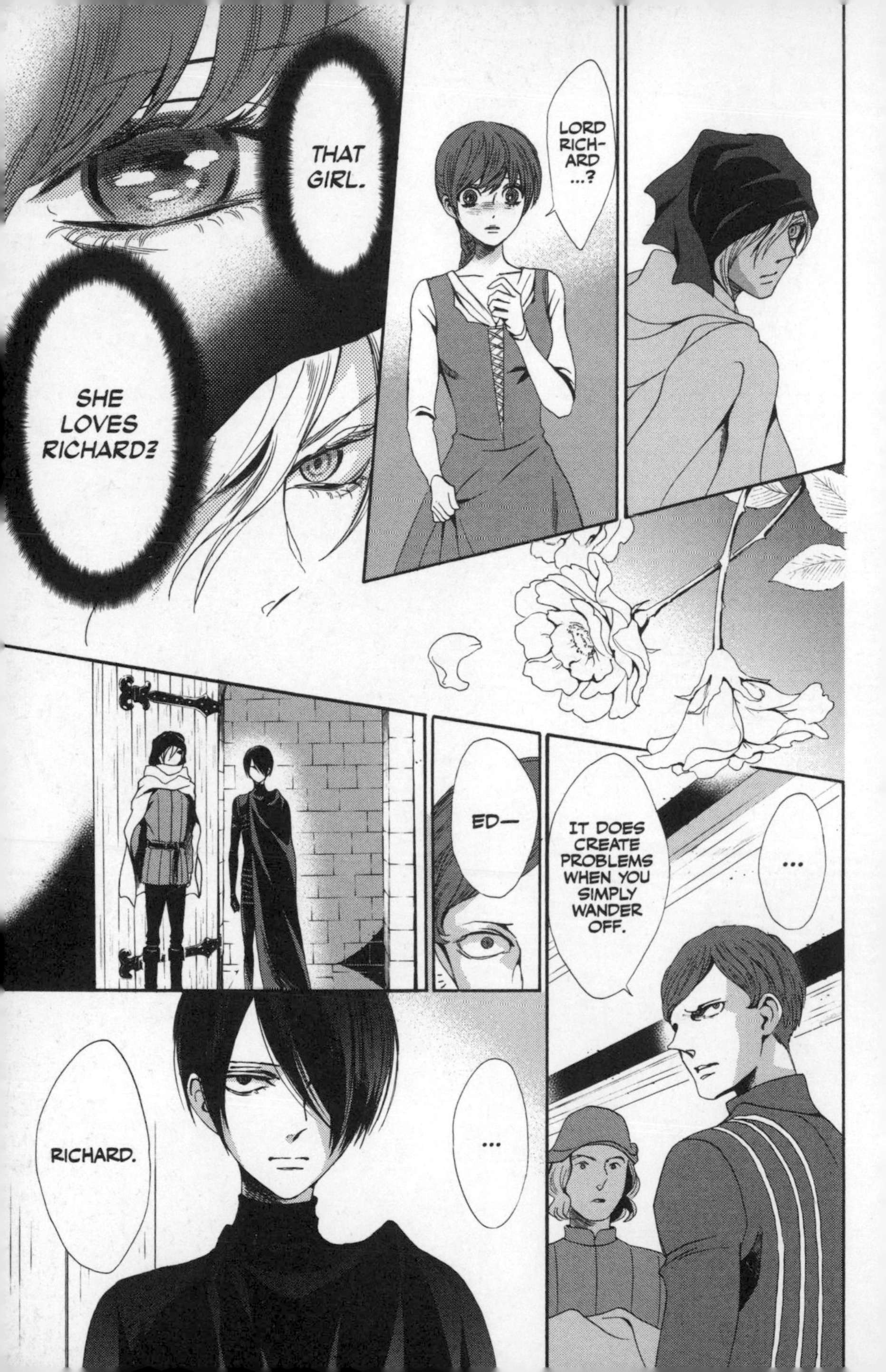
LORD RICH-ARD ...?
THAT GIRL.
SHE LOVES RICHARD?
...
IT DOES CREATE PROBLEMS WHEN YOU SIMPLY WANDER OFF.
ED—
...
RICHARD.

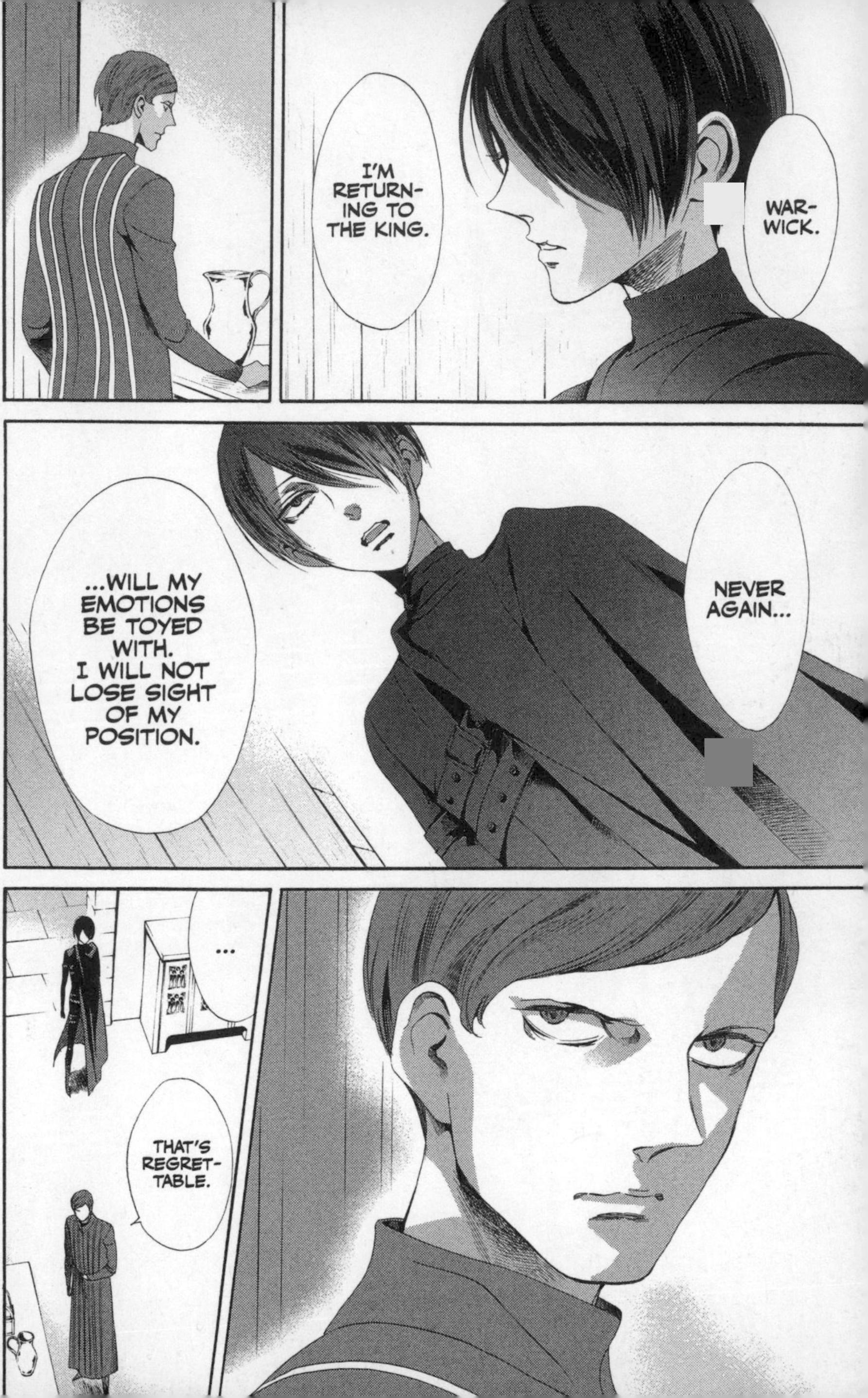
WAR-
WICK.
I'M RETURN-
ING TO
THE KING.
NEVER
AGAIN...
...WILL MY
EMOTIONS
BE TOYED
WITH.
I WILL NOT
LOSE SIGHT
OF MY
POSITION.
...
THAT'S
REGRET-
TABLE.

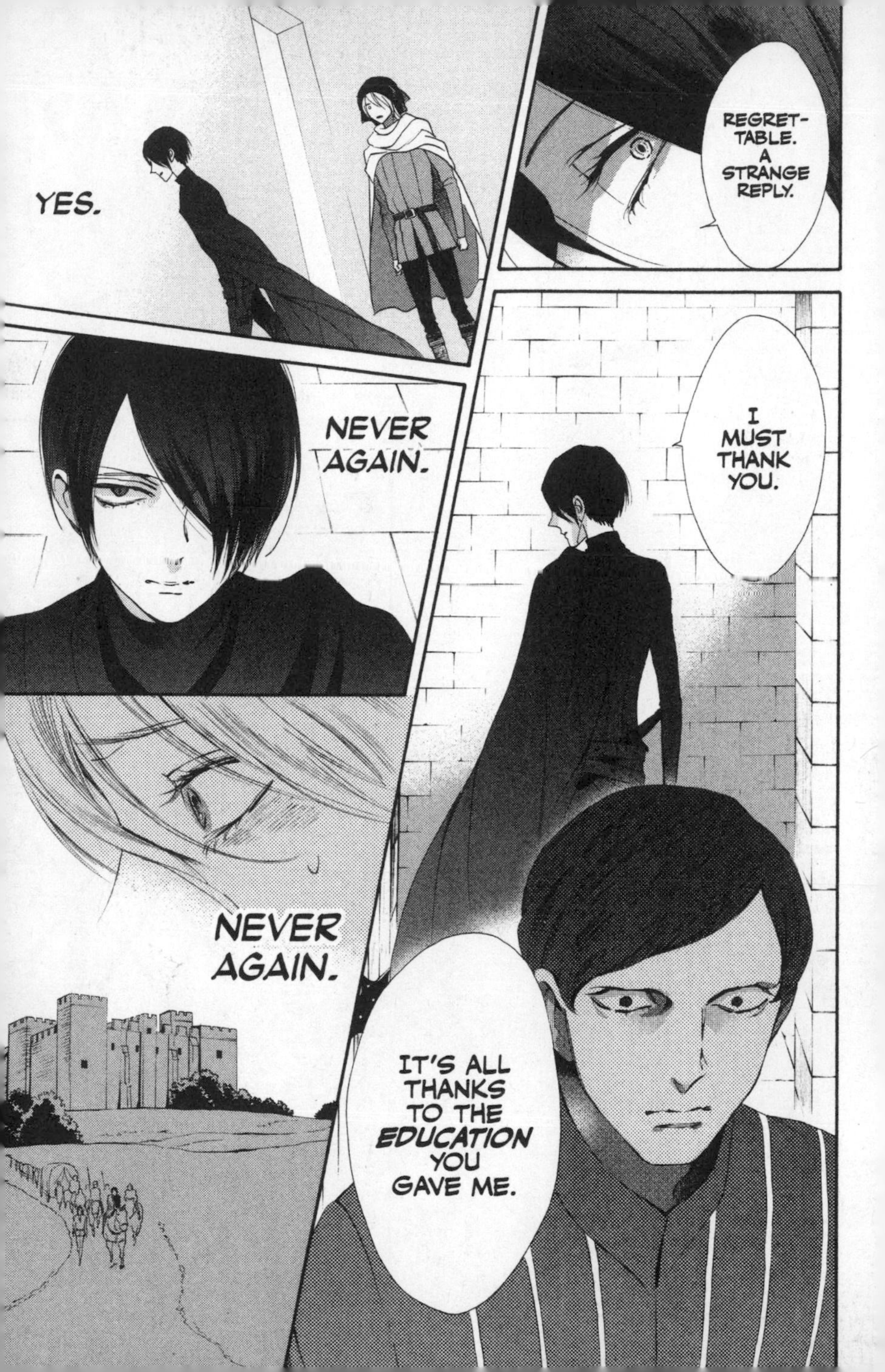
REGRET-TABLE. A STRANGE REPLY.
YES.
I MUST THANK YOU.
IT'S ALL THANKS TO THE EDUCATION YOU GAVE ME.
NEVER AGAIN.
NEVER AGAIN.

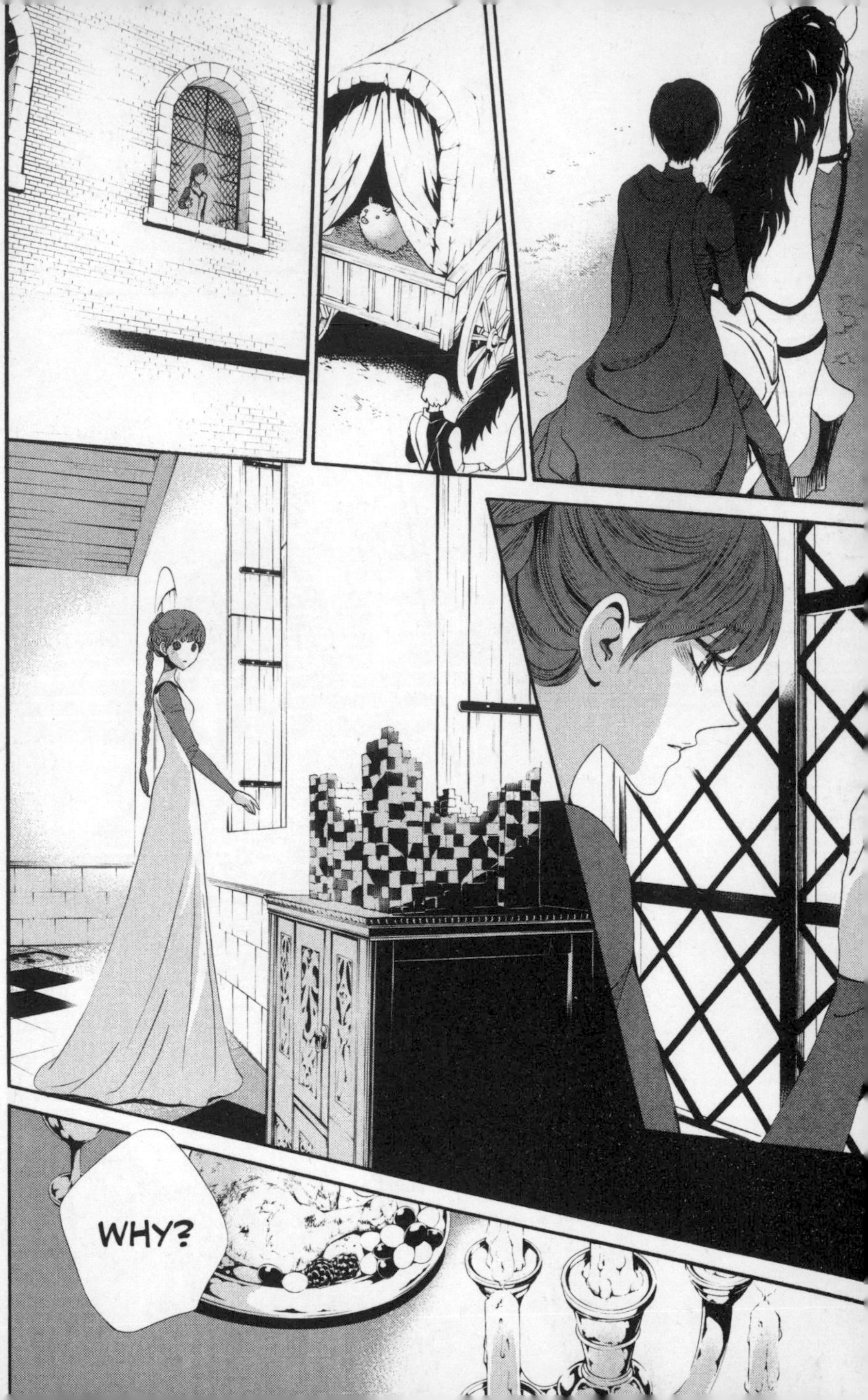
WHY?

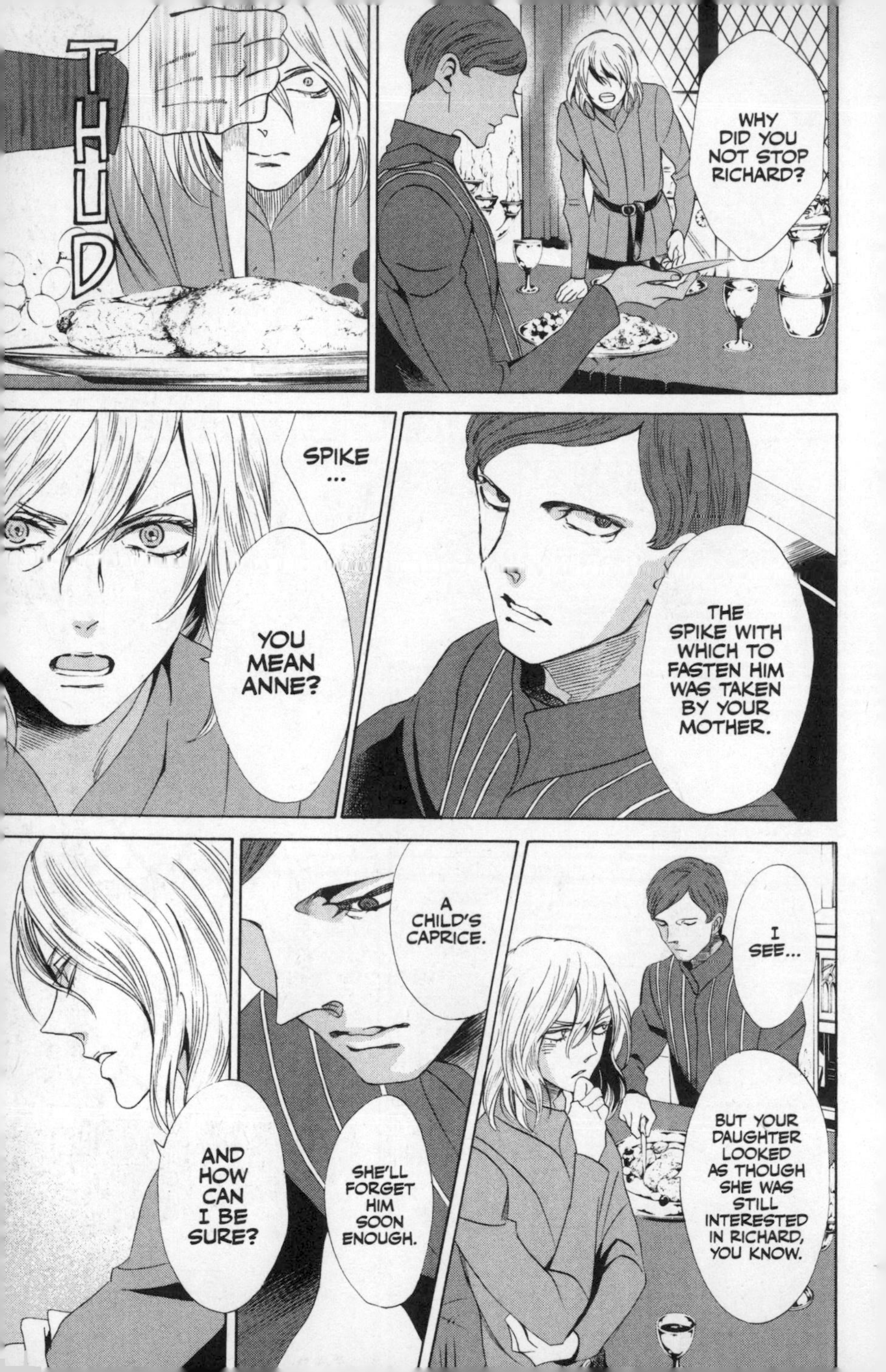
WHY DID YOU NOT STOP RICHARD?
THUD
THE SPIKE WITH WHICH TO FASTEN HIM WAS TAKEN BY YOUR MOTHER.
SPIKE ...
YOU MEAN ANNE?
I SEE...
BUT YOUR DAUGHTER LOOKED AS THOUGH SHE WAS STILL INTERESTED IN RICHARD, YOU KNOW.
A CHILD'S CAPRICE.
SHE'LL FORGET HIM SOON ENOUGH.
AND HOW CAN I BE SURE?

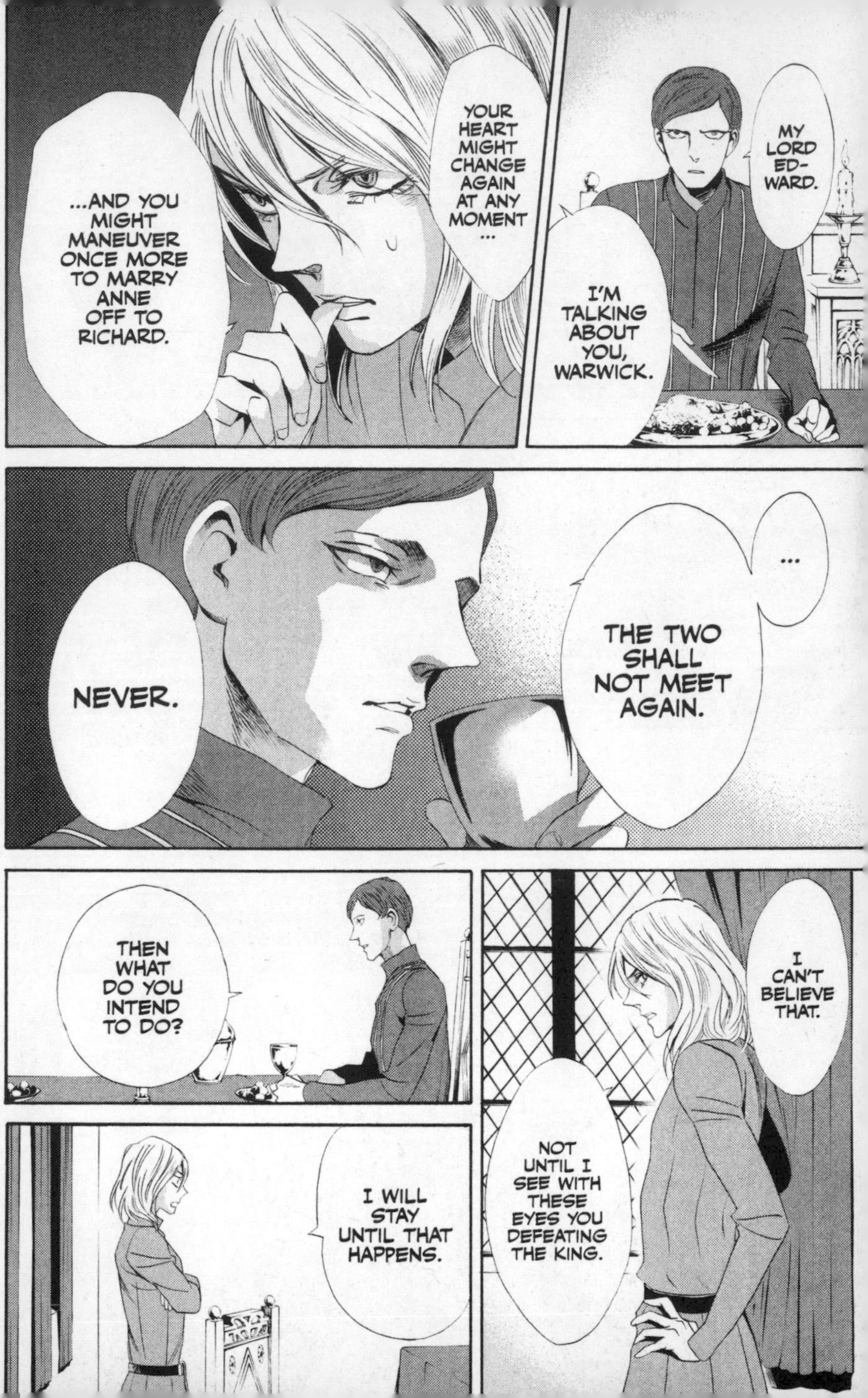
MY LORD ED-WARD.
I'M TALKING ABOUT YOU, WARWICK.
YOUR HEART MIGHT CHANGE AGAIN AT ANY MOMENT ...
...AND YOU MIGHT MANEUVER ONCE MORE TO MARRY ANNE OFF TO RICHARD.
...
THE TWO SHALL NOT MEET AGAIN.
NEVER.
I CAN'T BELIEVE THAT.
NOT UNTIL I SEE WITH THESE EYES YOU DEFEATING THE KING.
THEN WHAT DO YOU INTEND TO DO?
I WILL STAY UNTIL THAT HAPPENS.

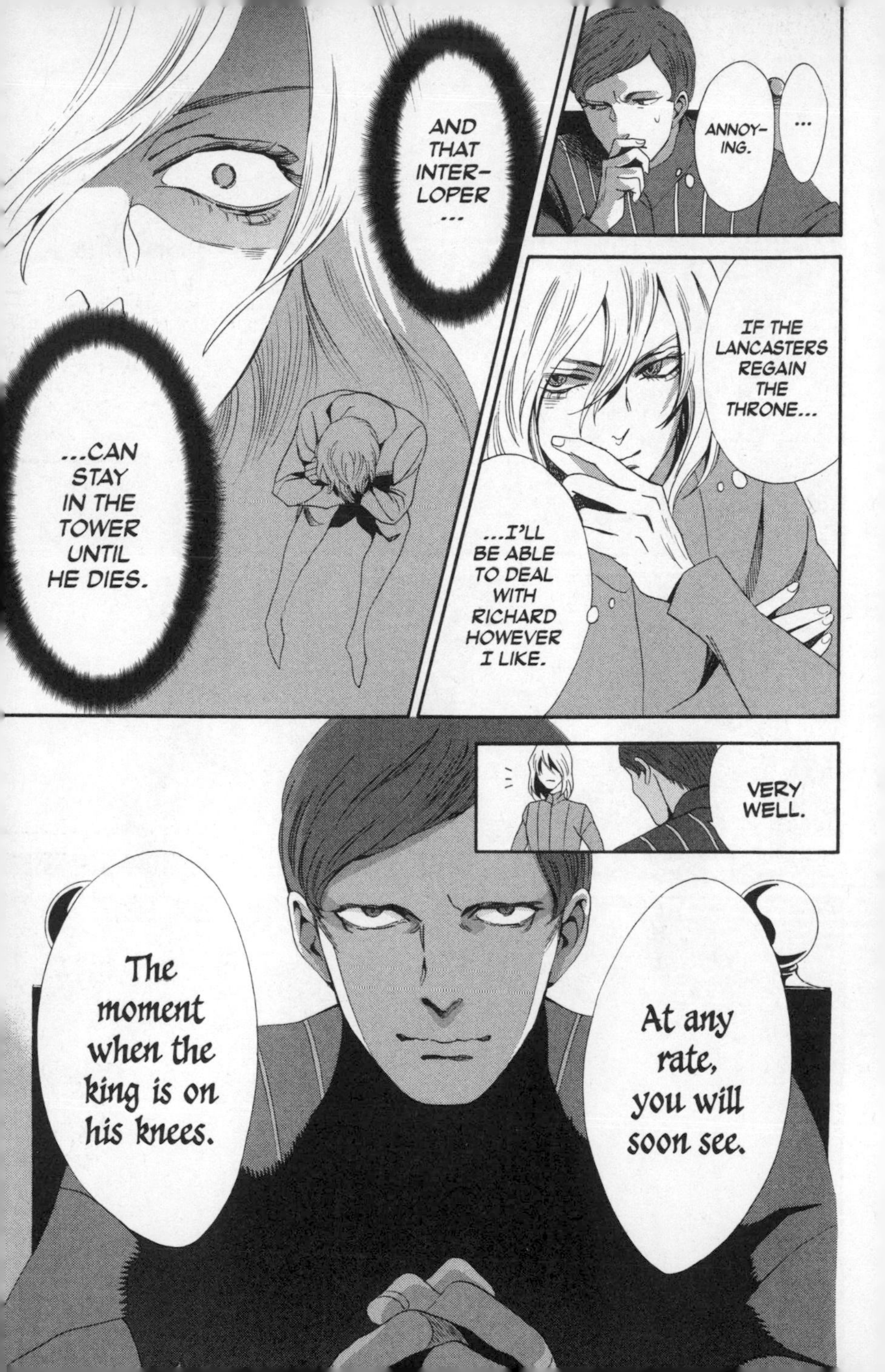
...
ANNOY-ING.
IF THE LANCASTERS REGAIN THE THRONE...
...I'LL BE ABLE TO DEAL WITH RICHARD HOWEVER I LIKE.
AND THAT INTER-LOPER...
...CAN STAY IN THE TOWER UNTIL HE DIES.
VERY WELL.
At any rate, you will soon see.
The moment when the king is on his knees.

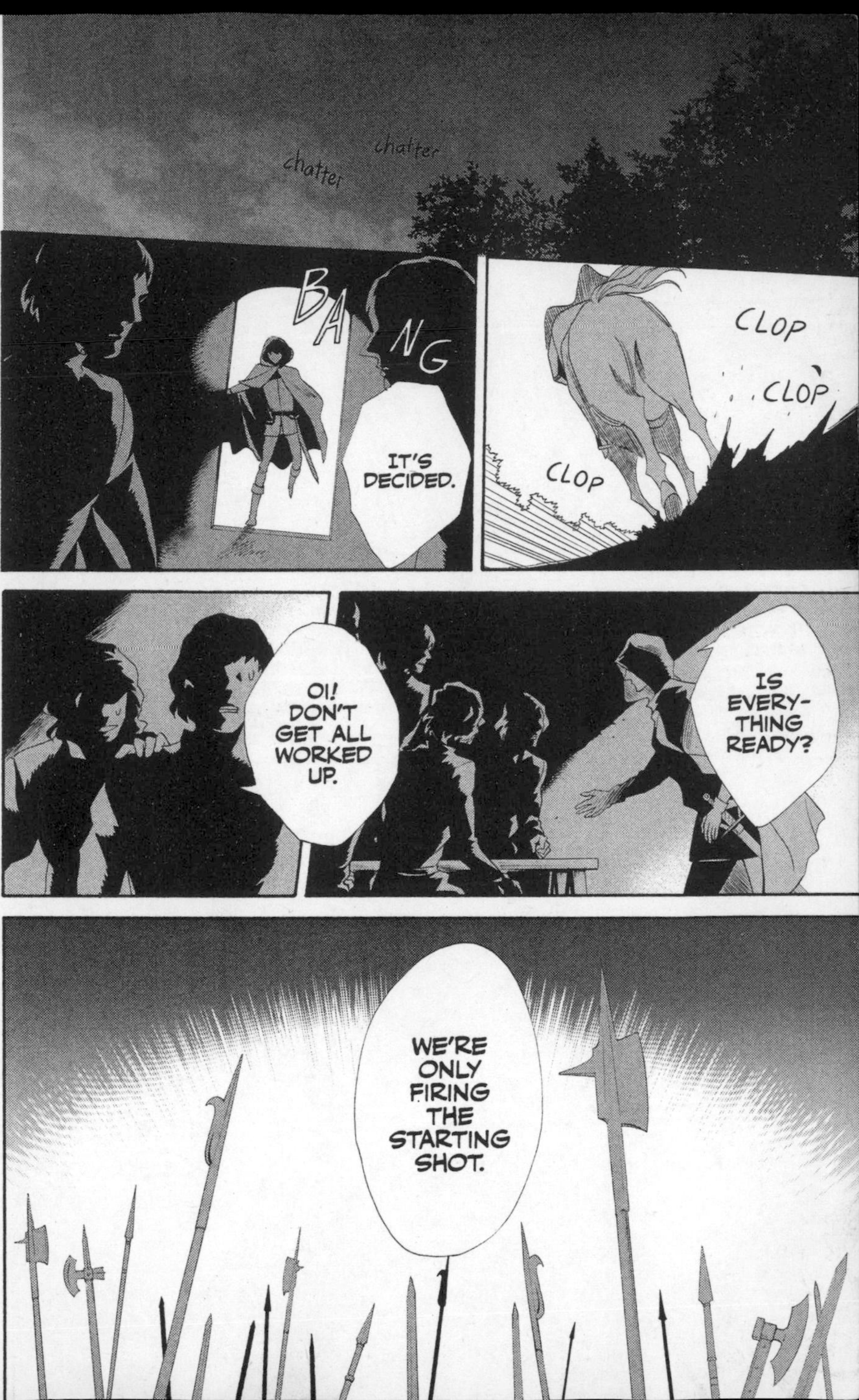
chatter
chatter
CLOP
CLOP
CLOP
BANG
IT'S DECIDED.
IS EVERYTHING READY?
OI! DON'T GET ALL WORKED UP.
WE'RE ONLY FIRING THE STARTING SHOT.

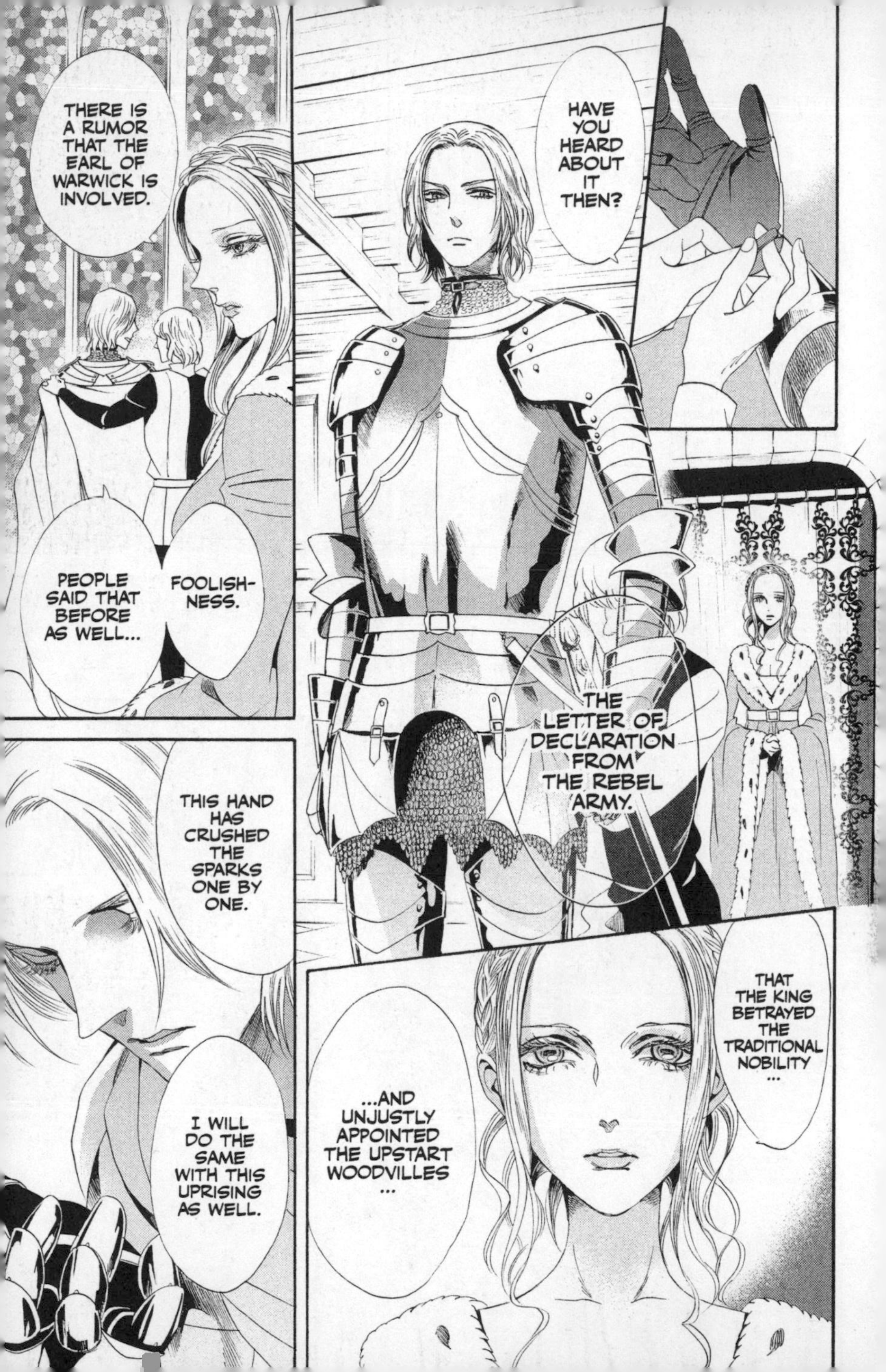
HAVE YOU HEARD ABOUT IT THEN?
THE LETTER OF DECLARATION FROM THE REBEL ARMY.
THERE IS A RUMOR THAT THE EARL OF WARWICK IS INVOLVED.
FOOLISHNESS.
PEOPLE SAID THAT BEFORE AS WELL...
THAT THE KING BETRAYED THE TRADITIONAL NOBILITY ...
...AND UNJUSTLY APPOINTED THE UPSTART WOODVILLES ...
THIS HAND HAS CRUSHED THE SPARKS ONE BY ONE.
I WILL DO THE SAME WITH THIS UPRISING AS WELL.

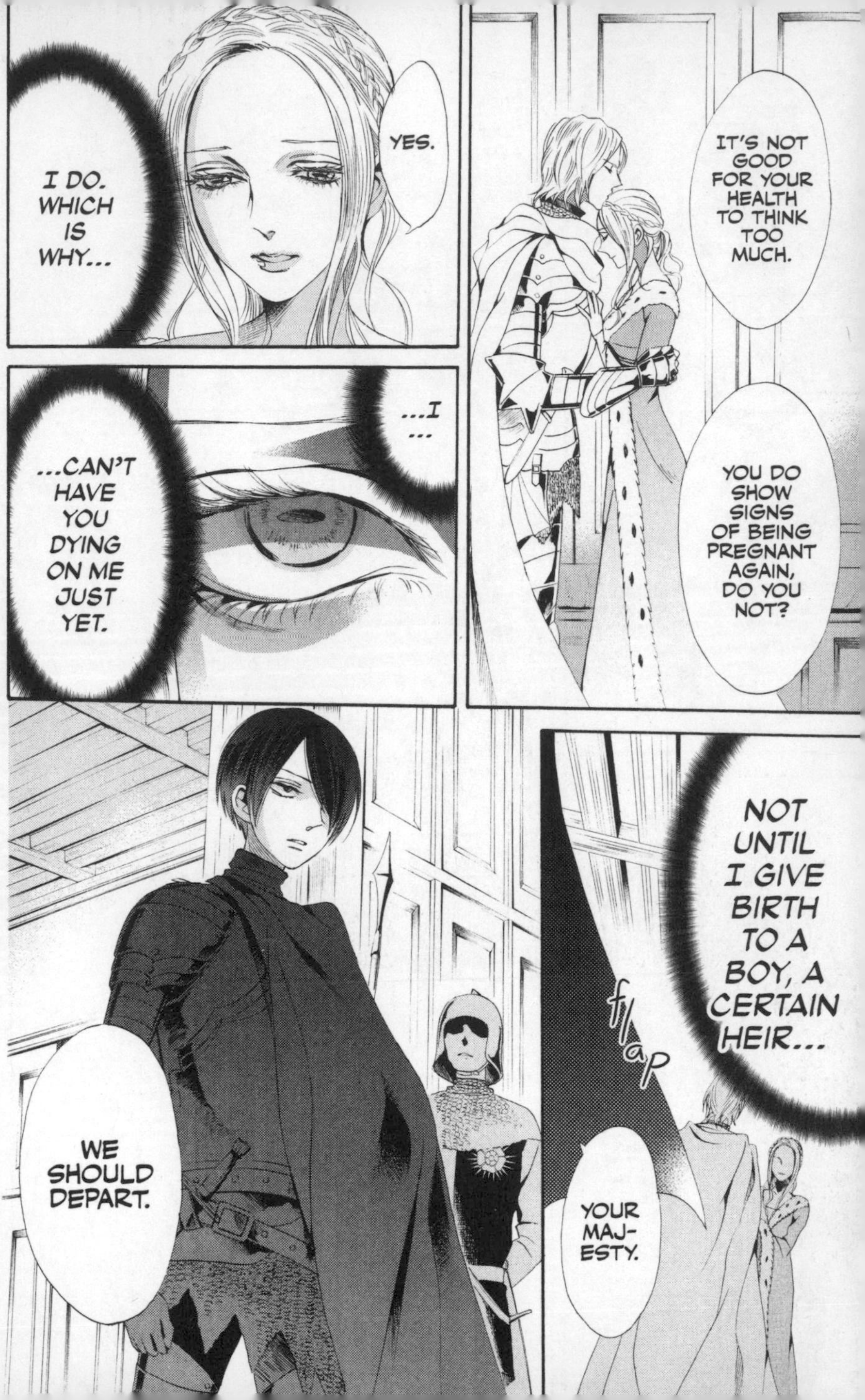
IT'S NOT GOOD FOR YOUR HEALTH TO THINK TOO MUCH.
YOU DO SHOW SIGNS OF BEING PREGNANT AGAIN, DO YOU NOT?
YES.
I DO. WHICH IS WHY...
...I ...
...CAN'T HAVE YOU DYING ON ME JUST YET.
NOT UNTIL I GIVE BIRTH TO A BOY, A CERTAIN HEIR...
flap
YOUR MAJ-ESTY.
WE SHOULD DEPART.

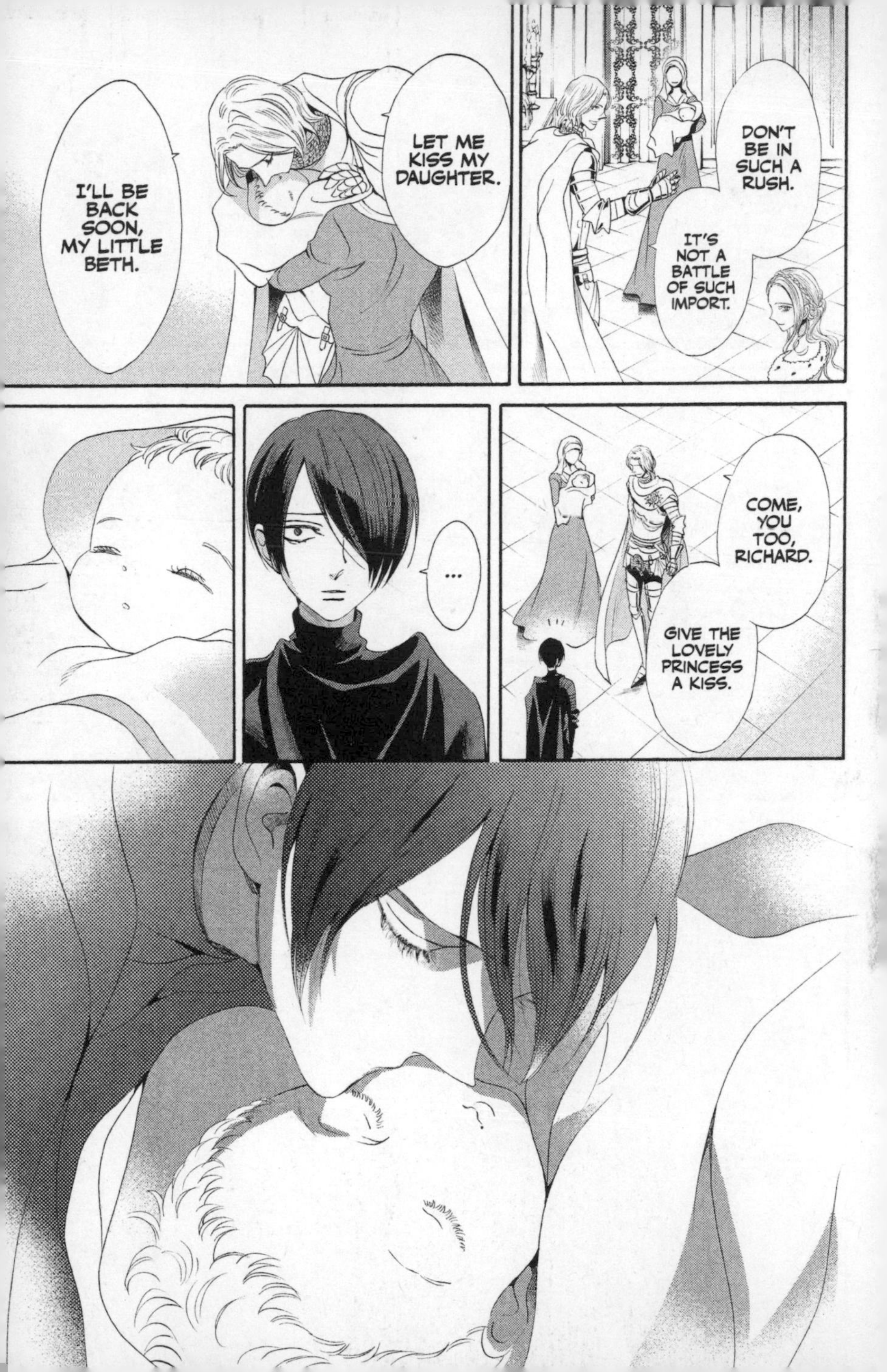
DON'T BE IN SUCH A RUSH.
IT'S NOT A BATTLE OF SUCH IMPORT.
LET ME KISS MY DAUGHTER.
I'LL BE BACK SOON, MY LITTLE BETH.
COME, YOU TOO, RICHARD.
GIVE THE LOVELY PRINCESS A KISS.
...

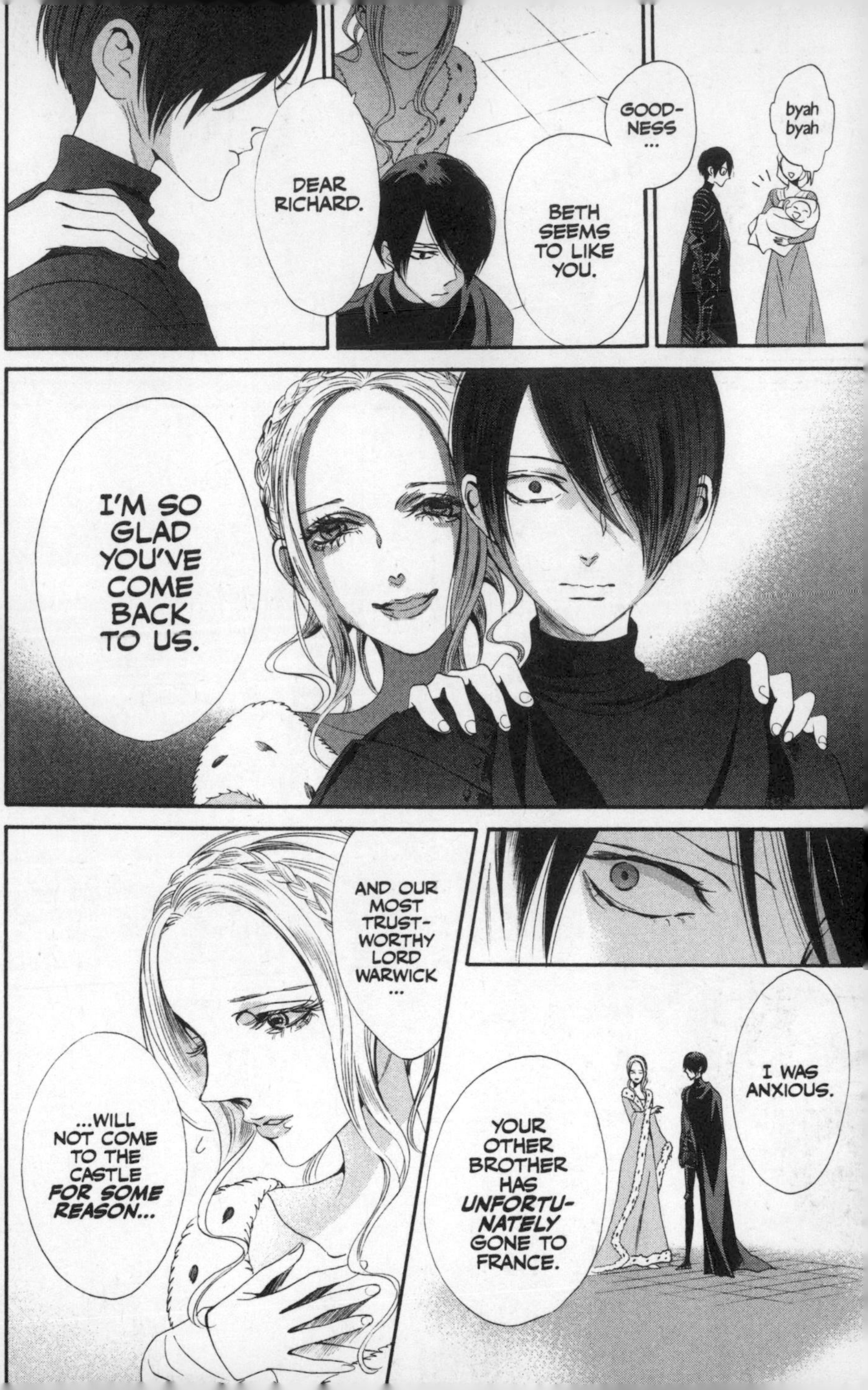
byah byah
GOODNESS...
BETH SEEMS TO LIKE YOU.
DEAR RICHARD.
I'M SO GLAD YOU'VE COME BACK TO US.
I WAS ANXIOUS.
YOUR OTHER BROTHER HAS *UNFORTUNATELY* GONE TO FRANCE.
AND OUR MOST TRUSTWORTHY LORD WARWICK...
...WILL NOT COME TO THE CASTLE *FOR SOME REASON...*

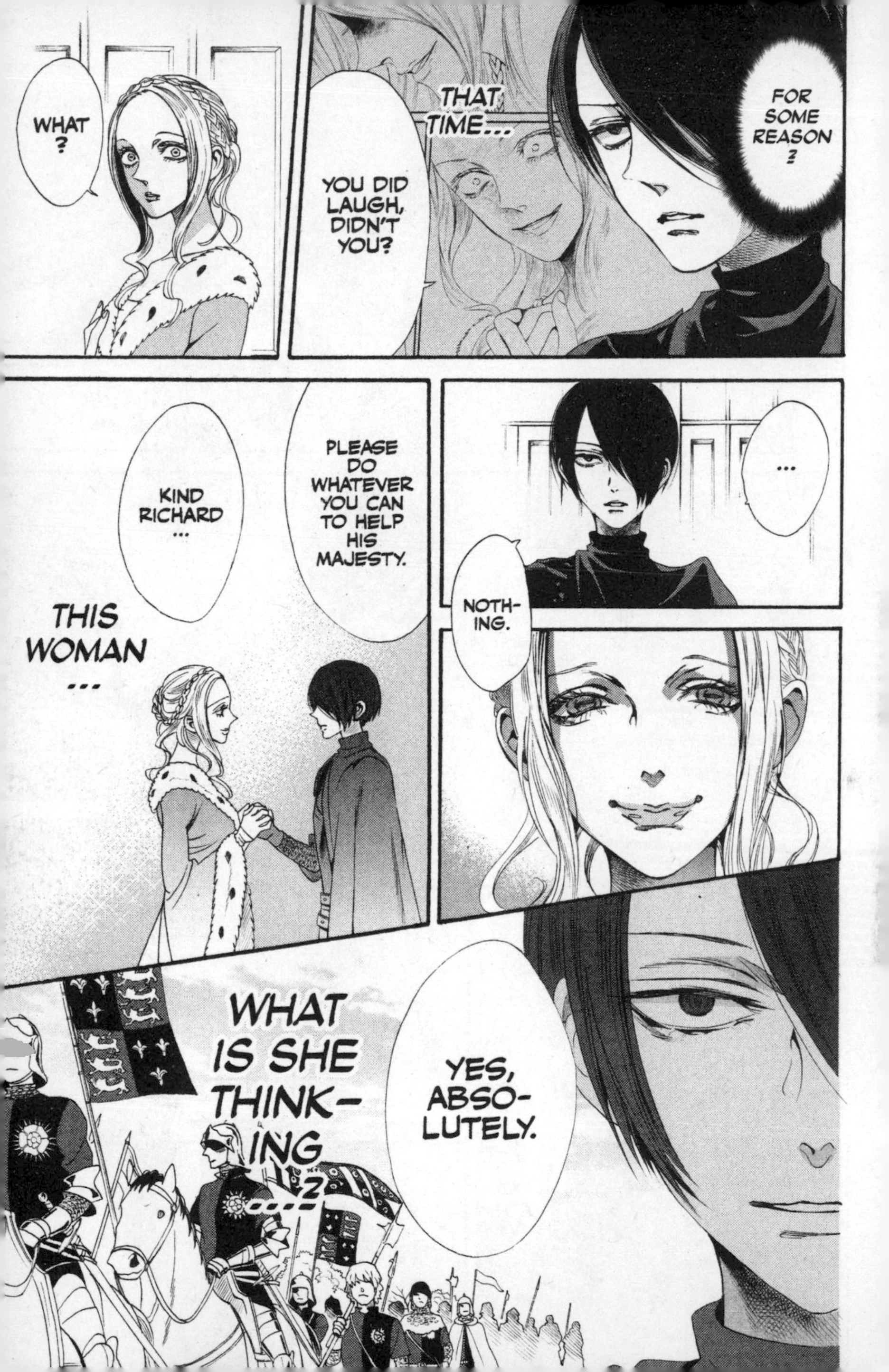
FOR SOME REASON?
THAT TIME...
YOU DID LAUGH, DIDN'T YOU?
WHAT?
...
NOTHING.
PLEASE DO WHATEVER YOU CAN TO HELP HIS MAJESTY.
KIND RICHARD...
THIS WOMAN...
YES, ABSOLUTELY.
WHAT IS SHE THINKING...?

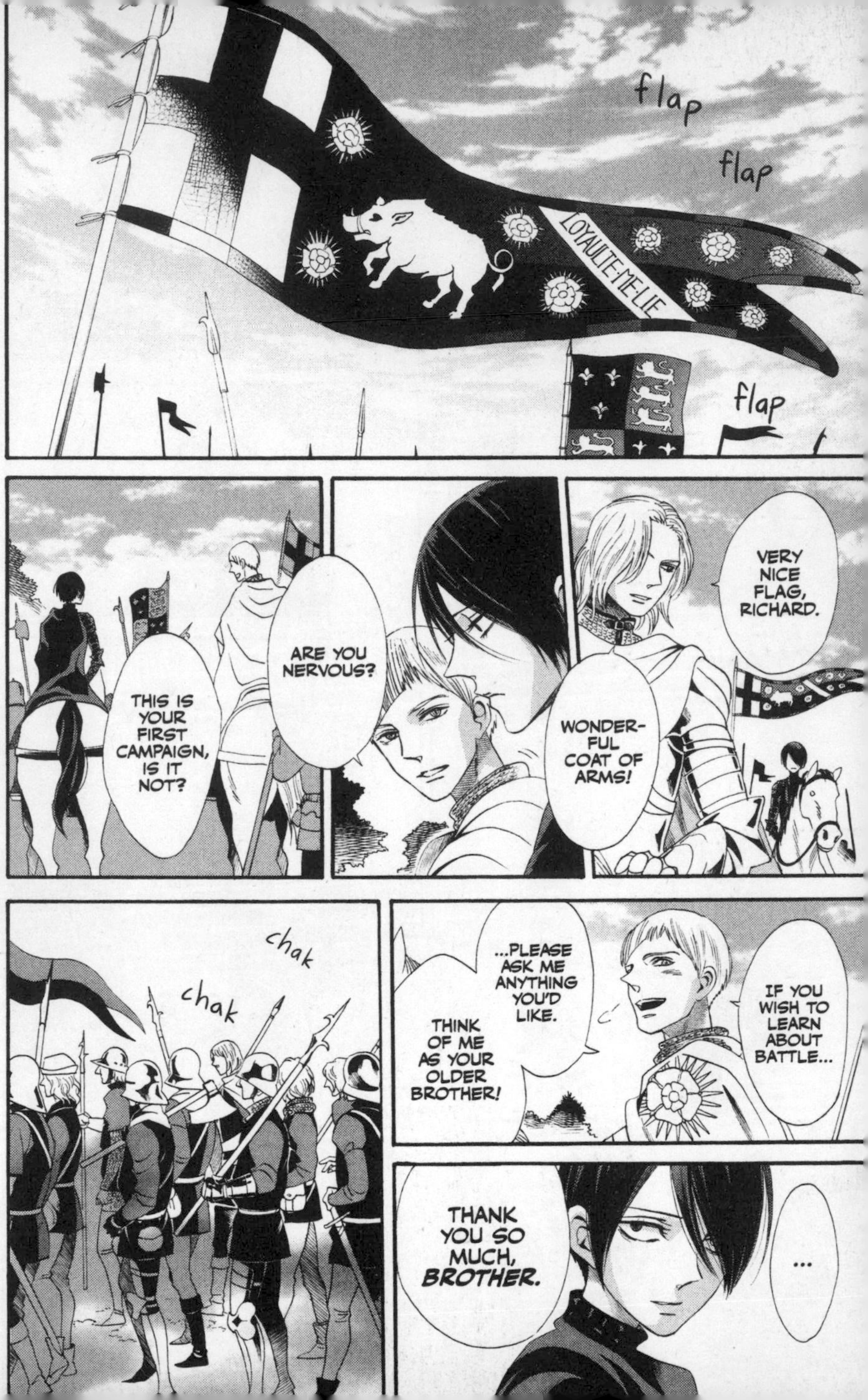
LOYAULTE·ME·LIE
flap
flap
flap
VERY NICE FLAG, RICHARD.
WONDERFUL COAT OF ARMS!
ARE YOU NERVOUS?
THIS IS YOUR FIRST CAMPAIGN, IS IT NOT?
IF YOU WISH TO LEARN ABOUT BATTLE...
...PLEASE ASK ME ANYTHING YOU'D LIKE.
THINK OF ME AS YOUR OLDER BROTHER!
...
THANK YOU SO MUCH, *BROTHER*.
chak
chak

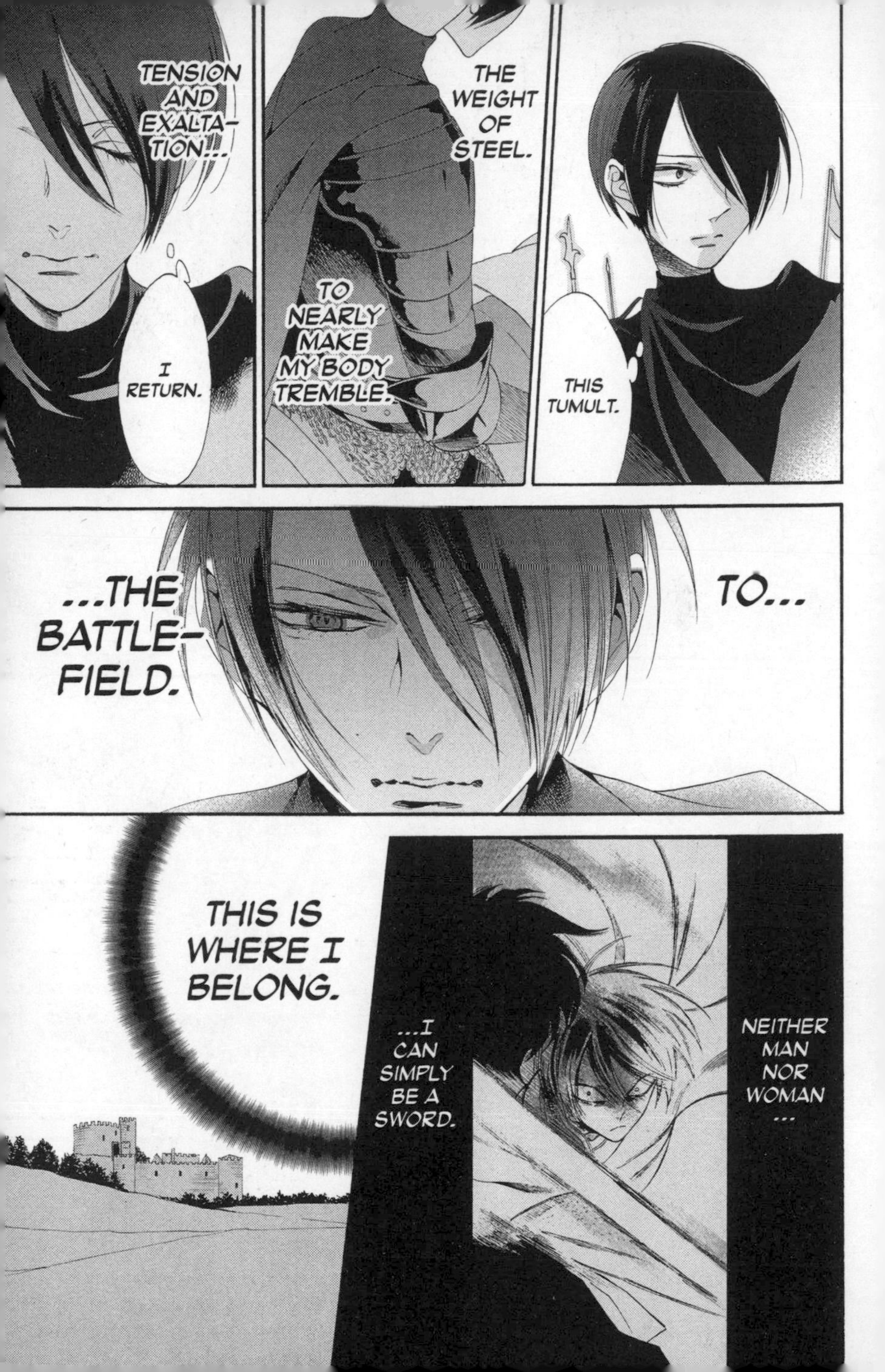
THIS TUMULT.
THE WEIGHT OF STEEL.
TO NEARLY MAKE MY BODY TREMBLE.
TENSION AND EXALTATION...
I RETURN.
TO...
...THE BATTLEFIELD.
NEITHER MAN NOR WOMAN...
...I CAN SIMPLY BE A SWORD.
THIS IS WHERE I BELONG.

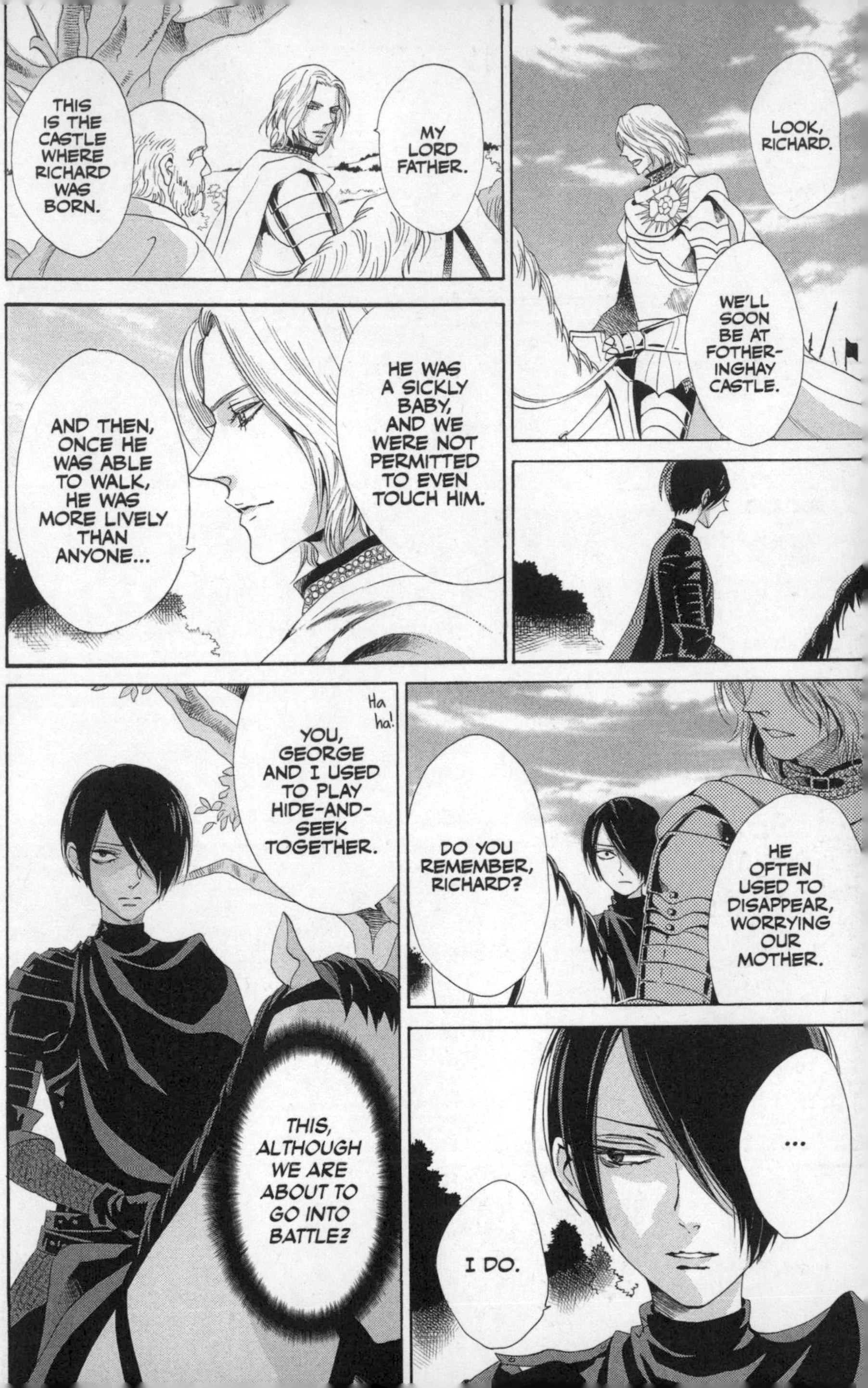
LOOK, RICHARD.
WE'LL SOON BE AT FOTHER-INGHAY CASTLE.
MY LORD FATHER.
THIS IS THE CASTLE WHERE RICHARD WAS BORN.
HE WAS A SICKLY BABY, AND WE WERE NOT PERMITTED TO EVEN TOUCH HIM.
AND THEN, ONCE HE WAS ABLE TO WALK, HE WAS MORE LIVELY THAN ANYONE...
HE OFTEN USED TO DISAPPEAR, WORRYING OUR MOTHER.
DO YOU REMEMBER, RICHARD?
...
I DO.
Ha ha!
YOU, GEORGE AND I USED TO PLAY HIDE-AND-SEEK TOGETHER.
THIS, ALTHOUGH WE ARE ABOUT TO GO INTO BATTLE?

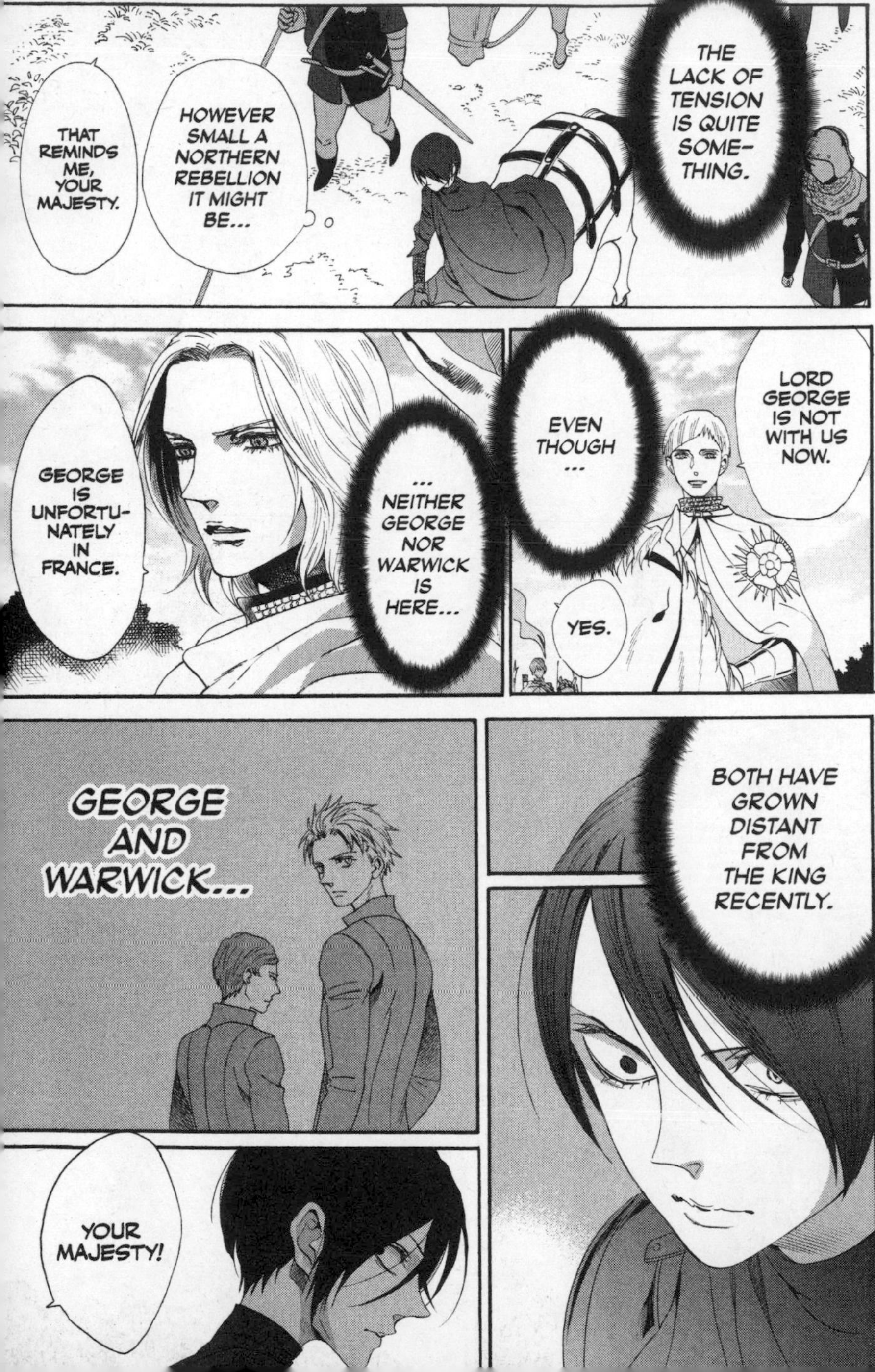
THE LACK OF TENSION IS QUITE SOME-THING.
HOWEVER SMALL A NORTHERN REBELLION IT MIGHT BE...
THAT REMINDS ME, YOUR MAJESTY.
LORD GEORGE IS NOT WITH US NOW.
EVEN THOUGH ...
YES.
...NEITHER GEORGE NOR WARWICK IS HERE...
GEORGE IS UNFORTU-NATELY IN FRANCE.
BOTH HAVE GROWN DISTANT FROM THE KING RECENTLY.
GEORGE AND WARWICK...
YOUR MAJESTY!

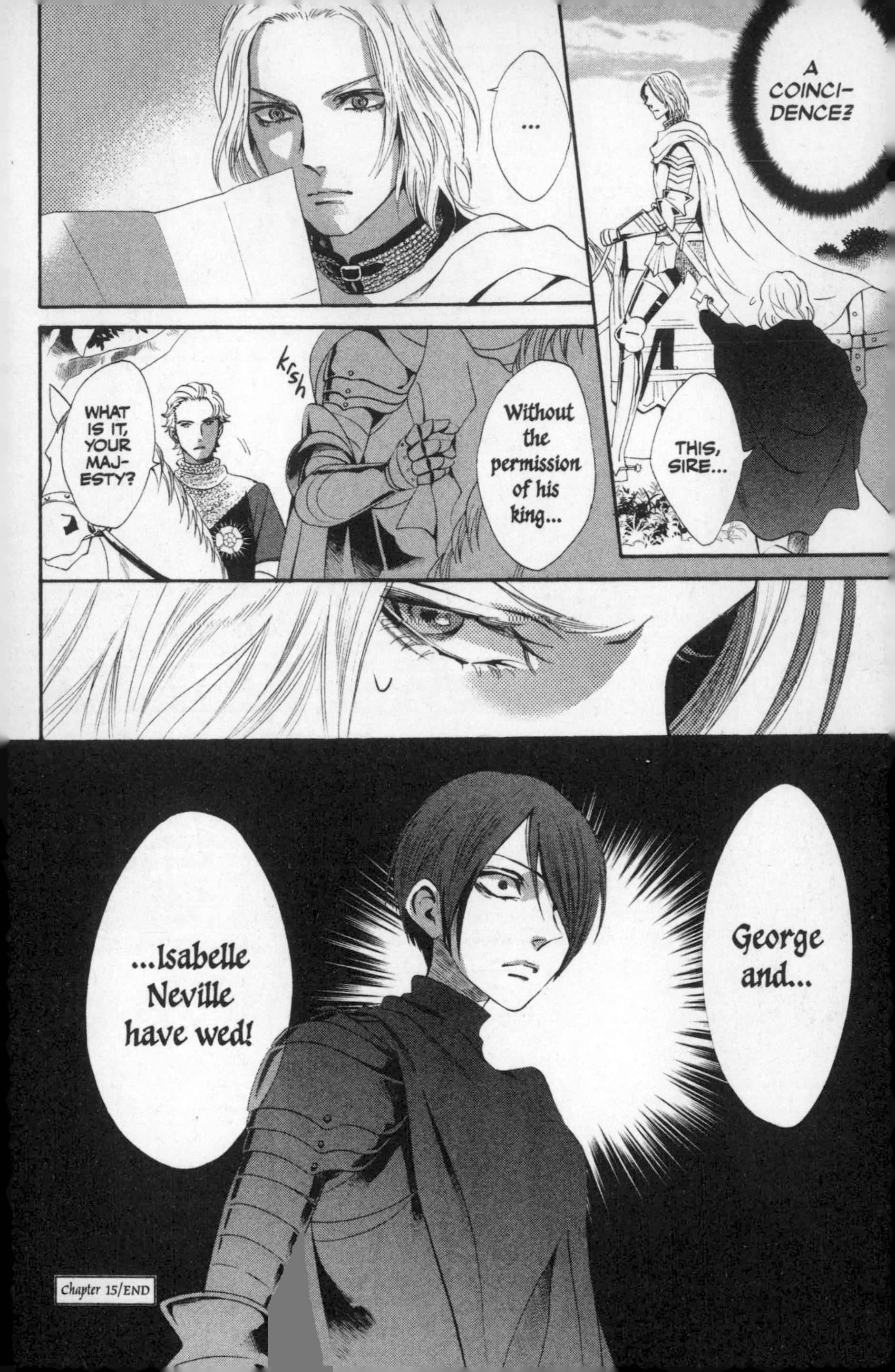
A COINCIDENCE?
THIS, SIRE...
...
Without the permission of his king...
krsh
WHAT IS IT, YOUR MAJESTY?
George and...
...Isabelle Neville have wed!
Chapter 15/END

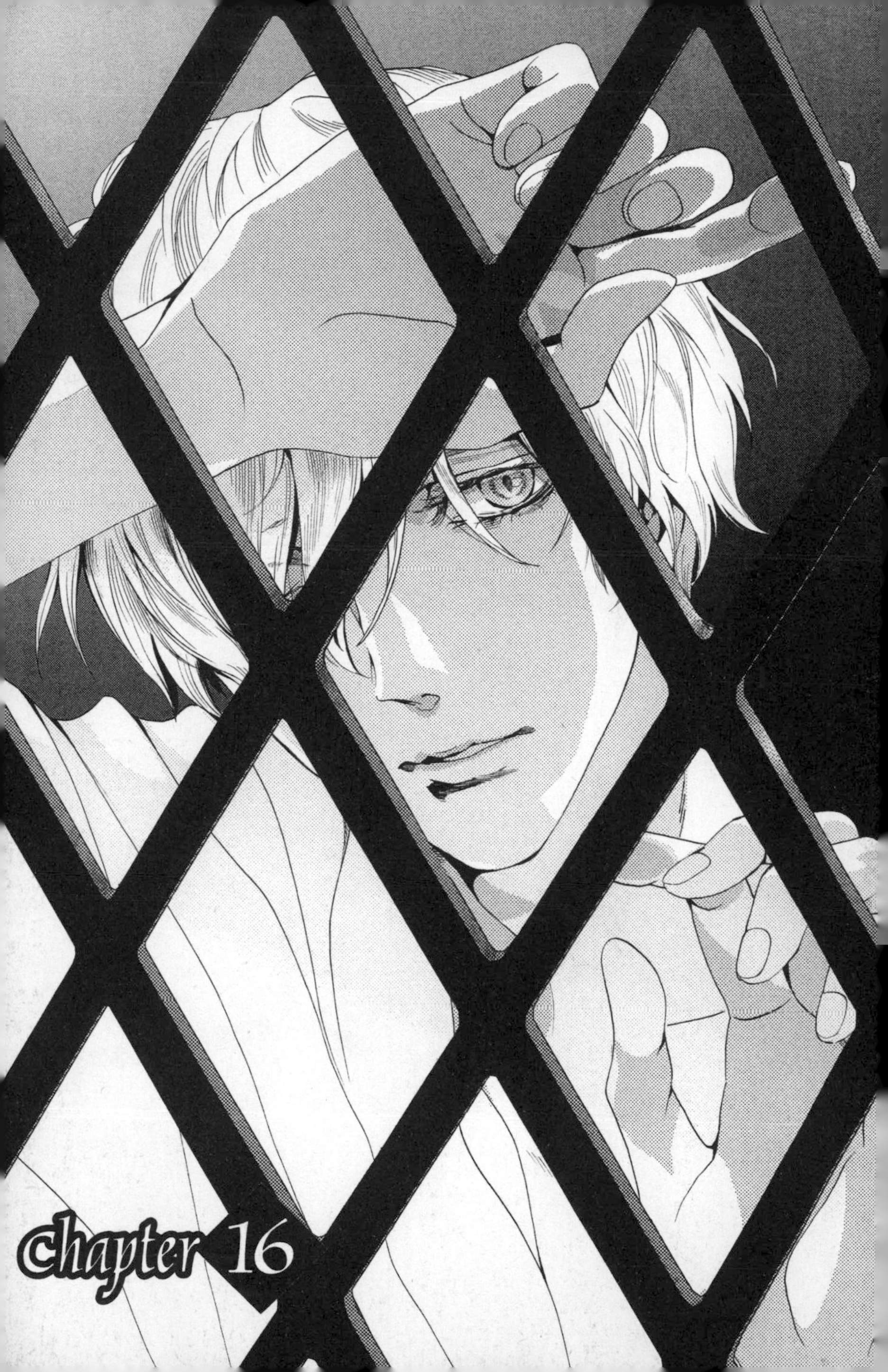
chapter 16

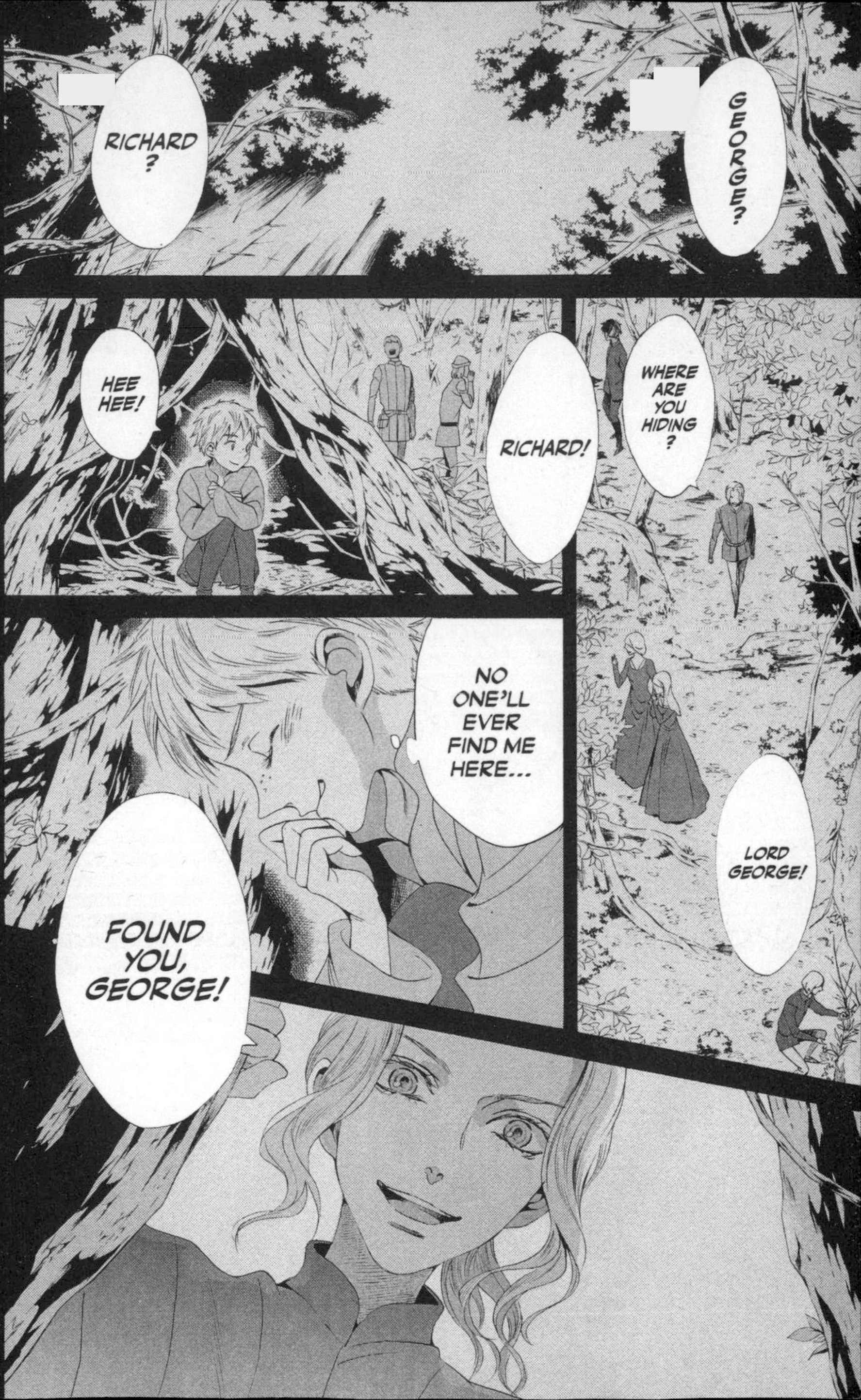
GEORGE?
RICHARD?
WHERE ARE YOU HIDING?
LORD GEORGE!
RICHARD!
HEE HEE!
NO ONE'LL EVER FIND ME HERE...
FOUND YOU, GEORGE!

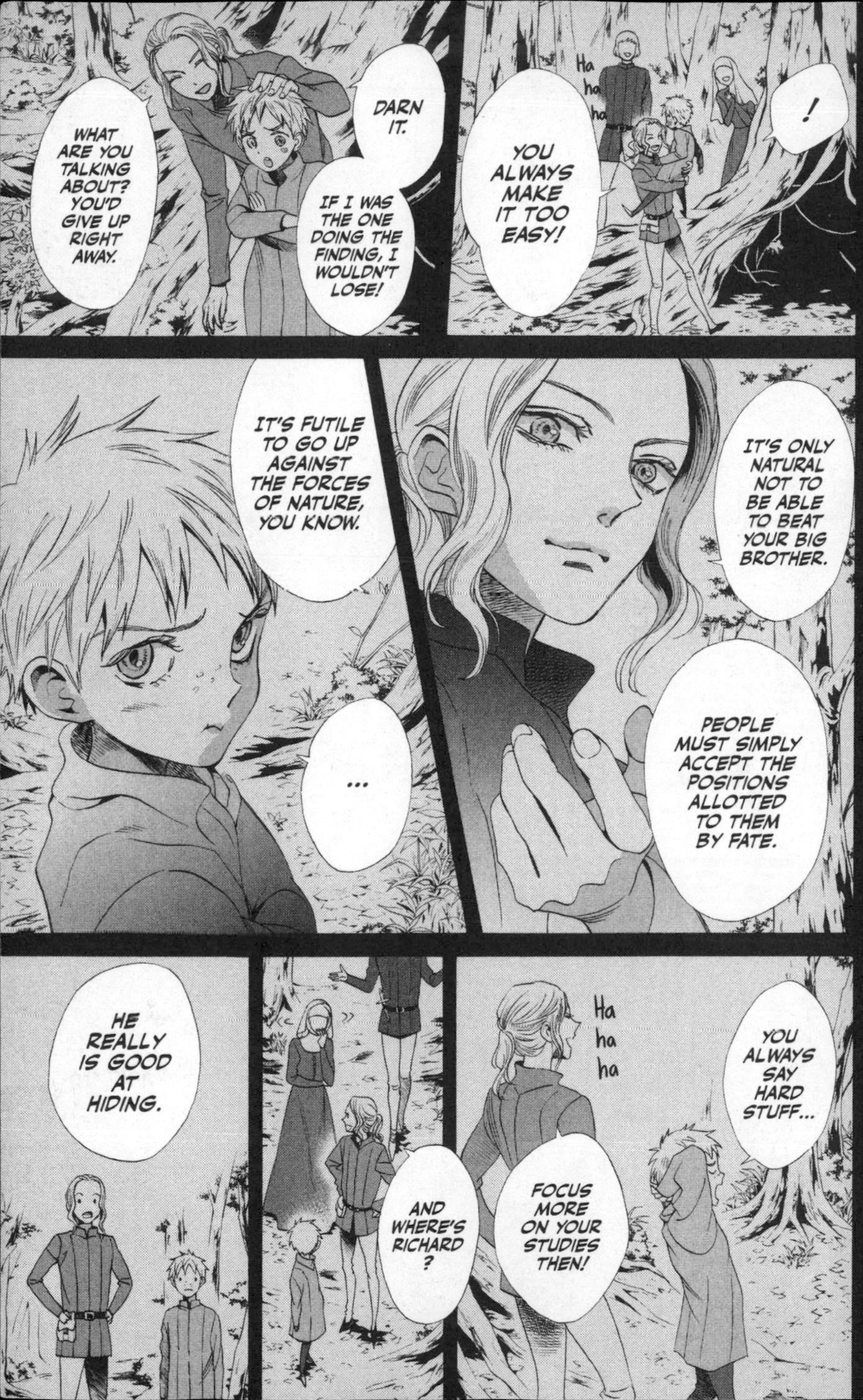
!
Ha ha ha
YOU ALWAYS MAKE IT TOO EASY!
DARN IT.
IF I WAS THE ONE DOING THE FINDING, I WOULDN'T LOSE!
WHAT ARE YOU TALKING ABOUT? YOU'D GIVE UP RIGHT AWAY.
IT'S ONLY NATURAL NOT TO BE ABLE TO BEAT YOUR BIG BROTHER.
PEOPLE MUST SIMPLY ACCEPT THE POSITIONS ALLOTTED TO THEM BY FATE.
IT'S FUTILE TO GO UP AGAINST THE FORCES OF NATURE, YOU KNOW.
...
YOU ALWAYS SAY HARD STUFF...
Ha ha ha
FOCUS MORE ON YOUR STUDIES THEN!
AND WHERE'S RICHARD?
HE REALLY IS GOOD AT HIDING.

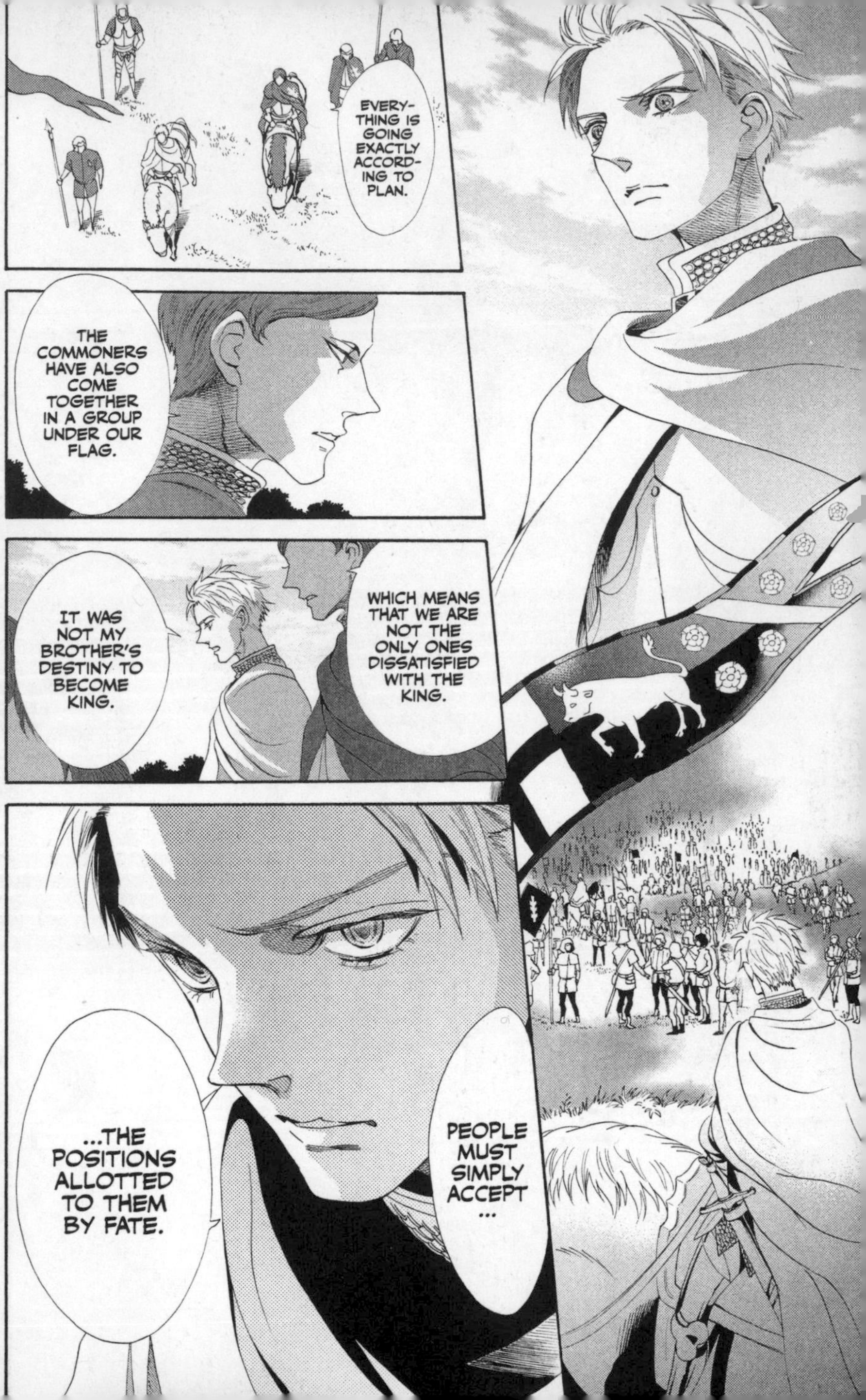

EVERY-THING IS GOING EXACTLY ACCORD-ING TO PLAN.
THE COMMONERS HAVE ALSO COME TOGETHER IN A GROUP UNDER OUR FLAG.
WHICH MEANS THAT WE ARE NOT THE ONLY ONES DISSATISFIED WITH THE KING.
IT WAS NOT MY BROTHER'S DESTINY TO BECOME KING.
PEOPLE MUST SIMPLY ACCEPT...
...THE POSITIONS ALLOTTED TO THEM BY FATE.

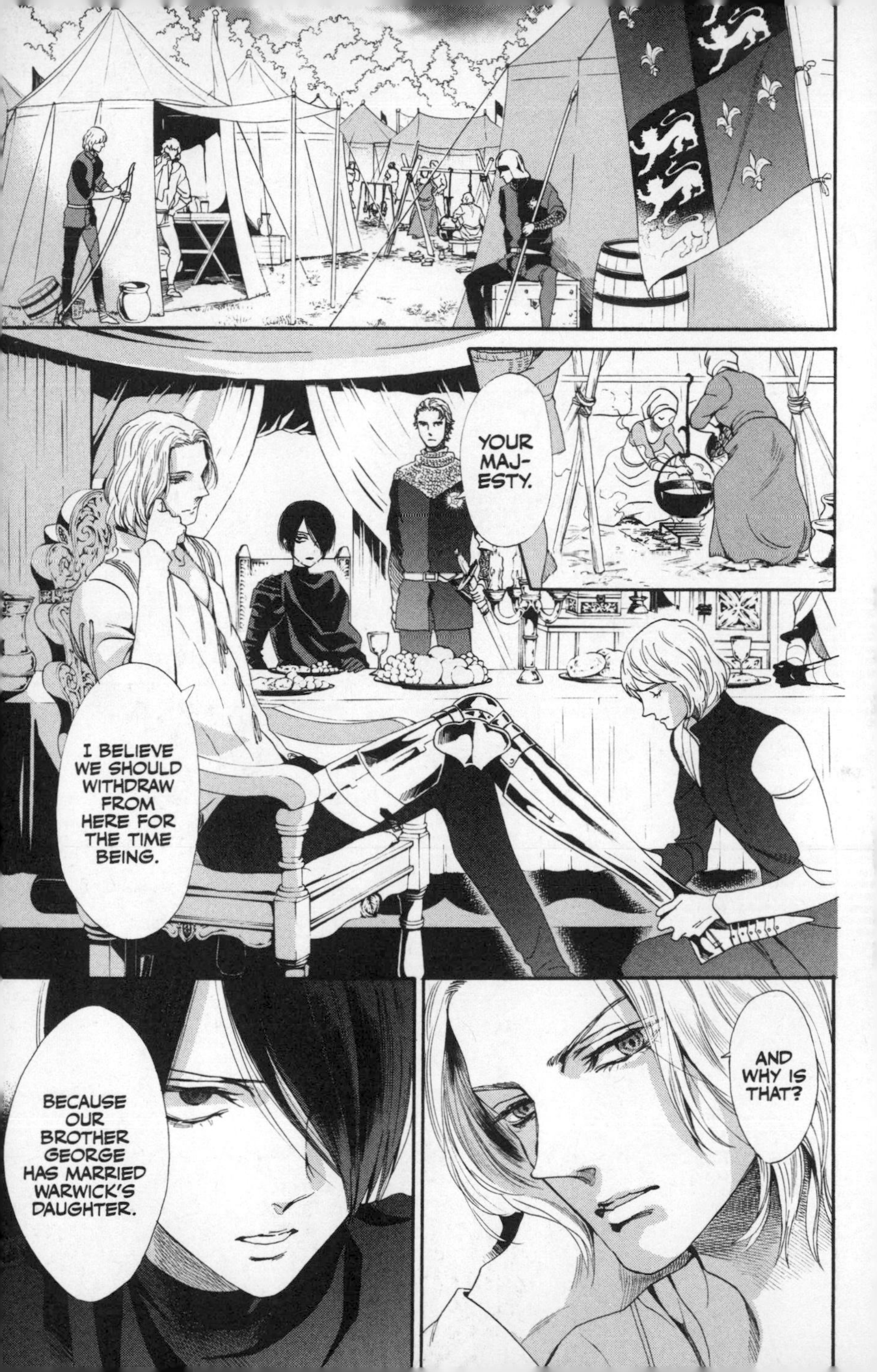
YOUR MAJ-ESTY.
I BELIEVE WE SHOULD WITHDRAW FROM HERE FOR THE TIME BEING.
AND WHY IS THAT?
BECAUSE OUR BROTHER GEORGE HAS MARRIED WARWICK'S DAUGHTER.

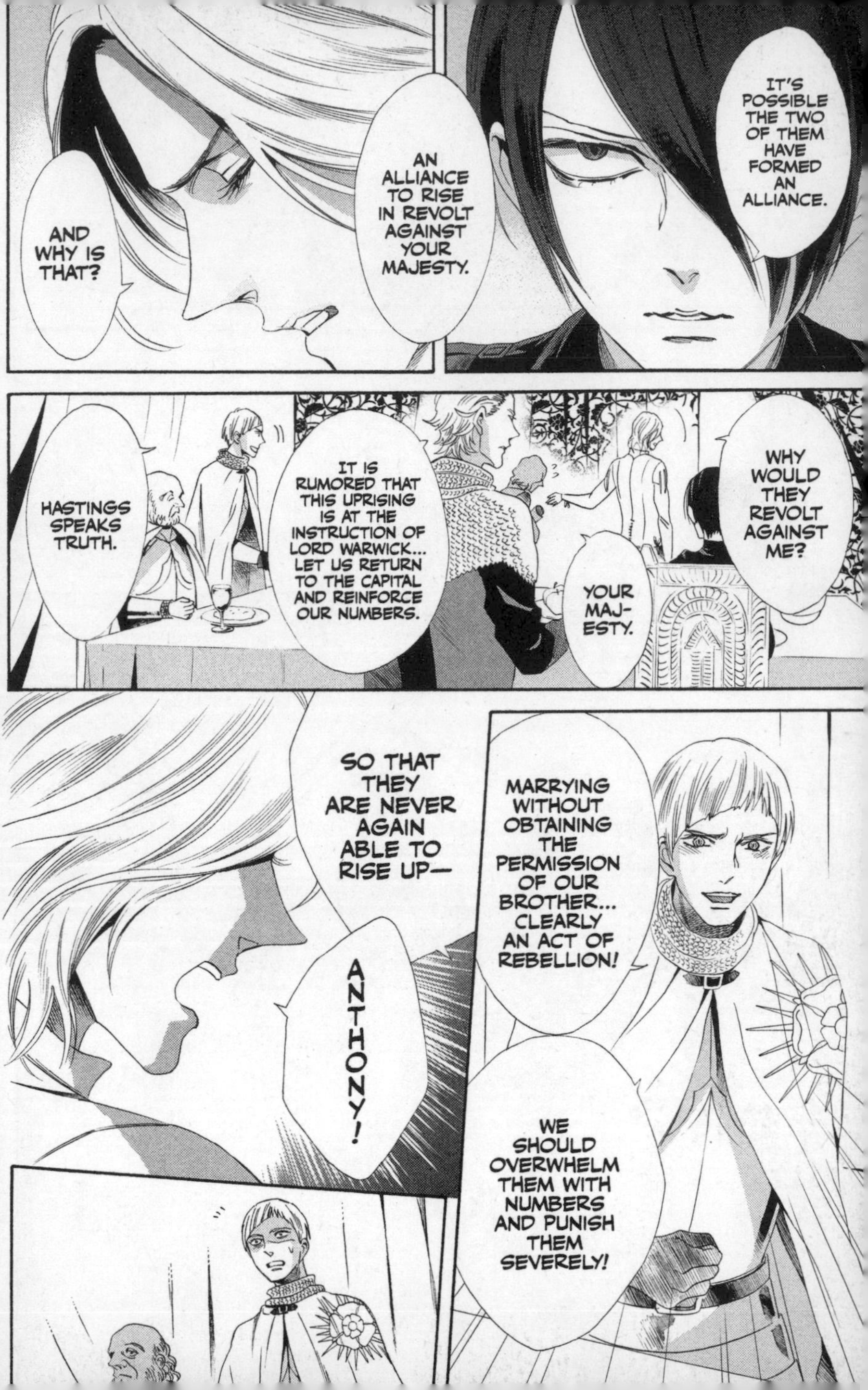
IT'S POSSIBLE THE TWO OF THEM HAVE FORMED AN ALLIANCE.
AN ALLIANCE TO RISE IN REVOLT AGAINST YOUR MAJESTY.
AND WHY IS THAT?
WHY WOULD THEY REVOLT AGAINST ME?
YOUR MAJ-ESTY.
IT IS RUMORED THAT THIS UPRISING IS AT THE INSTRUCTION OF LORD WARWICK... LET US RETURN TO THE CAPITAL AND REINFORCE OUR NUMBERS.
HASTINGS SPEAKS TRUTH.
MARRYING WITHOUT OBTAINING THE PERMISSION OF OUR BROTHER... CLEARLY AN ACT OF REBELLION!
WE SHOULD OVERWHELM THEM WITH NUMBERS AND PUNISH THEM SEVERELY!
SO THAT THEY ARE NEVER AGAIN ABLE TO RISE UP—
ANTHONY!

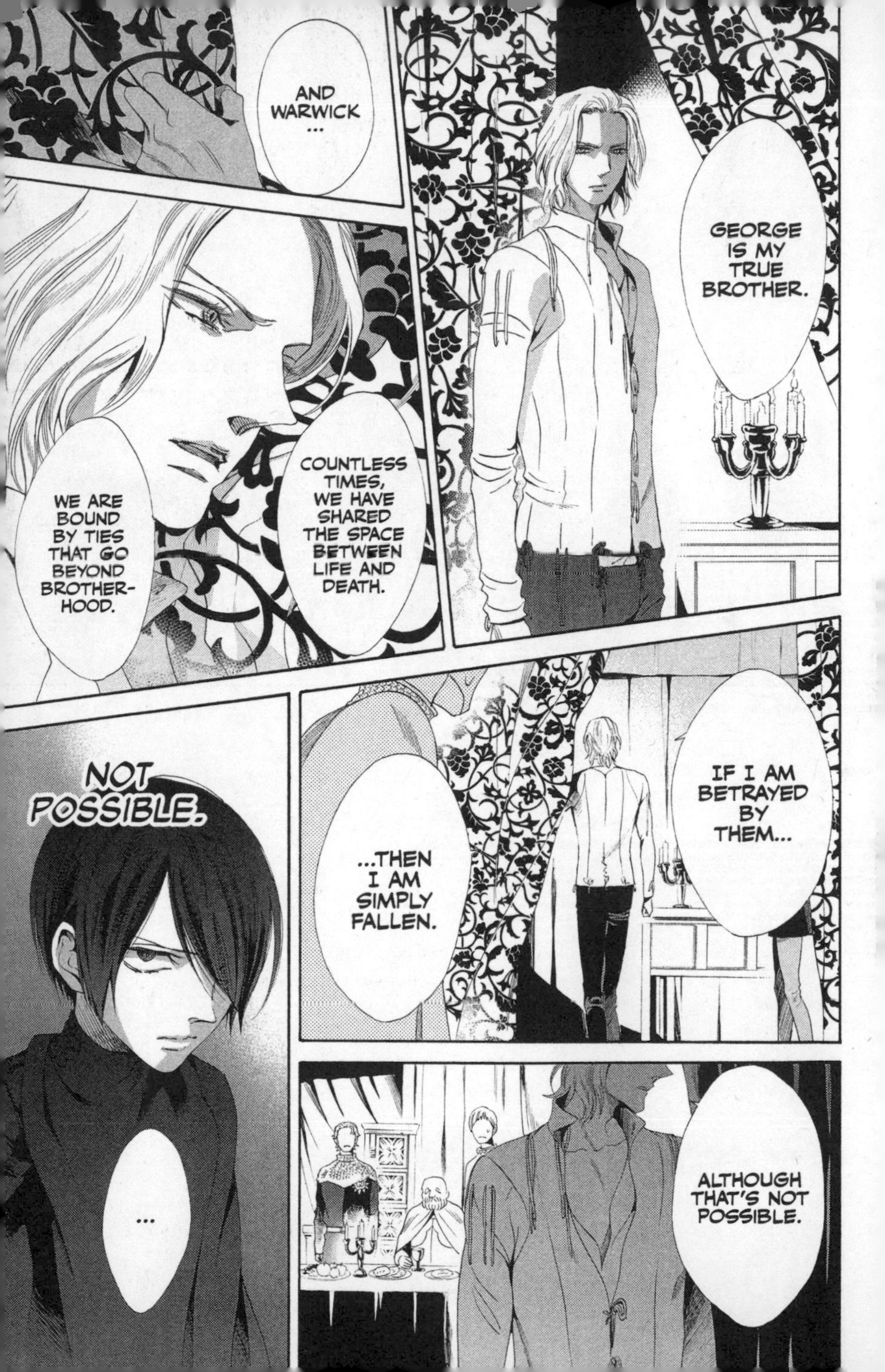
GEORGE IS MY TRUE BROTHER.
AND WARWICK ...
COUNTLESS TIMES, WE HAVE SHARED THE SPACE BETWEEN LIFE AND DEATH.
WE ARE BOUND BY TIES THAT GO BEYOND BROTHER-HOOD.
IF I AM BETRAYED BY THEM...
...THEN I AM SIMPLY FALLEN.
ALTHOUGH THAT'S NOT POSSIBLE.
NOT POSSIBLE.
...

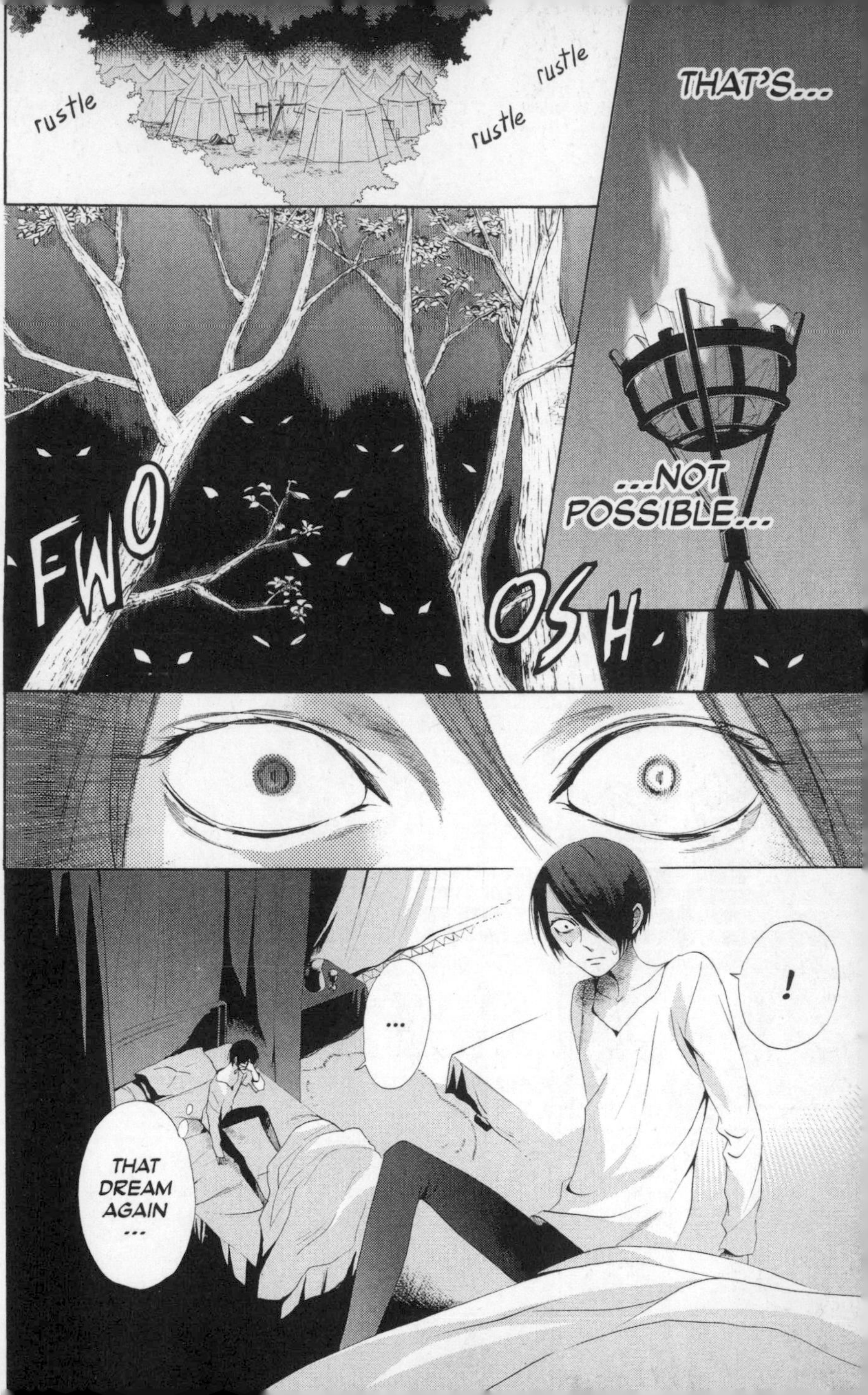
THAT'S...
...NOT POSSIBLE...
rustle
rustle
rustle
FWOOSH
!
...
THAT DREAM AGAIN...

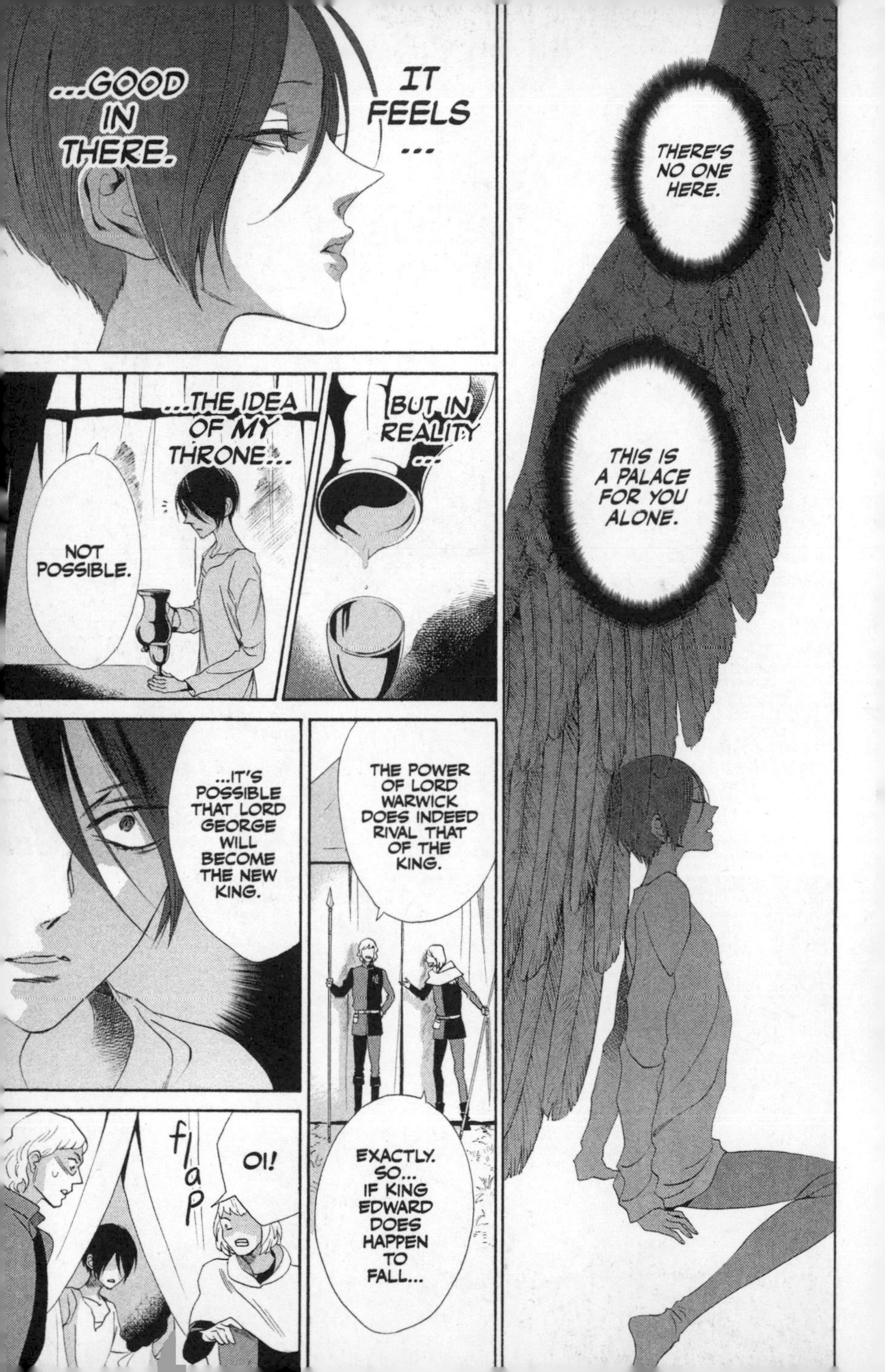
THERE'S NO ONE HERE.
THIS IS A PALACE FOR YOU ALONE.
IT FEELS...
...GOOD IN THERE.
BUT IN REALITY...
...THE IDEA OF MY THRONE...
NOT POSSIBLE.
THE POWER OF LORD WARWICK DOES INDEED RIVAL THAT OF THE KING.
EXACTLY. SO... IF KING EDWARD DOES HAPPEN TO FALL...
...IT'S POSSIBLE THAT LORD GEORGE WILL BECOME THE NEW KING.
OI!
flap

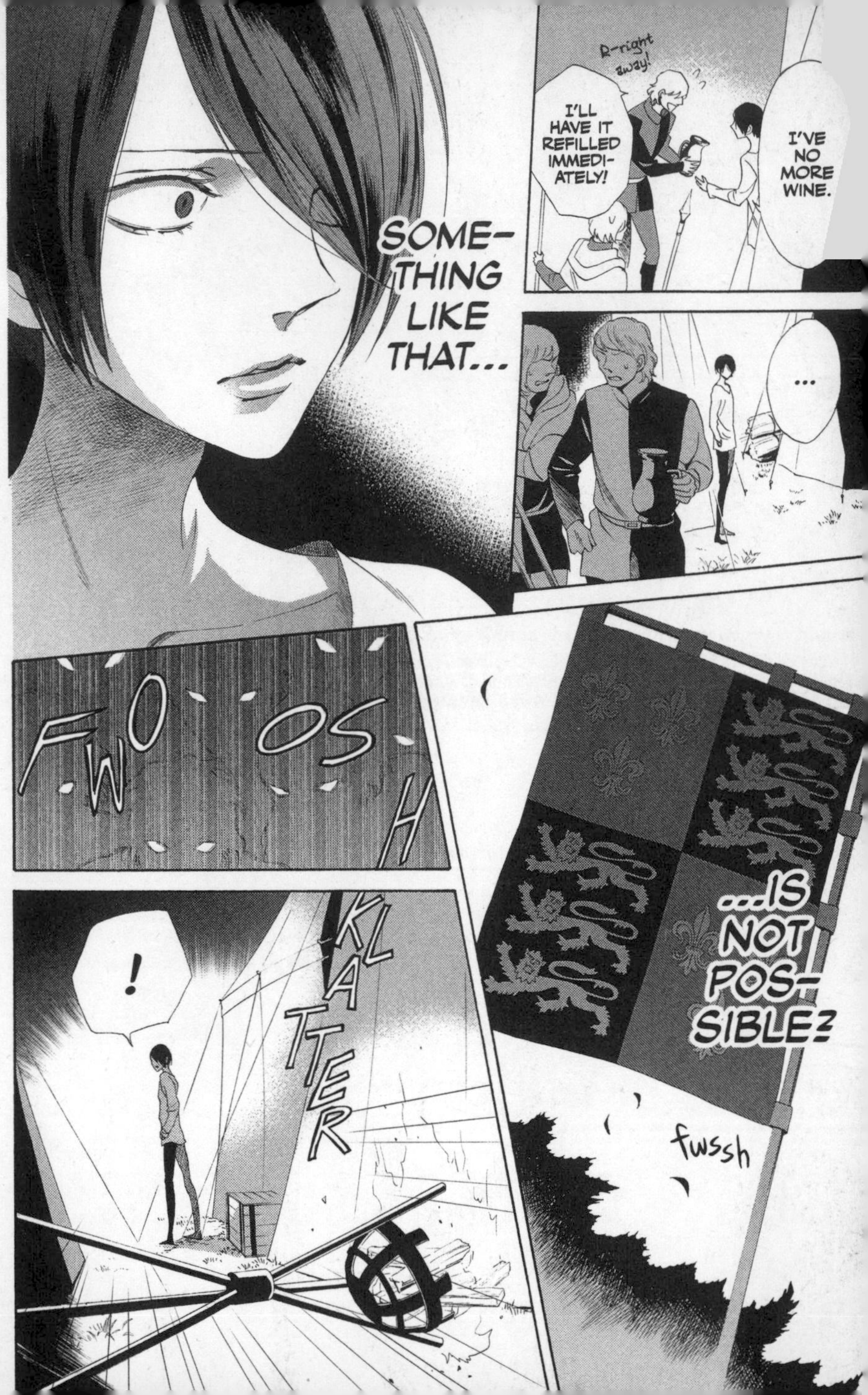
I'VE NO MORE WINE.
I'LL HAVE IT REFILLED IMMEDIATELY!
R-right away!
...
SOMETHING LIKE THAT...
...IS NOT POSSIBLE?
fwssh
FWOOSH
!
KLATTER

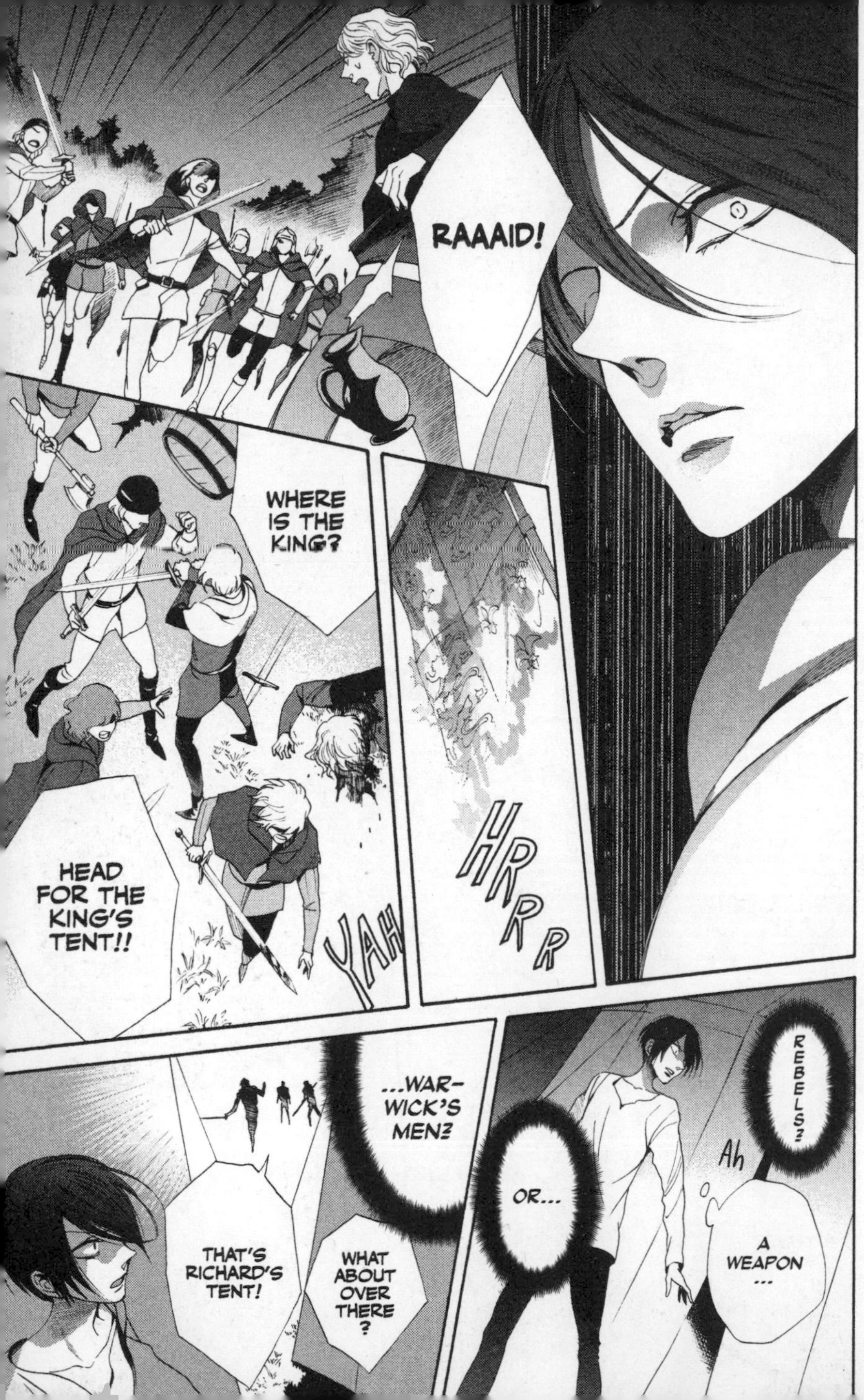
RAAAID!
HRRR
WHERE IS THE KING?
HEAD FOR THE KING'S TENT!!
YAH
REBELS?
OR...
...WARWICK'S MEN?
Ah
A WEAPON...
WHAT ABOUT OVER THERE?
THAT'S RICHARD'S TENT!

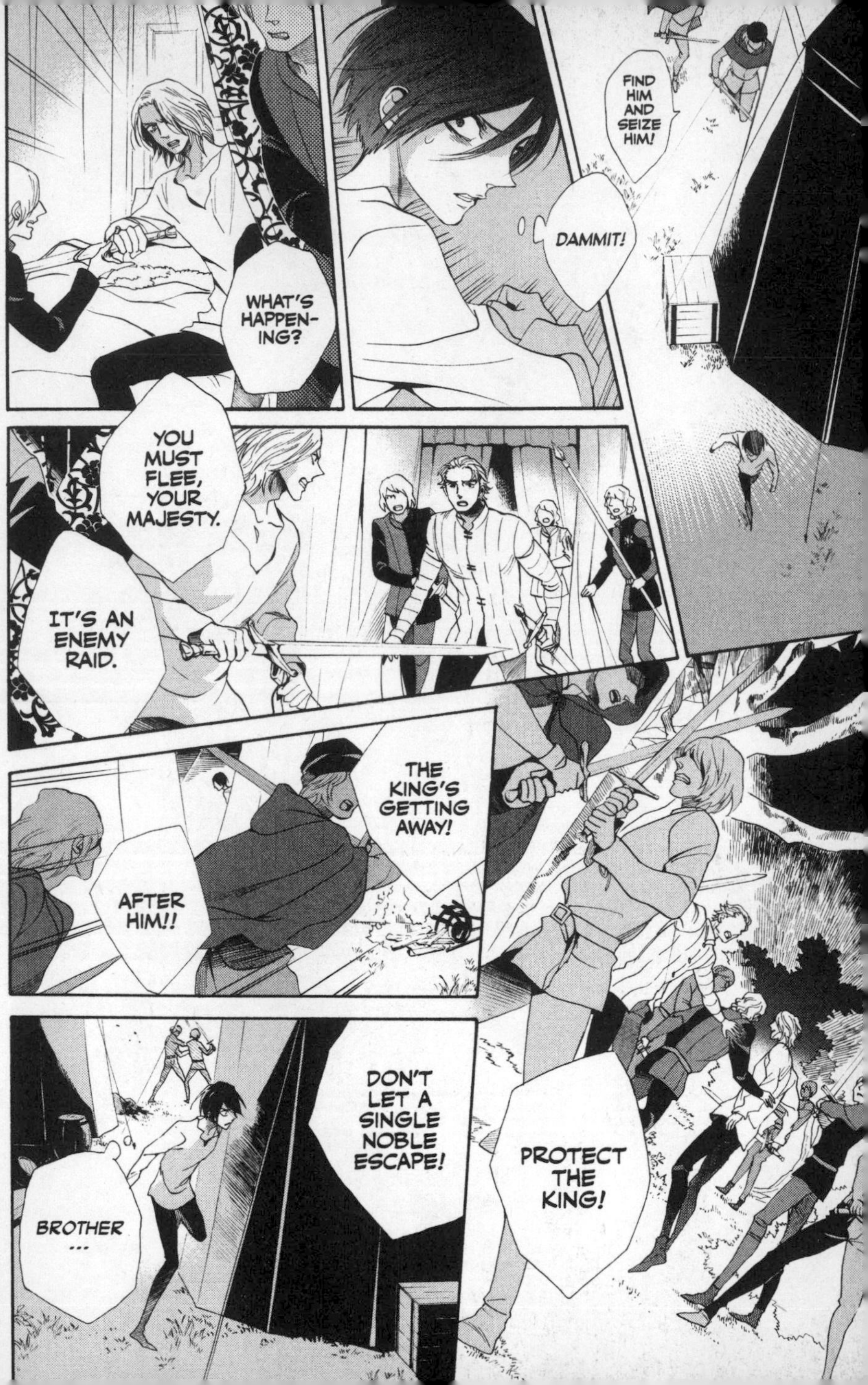
FIND HIM AND SEIZE HIM!
DAMMIT!
WHAT'S HAPPEN-ING?
YOU MUST FLEE, YOUR MAJESTY.
IT'S AN ENEMY RAID.
PROTECT THE KING!
THE KING'S GETTING AWAY!
AFTER HIM!!
DON'T LET A SINGLE NOBLE ESCAPE!
BROTHER ...

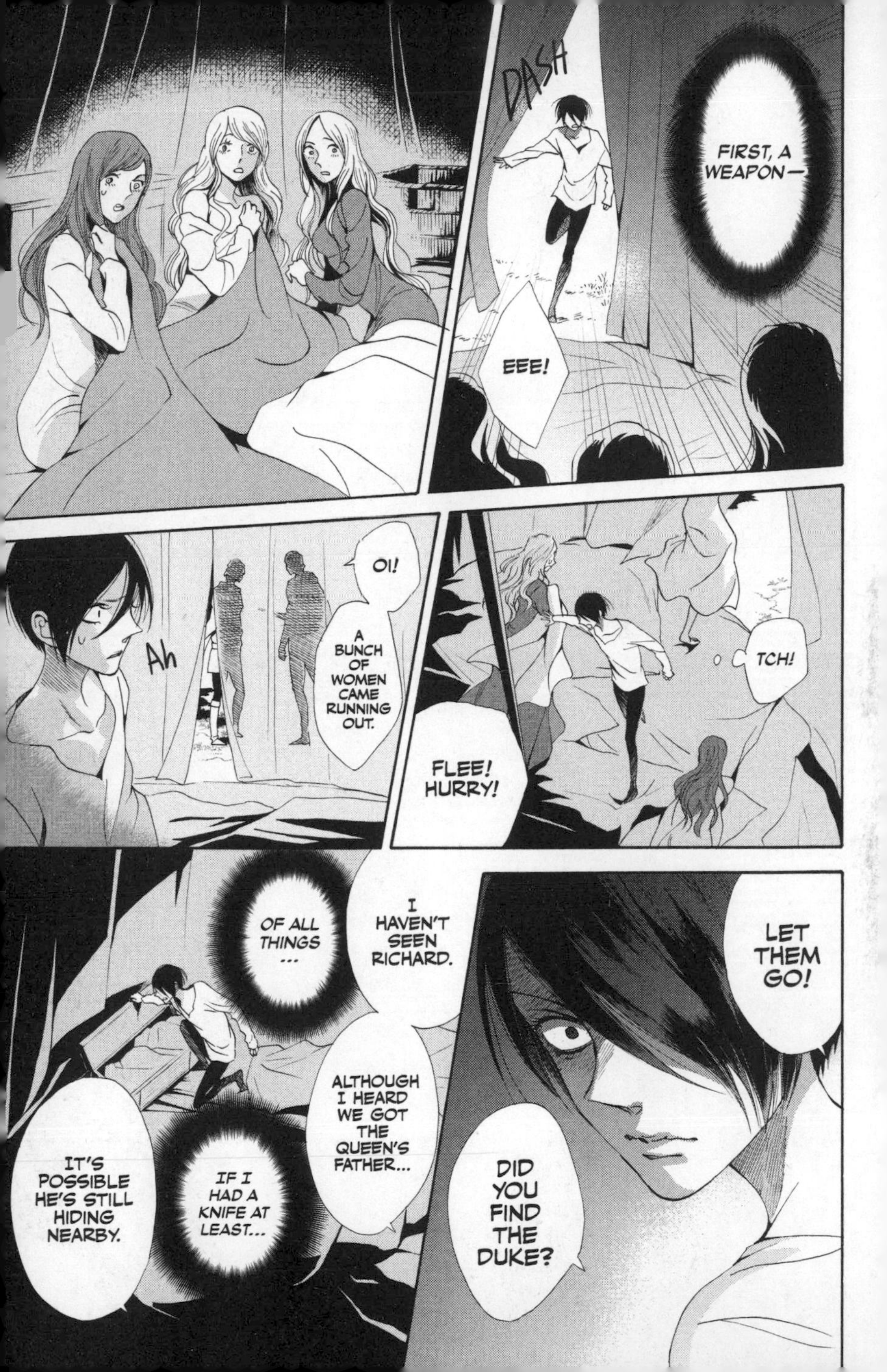
DASH
FIRST, A WEAPON—
EEE!
TCH!
FLEE! HURRY!
OI!
A BUNCH OF WOMEN CAME RUNNING OUT.
Ah
LET THEM GO!
DID YOU FIND THE DUKE?
I HAVEN'T SEEN RICHARD.
OF ALL THINGS ...
ALTHOUGH I HEARD WE GOT THE QUEEN'S FATHER...
IF I HAD A KNIFE AT LEAST...
IT'S POSSIBLE HE'S STILL HIDING NEARBY.

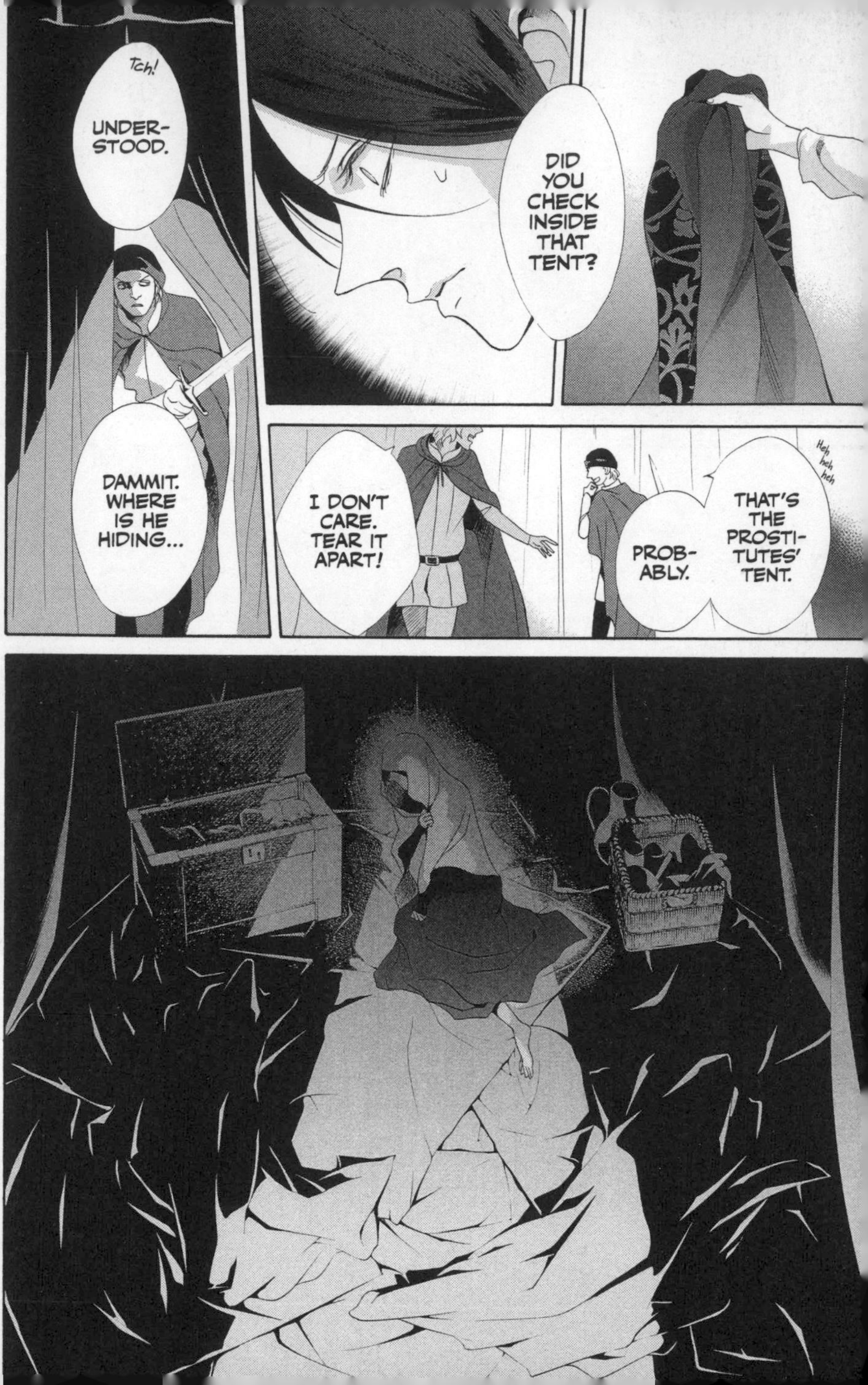
DID YOU CHECK INSIDE THAT TENT?
Heh heh heh
THAT'S THE PROSTITUTES' TENT.
PROBABLY.
I DON'T CARE. TEAR IT APART!
Tch!
UNDERSTOOD.
DAMMIT. WHERE IS HE HIDING...

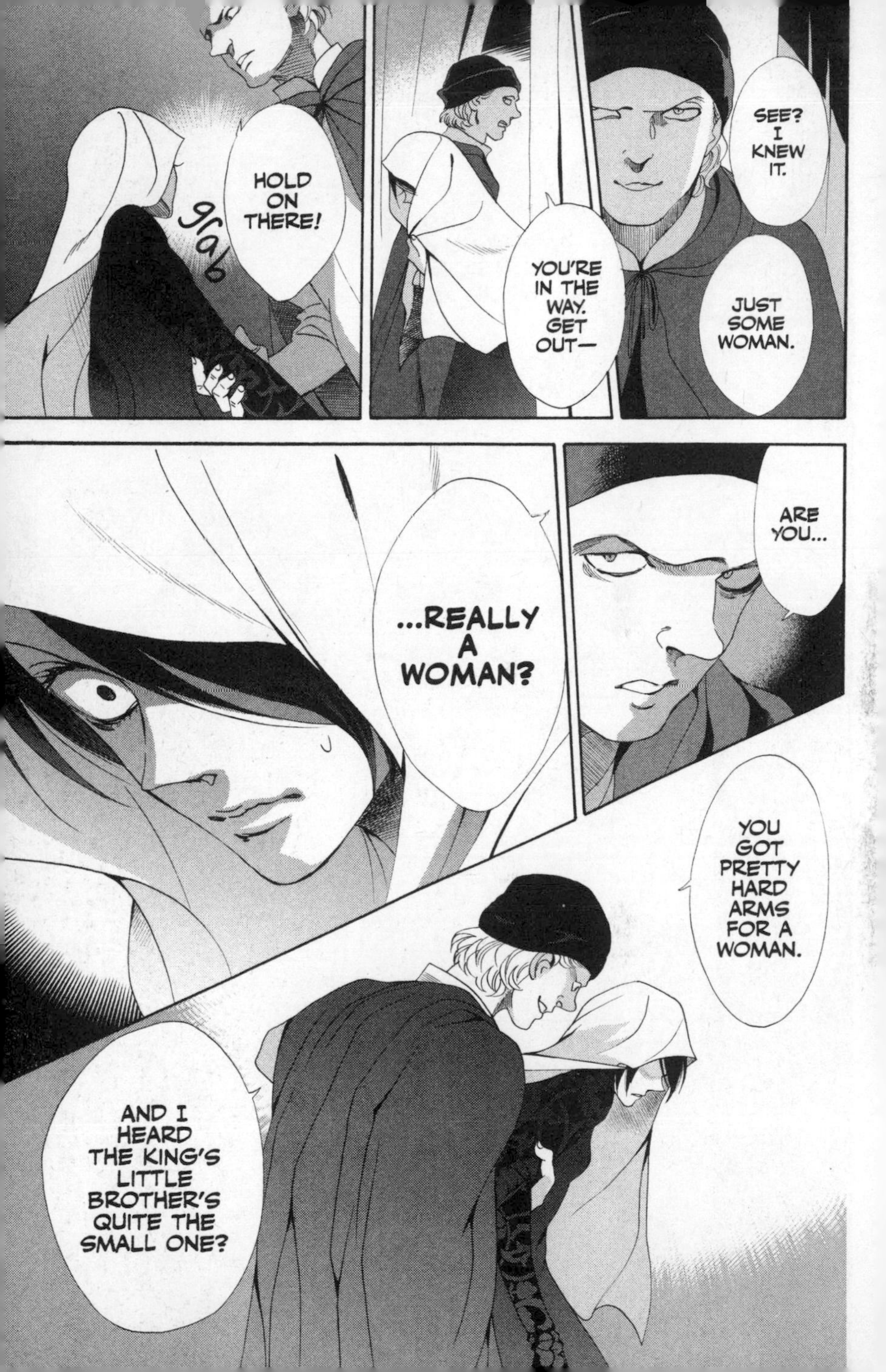
SEE? I KNEW IT.
JUST SOME WOMAN.
YOU'RE IN THE WAY. GET OUT—
HOLD ON THERE!
grab
ARE YOU...
...REALLY A WOMAN?
YOU GOT PRETTY HARD ARMS FOR A WOMAN.
AND I HEARD THE KING'S LITTLE BROTHER'S QUITE THE SMALL ONE?

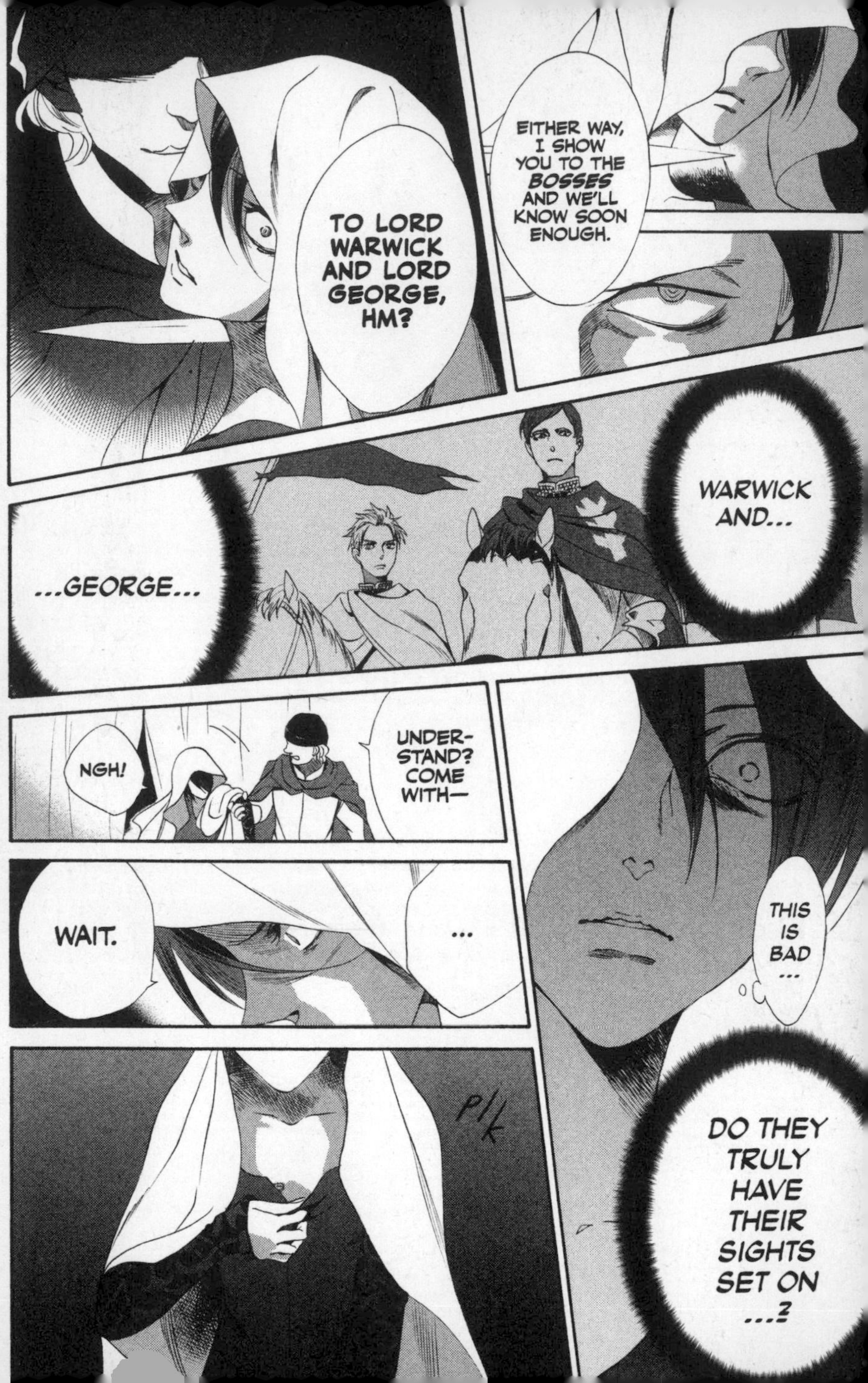
EITHER WAY, I SHOW YOU TO THE *BOSSES* AND WE'LL KNOW SOON ENOUGH.
TO LORD WARWICK AND LORD GEORGE, HM?
WARWICK AND...
...GEORGE...
THIS IS BAD...
DO THEY TRULY HAVE THEIR SIGHTS SET ON ...?
UNDER-STAND? COME WITH—
NGH!
...
WAIT.
P/K

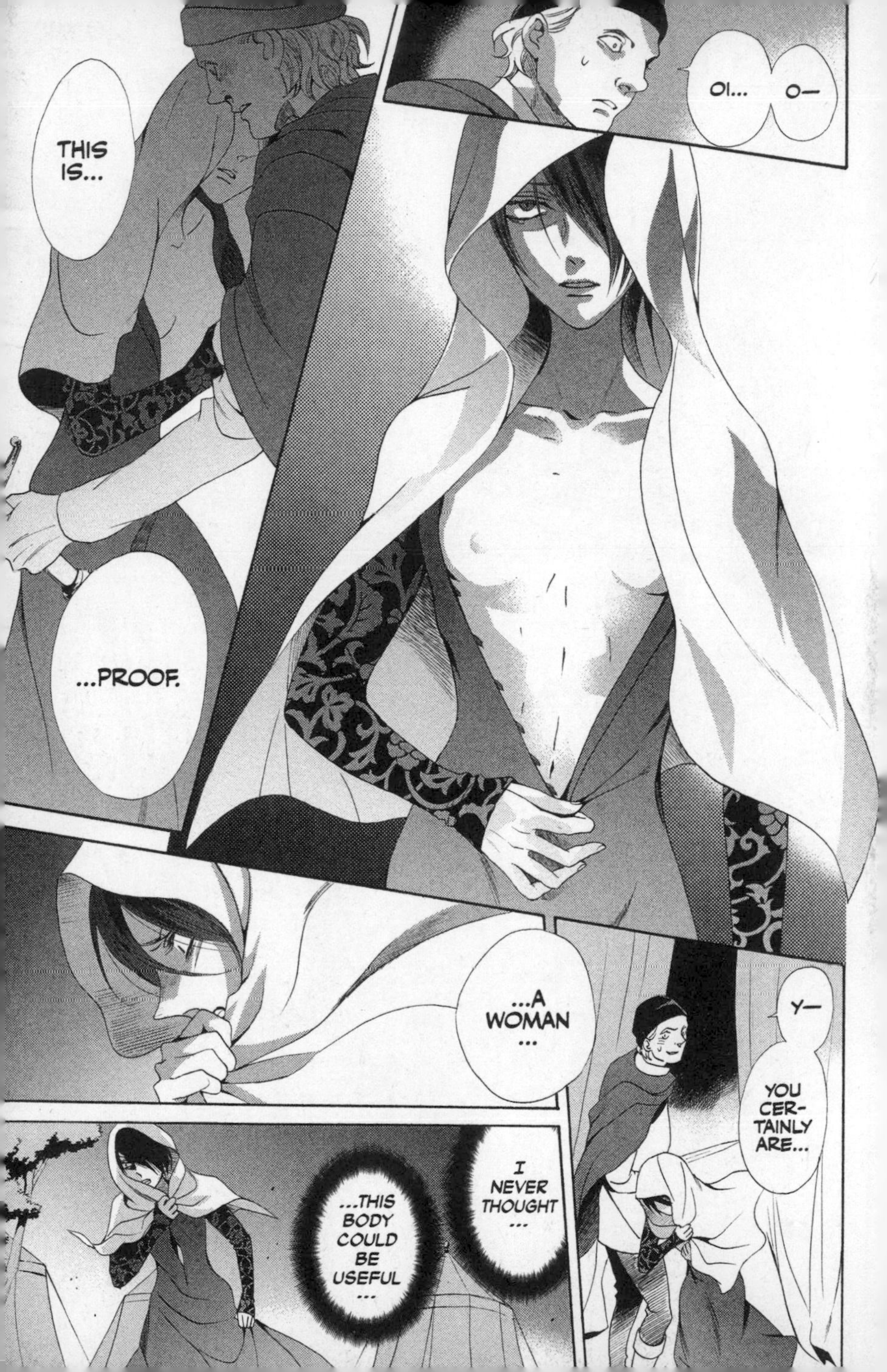
OI... O—
THIS IS...
...PROOF.
Y—
YOU CER-TAINLY ARE...
...A WOMAN ...
I NEVER THOUGHT ...
...THIS BODY COULD BE USEFUL ...

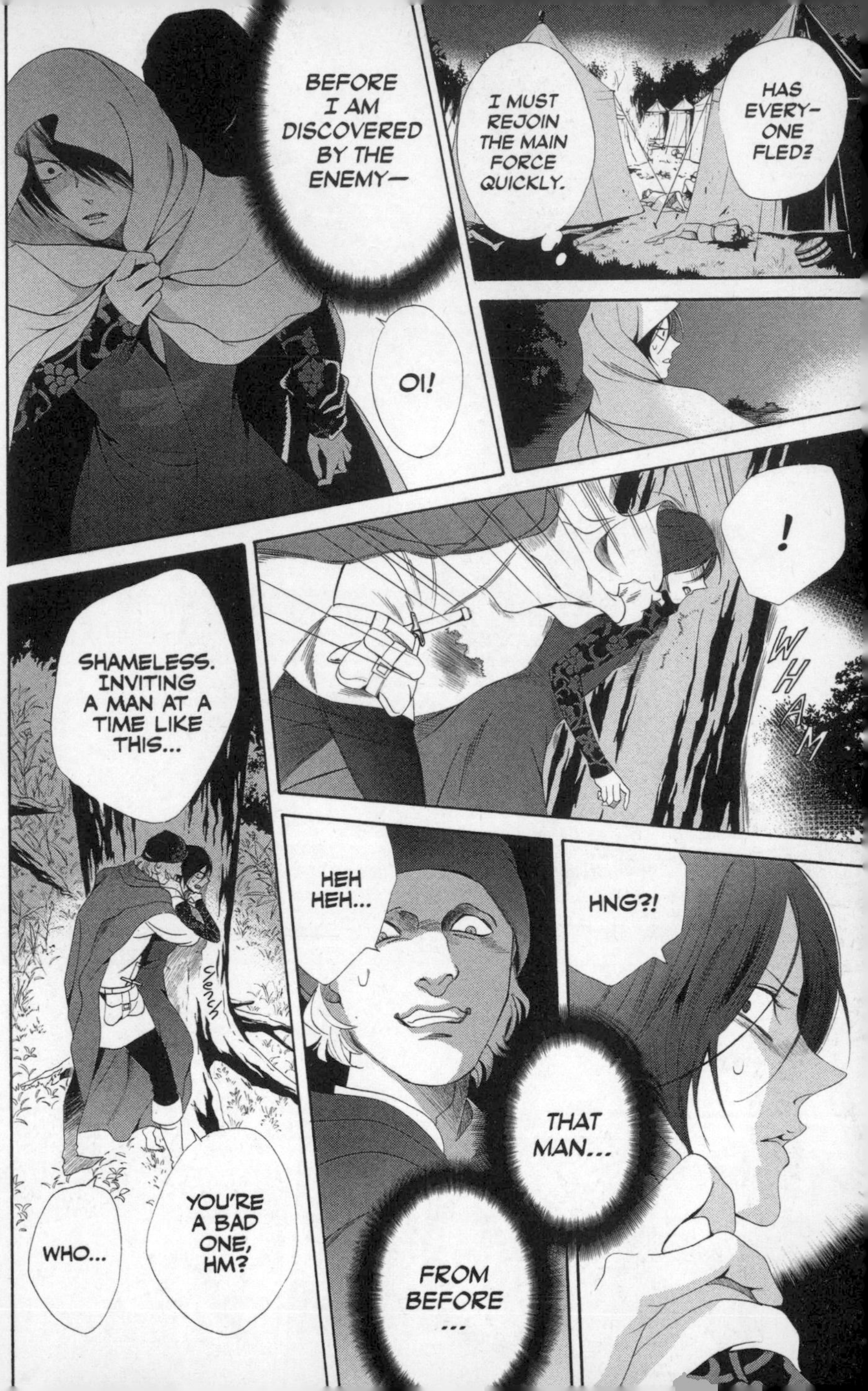
HAS EVERY-ONE FLED?
I MUST REJOIN THE MAIN FORCE QUICKLY.
BEFORE I AM DISCOVERED BY THE ENEMY—
OI!
!
WHAM
HNG?!
THAT MAN...
FROM BEFORE...
HEH HEH...
SHAMELESS. INVITING A MAN AT A TIME LIKE THIS...
clench
YOU'RE A BAD ONE, HM?
WHO...

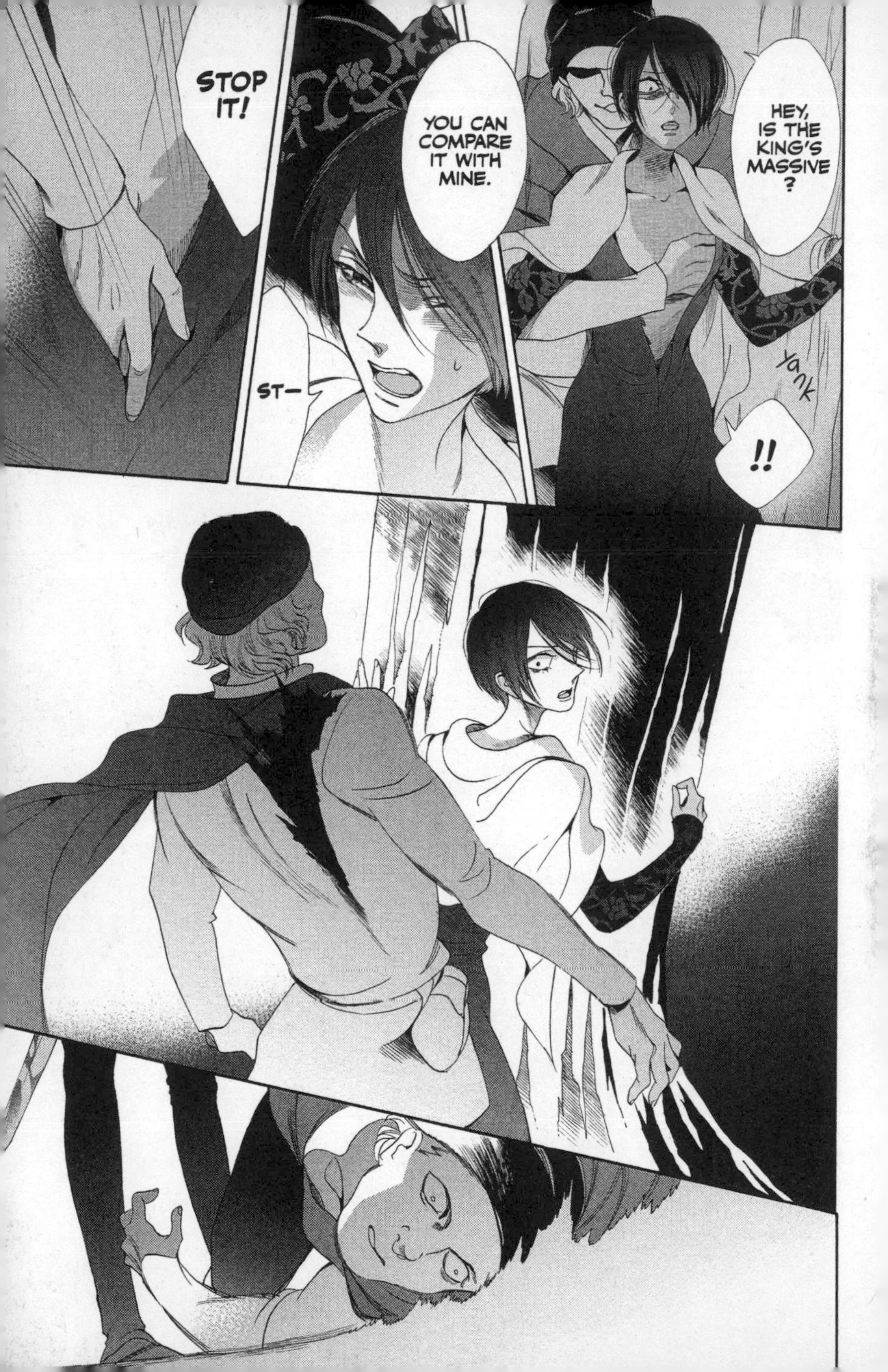
HEY, IS THE KING'S MASSIVE ?
yank
!!
YOU CAN COMPARE IT WITH MINE.
ST—
STOP IT!

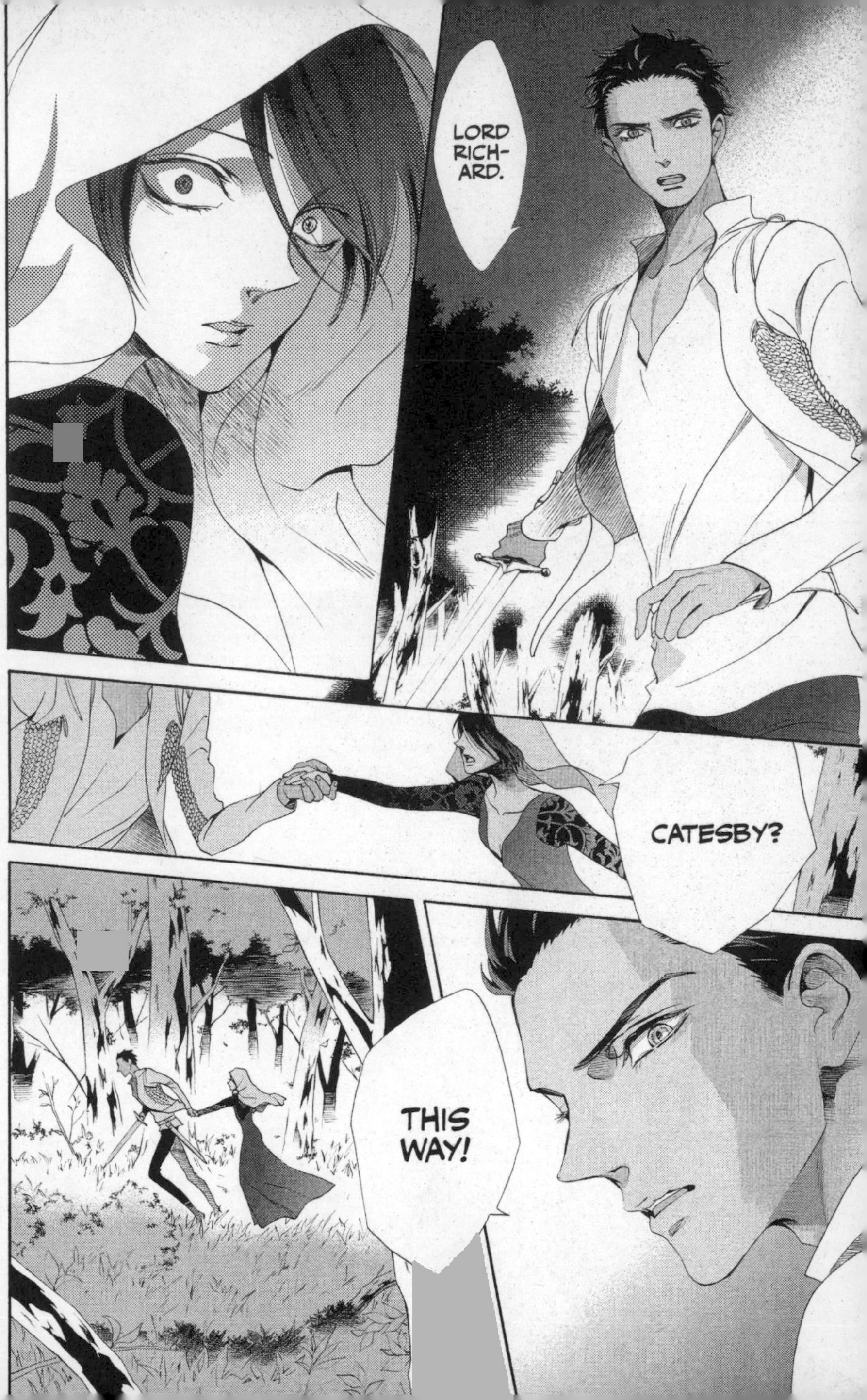
LORD RICH-ARD.
CATESBY?
THIS WAY!

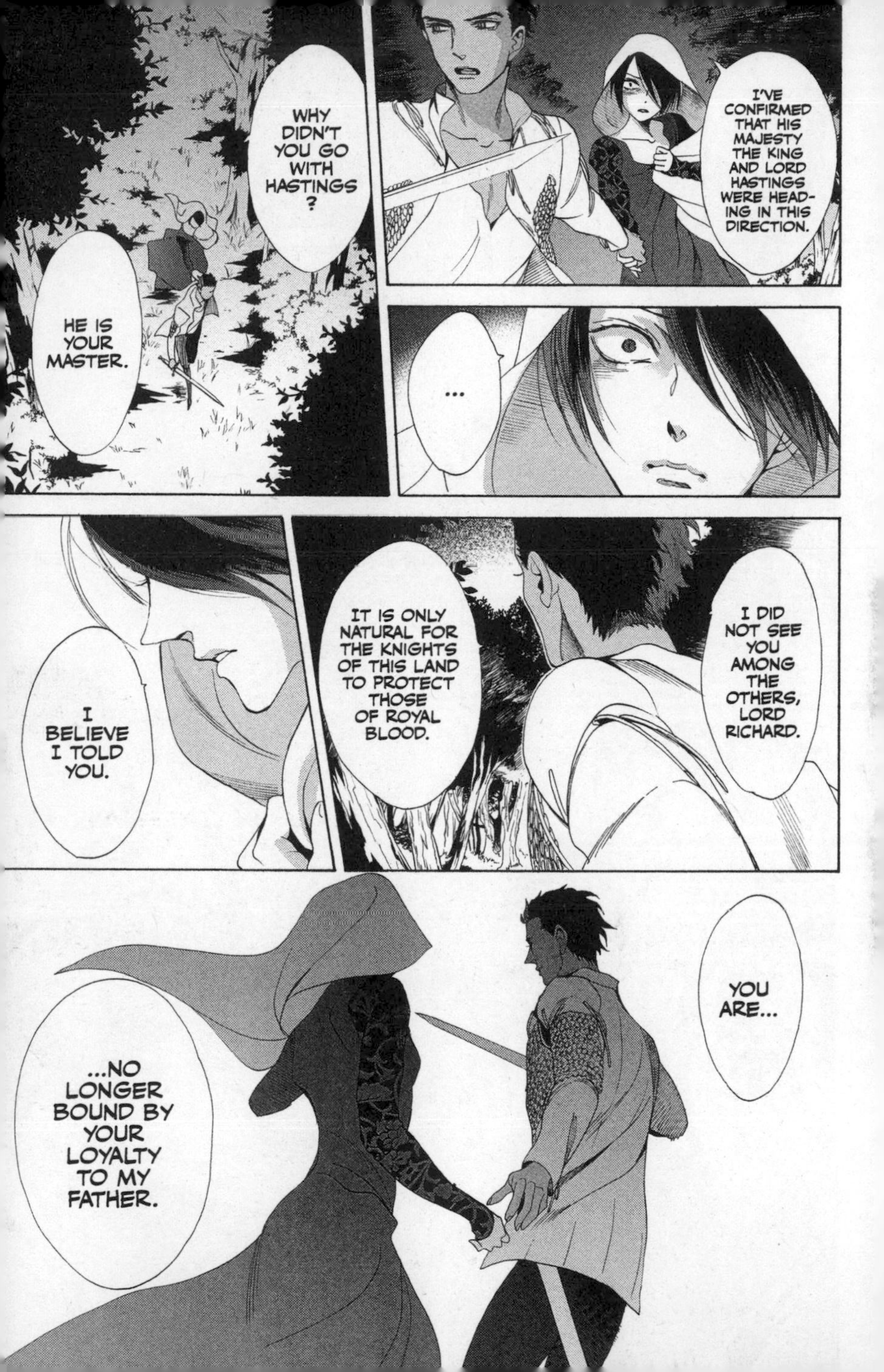
I'VE CONFIRMED THAT HIS MAJESTY THE KING AND LORD HASTINGS WERE HEADING IN THIS DIRECTION.
...
WHY DIDN'T YOU GO WITH HASTINGS?
HE IS YOUR MASTER.
I DID NOT SEE YOU AMONG THE OTHERS, LORD RICHARD.
IT IS ONLY NATURAL FOR THE KNIGHTS OF THIS LAND TO PROTECT THOSE OF ROYAL BLOOD.
I BELIEVE I TOLD YOU.
YOU ARE...
...NO LONGER BOUND BY YOUR LOYALTY TO MY FATHER.

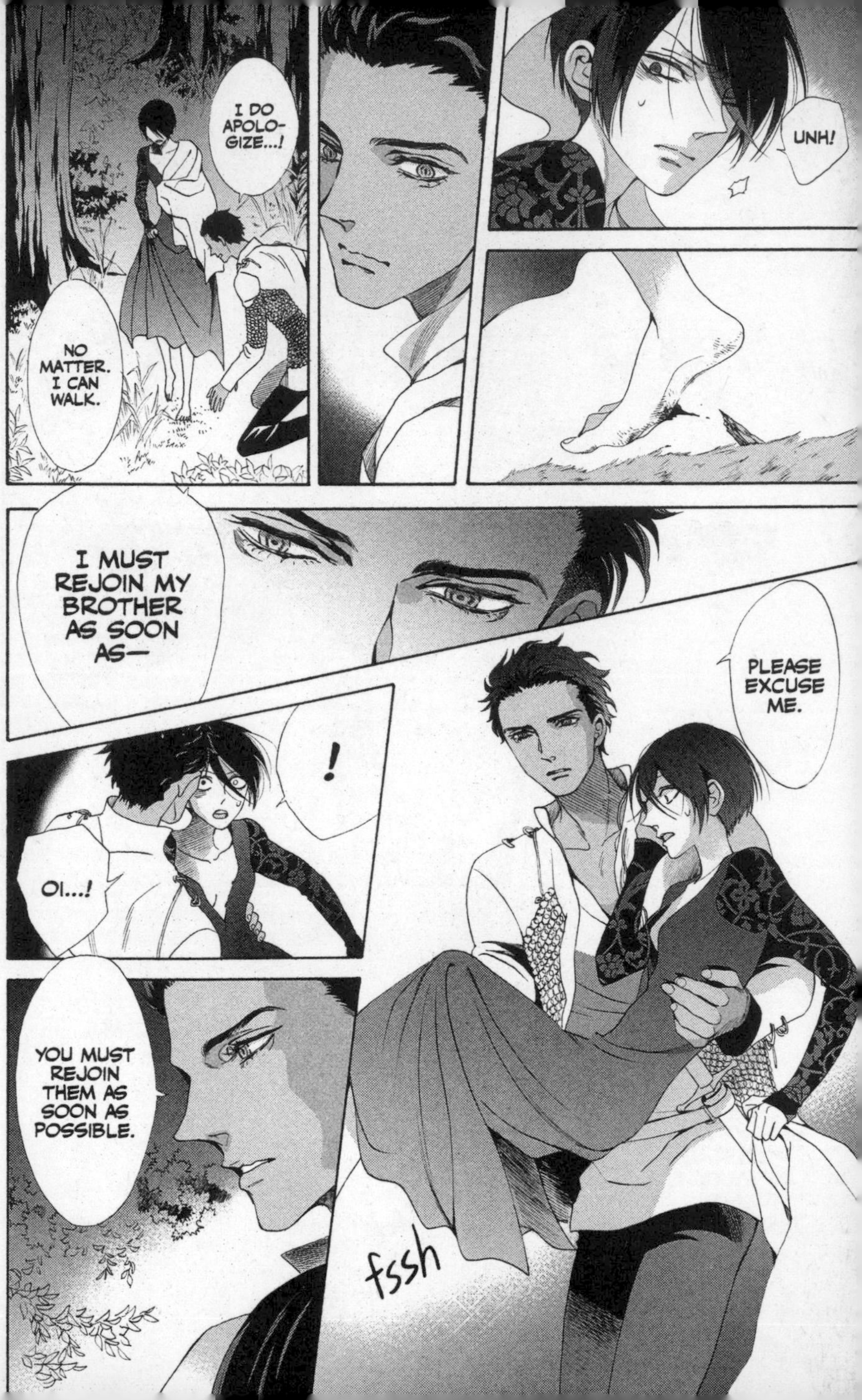
UNH!
I DO APOLOGIZE...!
NO MATTER. I CAN WALK.
I MUST REJOIN MY BROTHER AS SOON AS—
PLEASE EXCUSE ME.
fssh
!
OI...!
YOU MUST REJOIN THEM AS SOON AS POSSIBLE.

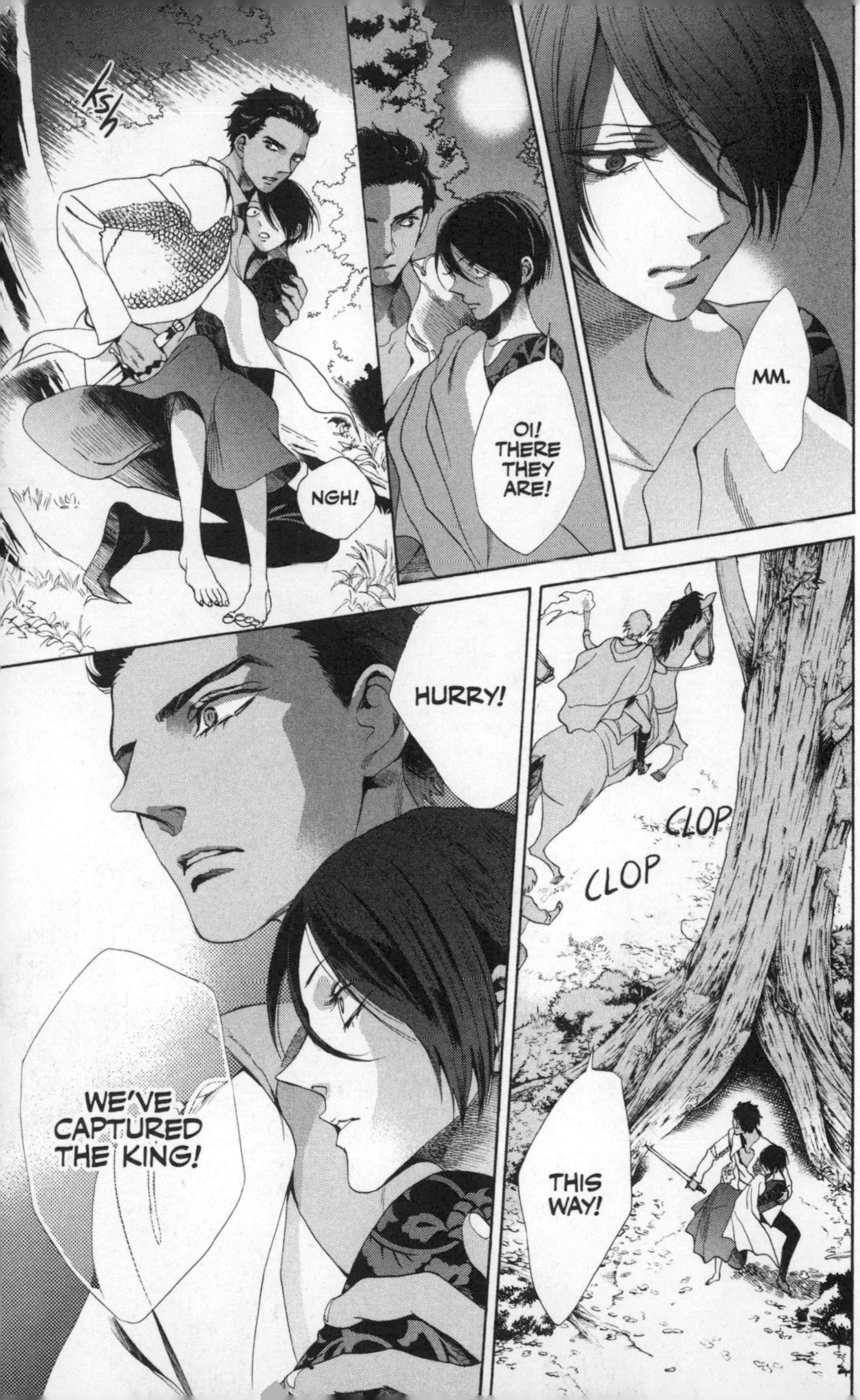
MM.
OI! THERE THEY ARE!
KSH
NGH!
CLOP
CLOP
THIS WAY!
HURRY!
WE'VE CAPTURED THE KING!

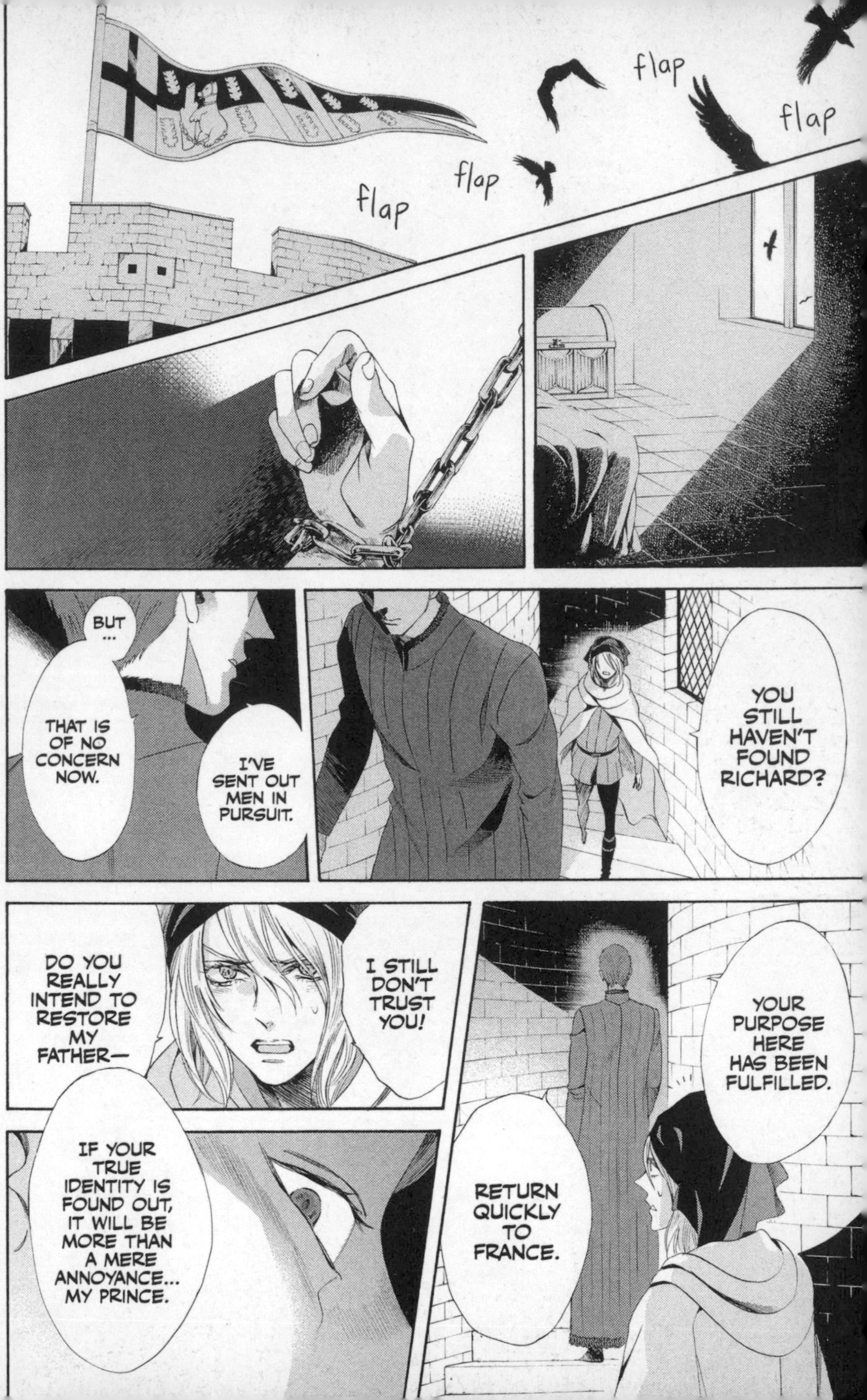
flap
flap
flap
flap
YOU STILL HAVEN'T FOUND RICHARD?
I'VE SENT OUT MEN IN PURSUIT.
BUT ...
THAT IS OF NO CONCERN NOW.
YOUR PURPOSE HERE HAS BEEN FULFILLED.
RETURN QUICKLY TO FRANCE.
I STILL DON'T TRUST YOU!
DO YOU REALLY INTEND TO RESTORE MY FATHER—
IF YOUR TRUE IDENTITY IS FOUND OUT, IT WILL BE MORE THAN A MERE ANNOYANCE... MY PRINCE.

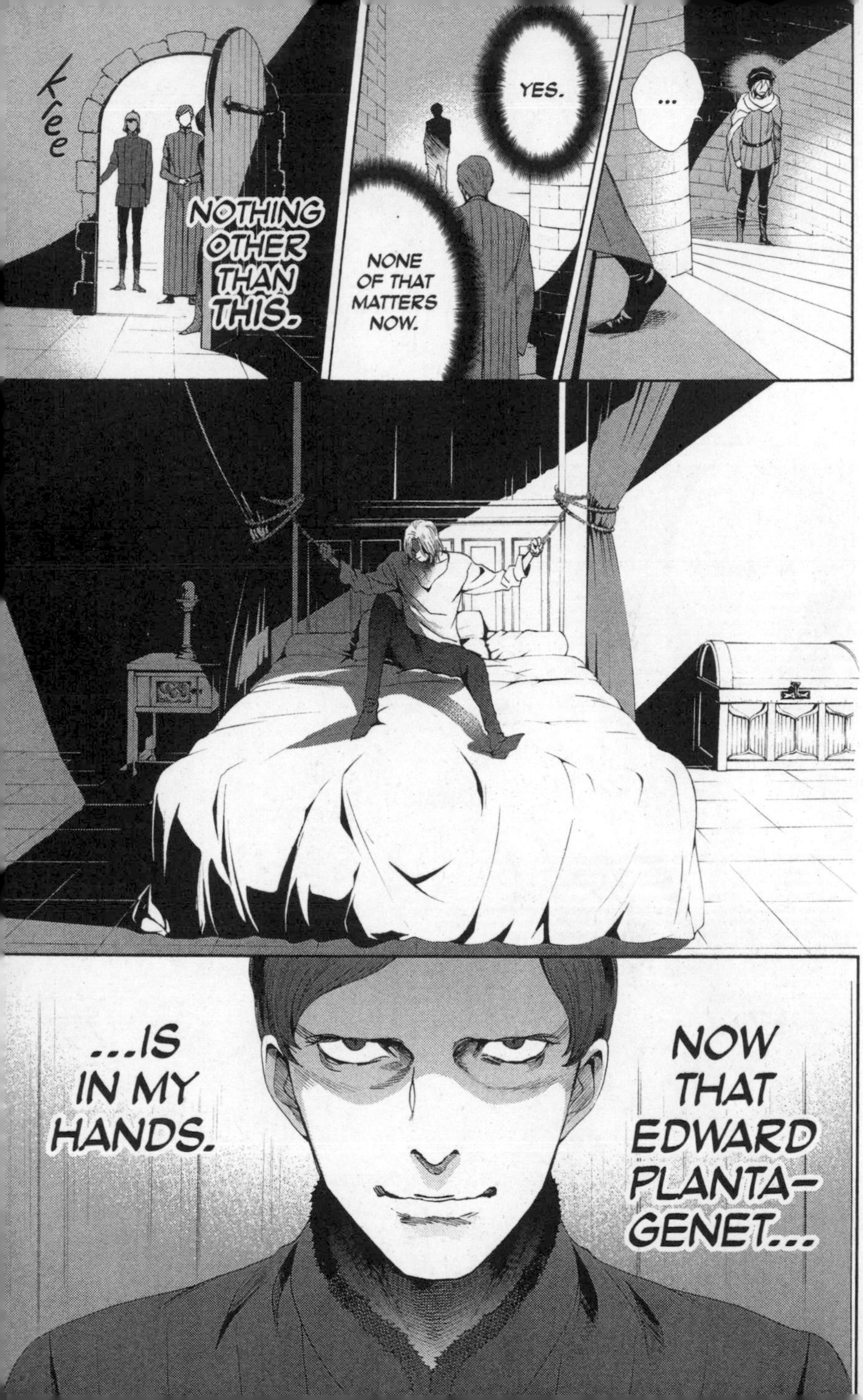
...
YES.
NONE OF THAT MATTERS NOW.
Kree
NOTHING OTHER THAN THIS.
NOW THAT EDWARD PLANTA-GENET...
...IS IN MY HANDS.

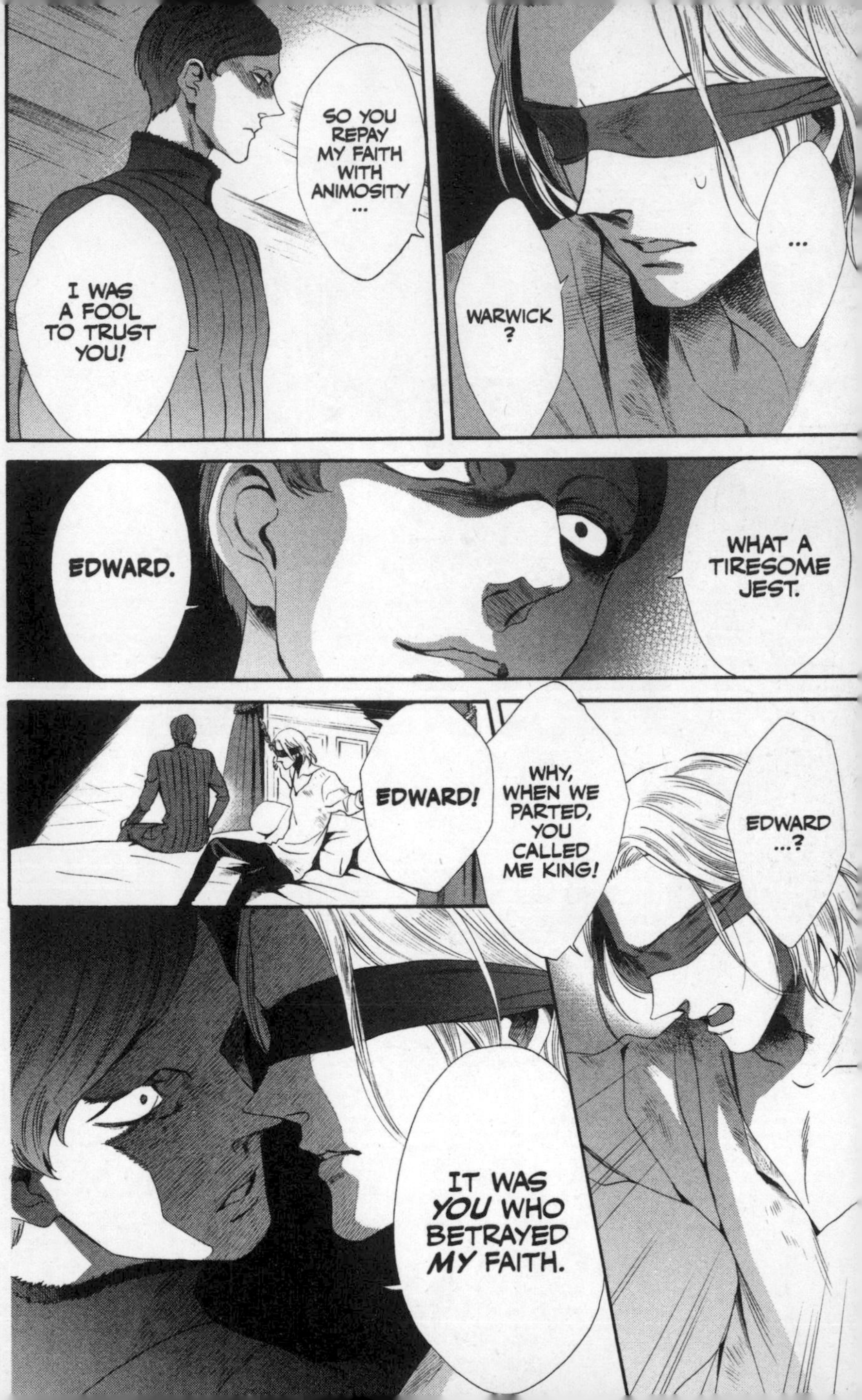
...
WARWICK ?
SO YOU REPAY MY FAITH WITH ANIMOSITY ...
I WAS A FOOL TO TRUST YOU!
WHAT A TIRESOME JEST.
EDWARD.
EDWARD ...?
WHY, WHEN WE PARTED, YOU CALLED ME KING!
EDWARD!
IT WAS *YOU* WHO BETRAYED *MY* FAITH.

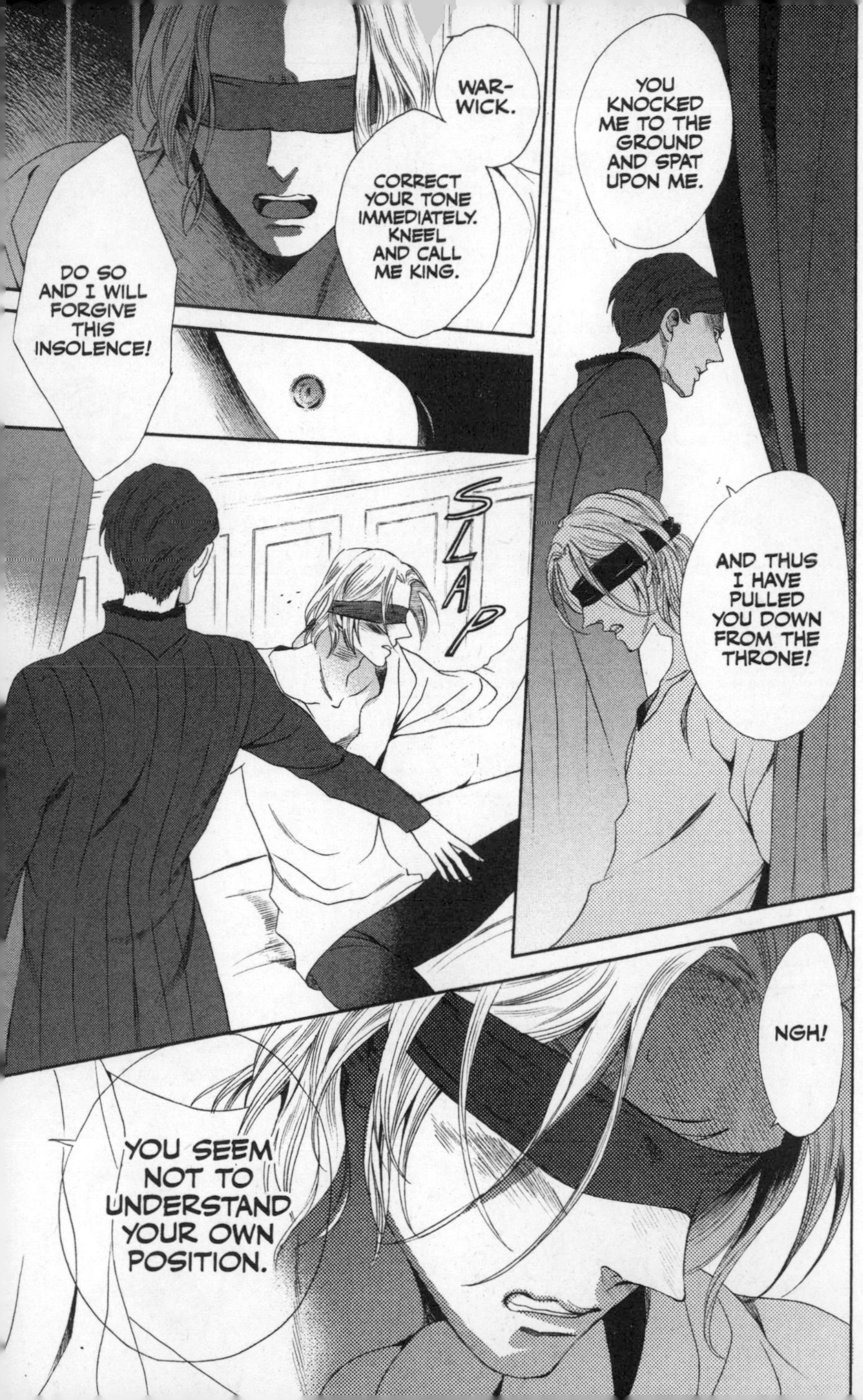
YOU KNOCKED ME TO THE GROUND AND SPAT UPON ME.
AND THUS I HAVE PULLED YOU DOWN FROM THE THRONE!
WAR-WICK.
CORRECT YOUR TONE IMMEDIATELY. KNEEL AND CALL ME KING.
DO SO AND I WILL FORGIVE THIS INSOLENCE!
SLAP
NGH!
YOU SEEM NOT TO UNDERSTAND YOUR OWN POSITION.

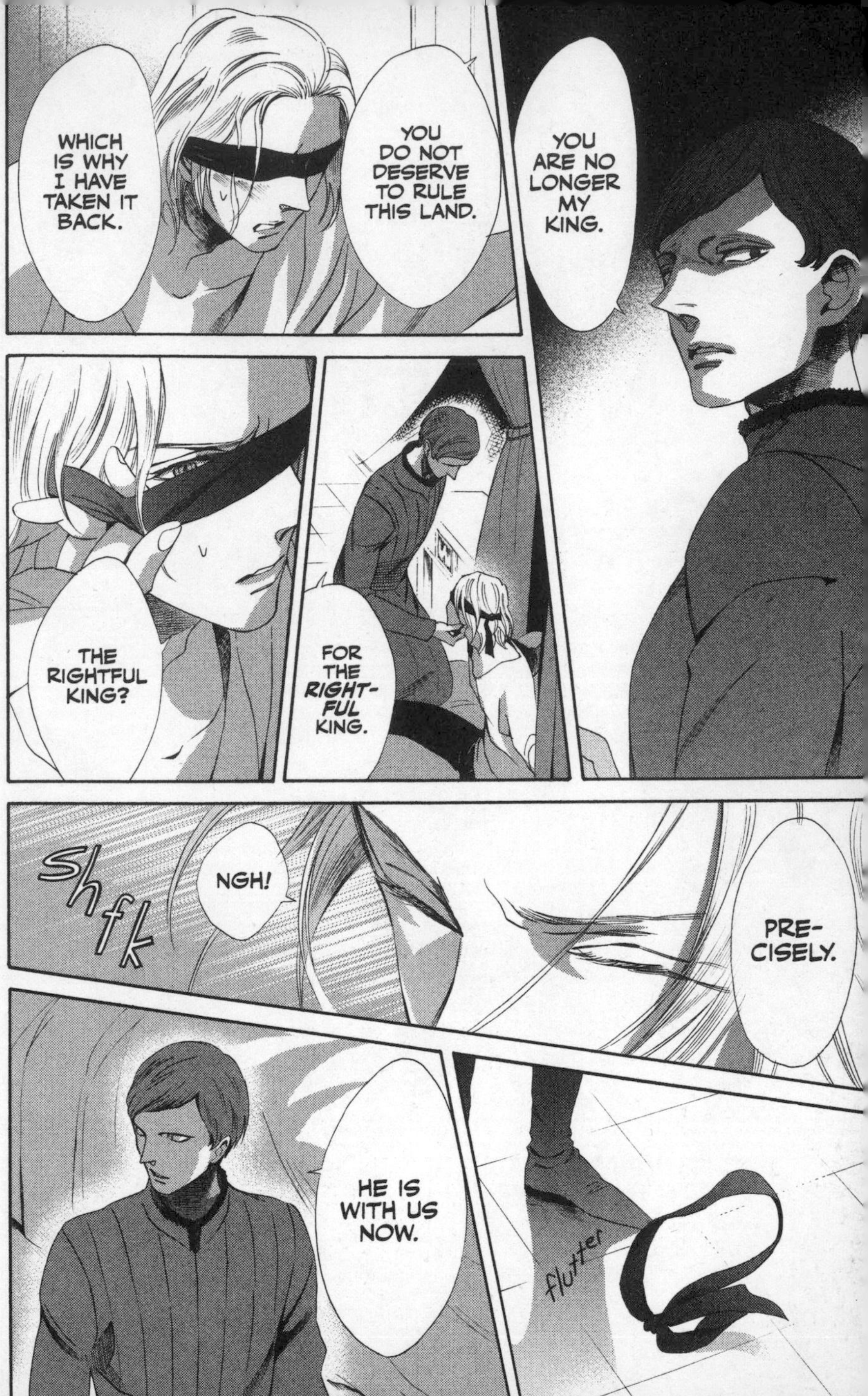
YOU ARE NO LONGER MY KING.
YOU DO NOT DESERVE TO RULE THIS LAND.
WHICH IS WHY I HAVE TAKEN IT BACK.
FOR THE *RIGHTFUL* KING.
THE RIGHTFUL KING?
PRE-CISELY.
NGH!
Shfk
flutter
HE IS WITH US NOW.

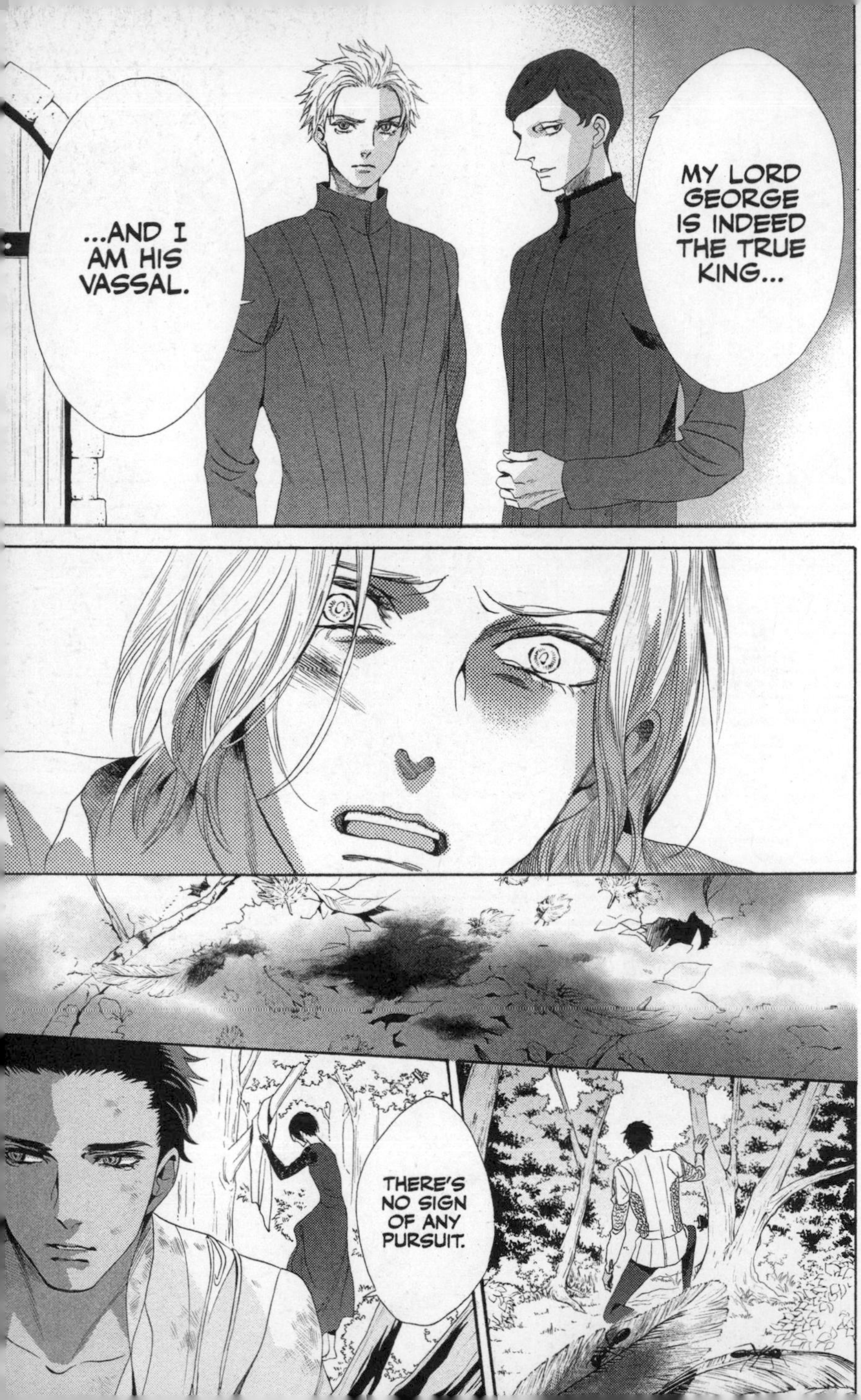
MY LORD GEORGE IS INDEED THE TRUE KING...
...AND I AM HIS VASSAL.
THERE'S NO SIGN OF ANY PURSUIT.

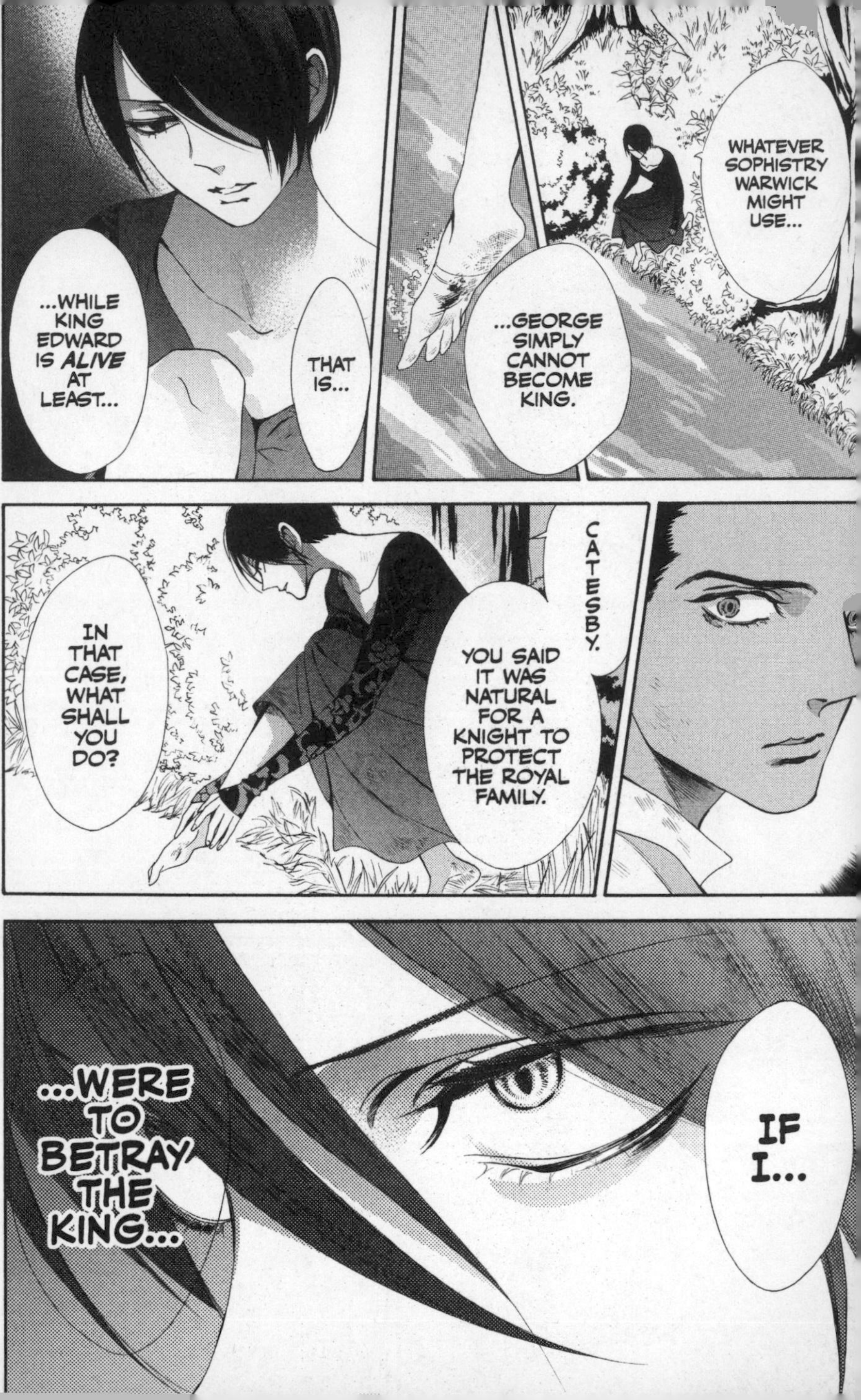
WHATEVER SOPHISTRY WARWICK MIGHT USE...
...GEORGE SIMPLY CANNOT BECOME KING.
THAT IS...
...WHILE KING EDWARD IS *ALIVE* AT LEAST...
CATESBY.
YOU SAID IT WAS NATURAL FOR A KNIGHT TO PROTECT THE ROYAL FAMILY.
IN THAT CASE, WHAT SHALL YOU DO?
IF I...
...WERE TO BETRAY THE KING...

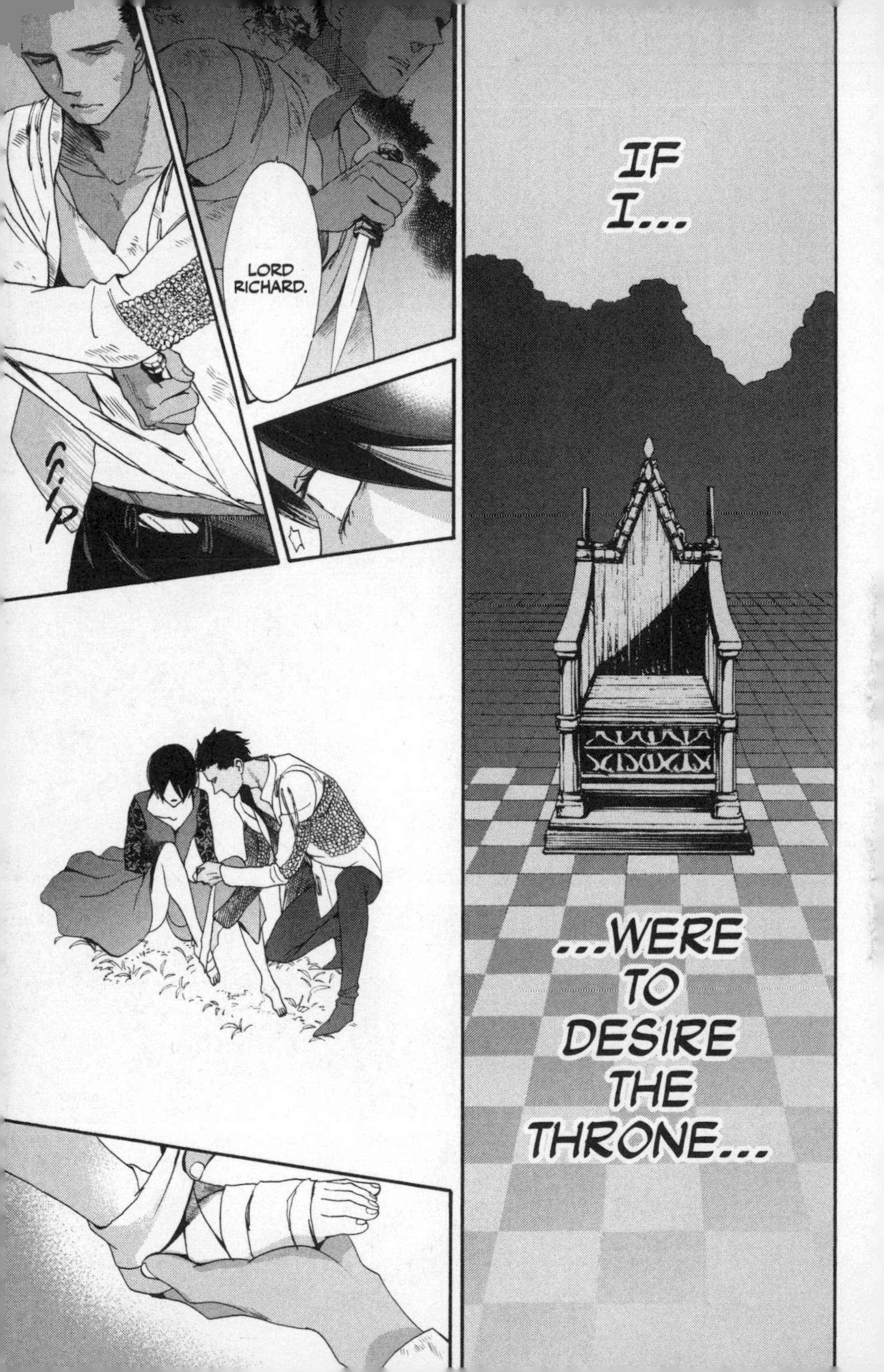

IF I...
...WERE TO DESIRE THE THRONE...
LORD RICHARD.
RRIP

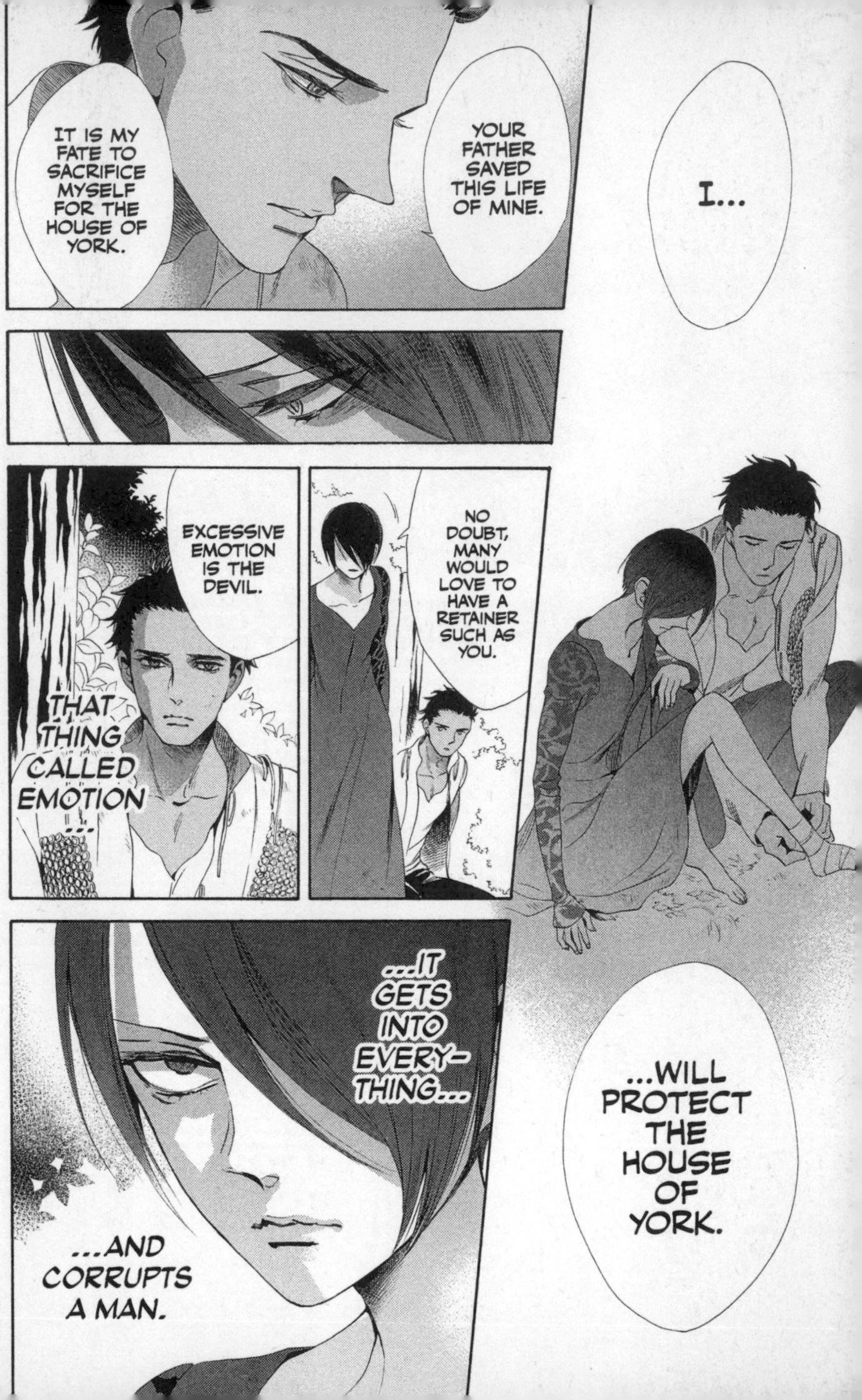
I...
...WILL PROTECT THE HOUSE OF YORK.
YOUR FATHER SAVED THIS LIFE OF MINE.
IT IS MY FATE TO SACRIFICE MYSELF FOR THE HOUSE OF YORK.
NO DOUBT, MANY WOULD LOVE TO HAVE A RETAINER SUCH AS YOU.
EXCESSIVE EMOTION IS THE DEVIL.
THAT THING CALLED EMOTION...
...IT GETS INTO EVERY-THING...
...AND CORRUPTS A MAN.

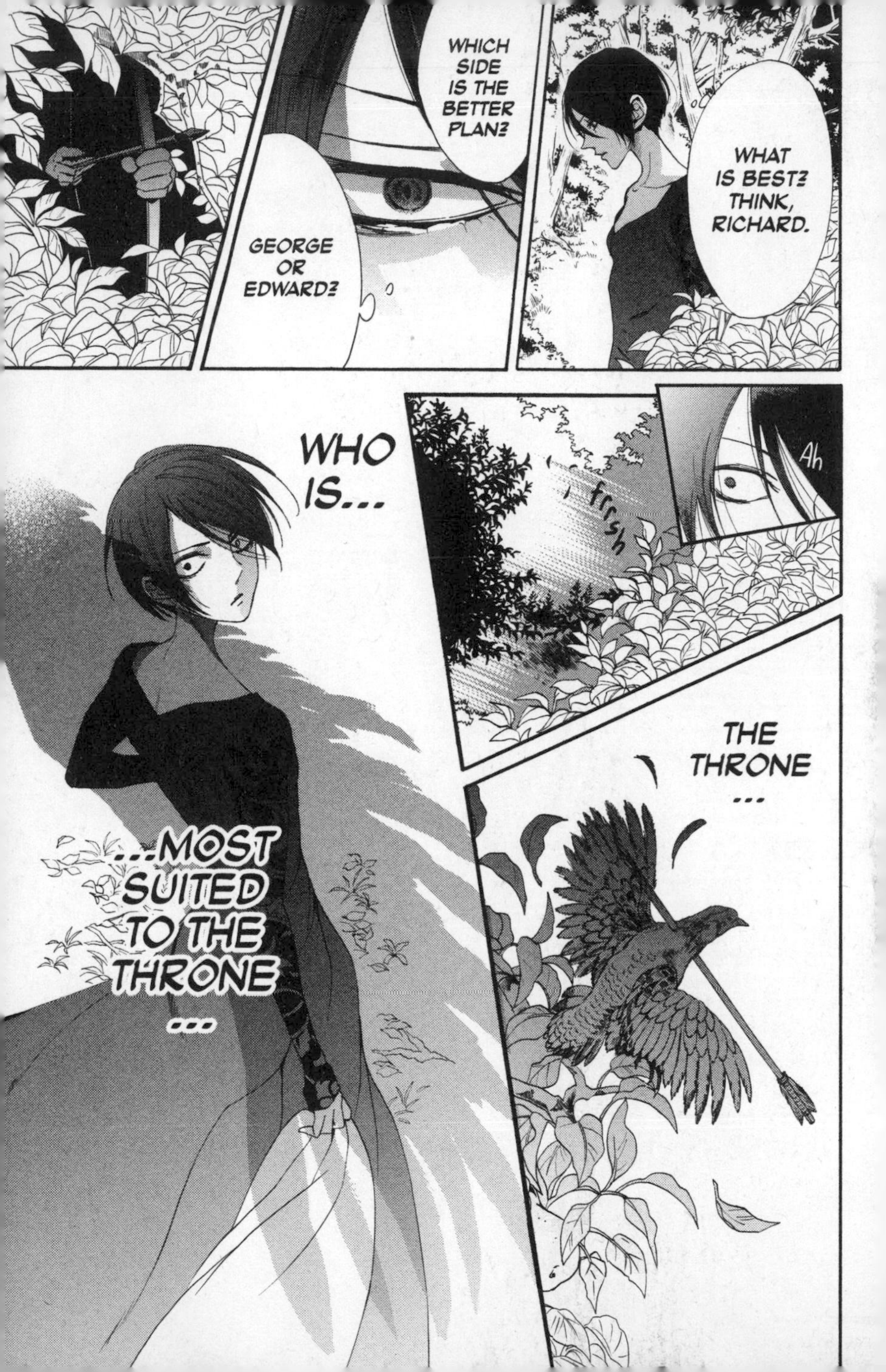
WHAT IS BEST? THINK, RICHARD.
WHICH SIDE IS THE BETTER PLAN?
GEORGE OR EDWARD?
Ah
frsh
THE THRONE ...
WHO IS...
...MOST SUITED TO THE THRONE ...

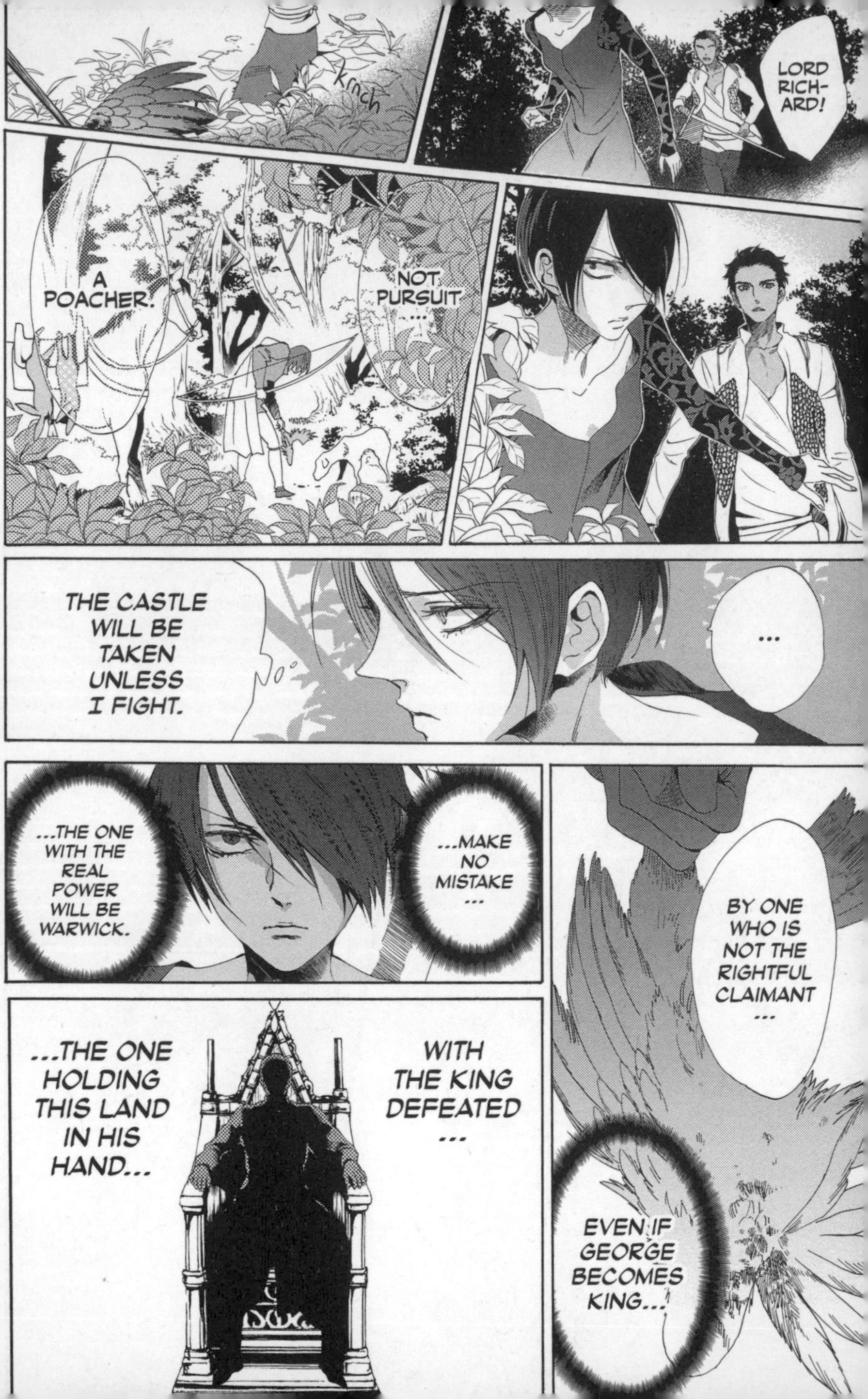
LORD RICH-ARD!
krnch
NOT PURSUIT...
A POACHER.
...
THE CASTLE WILL BE TAKEN UNLESS I FIGHT.
BY ONE WHO IS NOT THE RIGHTFUL CLAIMANT...
EVEN IF GEORGE BECOMES KING...
...MAKE NO MISTAKE...
...THE ONE WITH THE REAL POWER WILL BE WARWICK.
WITH THE KING DEFEATED...
...THE ONE HOLDING THIS LAND IN HIS HAND...

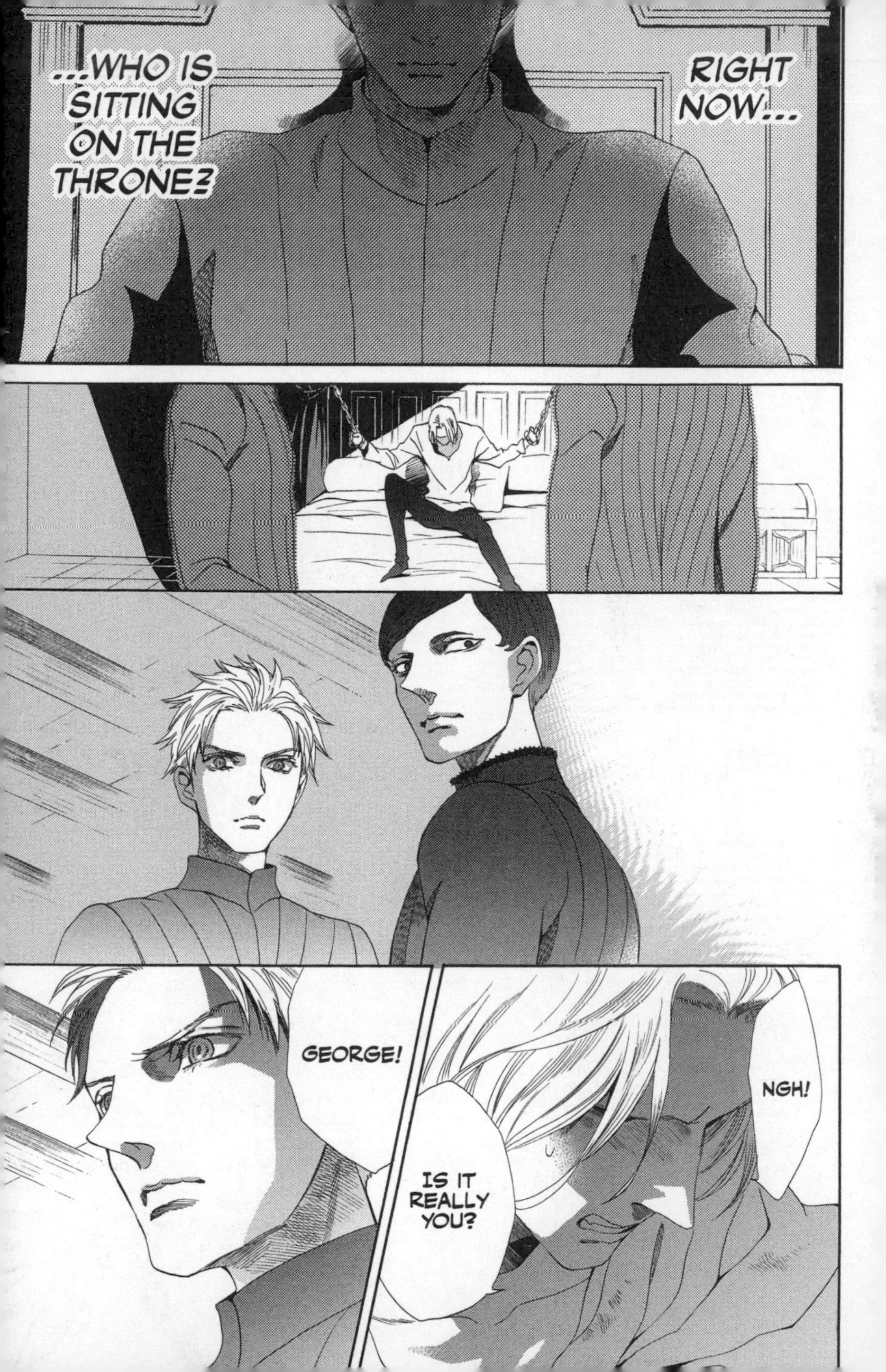
RIGHT NOW...
...WHO IS SITTING ON THE THRONE?
NGH!
IS IT REALLY YOU?
GEORGE!

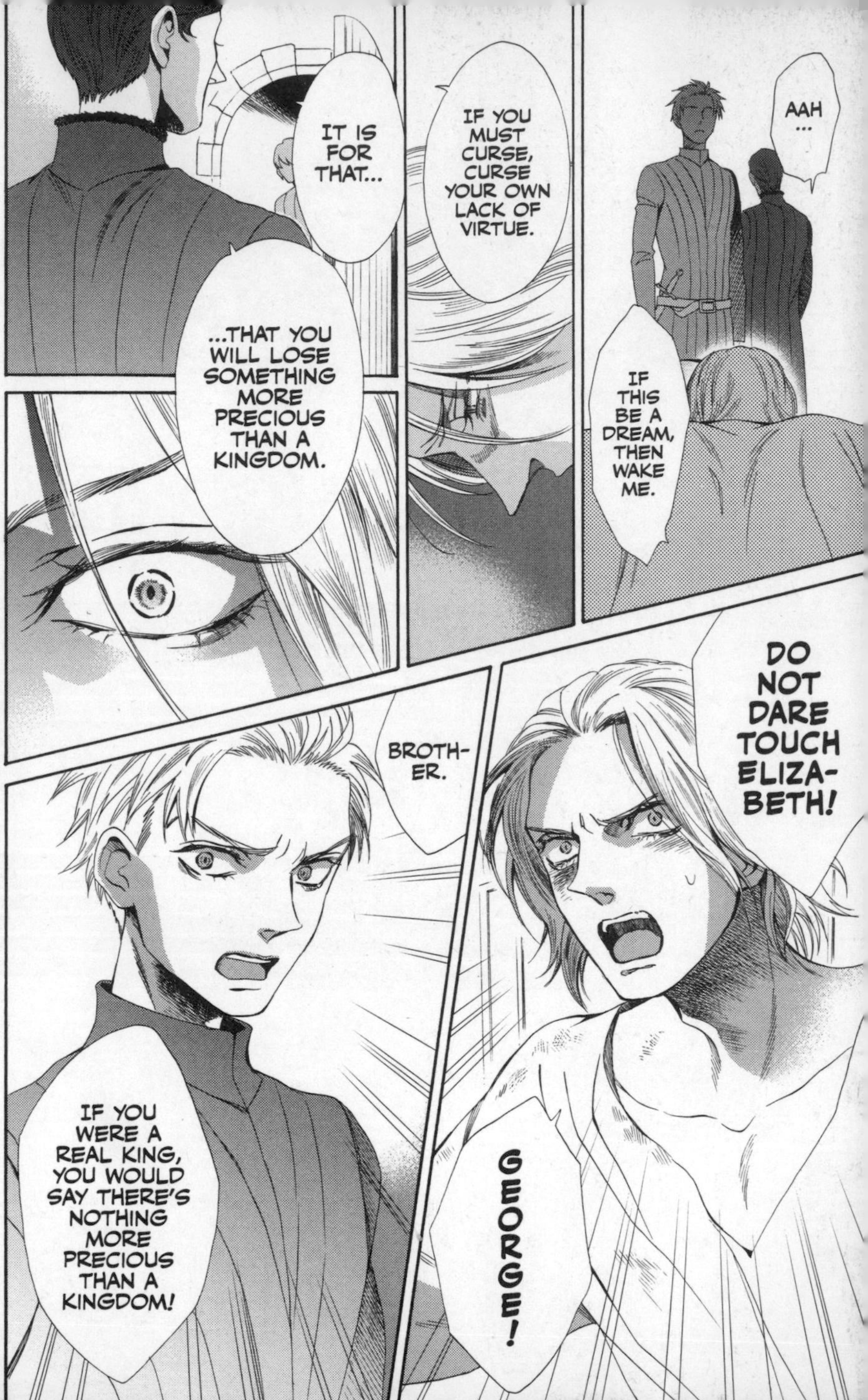
AAH ...
IF THIS BE A DREAM, THEN WAKE ME.
IF YOU MUST CURSE, CURSE YOUR OWN LACK OF VIRTUE.
IT IS FOR THAT...
...THAT YOU WILL LOSE SOMETHING MORE PRECIOUS THAN A KINGDOM.
DO NOT DARE TOUCH ELIZA-BETH!
GEORGE!
BROTH-ER.
IF YOU WERE A REAL KING, YOU WOULD SAY THERE'S NOTHING MORE PRECIOUS THAN A KINGDOM!

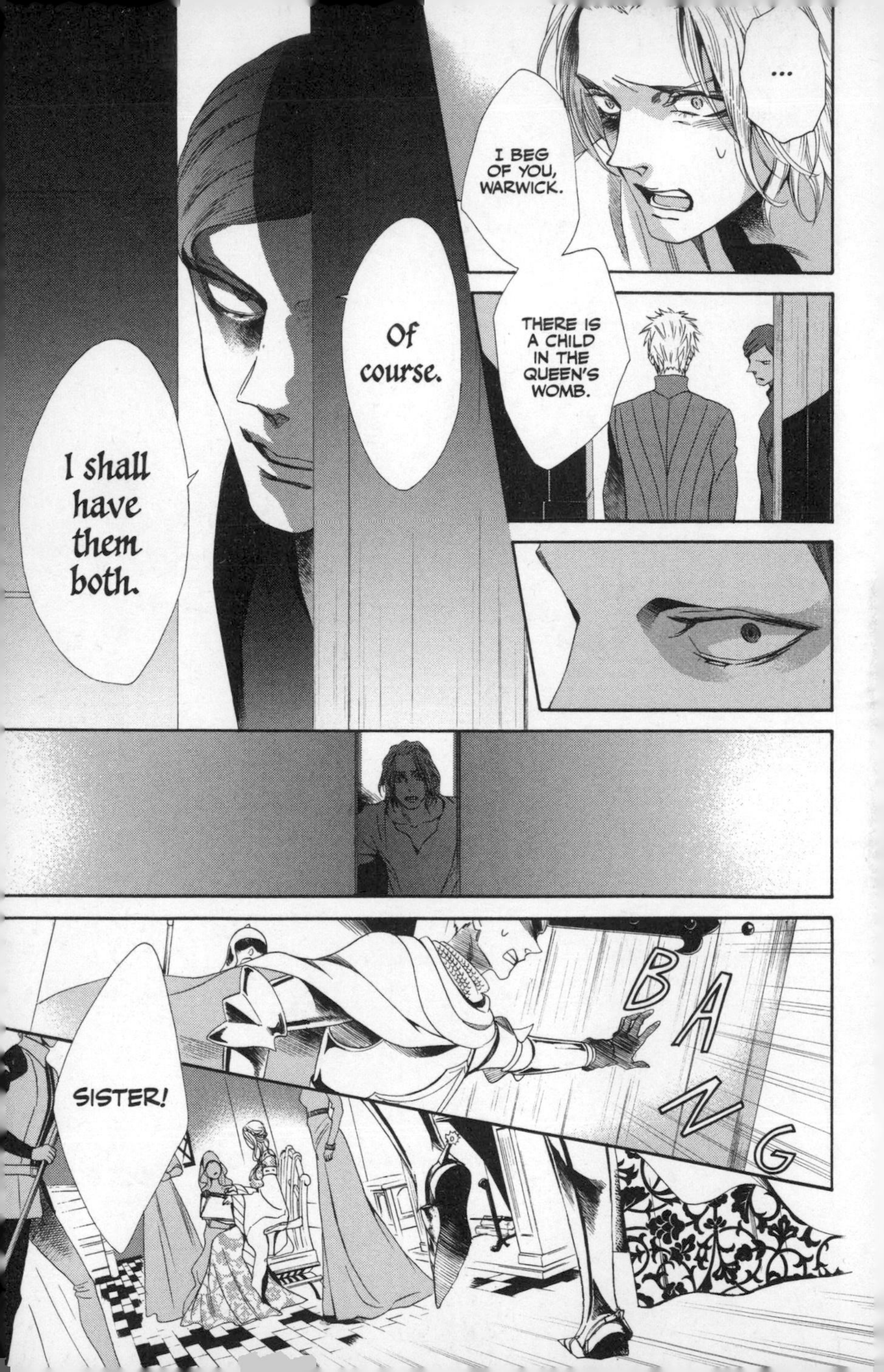
...
I BEG OF YOU, WARWICK.
THERE IS A CHILD IN THE QUEEN'S WOMB.
Of course.
I shall have them both.
BANG
SISTER!

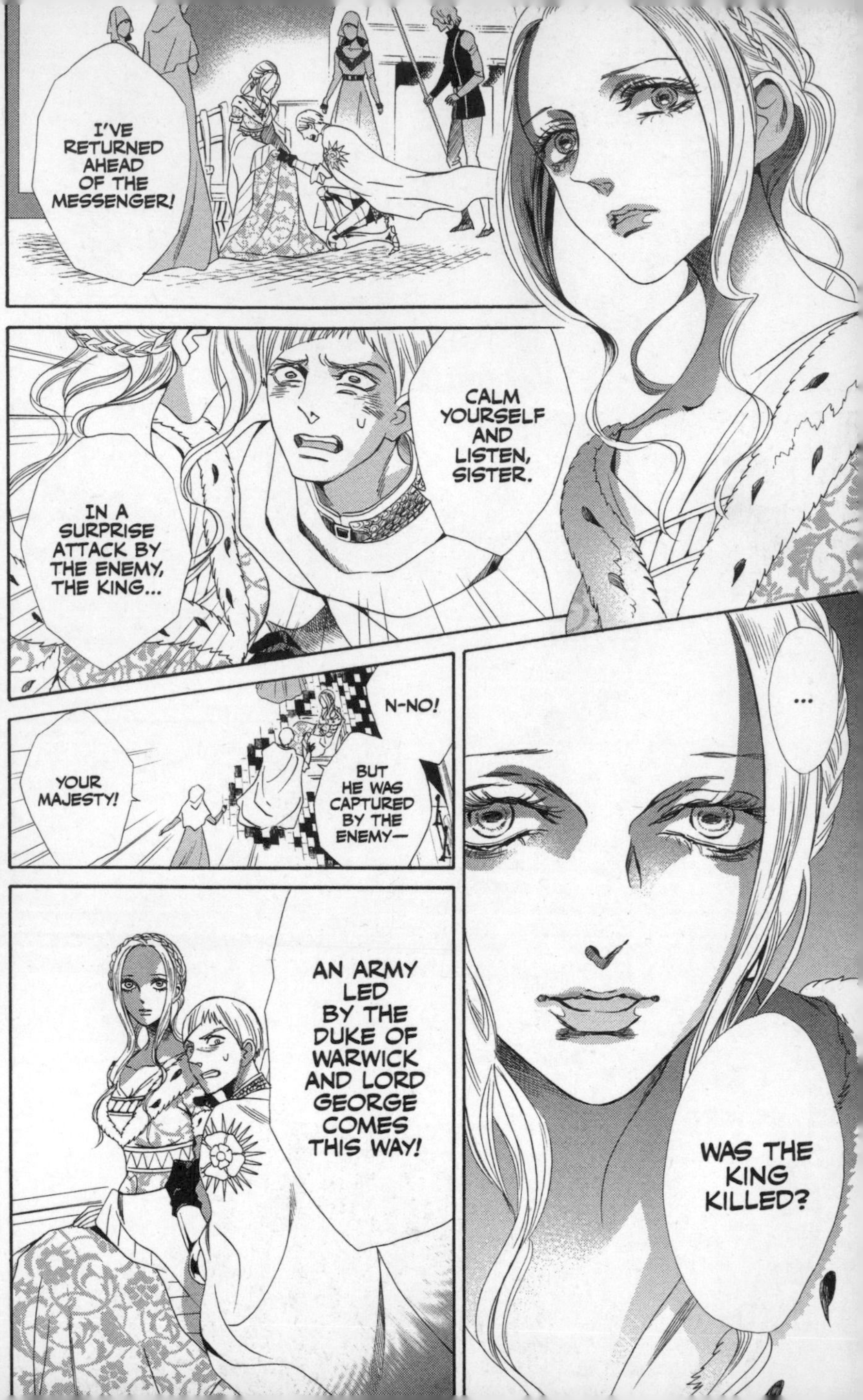
I'VE RETURNED AHEAD OF THE MESSENGER!
CALM YOURSELF AND LISTEN, SISTER.
IN A SURPRISE ATTACK BY THE ENEMY, THE KING...
...
WAS THE KING KILLED?
N-NO!
BUT HE WAS CAPTURED BY THE ENEMY—
YOUR MAJESTY!
AN ARMY LED BY THE DUKE OF WARWICK AND LORD GEORGE COMES THIS WAY!

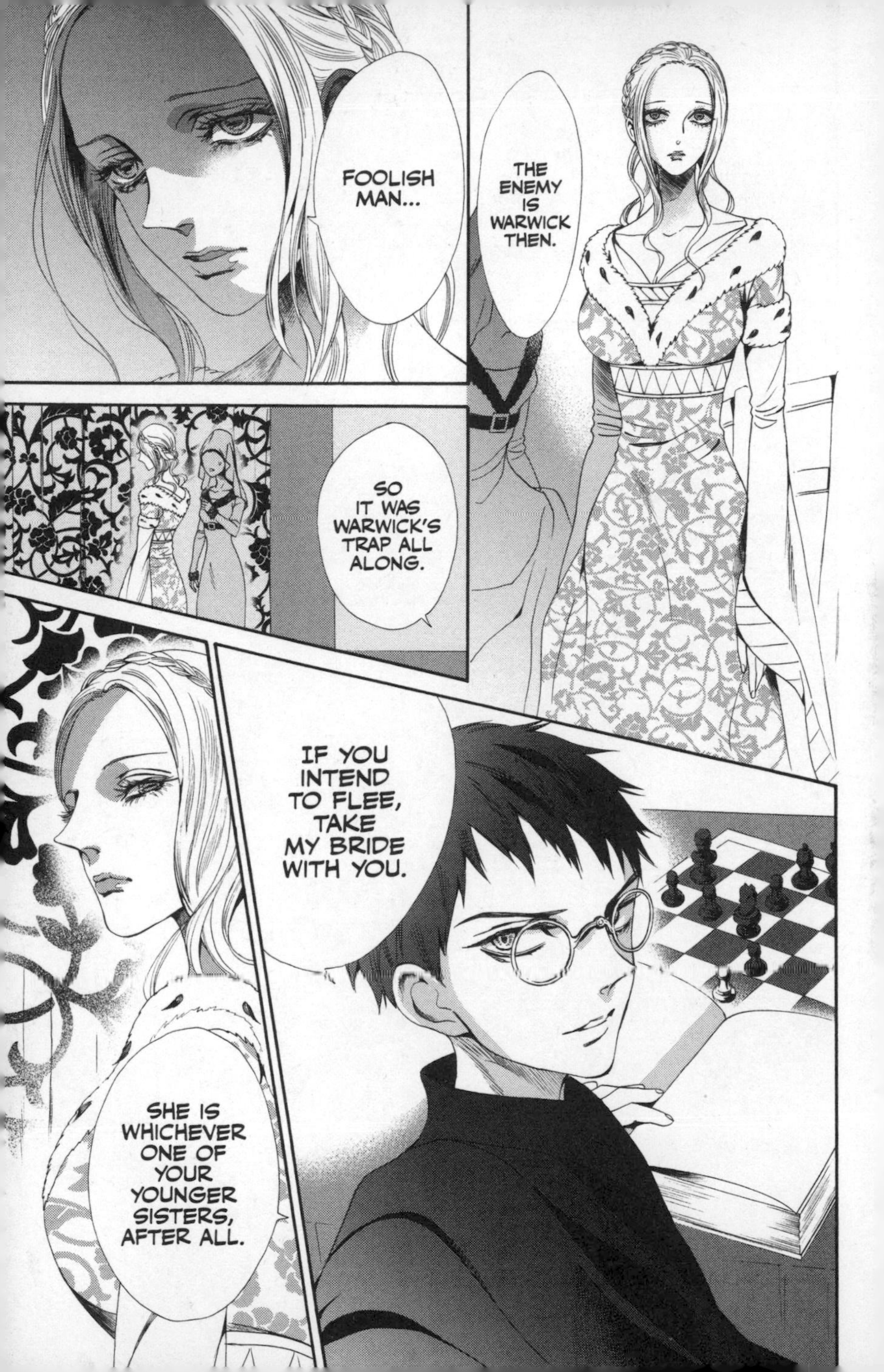
THE ENEMY IS WARWICK THEN.
FOOLISH MAN...
SO IT WAS WARWICK'S TRAP ALL ALONG.
IF YOU INTEND TO FLEE, TAKE MY BRIDE WITH YOU.
SHE IS WHICHEVER ONE OF YOUR YOUNGER SISTERS, AFTER ALL.

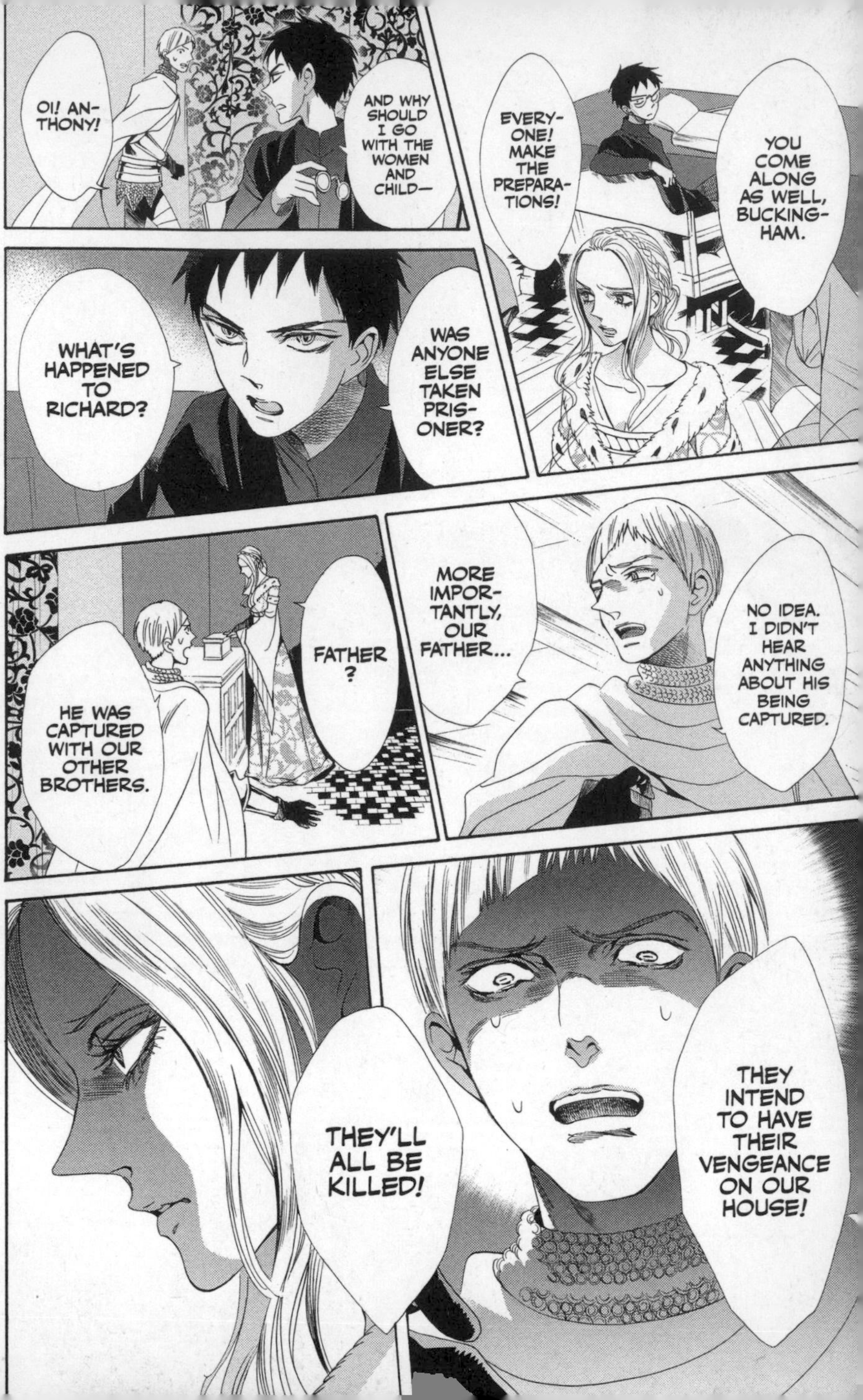

YOU COME ALONG AS WELL, BUCKINGHAM.
EVERYONE! MAKE THE PREPARATIONS!
AND WHY SHOULD I GO WITH THE WOMEN AND CHILD—
OI! ANTHONY!
WAS ANYONE ELSE TAKEN PRISONER?
WHAT'S HAPPENED TO RICHARD?
NO IDEA. I DIDN'T HEAR ANYTHING ABOUT HIS BEING CAPTURED.
MORE IMPORTANTLY, OUR FATHER...
FATHER?
HE WAS CAPTURED WITH OUR OTHER BROTHERS.
THEY INTEND TO HAVE THEIR VENGEANCE ON OUR HOUSE!
THEY'LL ALL BE KILLED!

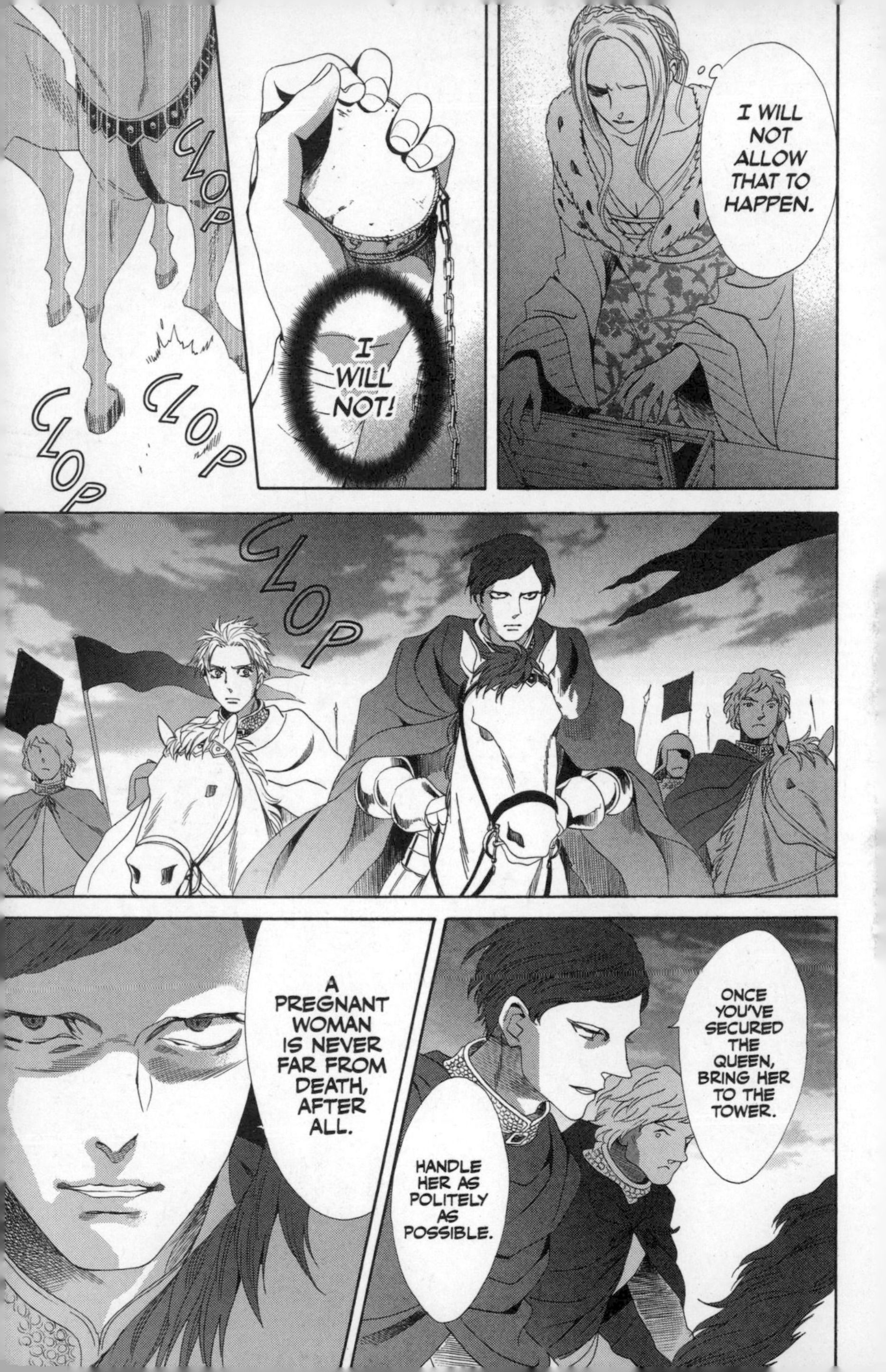
I WILL NOT ALLOW THAT TO HAPPEN.
I WILL NOT!
CLOP
CLOP
CLOP
CLOP
CLOP
ONCE YOU'VE SECURED THE QUEEN, BRING HER TO THE TOWER.
HANDLE HER AS POLITELY AS POSSIBLE.
A PREGNANT WOMAN IS NEVER FAR FROM DEATH, AFTER ALL.

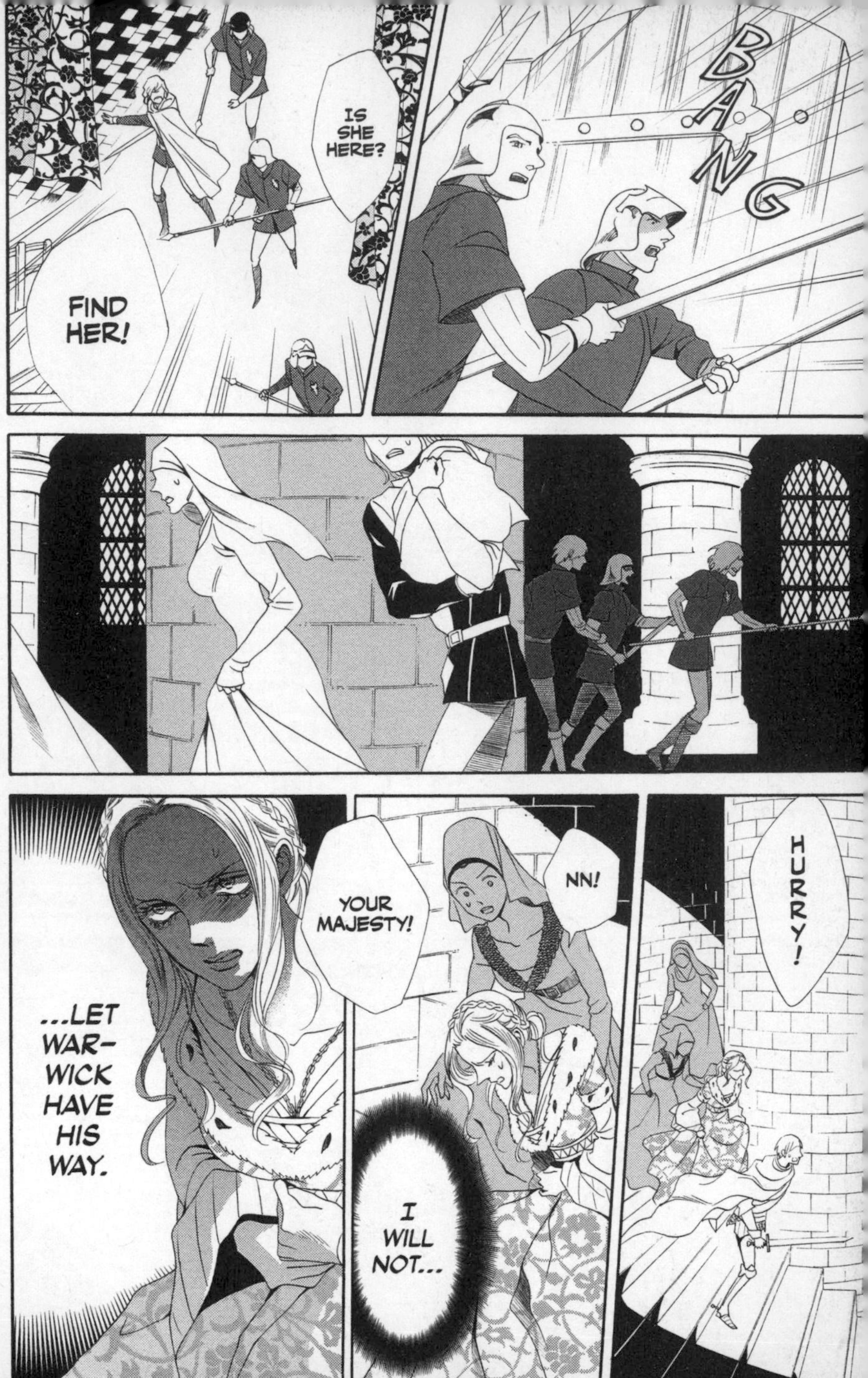
BANG
IS SHE HERE?
FIND HER!
HURRY!
NN!
YOUR MAJESTY!
I WILL NOT...
...LET WAR-WICK HAVE HIS WAY.

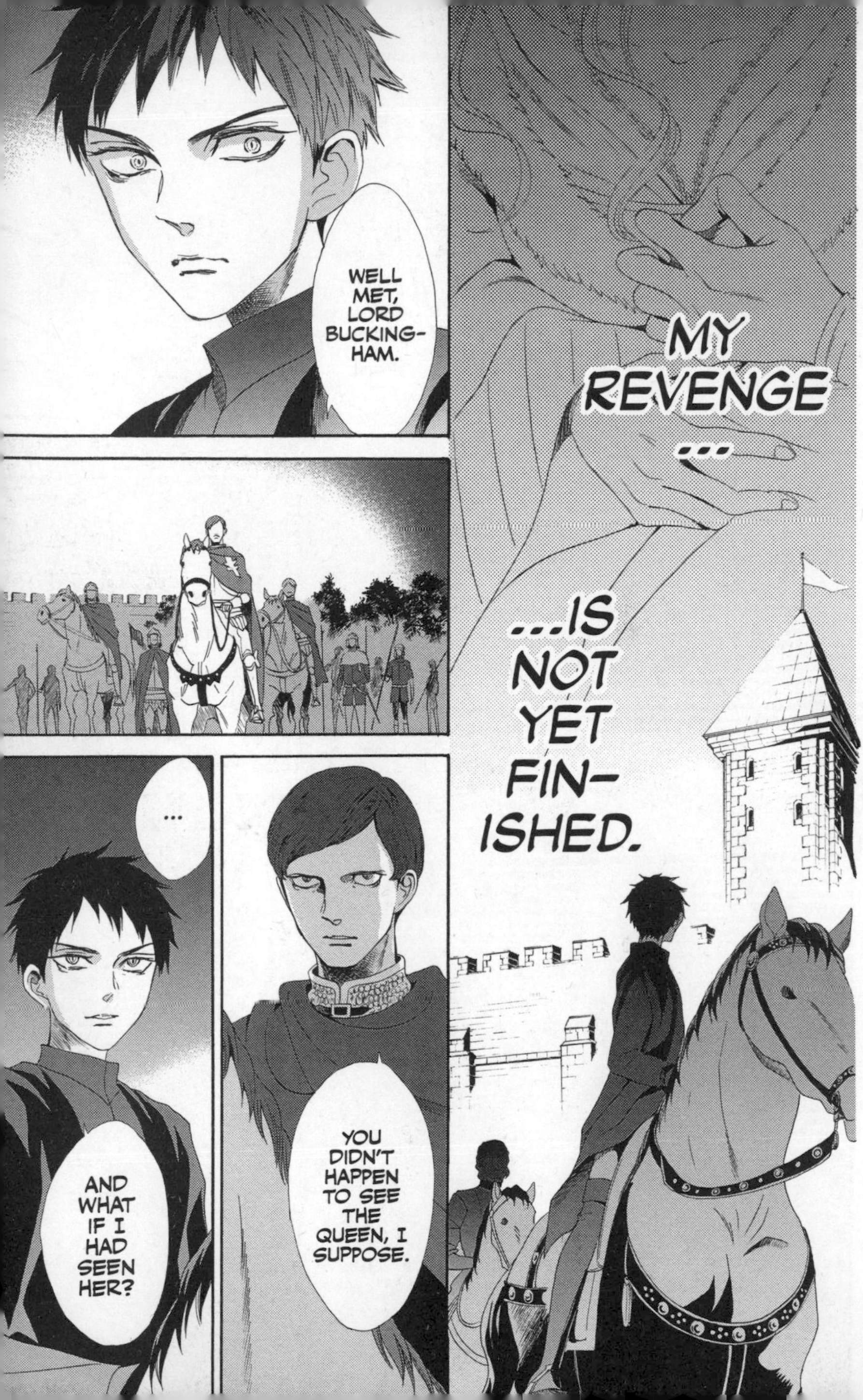
MY REVENGE...
...IS NOT YET FIN-ISHED.
WELL MET, LORD BUCKING-HAM.
YOU DIDN'T HAPPEN TO SEE THE QUEEN, I SUPPOSE.
...
AND WHAT IF I HAD SEEN HER?

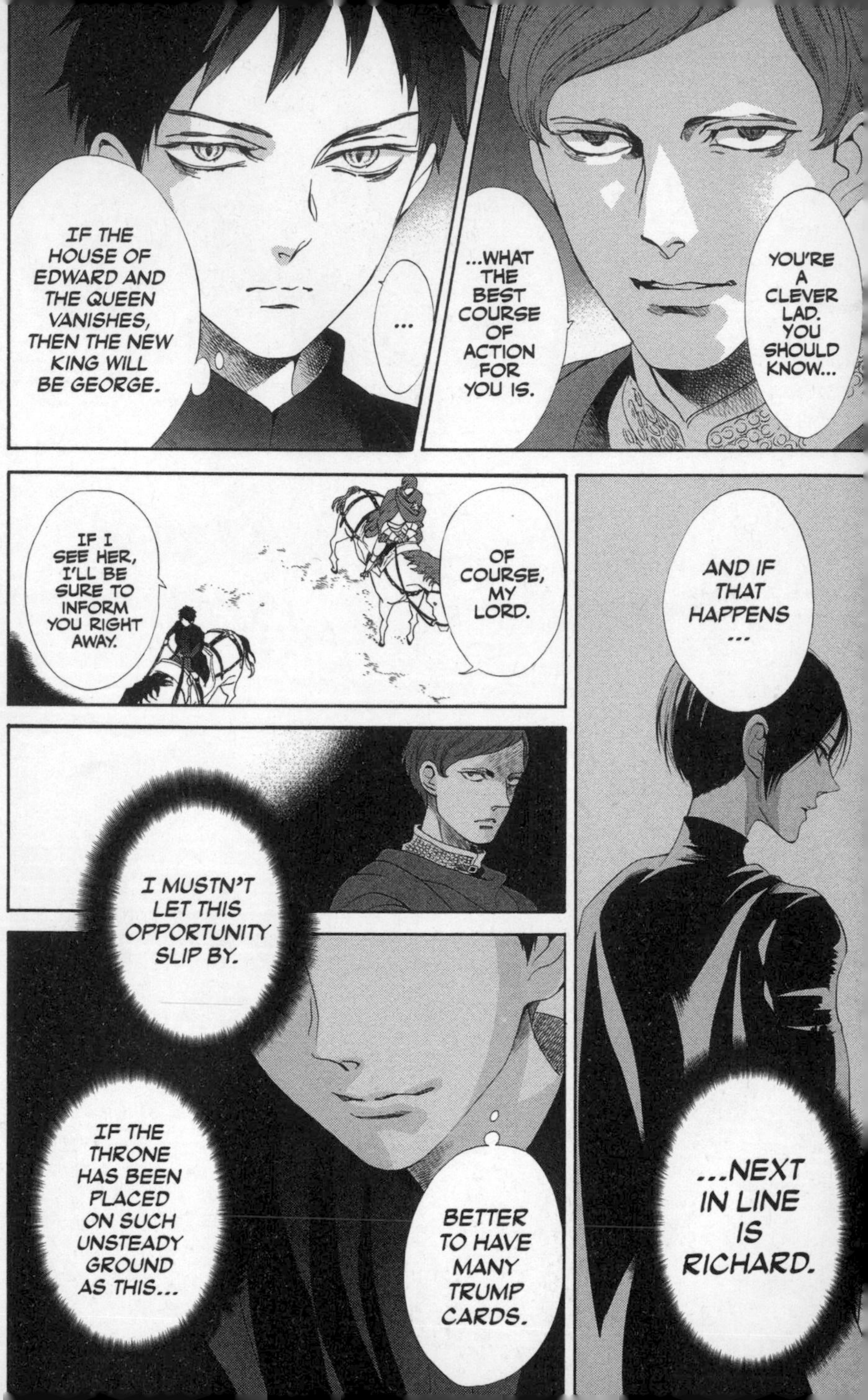
YOU'RE A CLEVER LAD. YOU SHOULD KNOW...
...WHAT THE BEST COURSE OF ACTION FOR YOU IS.
...
IF THE HOUSE OF EDWARD AND THE QUEEN VANISHES, THEN THE NEW KING WILL BE GEORGE.
AND IF THAT HAPPENS...
...NEXT IN LINE IS RICHARD.
OF COURSE, MY LORD.
IF I SEE HER, I'LL BE SURE TO INFORM YOU RIGHT AWAY.
I MUSTN'T LET THIS OPPORTUNITY SLIP BY.
BETTER TO HAVE MANY TRUMP CARDS.
IF THE THRONE HAS BEEN PLACED ON SUCH UNSTEADY GROUND AS THIS...

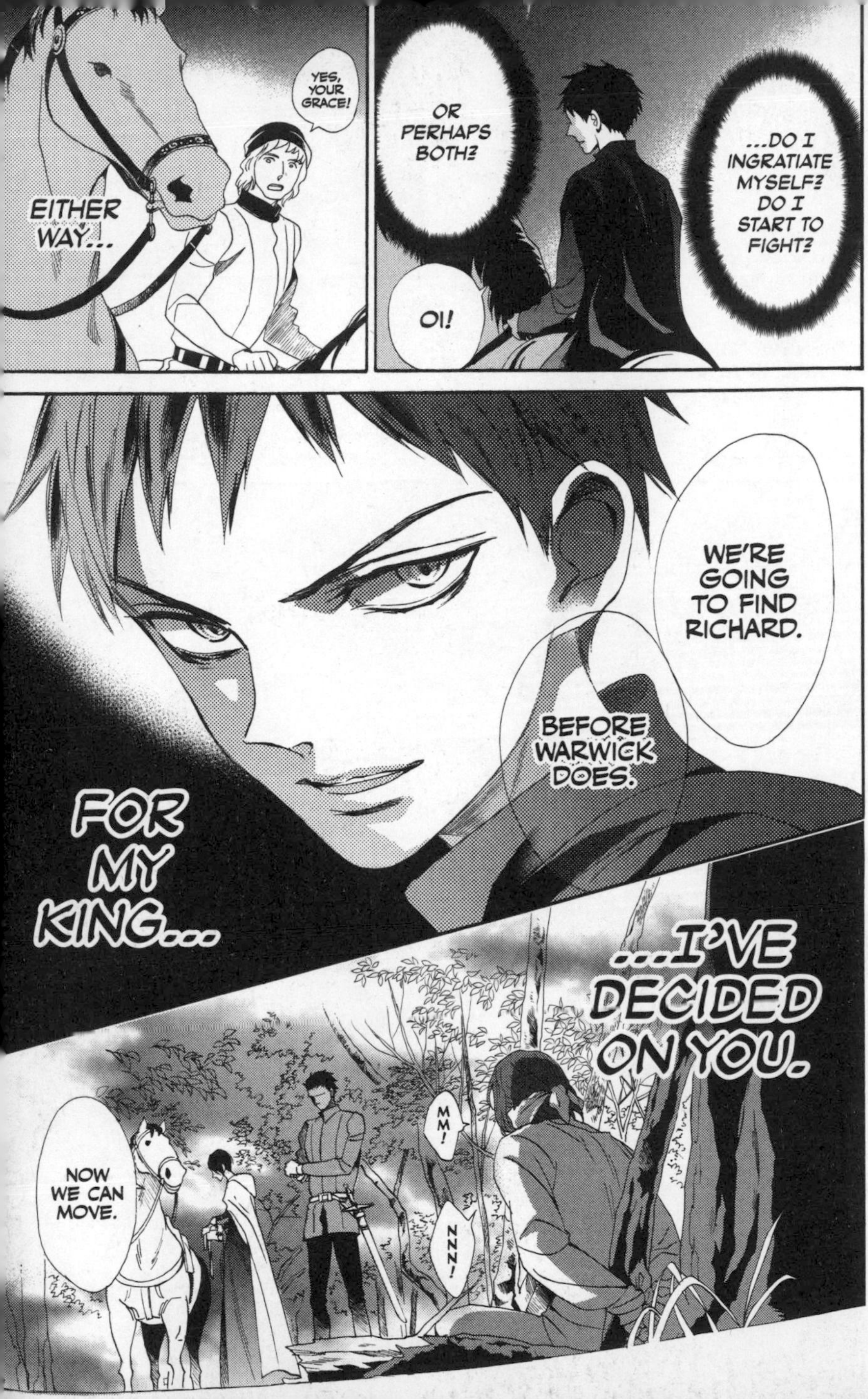
...DO I INGRATIATE MYSELF? DO I START TO FIGHT?
OR PERHAPS BOTH?
OI!
YES, YOUR GRACE!
EITHER WAY...
WE'RE GOING TO FIND RICHARD.
BEFORE WARWICK DOES.
FOR MY KING...
...I'VE DECIDED ON YOU.
MM!
NNN!
NOW WE CAN MOVE.

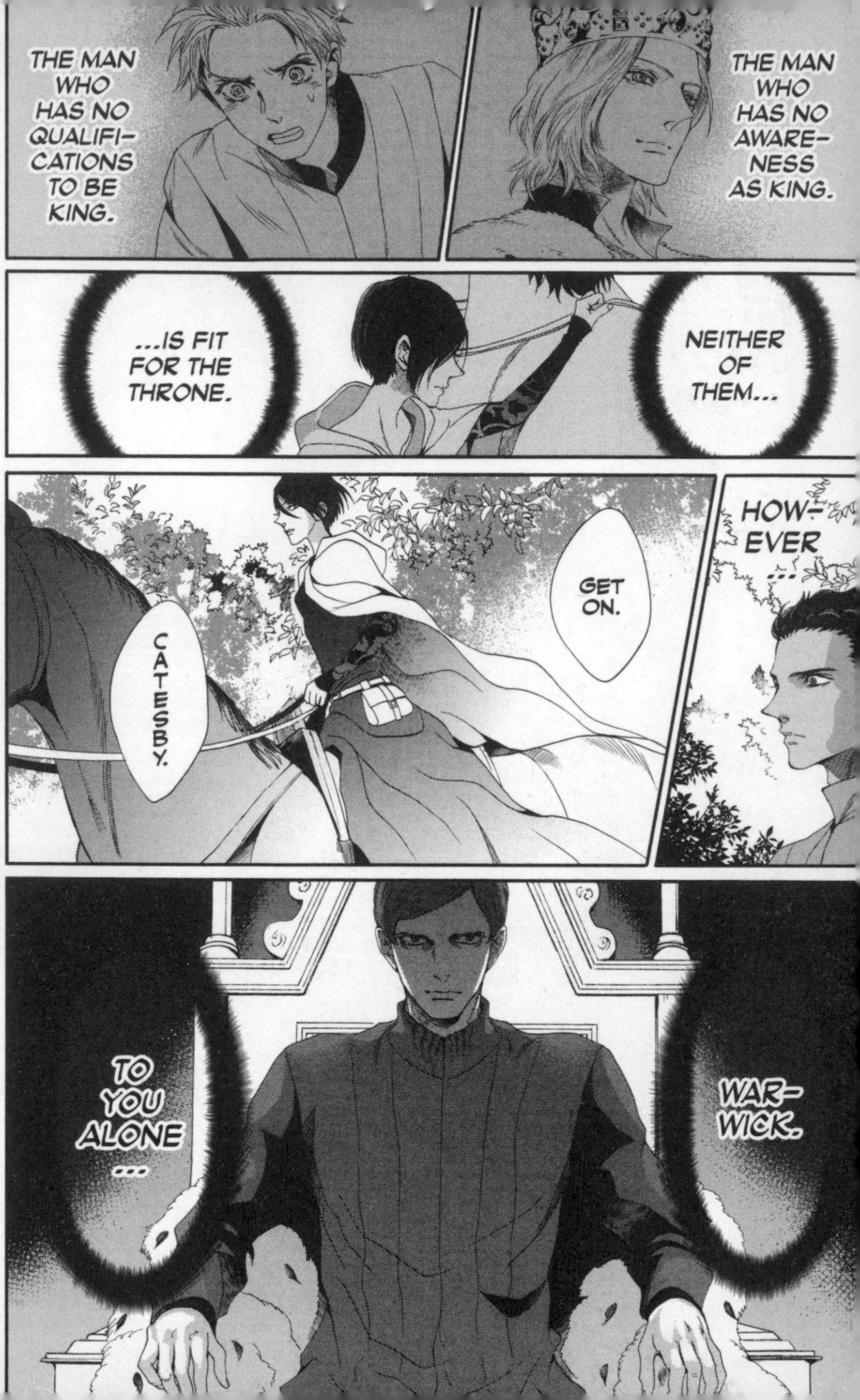
THE MAN WHO HAS NO AWARE-NESS AS KING.
THE MAN WHO HAS NO QUALIFI-CATIONS TO BE KING.
NEITHER OF THEM...
...IS FIT FOR THE THRONE.
HOW-EVER...
GET ON.
CATESBY.
WAR-WICK.
TO YOU ALONE...

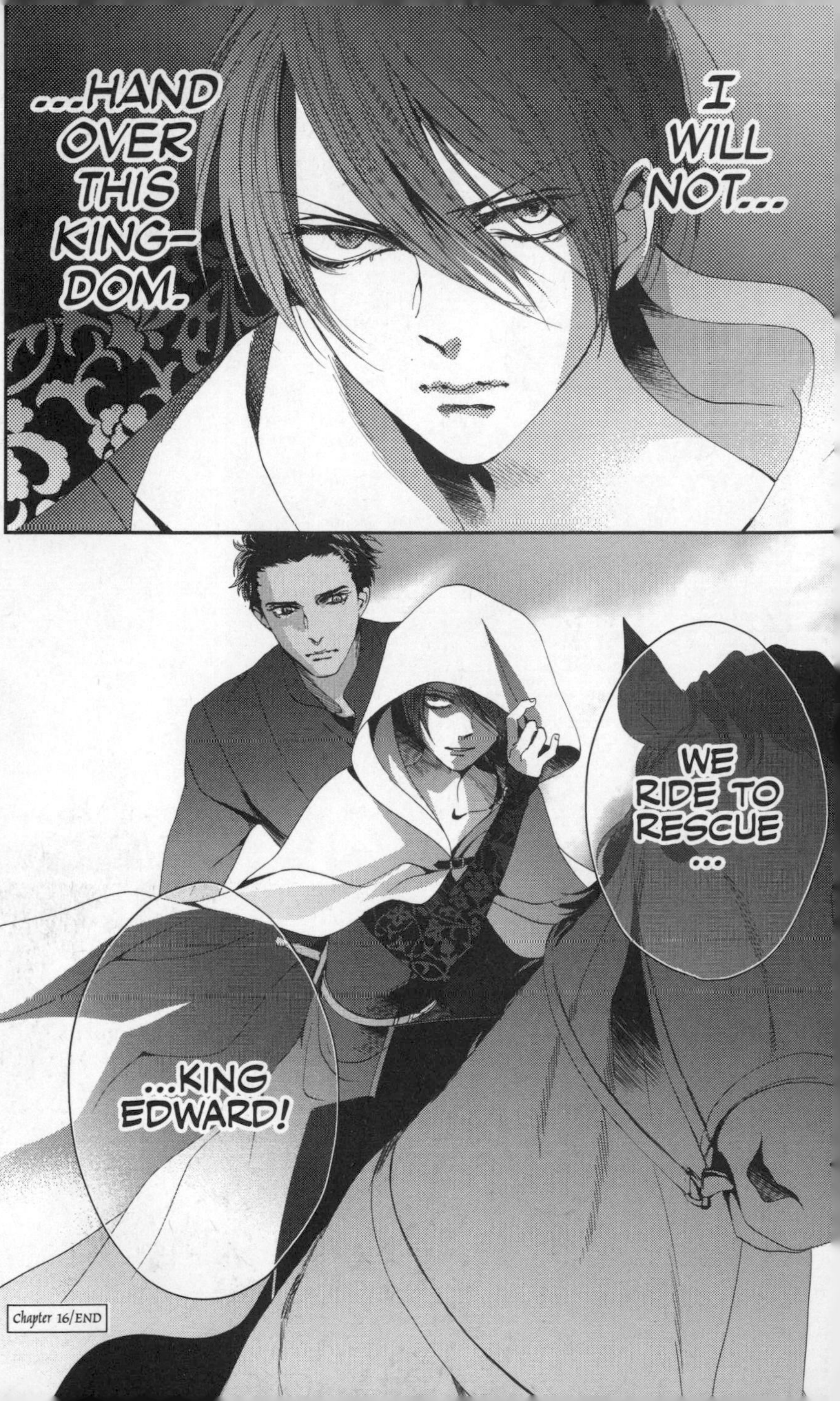
I WILL NOT...
...HAND OVER THIS KING-DOM.
WE RIDE TO RESCUE ...
...KING EDWARD!
Chapter 16/END

Everyone has feelings
for someone, and
yet no one shares
any of them in this
fourth volume.

Aya Kanno

was born in Tokyo, Japan.
She is the creator of
Soul Rescue, *Blank Slate* and the
New York Times best-selling
series *Otomen*.